Beiträge zum
ausländischen öffentlichen Recht und Völkerrecht

Edited by

the Max Planck Society
for the Advancement of Science
represented by Prof. Dr. Armin von Bogdandy
and Prof. Dr. Anne Peters

Volume 348

Philipp Sauter

Fusion Energy in Nuclear Weapons Law

Tackling the Climate Crisis while Addressing the Risk of Further Proliferation

Nomos

Open Access funding provided by Max Planck Society.

The Deutsche Nationalbibliothek lists this publication in the Deutsche Nationalbibliografie; detailed bibliographic data are available on the Internet at http://dnb.d-nb.de

a.t.: Frankfurt am Main, Univ., Diss., 2025

1st Edition 2026

Published by
Nomos Verlagsgesellschaft mbH & Co. KG
Waldseestraße 3–5 | 76530 Baden-Baden
www.nomos.de

Production of the printed version:
Nomos Verlagsgesellschaft mbH & Co. KG

Waldseestraße 3–5 | 76530 Baden-Baden

ISBN (Print): 978-3-7560-3561-8
ISBN (ePDF): 978-3-7489-6621-0

DOI: https://doi.org/10.5771/9783748966210

D30

Onlineversion
Inlibra

In loving memory of my Father

Acknowledgments

This book is based on my PhD thesis which has been accepted as doctoral dissertation by the Faculty of Law of the Goethe University Frankfurt during the summer semester of 2025.

I am indebted to many people who have accompanied me on this journey. *Marcel Dommer* first introduced me to the topic of fusion in 2015. *Thomas Eich* enabled me to do research in plasma physics between 2020 and 2022. *Karoly Olajos Tamas* integrated me into the legal fusion community. *Dieter Fleck* sparked my particular interest in nuclear weapons law. *Rob Goldston* and *Hartmut Zohm* offered valuable help with physics questions. I am also grateful to the two anonymous reviewers whose comments on a draft paper significantly improved my analysis.

Furthermore, I also wish to thank the Max Planck Society, the German Academic Scholarship Foundation (Studienstiftung des deutschen Volkes) as well as the German Federal Ministry of Research, Technology and Space (Funding Program Fusion 2040 – Research on the way to a fusion power plant, contract number 13F1002D) for their financial support, which made my research and extensive travels to conferences possible.

Moreover, I want to express my deepest gratitude to my colleagues at the Max-Planck-Institute for Comparative Public Law and International Law for their invaluable feedback on draft chapters and for contributing to the inspiring intellectual atmosphere at the institute. I am especially grateful to my supervisor, *Armin von Bogdandy*, for his support, guidance, and patience. I would like to also thank *Caroline Sommerfeld* for helping me with proofreading. I further thank *Stefan Kadelbach* for his prompt grading of my thesis and for his valuable feedback.

Finally, I am also deeply indebted to my friends and family, who, even if they did not always understand what I was doing, constantly supported me in my endeavours.

Heidelberg, September 2025

Philipp Sauter

Table of Contents

Table of Abbreviations

Abbreviation	Explanation
AP	Additional Protocol, based on INFCIRC/540(Corrected)
COP	Conference of Parties
CSA	Comprehensive Safeguards Agreements, based on INF-CIRC/153(Corrected)
CTBT	Comprehensive Test-Ban Treaty
CTBTO	Comprehensive Test-Ban Treaty Organization
D	Deuterium
ENDC	Eighteen Nations Committee on Disarmament
Euratom	European Atomic Energy Community
EU	European Union
H	Hydrogen
He	Helium
ICF	Inertial Confinement Fusion
INFCIRC	Information Circulars (IAEA series to communicate on matters of general interest to all IAEA Member States)
IAEA	International Atomic Energy Agency
ICJ	International Court of Justice
IFEA	International Fusion Energy Agency
ILC	International Law Commission
Li	Lithium
NNWS	Non-Nuclear Weapons State
NATO	North Atlantic Treaty Organization
NPT	Nuclear Non-Proliferation Treaty
NSG	Nuclear Suppliers Group
NWFZ	Nuclear Weapon Free Zone
NWS	Nuclear Weapons State
OECD	Organization for Economic Co-operation and Development
Pu	Plutonium

SDG	Sustainable Development Goals
TPNW	Treaty on the Prohibition of Nuclear Weapons
T	Tritium
UN	United Nations
UNSCR	United Nations Security Council Resolution
U	Uranium
UNFCCC	United Nations Framework Convention on Climate Change
VCLT	Vienna Convention on the Law of Treaties

Introduction: Sustainable Development and Securing Peace

The climate crisis is arguably the most pressing issue of the 21st century. Finding solutions to tackle this crisis is imperative for the continuation of the world and the functioning of society as we know it. The failure to do so will result in unprecedented consequences.[1] The climate crisis is driven by human-induced emissions of carbon dioxide (CO_2) and other greenhouse gases.[2] The majority of these emissions is caused by the world's hunger for energy.[3] Consequently, transforming the energy production to emission-free energy sources is of paramount importance in the effort to combat climate change.

Emission-free energy sources already exist today, including solar energy, wind energy, hydroelectric energy, geothermal energy and nuclear energy. These technologies, however, come with limitations. Both solar and wind energy depend on meteorological conditions, thus necessitating the technologically challenging process of storing electricity.[4] Hydroelectric and geothermal energy are limited to geographical conditions where there are suitable water bodies or sufficient geothermal activity. Nuclear energy, too, has its own downsides in light of safety and proliferation concerns as well as the unresolved question of how to deal with nuclear waste.

This is where nuclear fusion – or fusion for short – becomes important. Fusion is the process that powers the Sun and all other stars in our universe. Harvesting this energy has the potential to provide the world with a virtually unlimited source of energy. A bottle of water combined with less

1 *International Panel on Climate Change*, Sixth Assessment Report – Synthesis Report, 2022, at 68 ff.; *Sabine L. Perch-Nielsen/Michèle B. Bättig/Dieter Imboden*, Exploring the Link Between Climate Change and Migration, Climatic Change 91 (2008), 375–393; *J. Timmons Roberts*, Global Inequality and Climate Change, Society & Natural Resources 14 (2001), 501–509.

2 *International Panel on Climate Change*, Climate Change 2021: The Physical Science Basis, in: Sixth Assessment Report, Geneva: IPCC 2021, at 423 ff.

3 In 2022, global energy-related CO_2 emissions amounted to 36.8 Gt, *International Energy Agency*, CO2 Emissions in 2022, Paris: IEA 2023. On the different contributors to this number in a historic context, see *Zhu Liu/Zhu Deng/Steve Davis et al.*, Monitoring Global Carbon Emissions in 2022, Nature Reviews Earth & Environment 4 (2023), 205–206.

4 See Trevor M. Letcher (ed.), Storing Energy, Amsterdam: Elsevier 2022.

than a gram of lithium contains roughly as much fusion energy as can be generated by burning three tonnes of coal.[5] This energy source comes without the production of CO_2 or other greenhouse gases, as in fossil energy sources, and without the level of safety and waste concerns, as in nuclear fission energy. Additionally, fusion energy can provide a baseload supply of energy independent of meteorological or geographical conditions, unlike renewable energy sources. While fusion has been confined to academic research for decades, with continued promises of reaching a commercial scale within a few decades, recent times have shown substantial scientific breakthroughs,[6] as well as a significant increase in the number of start-ups and investor capital.[7] Fusion could be a key technology in solving the energy problem and playing a crucial role in the broader effort to combat climate change.

As has been emphasised by numerous scholars, the climate crisis represents a threat to peace.[8] The climate crisis will increase inequalities in socioeconomic development, can lead to a fight for resources and may cause large-scale migration movements.[9] As fusion plays a role in the fight against the climate crisis, fusion energy can contribute to peace. Indeed, fusion already served as a peace project between the United States and the

---

5 One liter of water contains roughly 10^{22} deuterium atoms, while one gram of natural lithium contains enough ^{6}Li to produce 10^{22} tritium atoms. Their fusion energy amounts to roughly 30 GJ, which correlates to 3 tonnes of brown coal with an energy density of 10 MJ/kg.

6 See for example *Michael Banks*, China's Experimental Advanced Superconducting Tokamak Smashes Fusion Confinement Record in: Physics World, https://physicsworld.com/a/chinas-experimental-advanced-superconducting-tokamak-smashes-fusion-confinement-record/#:~:text=This%20week%2C%20scientists%20working%20on,device%20located%20in%20Hefei%2C%20China., last accessed 17 July 2025; *Max-Planck-Institute for Plasma Physics*, JET Fusion Facility Sets a New World Energy Record in: https://www.mpg.de/18250857/jet-fusion-facility-new-world-energy-record, last accessed 17 July 2025; *U.S. Department of Energy*, DOE National Laboratory Makes History by Achieving Fusion Ignition (2022), https://www.energy.gov/articles/doe-national-laboratory-makes-history-achieving-fusion-ignition, last accessed 17 July 2025.

7 *Fusion Industry Association*, The Global Fusion Industry in 2024, Washington DC: FIA 2024.

8 *Katharine J. Mach/Caroline M. Kraan/W. Neil Adger et al.*, Climate as a Risk Factor for Armed Conflict, Nature 571 (2019), 193–197; *Vally Koubi*, Climate Change and Conflict, Annual Review of Political Science 22 (2019), 343–360; *Oli Brown/Robert McLeman*, A Recurring Anarchy? The Emergence of Climate Change as a Threat to International Peace and Security, Conflict, Security & Development 9 (2009), 289–305.

9 *Mach/Kraan/Adger et al.* (n 8).

Soviet Union during the Cold War in the 1980s.[10] However, as a nuclear technology, fusion also has military applications, especially with regard to nuclear weapons. Nuclear weapons are one of the greatest threats to peace.[11] Promoting a nuclear technology for sustainable development poses the risk of increasing the risk of nuclear proliferation, and in the worst case, nuclear war. Fusion intends to promote sustainable development in the fight against the climate crisis, while securing peace at the same time.

Law seeks to make these interests compatible. This introduction first explores how fusion as a technology to promote sustainable development stands in the broader context of international law (1), before focusing on the technology's role in international nuclear law (2), the legal regime that focuses on the specific risk-potential of nuclear technology. The introduction then proceeds to highlight the relevance of fusion in the context of nuclear weapons law (3), where the combined task of promoting sustainable development while preventing the further proliferation of nuclear weapons is prominent. The introduction concludes with a presentation of the outline of the book (4).

1 Fusion in International Law

Fusion is a technology that has the potential to play a significant role in the fight against the climate crisis. This transformative potential of fusion as a new energy source in realising an objective shared by the world community raises the question of fusion's role in the broader context of international law. As it is true for any energy source, the implications in international law are manifold and stretch into different sub-disciplines, emphasised by an increased focus of international law on various aspects of energy.[12]

As fusion may play a significant role in the context of the climate crisis and in finding solutions for climate mitigation, international climate law is of relevance. The United Nations Framework Convention on Climate Change (UNFCCC) has been in force for more than thirty years with

10 *Michel Claessens*, ITER: The Giant Fusion Reactor – Bringing a Sun to Earth, Cham: Springer 2020, at 19.

11 *John Mecklin*, Closer Than Ever: It Is Now 89 Seconds to Midnight in: Bulletin of the Atomic Scientists, https://thebulletin.org/doomsday-clock/2025-statement/, last accessed 17 July 2025.

12 *Jorge E. Viñuales*, Energy in International Law, Cambridge: Cambridge University Press 2022, at 1 ff.

almost universal adherence, aiming to stabilise "greenhouse gas concentrations in the atmosphere at a level that would prevent dangerous anthropogenic interference with the climate system."[13] Again, energy is the largest source of greenhouse gases, emphasising the role of sustainable energy sources within the climate law regime, including fusion.

The role of new technologies is further emphasised in the 2015 Paris Agreement, which introduced the limit of an increase in the global average temperature to well below 2°C above pre-industrial levels, with efforts to limit it to 1.5°C, into an international agreement.[14] To achieve this goal, Article 10 emphasises the role of technology within climate mitigation and the reduction of greenhouse gas emissions. In 2023, the so-called Global Stocktake, adopted during COP28 in Dubai, has introduced the yet biggest focus on energy within the regime. There, the Parties to the Paris Agreement recognised the need to accelerate efforts globally towards net zero emission energy systems, to transition away from fossil fuels in energy systems and to accelerate zero-emission technologies, such as nuclear technologies.[15] Fusion can provide pathways to keeping the increase of global temperature within the limits of the UNFCCC and the Paris Agreement.

Fusion as a clean energy source also plays a role within the United Nations Sustainable Development Goals (SDGs). In 2015, the United Nations General Assembly adopted 17 Sustainable Development Goals as "a plan of action for people, planet and prosperity."[16] Goal 7 aims to ensure access to affordable, reliable, sustainable and modern energy for all. Fusion has the potential to provide a pathway to achieve these goals in all of these four aspects: Fusion as a modern energy source is expected to be affordable,[17] to be reliable as fusion power plants can provide baseload energy, to be sustainable by being climate-neutral, while avoiding the social implications of fossil and renewable energy sources, and also offering enormous economic potential. Furthermore, fusion contributes to Goal 13 – the goal addressing

13 Article 2 UNFCCC.

14 Article 2.1.a Paris Agreement.

15 Decision 1/CMA.5, at para. 28.

16 Preamble of A/RES/70/1, at para. 1.

17 *Slavomir Entler/Jan Horacek/Tomas Dlouhy et al.*, Approximation of the Economy of Fusion Energy, Energy 152 (2018), 489–497. It must be noted that there are high uncertainties both with regard to the costs of fusion power plants and the development of costs for renewable energy sources.

climate change –, by taking urgent action to combat climate change and its impacts.[18]

Once commercialised, fusion energy will become a focal point within the mitigation obligations under international climate law and sustainable development regimes.

Moreover, energy sources – including fusion – impact numerous other facets of international law. The impact starts from the relevance of large-scale energy projects within international investment law,[19] the potential to contribute to disputes brought before the International Court of Justice,[20] having major implications in human rights,[21] their role in shaping international environmental law,[22] and stretching as far as playing a crucial role in addressing violations of international law, such as Western reactions following the Russian aggression in Ukraine[23] or the relevance of access to oil in the United States' intervention in Iraq.[24]

---

18 On fusion's role within the SDGs, see also *E. G. Carayannis/J. Draper/I. A. Iftimie*, Nuclear Fusion Diffusion: Theory, Policy, Practice, and Politics Perspectives, IEEE Transactions on Engineering Management 69 (2022), 1237–1251.

19 See the vast majority of contributions in Karoly Tamas Olajos/Fusion For Energy (eds.), Fusion For Energy Contracting Professionals Roundtable Proceedings 2022–2023, Barcelona: European Commission 2023.

20 *International Court of Justice*, Gabčikovo-Nagymaros Project (Hungary/Slovakia), Judgment, ICJ Reports 1997, p. 7.

21 On Human Rights regarding access to energy, see *Marc Clemson*, Human Rights and the Environment: Access to Energy, New Zealand Journal of Environmental Law 16 (2012), 39–81; *Stephen R. Tully*, The Contribution of Human Rights to Universal Energy Access, Northwestern University Journal of International Human Rights 4 (2005), 518–548. However, energy (even renwables) can also be in conflict with human rights, see *Mary Finley-Brook/Curtis Thomas*, Renewable Energy and Human Rights Violations: Illustrative Cases from Indigenous Territories in Panama, Annals of the Association of American Geographers 101 (2011), 863–872.

22 *Anguel Anastassov*, The Sovereign Right to Peaceful Use of Nuclear Energy and International Environmental Law, in: Jonathan L. Black-Branch/Dieter Fleck (eds.), Nuclear Non-Proliferation in International Law – Volume I, The Hague: T.M.C. Asser Press 2014, 159–197.

23 For example, Germany was highly critised for its continued support of the gas pipeline Nord Stream 2 after the annexation of Crimea by Russia. On that, see *Tobias Bunde*, Lessons (to be) learned? Germany's Zeitenwende and European Security After the Russian Invasion of Ukraine, Contemporary Security Policy 43 (2022), 516–530.

24 *Eric Bonds*, Assessing the Oil Motive After the U.S. War in Iraq, Peace Review 25 (2013), 291–298; *John. S. Duffield*, Oil and the Decision to Invade Iraq, in: Jane Cramer/A. Trevor Thrall (eds.), Why Did the United States Invade Iraq?, London: Routledge 2011, 145–166.

2 Fusion in International Nuclear Law

Nuclear fusion, being a nuclear process, plays a specific role within the framework of international nuclear law, a subset of international law. Nuclear law and the regulation of nuclear energy are unparalleled in comparison to the regulation of other forms of energy.[25] Unlike with other energy sources, the dual-use characteristic of nuclear technology gives rise to questions of international security, as well as the safety and security of nuclear materials and facilities, which often take precedence over economic interests.[26] Furthermore, potential transboundary effects caused by accidents necessitate international legal approaches. The regime is characterised by a centralised approach, whereby international organisations exert a high level of authority under a comprehensive governance framework.[27] The International Atomic Energy Agency (IAEA), and to some extent the European Commission and the OECD, centralise the governance mechanisms of nuclear law.

Nuclear law is defined as "the body of special norms created to regulate the conduct of legal or natural persons engaged in activities related to fissionable materials, ionizing radiation and exposure to natural sources of radiation."[28] Given the radioactivity involved in fusion, the technology is subject to the regulations of nuclear law, which cover four pillars: safety, security, safeguards and civil liability.

These four pillars are designed to cover the specific risks and challenges posed by the inherent risks and dual-use nature of nuclear energy. Safety is the body of norms which aims to protect people and the environment from hazardous effects of nuclear facilities and materials.[29] These efforts are encapsulated in various conventions and standards, including the 1994 Convention on Nuclear Safety or the 1997 Joint Convention on the Safety of Spent Fuel Management and on the Safety of Radioactive Waste Management, and several IAEA Safety Standards. These instruments ensure that nuclear facilities are constructed, operated and decommissioned safely by establishing a comprehensive set of rules, procedures and institutions.

25 *Viñuales* (n 12), at 291.

26 Ibid, at 291, 303 f.

27 Ibid, at 293.

28 *Carlton Stoiber/Alex Baer/Norbert Pelzer et al.*, IAEA Handbook on Nuclear Law, Vienna: International Atomic Energy Agency 2003, at 4.

29 *International Atomic Energy Agency*, IAEA Nuclear Safety and Security Glossary, Vienna: IAEA 2022, at 139.

Security is the set of rules that protect the facilities and materials from external influence, especially with a view to preventing and detecting criminal acts.[30] This includes the 1979 Convention on the Physical Protection of Nuclear Material, as well as UN Security Council Resolutions 1373 and 1540. The overarching objective of these instruments is to prevent external influence on nuclear facilities and material, with a particular emphasis on preventing non-State actors from acquiring nuclear material. Safeguards regulate the verification that nuclear material and activities remains in peaceful uses with the 1968 Nuclear Non-Proliferation Treaty (NPT) as the cornerstone of the regime.[31] As will be discussed in the next chapters, the safeguards regime contains of a vast web of legal sources with a view to preventing the further spread of nuclear weapons. With regard to civil liability, there are special international regimes in place for the case that a nuclear accident occurs. These regimes introduce specific rules tailored to the potential large-scale consequences of such accidents.[32]

30 Ibid, at 140.

31 *International Atomic Energy Agency*, IAEA Safeguards Glossary, Vienna: IAEA 2022, at 18 ff.

32 1960 Paris Convention on Third Party Liability in the Field of Nuclear Energy, 1963 Vienna Convention on Civil Liability for Nuclear Damage, 1988 Joint Protocol Relating to the Application of the Vienna Convention and the Paris Convention. For an overview of the regime, see *Andrea Gioia*, Nuclear Accidents and International Law, in: Andrea de Guttry/Marco Gestri/Gabriella Venturini (eds.), International Disaster Response Law, The Hague, The Netherlands: T.M.C. Asser Press 2012, 85–102, at 98 ff.

Recent initiatives have seen governments,[33] the European Union[34] and the IAEA,[35] in addition to scholars,[36] commence efforts to regulate the safety of fusion. The question of how to regulate a future fusion facility remains a subject of ongoing discussion. Should the regulatory framework for nuclear fission power plants apply? Should a regime for radiological sources be implemented? Or should a specific regime for fusion be established? These questions are the focus of extensive research and debate.

Regarding nuclear security, the IAEA has begun to analyse the implications of fusion on this pillar.[37] The broad scope of the existing instruments has been found to already cover fusion without the need of any specific changes to the regime. The question of civil liability in the case of a fusion accident has been addressed by scholars[38] and is currently being discussed at the level of international organisations acting as depositaries for the

33 The United Kingdom has published first thoughts on fusion safety regulation, *Department for Energy Security & Net Zero*, Towards Fusion Energy 2023 – The Next Stage of the UK's Fusion Energy Strategy, London: 2023. The US Government has taken first decisions in 2023, https://www.nrc.gov/cdn/doc-collection-news/2023/23-029.pdf, last accessed 25 February 2025. Germany develops a regulatory framework for fusion until mid 2026, https://www.faz.net/aktuell/wirtschaft/energiewende-gesetzlicher-rahmen-zur-kernfusion-in-deutschland-geplant-19669987.html, last accessed 25 February 2025.

34 See for example *Commission European/Directorate-General for Research and Innovation/L. Eriksson et al.*, Exploring Regulatory Options for Fusion Power Plants, Brussels: Publications Office of the European Union 2021; The European Commission also set up an expert meeting on 23 April 2024, entitled "The EU Blueprint for Fusion Energy".

35 See for example *International Atomic Energy Agency*, IAEA World Fusion Outlook 2023 – Fusion Energy: Present and Future, Vienna: IAEA 2023, at 28 ff. The IAEA has also started to host meetings on safety regulation, e.g. the First Meeting Focusing on Safety and Regulation of Fusion in October 2023.

36 *J. Elbez-Uzan/L. Williams/S. Forbes et al.*, Recommendations for the Future Regulation of Fusion Power Plants, Nuclear Fusion 54 (2024), 1–10; *N. P. Taylor*, Safety and Licensing of Nuclear Facilities for Fusion, in: 2015 IEEE 26th Symposium on Fusion Engineering (SOFE)2015; *Didier Perrault*, Nuclear Safety Aspects on the Road Towards Fusion Energy, Fusion Engineering and Design 146 (2019), 130–134.

37 *International Atomic Energy Agency* (n 35), at 25.

38 *Claire Portier*, Le droit de la responsabilité à l'épreuve des activités de fusion nucléaire, Aix-en-Provence: Aix-Marseille Université 2022; *William E. Fork/Charles H. Peterson*, Fusion Energy and Nuclear Liability Considerations, Nuclear Law Bulletin 93 (2014), 43–62; *Steven McIntosh*, Nuclear Liability and Post-Fukushima Developments, in: International Atomic Energy Agency (ed.), Nuclear Law: The Global Debate, The Hague: T.M.C. Asser Press 2022, 249–269.

relevant treaties.[39] Similar to the question of safety, there are discussions as to whether the framework developed for fission is applicable to fusion and, if fusion were to be included, whether it would be proportionate given the technology's different risk profile. For example, fusion technology is inherently safe from runaway reactions, which caused the Chernobyl accident, and from meltdowns caused by decay heat such as the Fukushima-Daiichi accident. Furthermore, radioactive by-products and waste from fusion differ significantly from those of fission technology.[40]

With regard to safeguards, the fourth pillar, so far, no comprehensive legal study has been conducted. Safeguards represent a fundamental aspect of both nuclear non-proliferation and disarmament law. While technological aspects have been identified already a decade ago,[41] calls from experts to addressing the legal framework with regard to fusion have been left unanswered. This book aims at filling this gap and to provide an analysis of fusion energy within the context of nuclear weapons law.

3 Fusion in Nuclear Weapons Law

Fusion energy is of particular interest with regard to nuclear weapons law. Nuclear technologies, including fusion, are dual-use technologies, meaning they have both peaceful and military applications. While intended to support sustainable development and thus, contributing to the prevention of conflicts, fusion – like fission – could be used in a military context for the development of nuclear weapons. In response to the dual-use nature of nuclear technology, nuclear weapons law has developed a unique system for verifying compliance by vesting international and supranational organisations with an unprecedented level of authority. The study of the role

39 The OECD as depositary of the 1960 Paris Convention on Third Party Liability in the Field of Nuclear Energy has started a Working Group to discuss a potential inclusion of fusion into the treaty regime. The role of fusion within the 1963 Vienna Convention on Civil Liability for Nuclear Damage is also discussed within the IAEA as depositary, *International Atomic Energy Agency* (n 35), at 25.

40 *Sehila M. Gonzalez de Vicente/Nicholas A. Smith/Laila El-Guebaly et al.*, Overview on the Management of Radioactive Waste From Fusion Facilities: ITER, Demonstration Machines and Power Plants, Nuclear Fusion 62 (2022), 085001.

41 See for example *Alexander Glaser/Robert J. Goldston*, Proliferation Risks of Magnetic Fusion Energy: Clandestine Production, Covert Production and Breakout, Nuclear Fusion 52 (2012), 043004; *Giorgio Franceschini/Matthias Englert/Wolfgang Liebert*, Nuclear Fusion Power for Weapons Purposes, The Nonproliferation Review 20 (2013), 525–544.

of new technology in nuclear weapons law offers a distinctive perspective on a sub-regime of international law that operates in a distinct manner compared to other domains of international law.

This section will first explore the relevance of studying nuclear weapons law in general (3.1) as well as nuclear proliferation (3.2), before focusing on the specific interest of studying fusion energy in nuclear weapons law (3.3).

3.1 The Interest to Study Nuclear Weapons Law

Nuclear weapons law seeks to regulate the development, possession, transfer, and use of nuclear weapons, which are classified as weapons of mass destruction. While the use of weapons in general is governed by the legal frameworks of *jus ad bellum* (the law on the use of force) and *jus in bello* (international humanitarian law), only a limited number of weapon types are subject to specific international treaties. Some conventional weapons – such as anti-personnel mines[42] and cluster munitions[43] – are regulated through dedicated conventions, but these are exceptions rather than the norm.

In contrast, weapons of mass destruction are treated more extensively under international law. Biological[44] and chemical weapons[45] are comprehensively prohibited. However, nuclear weapons remain an outlier: there is no treaty that fully prohibits or comprehensively regulates them. Instead, the legal regime surrounding nuclear weapons is fragmented and focuses on three areas: non-proliferation, disarmament, and arms control. Each of these areas is governed by different instruments with varying legal obligations and differing levels of participation by States.

The focus of nuclear non-proliferation law is to prevent the further spread of nuclear weapons and, for nuclear weapon-states, to at least maintain the status quo of nuclear powers. In this regard, the 1968 Treaty on the Non-Proliferation of Nuclear Weapons (NPT) is the most important instrument. Nuclear disarmament goes beyond non-proliferation and aims to establish a pathway to a world free of nuclear weapons. Nuclear arms

42 Convention on the Prohibition of the Use, Stockpiling, Production and Transfer of Anti-Personnel Mines and on Their Destruction.

43 Convention on Cluster Munitions.

44 Convention on the Prohibition of the Development, Production and Stockpiling of Bacteriological (Biological) and Toxin Weapons and on their Destruction.

45 Convention on the Prohibition of the Development, Production, Stockpiling and Use of Chemical Weapons and on their Destruction.

control law includes highly detailed agreements and verification mechanisms between States possessing nuclear weapons to limit or reduce the amount, type, or yield of their respective nuclear weapons arsenals.

Nuclear weapons law is an area in which, despite its importance for the maintenance of international peace and security – the primary purpose listed in the UN Charter[46] – the United Nations is of secondary importance. While the organs of the United Nations, most notably the International Court of Justice (ICJ) and the Security Council, are often at the centre of international law discourse, it is other specialised international organisations and actors that dominate the field of nuclear weapons law. In international law, these two UN organs typically determine the compliance of States with international obligations. However, within the domain of nuclear weapons law, they assume a more marginal role. Such a deviation from standard scenarios in international law and the relevance of different actors renders the topic of nuclear weapons law an interesting area of research.

The question of compliance is always a controversial topic in international law. Given the absence of an equivalent to an executive power at the international level, verifying and enforcing international law is from time to time complicated. Indeed, one of the prominent criticisms of international law is precisely this absence of comprehensive powers to enforce compliance.[47] The assessment of compliance with the obligations assumed under nuclear weapons law is of the utmost importance. A breach of these obligations, which in the worst case could be the acquisition of a nuclear weapon, has the potential to cause irreversible consequences for the international security order.

The ICJ is the principal judicial organ of the United Nations,[48] yet its powers in the context of nuclear weapons law are limited given the courts limited jurisdiction. The ICJ has jurisdiction over a case only in three cases: Two or more disputing States present a case to the court (so-called *compromis*)[49], a State has accepted the ICJ's compulsory jurisdiction,[50] or a treaty

---

46 Article 1 para. 1 of the UN Charter.

47 On the seminal question of enforceability in international law, see *Gerald Fitzmaurice*, The Foundations of the Authority of International Law and the Problem of Enforcement, The Modern Law Review 19 (1956), 1–13.

48 Article 92 of the UN Charter.

49 Article 36 para. 1 ICJ Statute.

50 Article 36 para. 2 ICJ Statute.

establishes the ICJ's jurisdiction in a *compromissory clause*.[51] In the context of nuclear weapons law several issues arise. For instance, in the event of an alleged breach of the fundamental obligation of the Nuclear Non-Proliferation Treaty – specifically the development of a nuclear weapon by a non-nuclear weapon State –, it is very unlikely that the proliferating State would accept an *ad-hoc* jurisdiction by the ICJ. Moreover, the NPT does not include a *compromissory clause*. In addition, only 74 out of the 193 UN Member States have accepted the ICJ's compulsory jurisdiction, many of them with reservations, some of which are quite extensive.[52] Even if such a judgment were to be rendered, it would often be issued at a point where a nuclear weapons programme is at an advanced stage, making corrective measures difficult. Thus, the ICJ's authority in contentious cases regarding non-proliferation law is limited. In instances where the ICJ has been called upon to adjudicate on a contentious matter concerning nuclear weapons,[53] the issue of non-proliferation was not addressed. While the ICJ pronounced itself on the topic in the *Nuclear Weapons Advisory Opinion*,[54] this advisory opinion is neither binding nor did it specifically address the question of non-proliferation. The ICJ's capacity to adjudicate and pronounce itself in question regarding nuclear weapons law is limited and it does not play a role in ensuring compliance.

The second organ is the UN Security Council. In contrast to the ICJ, it has played a role in nuclear non-proliferation. While the Security Council has often been and still is blocked by the veto rights of its permanent

51 Article 36 para. 1 ICJ Statute. On compromissory clauses, see *Jonathan I. Charney*, Compromissory Clauses and the Jurisdiction of the International Court of Justice, American Journal of International Law 81 (1987), 855–887.

52 *Gary L. Scott/Craig L. Carr*, The ICJ and Compulsory Jurisdiction: The Case for Closing the Clause, American Journal of International Law 81 (1987), 57–76; *Stanimir A. Alexandrov*, Accepting the Compulsory Jurisdiction of the International Court of Justice with Reservations: An Overview of Practice with a Focus on Recent Trends and Cases, Leiden Journal of International Law 14 (2001), 89–124.

53 *International Court of Justice*, Obligations concerning Negotiations relating to Cessation of the Nuclear Arms Race and to Nuclear Disarmament (Marshall Islands v. India), Jurisdiction and Admissibility, Judgment, I.C.J. Reports 2016, p. 255; Obligations concerning Negotiations relating to Cessation of the Nuclear Arms Race and to Nuclear Disarmament (Marshall Islands v. Pakistan), Jurisdiction and Admissibility, Judgment, I.C.J. Reports 2016, p. 552; Obligations concerning Negotiations relating to Cessation of the Nuclear Arms Race and to Nuclear Disarmament (Marshall Islands v. United Kingdom), Preliminary Objections, Judgment, I.C.J. Reports 2016, p. 833.

54 *International Court of Justice*, Legality of the Threat or Use of Nuclear Weapons, Advisory Opinion, ICJ Reports 1996, p. 226.

members,[55] the P5 – being also the only States recognised by the NPT as nuclear-weapon States – have historically found consensus in cases of enforcing nuclear non-proliferation. This commitment is evidenced by the Security Council's responses to Iraq's clandestine nuclear programme in the 1990s, as reflected in the establishment of UNSCOM under UNSCR 687, and its subsequent efforts to prevent the proliferation of nuclear weapons to non-state actors, as outlined in UNSCR 1540. These acts were all adopted under Chapter VII of the UN Charter, thereby conferring legal binding obligations upon all States. However, it is important to note that the Security Council, in isolation, is unable to ensure nuclear non-proliferation; rather, it functions as a pivotal actor within a complex network of other actors at a stage when a State has already engaged in a nuclear weapons programme.

In lieu of the main actors in international law, nuclear weapons law is a regime in which specialised international organisations exercise a significant degree of authority, directly interfering with the sovereignty of States. While there are cases in which an international organisation can directly oblige a Member State, such as the Security Council under Chapter VII of the Charter or (quasi-)judicial decisions from the ICJ or the World Trade Organization's Dispute Settlement Mechanism, or sometimes even individuals[56], such powers are rare. Instruments of international organisations frequently consist of non-binding recommendations[57] or mere information.[58]

55 Article 27 para. 3 of the UN Charter.

56 On the effect on individuals, see *Clemens A. Feinäugle*, The UN Security Council Al-Qaida and Taliban Sanctions Committee: Emerging Principles of International Institutional Law for the Protection of Individuals?, in: Armin von Bogdandy/Rüdiger Wolfrum/Jochen von Bernstorff/Philipp Dann/Matthias Goldmann (eds.), The Exercise of Public Authority by International Institutions, Berlin, Heidelberg: Springer 2010, 101–131.

57 See for example *Gefion Schuler*, Effective Governance through Decentralized Soft Implementation: The OECD Guidelines for Multinational Enterprises, in: Armin von Bogdandy/Rüdiger Wolfrum/Jochen von Bernstorff/Philipp Dann/Matthias Goldmann (eds.), The Exercise of Public Authority by International Institutions, Berlin, Heidelberg: Springer 2010, 197–226.

58 See for example *Erika de Wet*, Governance through Promotion and Persuasion: The 1998 ILO Declaration on Fundamental Principles and Rights at Work, in: Armin von Bogdandy/Rüdiger Wolfrum/Jochen von Bernstorff/Philipp Dann/Matthias Goldmann (eds.), The Exercise of Public Authority by International Institutions, Berlin, Heidelberg: Springer 2010, 377–403; *Joseph Windsor*, The WTO Committee on Trade in Financial Services: The Exercise of Public Authority within an Informational Forum, in, Berlin, Heidelberg: Springer 2010, 405–435.

Where there are concrete actions, they are usually limited to the role of the State within the international organisation,[59] such as the suspension of voting rights or access to funds, without having direct impact to a Member State's territory. While these instruments also show an exercise of authority,[60] the level of authority within nuclear weapons law is of another order of magnitude: An international organisation can send international civil servants to a State to verify its compliance with international legal instruments, at facilities often operated by private-owned entities. These civil servants might bring to light clandestine nuclear weapons programmes, potentially leading to (coercive) action by the IAEA or even the UN Security Council. The origin of this high level of authority is obvious: The dramatic and potentially irreversible consequences of a lack of compliance. Once a State has acquired nuclear weapons, any coercive actions to reinstate compliance is difficult, as such a State then has the elevated positions of nuclear deterrence and nuclear coercion.[61] The case of North Korea serves as a prominent example.

Such a high degree of authority is important to maintain international peace and security. In instances where the exercise of authority by international organisations is insufficient to prevent the proliferation of nuclear weapons, States may resort to unilateral measures including the use of force. The question of whether a (suspected) nuclear weapons programme is sufficient to justify military attacks under Article 51 of the UN Charter is a subject of a controversial debate.[62] Israel invoked the argument of self-defence against nuclear proliferation when it destroyed the Iraqi Osirak

---

59 See for example *Ute Mager*, The UNESCO Regime for the Protection of World Heritage, in: Armin von Bogdandy/Rüdiger Wolfrum/Jochen von Bernstorff/Philipp Dann/Matthias Goldmann (eds.), The Exercise of Public Authority by International Institutions, Berlin, Heidelberg: Springer 2010, 337–339.

60 See for example the influence of the OECD's PISA Policy to national policies, *Armin von Bogdandy/Matthias Goldmann*, The Exercise of International Public Authority through National Policy Assessment: The OECD's PISA Policy as a Paradigm for a New International Standard Instrument, International Organizations Law Review 5 (2008), 241–298.

61 More on these concepts below, Chapter 2 Section 1.1.

62 *Christian Henderson*, The Bush Doctrine: From Theory to Practice, Journal of Conflict & Security Law 9 (2004), 3–24; *Rachel A. Weise*, How Nuclear Weapons Change the Doctrine of Self-Defense Note, New York University Journal of International Law and Politics 44 (2011), 1331–1398; *Arman Sarvarian*, The Lawfulness of a Use of Force Upon Nuclear Facilities in Self-Defence, Journal on the Use of Force and International Law 1 (2014), 247–272.

reactor in 1981,[63] the Syrian Dair Alzour reactor[64] or attacked Iran's nuclear programme in 2025.[65] A similar argument was presented by the so-called *coalition of the willing* when it invaded Iraq in 2003.[66]

3.2 The Interest to Study Nuclear Proliferation

A central topic of this book is proliferation. Proliferation, in the context of nuclear weapons, refers to the spread and advancement of nuclear capabilities, and it shows in two dimensions: horizontal and vertical.[67]

Horizontal proliferation occurs when a non-nuclear-weapon State (NNWS) – a state that previously did not possess nuclear weapons – acquires nuclear weapons. This type of proliferation expands the number of states possessing such weapons. The proliferation of nuclear weapons has started in the 1940s during World War II. Following a letter sent by Albert Einstein to President Roosevelt and fueled by fears of a German nuclear weapon,[68] the United States initiated a nuclear weapons programme (the

63 *Istvan Pogany*, The Destruction of Osirak: A Legal Perspective, The World Today 37 (1981), 413–418.

64 Both attacks were carried out following the so-called Begin Doctrine, the Israeli policy to use force preventively to stop enemies from acquiring weapons of mass destruction. On the so-called "Operation Outside the Box" and the Begin Doctrine, see *Ori Wertman/Christian Kaunert*, Operation "Outside the Box": The Securitization of the Syrian Nuclear Reactor, in: Israel: National Security and Securitization: The Role of the United States in Defining What Counts, Cham: Springer International Publishing 2023, 123–148.

65 *Michael N. Schmitt*, Israel's Operation Rising Lion and the Right of Self-Defense in: Lieber Institute Articles of War, https://lieber.westpoint.edu/israels-operation-rising-lion-right-of-self-defense/, last accessed 17 July 2025.

66 See e.g. the Address given to the UN Security Council by the then US Secretary of State Colin Power, https://georgewbush-whitehouse.archives.gov/news/releases/2003/02/20030205-1.html, last accessed 25 February 2025.

67 *Tom Sauer*, Nuclear Arms Control, Harvard: Macmillan 1998, at 31; *Vitaly Goldansky*, Connection between Horizontal and Vertical Proliferation of Nuclear Weapons, in: Joseph Rotblat/Laszlo Valki (eds.), Coexistence, Cooperation and Common Security: Annals of Pugwash 1986, London: Palgrave Macmillan UK 1988, 21–36; *Sabine Bauer/Cormac O'Reilly*, The Comprehensive Nuclear-Test-Ban Treaty Organization (CTBTO): Current and Future Role in the Verification Regime of the Nuclear-Test-Ban Treaty, in: Jonathan L. Black-Branch/Dieter Fleck (eds.), Nuclear Non-Proliferation in International Law: Volume II – Verification and Compliance, The Hague: T.M.C. Asser Press 2016, 131–150, at 142.

68 On 2 August 1939, Albert Einstein wrote a letter to President Roosevelt, indicating the risk that Germany was underway to develop a nuclear weapon. On the German

so-called Manhattan Project) in 1942, conducted the first nuclear weapons test (Trinity Test) on 16 July 1945 and dropped two nuclear weapons on Hiroshima on 6 August 1945 and Nagasaki on 9 August 1945.[69] Intelligence insights from the German *Uranprojekt* and the Manhattan Project aided the Soviet nuclear weapons programme, resulting in a first test in 1949.[70] The United Kingdom followed in 1952, France in 1960 and China in 1964. While many other States pursued nuclear weapons programmes during this time, the adoption of the Nuclear Non-Proliferation Treaty in 1968 halted many – but not all – of them.[71] Israel constructed nuclear weapons in the 1960s or 1970s,[72] India in the 1970s,[73] Pakistan in the 1990s,[74] and North Korea in the 2000s.[75] Between the 1970s and 1990s, South Africa possessed nuclear weapons as well but later dismantled them.[76] Today, nine States possess nuclear weapons: United States, Russia, United Kingdom, France, China, Israel, India, Pakistan and North Korea. In addition, Iran has had an

---

nuclear programme, see *Helmut Rechenberg*, 50 Jahre Kernspaltung: Transurane, Uranspaltung und das deutsche Uranprojekt, Physikalische Blätter 44 (1988), 453–459.

69 On the Manhattan Project, see *Bruce Cameron Reed*, The History and Science of the Manhattan Project, Berlin, Heidelberg: Springer 2019.

70 On the role of intelligence, see *Robert Chadwell Williams*, Klaus Fuchs, Atom Spy, Cambridge: Harvard University Press 1987. On the Soviet nuclear programme, see *John Beyer/Julian Cooper/Gerald Holden et al.*, The Soviet Union, in: Scilla McLean (ed.), How Nuclear Weapons Decisions are Made, London: Palgrave Macmillan UK 1986, 1–31.

71 On nuclear weapons programmes during the 1950s and 1960s, see below Chapter 2, Section 1.1.

72 The so-called Vela incident occurred on 22 September 1979 when US satellites detected an unidentified double flash. The most common interpretation is that a nuclear weapons test took place: *Lars-Erik De Geer/Christopher M. Wright*, The 22 September 1979 Vela Incident: Radionuclide and Hydroacoustic Evidence for a Nuclear Explosion, Science & Global Security 26 (2018), 20–54. This test is attributed to Israel: *Leonard Weiss*, Israel's 1979 Nuclear Test and the U.S. Cover-Up, Middle East Policy XVIII (2011), 83–95.

73 *Elisabeth Röhrlich*, Inspectors for Peace, Baltimore: John Hopkins University Press 2022, at 1 ff.

74 *Samina Ahmed*, Pakistan's Nuclear Weapons Program: Turning Points and Nuclear Choices, International Security 23 (1999), 178–204.

75 *Hans M. Kristensen/Matt Korda*, North Korean Nuclear Weapons, 2021, Bulletin of the Atomic Scientists 77 (2021), 222–236.

76 *Waldo Stumpf*, South Africa's Nuclear Weapons Program: From Deterrance to Dismantlement, Arms Control Today 25 (1995), 3–8.

advanced nuclear weapons programme.[77] Those States possess more than 12,000 nuclear weapons.[78]

Vertical proliferation, by contrast, refers to the qualitative and quantitative enhancement of nuclear weapons by states that already possess them – referred to as nuclear-weapon States (NWS).[79] This form of proliferation involves the development of new warhead designs, improvements in delivery systems such as missiles or submarines, increased weapon accuracy, greater destructive yields, yield to weight ratio, or the expansion of existing arsenals. The United States can be taken as an example: The Manhattan Project produced three relatively simple one-stage fission-only nuclear gravity bombs.[80] At the height of the Cold War in the mid-1980s, the United States possessed more than 27,000 nuclear weapons.[81] These weapons came in a variety of sizes and configurations. The US stockpile includes multi-stage thermonuclear weapons, gravity bombs, intercontinental ballistic missiles, submarine-launched ballistic missiles and weapons with and adjustable yield.[82]

NWS are investing massively in vertical proliferation. The United States is expected to invest more than one trillion dollars in modernising its nuclear weapons arsenal within the next quarter century, not including inflation.[83] The United Kingdom's programme to replace submarines which are equipped with nuclear weapons amounts to GBP 41 billion over 35 years.[84] Russia spends around USD 300 billion on the modernisation and

---

77 *Paul K. Kerr*, Iran and Nuclear Weapons Production, Washington DC: Congressional Research Service 2024. The current state of Iran's nuclear programme following the US-Israel attacks is unknown.

78 *Hans M. Kristensen/Matt Korda*, World Nuclear Forces, in: Stockholm International Peace Research Institute (ed.), SIPRI Yearbook 2024: Armaments, Disarmament and International Security, Stockholm: Stockholm International Peace Research Institute 2024, 271–376.

79 *Mark P. Hilborne*, The Non-Proliferation Treaty. Foundation of Disarmament Policy, in: Harsh V. Pant (ed.), Handbook of Nuclear Proliferation, London, New York: Routledge 2012, 251–260, at 251; *Victor W. Sidel*, Vertical Nuclear Proliferation, Medicine, Conflict and Survival 23 (2007), 249–258.

80 On different weapon technologies, see below Chapter 1, Section 4.

81 *Robert S. Norris/Hans M. Kristensen*, Global Nuclear Weapons Inventories, 1945–2010, Bulletin of the Atomic Scientists 66 (2010), 77–83.

82 *U.S. Department of Defense*, Nuclear Posture Review, Washington DC: U.S. Government 2022.

83 *Congressional Budget Office*, Approaches for Managing the Costs of U.S. Nuclear Forces, 2017 to 2046, 2017.

84 *Claire Mills/Esme Kirk-Wade*, The Cost of the UK's Strategic Nuclear Deterrent, London: House of Commons Research Briefing 2023.

expansion of its nuclear arsenal.[85] In this decade, France spends EUR 52 billion on modernising its nuclear arsenal.[86] In other numbers: All nine NWS spend combined almost USD 3,000 per second on maintaining and expanding their nuclear arsenals.[87]

Technological developments can influence both horizontal and vertical proliferation. New technologies may allow NNWS to acquire material or knowledge necessary to develop a nuclear weapon more easily. Such a scenario could pose a threat of horizontal nuclear proliferation. Such developments can also be utilised by NWS. New technologies may facilitate the production of material necessary for nuclear weapons, and thus facilitating the expansion of nuclear weapons arsenals. In such a scenario, a horizontal threat of NNWS acquiring nuclear weapons is also a vertical threat that NWS are consequently motivated to expand their arsenals. In addition, technologies developed for civilian use can also be beneficial for increasing the sophistication of a nuclear weapon. For example, they could allow for the construction of smaller more versatile weapons or bigger more destructive weapons. Moreover, new technologies may provide NWS with means to facilitate the maintenance of their arsenals.

3.3 The Interest and Scope of This Study

As fusion energy may play a significant role in the fight against the climate crisis, it is of particular interest how nuclear weapons law ensures that the use of fusion remains exclusively peaceful in order to help fully harnessing the potential of this technology. There is a tension between sustainable development and securing peace:[88] on the one hand, no application of nuclear weapons law might lead to a scenario in which fusion leads to the further proliferation of nuclear weapons. On the other hand, a regime that

---

85 *Julian Cooper*, How Much Does Russia Spend on Nuclear Weapons? in: SIPRI, https://www.sipri.org/commentary/topical-backgrounder/2018/how-much-does-russia-spend-nuclear-weapons, last accessed 17 July 2025.

86 https://www.bfmtv.com/economie/entreprises/defense/budget-des-armees-la-dissuasion-nucleaire-questionnee-a-l-assemblee-nationale_AD-202305240081.html, last accessed 25 February 2025.

87 *ICAN*, Surge 2023: Global Nuclear Weapons Spending, Geneva: ICAN 2024, at 4.

88 On the tension between nuclear energy to mitigate climate change and the risk of further proliferation, see Robert J. Goldston, Climate Change, Nuclear Power, and Nuclear Proliferation: Magnitude Matters, Science & Global Security 19 (2011), 130-165.

is not adapted to a specific technology, which is still in its infancy, may impose to burdens and costs, capable to limit the technology's potential. The regime of nuclear weapons law – developed for fission and its specific risk potential – is faced with the developed of a new technology with a different risk profile. Moreover, the regime of nuclear weapons law is characterised by many shortcomings, ongoing conflicts and an increased level of contestation. This book will analyse the role of fusion within the regime and explore how nuclear weapons law can find a convincing way forward.

The development of fusion energy will be of particular interest for non-proliferation and disarmament law as fusion technology can be used to develop nuclear weapons against existing obligations not to develop nuclear weapons and corresponding verification regimes. While nuclear weapons law also comprises arms control law, fusion is of less relevance for this domain of law. Arms control commitments are independent of the physical processes within a weapon and thus, the development of fusion energy only has a limited influence on the regime of nuclear arms control.[89] For example, one of the most relevant arms control instruments was the New START Treaty between the United States and Russia. This treaty limits the number of deployed missiles, warheads and bombers as well as launchers. Whether the warhead is powered by fission-only or a combination of fission and fusion or whether a bomber deploys a simple uranium bomb or a hydrogen bomb is of no relevance for the New START Treaty. Consequently, as fusion does not pose specific challenges to this are of law, this book does not engage in an analysis of arms control law.

4 Outline of the Book

In the evolving landscape of energy technology, the introduction of fusion energy presents a complex array of challenges and opportunities for the legal framework governing nuclear non-proliferation and disarmament. This book is the first comprehensive study of fusion within the context of the legal framework of nuclear weapons. It delves into these intricacies in five

89 It should also be noted that relevant international legal instruments in nuclear arms control have ceased to exist. On this, see *Philipp Sauter*, Russia's Withdrawal from New START – The End of a Cold War Relic, but Not the Beginning of a New Nuclear Arms Race (2023), in: Völkerrechtsblog, https://voelkerrechtsblog.org/russias-withdrawal-from-new-start/.

chapters, each addressing a distinct aspect of the fusion technology's implications on nuclear weapons law. The book's central objective is to provide a comprehensive analysis of how the legal framework of nuclear weapons can effectively regulate the peaceful use of fusion for energy production.

Chapter 1 sets the stage by exploring the technological aspect associated with nuclear fusion. The chapter will explain the basic concepts of physics necessary to understand the legal analysis that follows. It focuses on the differences between fusion and fission technologies as well as the functioning of nuclear weapons. The chapter further provides a detailed analysis of the proliferation potential of fusion.

Chapter 2 examines the legal background of nuclear weapons law. It examines the politics and interests of actors within the regime, supported by historic examples of the evolution of the regime. In addition, the chapter provides an overview of the institutional framework and the various legal sources which are of relevance for addressing fusion. It further explores the different regimes of nuclear non-proliferation and nuclear disarmament law. Additionally, the chapter analyses the role of law within the broader context of nuclear weapons.

Chapter 3 undertakes a critical examination of the existing framework of nuclear weapons law with respect to the proliferation concerns of fusion technology. It analyses the applicability of existing frameworks to fusion and identifies areas where the legal provisions may be too stringent or, conversely, insufficiently comprehensive. This analysis highlights the gaps and ambiguities within the legal structures that govern nuclear non-proliferation and disarmament, particularly as applied to fusion.

Chapter 4 proposes approaches to bridge the identified gaps by adapting the legal framework. It discusses evolutionary interpretation, which could offer flexibility in applying existing laws to fusion technology. The chapter further explores the role of exercising authority by the relevant actors involved in nuclear weapons law in adapting the regime for fusion. Furthermore, the chapter will explore where treaty changes are required and how they can be implemented.

Chapter 5 offers a forward-looking perspective on the potential for treaty changes in light of fusion technology's emergence and proposes the adoption of a Fusion Treaty that comprehensively covers all aspects of fusion regulation. This chapter discusses the rational of such a comprehensive approach and the structure of such a treaty.

The book concludes with a summary of the findings.

Chapter 1: Technological Background

This chapter explores the scientific and technological background relevant to fusion and the technology's role in nuclear weapons. First, this chapter explains the fundamentals of nuclear physics relevant for energy production and proliferation, thereby establishing a baseline of scientific comprehension for the subsequent legal analysis (1). The chapter delves into the underlying physical principles of nuclear fusion and the commercialisation pathways of this technology for energy production (2). Subsequent to this section, a comparison is drawn between fusion and fission (3). The chapter then goes on to provide a concise overview of the relevant fundamentals of nuclear weapons (4). Following the establishment of the fundamentals, the subsequent section explores the specific applications of fusion in the context of nuclear weapons and the potential for proliferation (5).

1 Fundamentals of Nuclear Physics

This section explores the fundamentals of nuclear physics to a degree that is necessary to understand the functioning of nuclear weapons as well as the role of fusion. It explains the modern understanding of the atom and its nucleus, what isotopes are and relevant nuclear processes.

1.1 Atom and its Nucleus

Atoms are the fundamental building blocks of all matter. In its simplest model, an atom consists of a nucleus and a shell. The shell consists of negatively charged electrons, while the nucleus is made of positively charged protons, and neutrons that carry no charge. Electrons are negative, protons are positive, and neutrons are neutral. Atoms are electrically neutral, with the number of protons being equal to the number of electrons. While the atomic nucleus accounts for less than 0.01 % of the total volume of the atom, it bears almost the entire weight. The weight of an electron is negligible in comparison to that of a proton or a neutron. Conversely, the weight of a proton is approximately equivalent to that of a neutron. The number of protons in an atom is what defines it. Hydrogen has one proton, helium has two, lithium has three, and so on in the periodic table.

The constituents of the nucleus (i.e., protons and neutrons) are bound together by the so-called strong nuclear force, which is the strongest force in the universe and one of the four fundamental forces in physics.[90] The strong nuclear force is so potent that it allows for the harvesting of energy at a level several (about six) orders of magnitude higher than in chemical reactions, such as the burning of coal or the explosion of TNT, where electromagnetic energy is released.

1.2 Isotopes

In the context of atomic structure, the number of neutrons within an atom can vary. Atoms that possess the same number of protons but a different number of neutrons are called isotopes. They share the same chemical properties but they differ in mass. The mass of an atom is typically denoted by a small number as a superscript or is added to the element name by a dash. This number is the sum of protons and neutrons. For instance, hydrogen (H) comprises three isotopes: regular hydrogen ^{1}H, deuterium ^{2}H and tritium ^{3}H. Specifically for hydrogen isotopes, other abbreviations are used: D for deuterium and T for tritium. The atomic nucleus of regular hydrogen ^{1}H (sometimes also called protium) consists solely of a proton, deuterium ^{2}H consists of one proton and one neutron, and tritium ^{3}H contains one proton and two neutrons. In a smilar manner, uranium exists in different isotopes. The most abundant isotope of uranium is ^{238}U (or denoted as uranium-238 or U-238) which consists of 92 protons and 146 neutrons. The isotopes ^{235}U and ^{233}U are of particular relevance to this book; ^{235}U consists of 92 protons and 143 neutrons, ^{233}U consists of 92 protons and 141 neutrons. Another pertinent example is plutonium, which has 94 protons and, in its standard form ^{244}Pu, 150 neutrons. Of relevance for this book is the isotope ^{239}Pu with 145 neutrons and 94 protons.

1.3 Radioactivity

Some isotopes are unstable. For instance, tritium consists of two neutrons more than regular hydrogen. The nucleus of this hydrogen isotope is three

90 The four fundamental forces are: the strong nuclear force, the weak nuclear force, the electromagnetic force and gravity.

times its typical size and is unstable. The process of nuclear instability is characterised by the tendency of a nucleus to undergo a radioactive decay, which in turn gives rise to the phenomenon of radioactivity. Notable examples of radioactive elements include tritium, uranium, and plutonium. Following the decay process, the nucleus transforms into another nucleus. This decay is a statistical process, characterised by the half-life, which is defined as the time after which half of the nuclei have decayed. For instance, tritium has a half-life of approximately twelve years. If one were to start with one kilogram of tritium today, after a period of about twelve years there would be only 500 grams remaining. After around twenty four years, there would be 250 grammes, circa thirty six years later only 125 grammes would remain and so on. During this decay, tritium turns into helium-3, a rare yet stable isotope of helium.

1.4 Neutron Capture

Another improtant nuclear process is neutron capture. Atomic nuclei have the capacity to capture a free neutron and to integrate it into its structure. For instance, ^{235}U can capture a neutron and subsequently transform into ^{236}U. Sometimes, if a nucleus catches a neutron, a neutron transforms into a proton. In the event of this occurence, the identity of the element changes, given that the number of protons is what defines an atom. This phenomenon is called transmutation. To illustrate, in the instance of ^{238}U catching a neutron, the resultant nucleus subsequently turns into ^{239}Pu.

In addition to the process of neutron capture, atomic nuclei have the capacity to undergo fission, whereby they divide into smaller nuclei, or fusion, whereby smaller nuclei combine to form a larger atomic nucleus. The capability of a nucleus to undergo fission or fusion is contingent upon its mass. Atomic nuclei that are heavier than iron are capable of undergoing fission, whereas nuclei that are lighter than iron are capable of undergoing fusion.

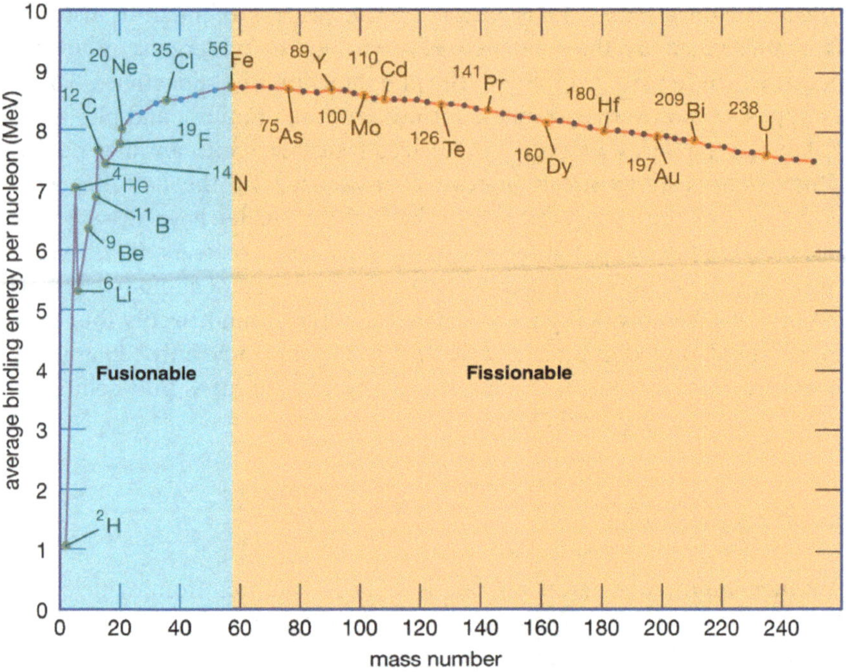

Figure 1: Comparison of the binding energy per nucleus as a function the mass number of the atomic nucleus. Due to the maximum at A=56, which is the mass of iron, iron is the defining element that separates fusionable (on the left) and fissionable (on the right) nuclei.[91]

2 Nuclear Fusion

Nuclear fusion – also referred to fusion for short – is the process that powers the stars. The harnessing of this energy has been an objective of scientists for decades. Historically, fusion research advanced more gradually than the optimistic predictions of its early decades, though it has now delivered the scientific basis for moving toward fusion pilot plants. Recent advancements in research and heightened interest from policy makers as well as private investors have led to the promises of commercial fusion within the next decade or two. Nuclear fusion has the potential to provide

91 Adopted and edited from https://cdn.britannica.com/46/6046-050-D533C3B3/energies-function-atomic-mass-number.jpg, last accessed 17 July 2025.

the world with a safe, greenhouse gas free and inexhaustable energy source without the downsides associated with today's nuclear energy. Fusion reactions do not produce radioactive waste that needs to be taken care of for several centuries or even millenia. Similarly, fusion reactors do not pose the risk of accidents like nuclear fission power plants. This section will explore the fundamental principles of nuclear fusion and the pathway towards its commercialisation.

2.1 Basics of Nuclear Fusion

The process of fusing atomic nuclei on Earth is an outstandingly difficult endeavour. Despite the experimental discovery of nuclear fusion[92] five years earlier than fission,[93] to date no fusion power plant exists, whereas there are hundreds of fission power plants in operation. Fusion has yet to leave the realm of fundamental research at universities and national laboratories. Today's fusion machines are among the most complex technical devices ever built. This is due to the fact that certain conditions must be met for fusion to occur. In fusion, two atomic nuclei have to be brought that closely together so the strong nuclear force attracts them. However, since atomic nuclei are positively charged, they repel each other due to the so-called Coulomb repulsion. The atomic nucleus, composed of positive protons and neutral neutrons, exhibits a net positive charge. Like charges repel each other, opposite charges attract each other. It is only when this repulsion is overcome that the strong nuclear force becomes dominant and fusion can occur. To overcome this repulsion, high temperatures in the order of tens to hundreds of millions of degrees Celsius are necessary. At these temperatures, matter exists in its fourth state, known as the plasma state. A plasma is a gas in which atoms disintegrate into their consituents, nuclei and electrons. Due to the high temperatures required for a nuclear reaction, such fusion reaction are called *thermonuclear*.

92 *Marcus Laurence Elwin Oliphant/Ernest Rutherford*, Experiments on the Transmutation of Elements by Protons, Proceedings of the Royal Society of London. Series A, Containing Papers of a Mathematical and Physical Character 141 (1933), 259–281.

93 *Otto Hahn/Fritz Strassmann*, Über den Nachweis und das Verhalten der bei der Bestrahlung des Urans mittels Neutronen entstehenden Erdalkalimetalle, Naturwissenschaften 27 (1939), 11–15.

In order for fusion reactions to be efficient, it is necessary that the so-called *Lawson criterion* is fulfilled.[94] In this context, the triple product

$$Tn\tau_E \quad (1)$$

of temperature T, density n and energy confinement time τ_E must exceed a certain threshold. To put this formula into (a simplified) context: The higher the temperature, the more energy each atomic nucleus has, and the greater the probability is to overcome the Coulomb barrier and thus of a fusion reaction. Similarly, the closer the particles are together, i.e., the higher the density is, the more likely the nuclei are to come close enough to fuse. Moreover, the longer the energy is confined, the more reactions are likely to occur.

In stars, this criterion is met by high gravitational pressure. Stars are extremely heavy, resulting in gravitational attraction of all matter of the star to its center. On Earth, complex technology is required, making the commercialisation of fusion a lengthy process. Over the past decades of fusion research, a number of different technologies have been developed. They differ both in the type of atoms to be fused and in the technology used to confine the plasma, which is over 150 million degrees hot.

2.2 Confinement Technologies

Fusion occurs at temperatures in the millions of degrees Celsius. One cannot simply put a 150 million degree hot plasma in a pot. Since no material can withstand these temperatures, fusion requires special confinement methods, sometimes described as bottling the artificial star.

The majority of fusion research facilities and start-ups follow the concept of *magnetic confinement,* wherein a series of magnetic coils confine the plasma. Magnetic fields keep together the plasma in a vacuum chamber. Typically, these machines are toroidal in shape and are often compared to the shape of a doughnut. Different mechanisms are employed to heat the plasma to the required temperatures. One such mechanism is a complex

94 *J. D. Lawson*, Some Criteria for a Power Producing Thermonuclear Reactor, Proceedings of the Physical Society – Section B 70 (1957), 6. On the role of the Lawson criterion for today's research, see: *Samuel E. Wurzel/Scott C. Hsu*, Progress Toward Fusion Energy Breakeven and Gain as Measured Against the Lawson Criterion, Physics of Plasmas 29 (2022), 062103.

version of a microwave oven,[95] utilising electromagnetic waves to heat the particles of the plasma. Another mechanism involves the introduction of particles at a high velocity, leading to collisions between particles, which in turn deposits heat into the plasma. A third, comparably minor, mechanism is the application of an electric current to the plasma. As known from chargers of phones or notebooks, an electric current produces heat.

Most magnetic confinement fusion facilities fall into two configurations: *tokamaks* and *stellarators*. The primary distiction between these two types of fusion devices pertains to the configuration of magnets. Tokamaks have two different sets of magnets but a rather simple geometry, while stellarators only have a single set of magnets but a highly complex geometry. Research facilities predominantly use tokamaks. While plasma physics in tokamaks is fairly well understood, there are significant challenges associated with their operation. The use of high magnetic fields necessitates the shutdown and subequent cooling down of magnets after a certain period of time. In addition, periodic plasma eroptions expose the material to extreme heat deposition.[96] A continuous operation is not possible with tokamaks, only a pulsed one, meaning that the machine has to be switched off after a certain period of time. Conversely, stellarators offer the potential for continuous operation; however, the comprehension of plasma physics in stellarators is comparatively underdeveloped relative to that in tokamaks.[97]

To date, the only fusion experiment that has achieved $Q > 1$, meaning a net-energy output, is the National Ignition Facility (NIF). It employs a different approach to confine the plasma: intertial confinement fusion (ICF), also called laser fusion. Rather than utilising magnetic fields to confine the plasma, NIF employs extremely power lasers that are focused on a target which contains the fusion fuel. The laser pulse drives the implosion to the required density, while the fuel's own inertia confines the plasma for the brief interval before the target disassembles. The energy of the laser heats the plasma to the required temperature threshold.

95 To be precise, fusion machines typically use a combination of electron cyclotron resonance heating (ECRH) and ion cyclotron resonance heating (ICRH).

96 So-called Edge-Localised Modes (ELMs). On the phenomenology of ELMs, see *Hartmut Zohm*, Edge Localized Modes (ELMs), Plasma Physics and Controlled Fusion 38 (1996), 105.

97 *Per Helander/Craig D. Beidler/T. M. Bird et al.*, Stellarator and Tokamak Plasmas: A Comparison, Plasma Physics and Controlled Fusion 54 (2012), 124009.

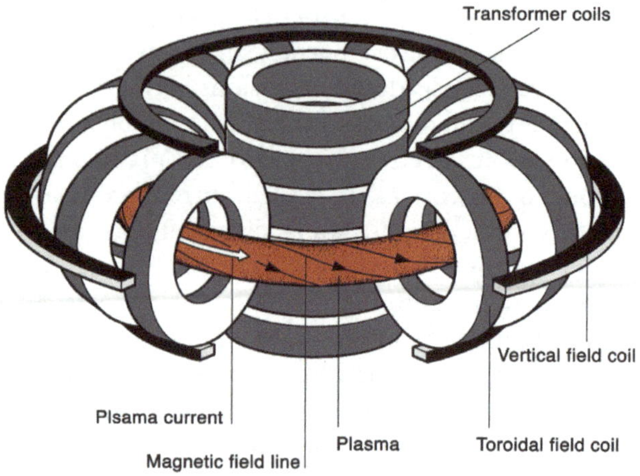

Figure 2: Schematic Depiction of a Tokamak[98]

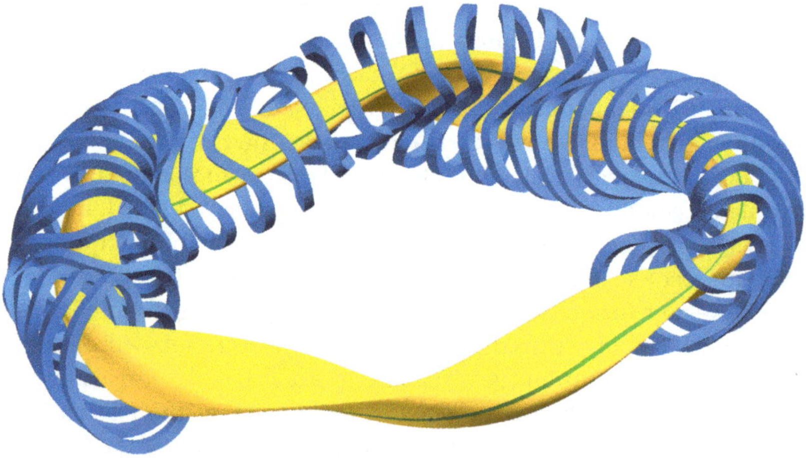

Figure 3: Schematic Depiction of a Stellarator[99]

98 Max-Planck-Institute for Plasma Physics, https://www.ipp.mpg.de/14869/tokamak, last accessed 17 July 2025.

99 Max-Planck-Institute for Plasma Physics, https://www.ipp.mpg.de/4326243/original-1673955102.webp?t=eyJ3aWR0aCI6NjgyLCJmaWxlX2V4dGVuc2lvbiI6IndlYnAiLCJvYmpfaWQiOjQzMjYyNDN9--21888a527ee4a6596ff10bf4dad6b5c56b56dfc1, last accessed 17 July 2025.

2.3 Fusionable Materials

The primary fusion fuel of our Sun is the fusion of two protons – regular hydrogen nuclei. Combined with an electron, they fuse to form the hydrogen isotope deuterium ^2H by releasing an electron neutrino v_e (which is not of interest for this book and is just added for physical correctness) and – most importantly – energy:

$$^1H + {}^1H + e^- \rightarrow {}^2H + \nu_e + 1.442\ \text{MeV} \quad (2)$$

The energy released is measured in the unit MeV which is the most common unit of energy in the field of nuclear physics.[100] As the energy released is comparatively low, other atomic nuclei are used for fusion experiments and future fusion power plants on Earth.

Current scientific experiments such as ASDEX Upgrade, Wendelstein 7-X, JT-60SA, EAST or DIII-D fuse two deuterium nuclei ^2H to form the helium isotope ^3He, a neutron n and energy:

$$^2H + {}^2H \rightarrow {}^3He + n + 3.3\ \text{MeV} \quad (3)$$

To further increase the amount of energy produced, deuterium can be fused with tritium ^3H to produce regular helium ^4He. This process, termed D-T reaction, is the reaction that will most likely power future fusion power plants.

$$^2H + {}^3H \rightarrow {}^4He + n + 17.6\ \text{MeV} \quad (4)$$

In other terms:

$$D + T \rightarrow {}^4He + n + 17.6\ \text{MeV} \quad (5)$$

It is important to put the amount of energy produced into context. One kilogram of coal contains approximately 20 MJ of energy. When the deuterium contained in one litre of regular water (i.e., one kilogram) is fused with tritium, approximately 30,000 MJ of energy are released.[101] To contextualise further: One kilogram of coal contains enough energy to drive a Tesla Model S for the distance of a marathon, while the deuterium in one

100 In nuclear physics, the typical unit for energy ins nuclear processes is MeV, short for mega electronvolt. In SI units, 1 MeV = 1.602×10^{-13} J.

101 One liter of water contains roughly 10^{22} deuterium atoms.

litre of water contains enough fusion energy to circumference the entire globe one and a half times in the same car.[102]

As tritium does not occur naturally, it must be produced artificially. This process is called *breeding*. The world's current main supply source of tritium is a by-product of fission reactions, specifically from heavy-water (i.e., deuterium replacing regular hydrogen in water molecules) moderated reactors of the CANDU type.[103] Within these reactors, a neutron, produced by the fission of uranium, is periodically captured by a deuterium nucleus, resulting in the formation of tritium. This is an example of the earlier outlined process of neutron capture. The significant demand for tritium in fusion research has led to plans to breed tritium (^3H) through the irradition of lithium (^6Li)with neutrons. ^6Li is an isotope of lithium with a natural abundance of approximately 7.5 %.

$$^6\text{Li} + \text{n} \rightarrow {}^4\text{He} + {}^3\text{H} \quad (6)$$

In this reaction, a ^6Li nucleus captures a neutron and transforms into ^4He and tritium.

2.4 Fusion in a Power Plant

The basic idea behind a fusion power plant is ambitious: Liberating the strongest force in the universe and using it for humanity's energy needs, based on simple water and lithium. Such a fusion power plant will comprise two primary constituents: Firstly, a fusion reactor and secondly, the energy generation section. Within the reactor, the aforementioned nuclear reactions occur, resulting in the release of energy. This energy is not electric energy, but kinetic or thermal energy, requiring an energy conversion process. The conceptual framework of a fusion power plant bears resemblance

102 For these calculations it is assumed that the car consumes 130 Wh per km and that 100 % of the energy could be converted into electricity.

103 On the tritium production in CANDU reactors, see: *Tae-Keun Park/Seon-Ki Kim*, Tritium: Its Generation and Pathways to the Environment at CANDU 6 Generating Stations, Nuclear Engineering and Design 163 (1996), 405–411. On the relevance of CANDU reactors for fusion research, see: *Richard J. Pearson/Armando B. Antoniazzi/William J. Nuttall*, Tritium Supply and Use: a Key Issue for the Development of Nuclear Fusion Energy, Fusion Engineering and Design 136 (2018), 1140–1148; *Muyi Ni/Yongliang Wang/Baoxin Yuan et al.*, Tritium Supply Assessment for ITER and DEMOnstration Power Plant, Fusion Engineering and Design 88 (2013), 2422–2426.

to that of conventional power plant technologies, such as coal, oil, gas, and nuclear fission. In essence, a fusion power plant can be conceptualised as a giant kettle. Physical and chemical processes – the burning of coal, oil, gas, the fission of an atomic nucleus, the fusion of two atomic nuclei – generate heat. Turning heat into electricity requires a steam generator and a turbine. The heat generates steam, the steam in turn powers turbine, which powers a generator that subsequently produces the actual electricity which is then transmitted to the power grid.

The operation of a fusion power plant necessitates a specific fuel cycle, providing deuterium and tritium. Deuterium gas is produced from regular water which is treated by specific chemical processes, the so-called Girdler sulfide process[104] and further distillation. On average, there is one molecule containing deuterium in 3,200 water molecules. These processes enable the separation of heavy water (first HDO, then D_2O) from regular water (H_2O). Subsequently, the heavy water undergoes electrolysis to separate deuterium from oxygen.

The supply with tritium is more complicated. In operation, a fusion power plant will produce its own tritium. For the start-up of a fusion power plant, an external supply – either from CANDU reactors or other fusion power plants – is required. The tritium produced in the fusion plant must be extracted and stored. A tritium supply cycle will be one of the most essential parts of a future fusion power plant.[105]

Inertial confinement fusion requires an additional step. This confinement technology utilizes small pellets of fuel, which are spheres containing a mixture of deuterium and tritium gas. The production of these pellets constitutes an additional step in the fuel cycle compared to magnetic confinement.

The fusion process itself does not generate waste, with the reaction product being helium, a gas that can be easily released into the atmosphere. However, waste will be produced from the fusion facility itself. The reactor components will require a specific handling after decommissioning due to their radioactivity. Neutrons produced in fusion reactions activate material, also leading to a certain degree of radioactivity. In addition, the reactor components will contain small traces of tritium which is radioactive. However, in comparison with fission power plants, the intensity and duration of

---

104 On hydrogen isotope separation, see. *Howard K. Rae*, Separation of Hydrogen Isotopes, Washington DC: American Chemical Society 1978.

105 *Ni/Wang/Yuan et al.* (n 103); *Pearson/Antoniazzi/Nuttall* (n 103).

radioactivity is severely limited. While fission waste needs to be taken care of for thousands of years, the majority of fusion waste will be recyclable and reusable after around 100 years.[106]

2.5 The Road to Commercial Fusion Energy

Despite the considerable promise of fusion technology, decades of research have yet to yield electricity generated by fusion. Among fusion scientists, a joke is regularly told: Fusion is only thirty years away and always will be. However, tremendous progress has been made in recent years, and various actors – both public and private – are pursuing roadmaps towards the commercialisation of fusion.

Currently, there are more than sixty fusion research facilities in operation, mostly located in Europe, North America and Asia. These facilities serve as experimental platforms for the exploration of confinement technologies, sizes, configurations, and other physical parameters, facilitating a deeper understanding of plasma physics. While a proportion of these facilities are involved in military programmes, the majority are dedicated to peaceful research. The JT-60SA, situated in Naka, Japan, and operated in collaboration by Japan and EUROfusion,[107] is currently the largest tokamak. Other important tokamaks include the recently decommissioned Joint European Torus (JET) or ASDEX-Upgrade. Within the domain of stellarators, Wendelstein 7-X, located in Greifswald, Germany and operated by the Max-Planck-Institute for Plasma Physics, represents the largest and most important facility. With regard to inertial confinement fusion, the National Ignition Facility, situated in the United States and operated by the US Department of Energy, is the most important facility.

In the coming years, ITER, short for International Thermonuclear Experimental Reactor or latin for *path*, is expected to become a pivotal fusion research facility. Located in Cadarache, France, the tokamak is currently under construction and is designed to be the first magnetic confinement

106 On fusion waste, see *M. Zucchetti/Z. Chen/L. El-Guebaly et al.*, Progress in International Radioactive Fusion Waste Studies, Fusion Science and Technology 75 (2019), 391–398; *Sehila M. Gonzalez de Vicente/Nicholas A. Smith/Laila El-Guebaly et al.*, Overview on the Management of Radioactive Waste From Fusion Facilities: ITER, Demonstration Machines and Power Plants, Nuclear Fusion 62 (2022), 085001.

107 EUROfusion is a consortium of fusion research institutions which is funded to 50 % by Euratom and to 50 % by the State the research institute is located in.

device to achieve the net production of energy via fusion. Originally conceptualised as a peace project in the final stages of the Cold War by uniting superpowers via the joint advancement of science, ITER is now an international consortium involving the United States, Russia, Euratom, Japan, China, South Korea and India. ITER is expected to be operational in 2034.[108]

In continental Europe, numerous fusion research facilities – funded to a significant extent by Euratom[109] – are following the roadmap developed by EUROfusion.[110] This roadmap delineates a series of milestones leading to the commericalisation of fusion. The first step is the completion of ITER in the mid 2030s. Following the successful demonstration of a net energy gain around that time, the plan is to construct a machine capable of producing not only net energy but also net electricity. This is envisioned to be achieved in DEMO, a demonstration power plant scheduled to be built in the mid-2040s. The primary objective of DEMO is to establish a foundation for the subsequent commercialisation of fusion power plants, which is anticipated to occur in the latter half of the 21st century. Given construction delays by ITER, it is unclear whether the roadmap will be pursued as anticipated.

The United Kingdom is adopting a different approach, not waiting for the completion of ITER as the UK ended its participation in the project with Brexit. The UK Atomic Energy Authority (UKAEA) is currently engaged in developing a demonstration fusion power plant, STEP, with an operational target of 2040.

In the United States, the Department of Energy is also pursuing a roadmap, with the objective to commercialise fusion in the late 2030s or early 2040s.[111] In contrast to the approach of relying on government-backed projects such as Euratom or the United Kingdom, the United States strategy places emphasis on public-private partnerships, with the private sector demonstrating notable activity. At present, approximately fifty fusion start-ups worldwide have secured several billions of USD in funding from public

108 *Pietro Barabaschi/Arnaud Fossen/Alberto Loarte et al.*, ITER Progresses into New Baseline, Fusion Engineering and Design 215 (2025), 114990.

109 Euratom funds fusion research with €1.38 billion between 2021 and 2024 as part of the Horizon Europe research and development initiative.

110 *EUROfusion*, European Research Roadmap to the Realisation of Fusion Energy (Long Version), 2018.

111 *U.S. Department of Energy*, Fusion Energy Strategy 2024, 2024.

and private investors.[112] The private sector anticipates the availability of commercial fusion technology within the next decade.[113]

Nevertheless, there are still problems to be solved for the commercialisation of fusion. One pressing question is the start-up quantity of tritium. Current estimates suggest that ITER will consume almost all of the available tritium on the world market during its lifetime.[114] ITER itself, however, will not produce any tritium unlike future fusion plants. How will fusion power plant projects – either in research such as DEMO or commercially – be able to start their power plant if there is no tritium on the world market? Furthermore, the tritium breeding technology is still in its infancy and research in this field is ongoing.[115] In addition, plasma physics itself remains a complex topic with challenges which are object of current research, such as plasma instabilities.[116] Further challenges concern the handling of heat fluxes and the handling of materials due to neutron bombardment. Finally, there are still open questions regarding the dimension of a fusion power plant.[117]

3 Nuclear Fission

In order to comprehend the existing non-proliferation and disarmament regime, as well as the challenges posed by the commercialisation of fusion, it is imperative to understand the fundamentals of nuclear fission and the fuel cycle of a nuclear (fission) power plant. Nuclear fission is the process by which a nucleus splits into at least two smaller nuclei. Both civilian and

112 https://www.nuclearbusiness-platform.com/media/insights/62-billion-fusion-energy-funding-race-turning-the-dream-of-creating-a-star-on-earth-into-reality, last accessed 25 February 2025.

113 For instance, Helion Energy envisages their first power plant in 2028. Commonwealth Fusion Systems plans to have a fusion power plant operational in the first half of the 2030s.

114 *Pearson/Antoniazzi/Nuttall* (n 103).

115 For an overview, see *Marek Rubel*, Fusion Neutrons: Tritium Breeding and Impact on Wall Materials and Components of Diagnostic Systems, Journal of Fusion Energy 38 (2019), 315–329.

116 See for example *Thomas Eich/Robert J. Goldston/Arne Kallenbach et al.*, Correlation of the Tokamak H-Mode Density Limit With Ballooning Stability at the Separatrix, Nuclear Fusion 58 (2018), 034001.

117 *Hartmut Zohm*, On the Size of Tokamak Fusion Power Plants, Philosophical Transactions of the Royal Society A: Mathematical, Physical and Engineering Sciences 377 (2019), 20170437.

military applications utilise chain reactions of the elements uranium and plutonium. Natural uranium consists of mainly two isotopes, ^{238}U and ^{235}U. ^{235}U is a rare isotope with an abundance of only 0.72 %.[118] This means, that in 1 kg of natural uranium, only about 7 g of that uranium is ^{235}U. The remaining mass of uranium consists of the more abundant isotope of uranium ^{238}U, which has an abundance of 99.27 %.[119] Plutonium does not exist in nature; it is artificially bred in plutonium production plants.

In order to utilise the strong nuclear force of the atomic nucleus via fission in an efficient manner, it is necessary to induce a chain reaction. This means that any step produces more neutrons than it consumes. The ratio between produced and consumed neutrons needs to be greater than one. However, reactions involving ^{238}U do not release neutrons, rendering it unsuitable for sustaining chain reactions, and consequently is of no use for both nuclear reactors and nuclear weapons. In contrast, the uranium isotopes ^{233}U and ^{235}U as well as the plutonium isotope ^{239}Pu are suitable materials for nuclear chain reactions. These materials are classified as fissile material.

$$^{233}U + n \longrightarrow {}^{234}U \rightarrow \text{Fission Fragments} + 2.50n + 198\ \text{MeV} \quad (7)$$

$$^{235}U + n \longrightarrow {}^{236}U \rightarrow \text{Fission Fragments} + 2.43n + 207\ \text{MeV} \quad (8)$$

$$^{239}Pu + n \longrightarrow {}^{240}Pu \rightarrow \text{Fission Fragments} + 2.87n + 214\ \text{MeV} \quad (9)$$

The fissile material (^{239}Pu, ^{233}U or ^{235}U) captures a neutron, thereby transmuting into an unstable atomic nucleus, either ^{240}Pu, ^{234}U or ^{236}U. This nucleus subsequently decays into fission fragments, releasing free neutrons and energy in the process. These neutrons then initiate the next fission process, thus leading to a chain reaction.

As ^{235}U is the only naturally occuring[120] uranium isotope that produces neutrons in order to keep up chain reactions, it is the main isotope of uranium used in reactors and weapons. However, at natural abundance levels of 99.27 % of unusable uranium ^{238}U compared to the fissile ^{235}U, the utilisation of uranium in sustained chain reactions necessitates the enriche-

118 *Zsolt Sóti/Joseph Magill/Raymond Dreher*, Karlsruhe Nuclide Chart – New 10th Edition 2018 EPJ Nuclear Sciences and Technologies 5 (2019), 6.

119 Ibid.

120 The uranium isotope ^{233}U is bred via neutron capture from ^{232}Th, often in molten-salt reactors.

ment of uranium in that isotope. This process is typically accomplished through the utilisation of gaseous diffusion[121] or gas centrifuges[122], and in the future maybe even with lasers[123]. While the enrichment level for power plants typically ranges from three to five per cent[124], the level for nuclear weapons required is about 90 per cent.[125] The facts that the same chemical element is used, in conjunction with the necessity for the same enrichment process, require the implementation of a safeguards regime for *fission*. Fission is a dual-use technology: The physical processes involved can be applied to both civilian and military application, including nuclear power plants and nuclear weapons respectively.

The fission fuel cycle is characterised by a greater diversity of processes when compared to the fusion fuel cycle. It commences with the mining of uranium ore. The uranium ore is subsequently processed and enriched. The enriched material is used to produce fuel rods. After operation, the fuel might get reprocessed to extract remnants of fissile material and plutonium. In the end, there is waste that needs to be disposed of.

Within the fission fuel cycle, there exists a range of facilities with varying degrees of proliferation potential. First, there is the fission reactor itself.

---

121 Enrichment is a technologically challenging process, as two isotopes are identical in their chemical properties. The only difference is the weight. ^{235}U is three atomic mass units (i.e. 3×10^{-27} g) or 1.3 % lighter than ^{238}U. Gas diffusion devices use the chemical compound uranium hexafluoride UF_6 in a gaseous state, instead of uranium ore. This gas then forced through semi-permeable membranes. Due to the difference in weight – a UF_6 molecule containing ^{238}U is heavier than a UF_6 molecule containing ^{235}U – the diffusion velocity differs between the two types of molecules, leading to an isotope separation. After the isotope separation, the fluoride is removed from UF_6 to get pure uranium.

122 Gas centrifuges exploit both the gaseous properties of UF_6 and the weight difference of isotopes. Due to centrifugal forces, heavier molecules are pushed farther outwards than lighter molecules. On the physics behind gas centrifuges, see *Donald R. Olander*, The Theory of Uranium Enrichment by the Gas Centrifuge, Progress in Nuclear Energy 8 (1981), 1–33.

123 Laser enrichment technology works by exciting UF_6 molecules. On its proliferation potential, see *Ryan Snyder*, A Proliferation Assessment of Third Generation Laser Uranium Enrichment Technology, Science & Global Security 24 (2016), 68–91.

124 *Shuichi Hasegawa*, Isotope Separation Methods for Nuclear Fuel, in: Nicholas Tsoulfanidis (ed.), Nuclear Energy: Selected Entries from the Encyclopedia of Sustainability Science and Technology, New York: Springer 2013, 59–76, at 60.

125 *Alexander Glaser*, On the Proliferation Potential of Uranium Fuel for Research Reactors at Various Enrichment Levels, Science & Global Security 14 (2006), 1–24; *Alexander Glaser*, Characteristics of the Gas Centrifuge for Uranium Enrichment and Their Relevance for Nuclear Weapon Proliferation, Science & Global Security 16 (2008), 1–25.

Nuclear safeguards are implemented to verify the use of uranium and the handling of the spent fuel. Spent uranium fuel may contain plutonium, which can be utilised to construct a nuclear weapon. A significant proliferation potential exists outside the reactors, particularly within enrichment facilities and spent fuel facilities.[126] As previously mentioned, while both nuclear fission power plants and nuclear weapons require enriched uranium, the enrichment levels differ. In enrichment facility the duration of operation determines the achievable enrichment level. If such a facility is operated long enough and reconfigured, reactor-grade material can turn into weapons-grade material, thereby emphasising a focus of safeguards on material within enrichment facilities. Concerning spent fuel, the objective is to safeguard against the separation of plutonium from the spent fuel for the purpose of producing nuclear weapons. Consequently, safeguards extend to the entire fuel cycle, with a particular emphasis on nuclear material before and after its utilisation in a reactor.[127]

4 Nuclear Weapons

In order to comprehend the legal framework of nuclear weapons and the role of fusion in it, it is imperative to establish the fundamental principles of the categories and operational mechanisms of nuclear weapons. Next to biological and chemical weapons, nuclear weapons are weapons of mass destruction. Nuclear weapon is an umbrella term for different types of weapons that all utilise the energy released from nuclear reactions in an uncontrolled manner, resulting in an explosion, for military applications. Within the domain of nuclear weapons, various categorisations exist with regard to the yield or range and the nuclear processes involved.

4.1 Tactical and Strategic Nuclear Weapons

There are different approaches to categorising nuclear weapons. One category is to differentiate by yield and range between strategic and tactical nuclear weapons. In this sense, strategic weapons are defined as those used

---

126 *IAEA*, Safeguards for Reprocessing and Enrichment Plants, IAEA Bulletin 19 (1977), 30–33.

127 For an overview of the legal framework, see Chapter 2.

for nuclear deterrence[128] due to their high yield in the range of megaton equivalents of TNT, capable of destroying entire cities, and characteristically have a high range of thousands of kilometres.[129] In contrast, tactical (also called non-strategic) nuclear weapons are characterised by a lower yield of several kilotons of TNT equivalent, and a shorter range.[130] However, this distinction has been subject of criticism. Not only is any use of nuclear weapons of strategic nature,[131] the question of range or yield is also mainly an operational question. Consequently, under such a categorisation, both nuclear weapons deployed in the atomic bombings of Hiroshima and Nagasaki on 6 and 9 August 1945 would be classified as tactical weapons; despite the fact that they resulted in the elimitation of entire cities and the death of over 200,000 people.[132] Nuclear weapons deemed strategic typically contain fusionable material.

4.2 Nuclear Weapons Delivery Systems

There are various delivery systems for nuclear weapons.[133] One option is gravity bombs, such as those deployed over Japan in 1945. In this scenario, the bomb is mounted to an airplane and released over the target. Another option is to mount a nuclear warhead onto a missile, especially intercontinental ballistic missiles (ICBMs), submarine-launched ballistic missiles (SLBMs) or cruise missiles. A ballistic missile follows the ballistic trajectory from the launch with a relatively short powering phase, while cruise missiles have an additional guiding system and can change its trajectory

---

128 On nuclear deterrence, see Chapter 2, Section 1.1.

129 *Office of the Deputy Assistant Secretary of Defense for Nuclear Matters*, Nuclear Matters Handbook 2020, US Department of Defense 2018, at 44.

130 Ibid, at 4; *Amy F. Woolf*, Nonstrategic Nuclear Weapons, Washington DC: CRS Report for Congress 2010, at 4 f.

131 Former US Secretary of Defense Mattis called any use of a nuclear weapon "a strategic gamechanger", *James N Mattis*, The National Defense Strategy and the Nuclear Posture Review – Committee on Armed Services of the House of Representatives, Washington DC: U.S. Government Publishing Office 2018.

132 *Masao Tomonaga*, The Atomic Bombings of Hiroshima and Nagasaki: A Summary of the Human Consequences, 1945–2018, and Lessons for Homo sapiens to End the Nuclear Weapon Age, Journal for Peace and Nuclear Disarmament 2 (2019), 491–517.

133 *Jeff Richardson*, Shifting from a Nuclear Triad to a Nuclear Dyad, Bulletin of the Atomic Scientists 65 (2009), 33–42.

mid-journey.[134] As fission-only warheads are heavy (the bombs deployed on Hiroshima and Nagasaki had to be dropped from a bomber plane), mounting a nuclear weapon onto a missile usually requires miniaturisation, which is achieved by a combination of fission and fusion technology.

4.3 Fission and Fusion Bombs

A significant distinction between types of nuclear weapons is the nuclear process which powers the explosion. As nuclear weapons are weapons that use nuclear processes, they can encompass not only nuclear fission, but also nuclear fusion, a combination which is incorporated into the arsenals of all nuclear weapons States.

4.3.1 Pure Fission Bombs

The first generation of nuclear weapons, such as those deployed in Japan in 1945, utilised only fissile material in the explosion, i.e., either ^{235}U or ^{239}Pu. Within the context of a nuclear power plant, a moderator medium and associated control mechanisms are employed to ensure controlled fission chain reactions. The number of neutrons produced remains the same level as the number of neutrons captured by the reactor fuel. In contrast, a nuclear weapon does not possess moderators or other control mechanisms, as it induces uncontrolled chain reactions, leading to an explosion. Physically, both a fission reactor and a nuclear weapon are powered by the same nuclear reaction.

Pure fission nuclear weapons exist in different designs. To initiate a nuclear chain reaction, a critical mass is required. Once the material is critical, the chain reaction is initiated. However, in a weapon, (super-)criticality must only occur once the weapon is supposed to detonate. To achieve super-criticality only at detonation, different approaches were developed. Uranium-based weapons, such as *Little Boy*, the weapon that destroyed Hiroshima, used a gun-type approach. The uranium is split into two parts and placed at both ends of a tube. At detonation, a classical explosive pushes one part into the other, leading to criticality and finally the nuclear explosion. Plutonium-based weapons, such as *Fat Man*, the bomb that

134 *Richard K. Betts*, Cruise Missiles: Technology, Strategy, Politics, The Washington Quarterly 4 (1981), 66–80.

destroyed Nagasaki, as well as modern uranium-based weapons, use an implosion mechanism. The plutonium is shaped into a sphere. This sphere is surrounded by classical explosives. Once the classical explosives detonate, the fissile material is pushed inwards, leading to super-criticality and then an explosion. Both designs have an inherent limitation: only a fraction of the fissile material contributes to the final explosion. To increase the percentage of fissile material contributing to the explosion, fusion has to be included into the weapon design.

4.3.2 Thermonuclear Weapons

The majority of modern nuclear weapons are thermonuclear weapons, combining fission and fusion. The utilisation of fusion serves to increase the yield of the weapon and allows for lighter and more compact weapon designs (minituarisation). The influence of fusion ranges from a minor fusion component, limited to increasing the number of neutrons to boost the chain reaction, to full-scale hydrogen bombs where fusion contributes significantly to the explosion. The more neutrons there are, the more fission reaction occur, the bigger the explosion is. More advanced designs, sometimes called hydrogen bomb or just H-Bomb, use a two (or sometimes even more) staged mechanism. First, a fission primary detonates. The energy and radiation released then initiates fusion reactions within the fusion secondary. The explosion of the hydrogen bomb is then a combination of both uncontrolled fission and fusion reactions.

Such a combination of fission and fusion increases the percentage of fissile fuel burnt, thereby significantly increasing the yield of a nuclear weapon. The biggest man-made explosion ever, the *Tsar Bomba* by the Soviet Union, was such a thermonuclear weapon. It had a yield of more than 50 Mt, which is approximately 1,500 times the combined yield of both nuclear weapons deployed on Japan.[135] The development of thermonuclear weapons played a pivotal role in propelling the nuclear arms race that characterised the Cold War.

135 On the yield of the Tsar Bomba, Little Boy and Fat Man, see *F. A. Khan*, On Tsar Bomba – The Most Powerful Nuclear Weapon Ever Tested, Physics Education 56 (2021), 013002.

5 Fusion and the Risk of Nuclear Proliferation

Fusion energy is a dual-use technology, with the potential for proliferation, albeit to a significantly lesser extent than fission. While the development of fusion energy is driven by the demand for a clean source of energy for civilian purposes, fusion can also support nuclear weapons programmes. Fusion poses three proliferation risks. Firstly, fusion is an intense neutron source. Irradiating an atomic nucleus with neutrons can transform one element into another, thereby converting fertile[136] material into fissile[137] material. In other words, it is possible to create nuclear weapons material with fusion as an intense neutron source (5.1). Secondly, tritium – a radioactive isotope of hydrogen – plays a crucial role in fusion energy production and is also a vital component in boosted fission weapons and thermonuclear weapons (5.2). Thirdly, a specific fusion technology – inertial confinement or laser fusion – poses a proliferation risk due to potential insights gained into the functioning of thermonuclear weapons (5.3). After having explored fusion's three main proliferation concerns, this section then briefly focuses on the possibility of fission-fusion hybrid systems (5.4), before pinpointing the exact differences between the proliferation potential of fission and fusion (5.5).

5.1 Transmutation – Fusion to Produce Nuclear Weapons Material

Nuclear fusion technology has the potential be utilised in the production of nuclear weapons material. The neutrons produced in the fusion processes possess the capability to transform certain material into fissile material.[138] These materials are the key component of nuclear weapons.

---

136 Fertile material is a material that can be transformed into fissile material through neutron capture. An example for fertile materials is the uranium isotope ^{238}U.

137 Fissile material is a material that undergoes fission by neutrons of all energies. The best example is ^{235}U. *International Atomic Energy Agency*, IAEA Safeguards Glossary, Vienna: IAEA 2022, at 36.

138 See *Alexandre Obertelli/Hiroyuki Sagawa*, Modern Nuclear Physics – From Fundamentals to Frontiers, Singapore: Springer Singapore 2021, at 669 ff.

5.1.1 Transmutation of Uranium and Thorium

As previously stated, atomic nuclei possess a very distinctive property: When a nucleus catches a neutron, it can turn into another element. Depending on the element and the energy of the neutron, this process occurs with a certain probability that allows to artificially produce elements (so-called cross-section). This process of transmutation can play a pivotal role in nuclear weapons programmes to transform fertile material into fissile material. ^{238}U can be transformed into the fissile material ^{239}Pu.[139]

$$^{238}U + n \rightarrow {}^{239}U \rightarrow {}^{239}Np + \beta^- \rightarrow {}^{239}Pu + \beta^- \quad (10)$$

The ^{238}U nucleus captures a neutron and is thereby transmuted into the unstable isotope ^{239}U. This, in turn, decays into another unstable isotope of neptunium, which decays into the weapon-grade isotope of plutonium ^{239}Pu.[140] The β^- denotates the decay process, referred to as beta decay, which is of no importance for this book and is only added for the purpose of physical accuracy. The important point is the observation that a neutron induces the decay of a nucleus. Irradiating uranium with neutrons can result in the production of plutonium. Plutonium is the core material of the US nuclear weapon *Fat Man* that was deployed on Nagasaki on 9 August 1945.

Similar to plutonium breeding from uranium, it also possible to breed the fissile material ^{233}U from the thorium isotope ^{232}Th via neutron capture and beta decays:

$$^{232}Th + n \rightarrow {}^{233}Th \rightarrow {}^{233}Pa + \beta^- \rightarrow {}^{233}U + \beta^- \quad (11)$$

By capturing a neutron, ^{232}Th turns into ^{233}Th, which then first decays to ^{233}Pa and ultimately to ^{233}U.

It is important to note that other intense neutron source might be utilised for the purposes of breeding fissile material from fertile material.[141]

---

139 *David Hafemeister*, Physics of Societal Issues: Calculations on National Security, Environment, and Energy, Springer 2016, at 13.

140 The decay processes are so-called beta decays, indicated by the Greek letter β. A β^- decay involves a neutron that decays into a proton, an electron and a neutrino.

141 On the broader question of safeguards on intense neutron sources, see *Matthias Englert/Anne Harrington*, Next Generation Nuclear Technologies: New Challenges to the Legal Framework of the IAEA from Intense Neutron Sources, in: Jonathan L. Black-Branch/Dieter Fleck (eds.), Nuclear Non-Proliferation in International Law:

Both fission and fusion processes generate neutrons with energies, which allow for the breeding of fissile material. In addition, particle accelerators and some research institutions (such as the particle accelerators at CERN or the the high-flux reactor at the Institut Laue-Langevin) are also intense neutron sources, yet with significantly lower neutron fluxes.

5.1.2 From Fertile to Fissile Material with Fission

In order to comprehend the potential of fusion to produce fissile material, it is first necessary to understand the current methods of producing fissile material using fission technology.

As explained above in Section 4.3.1, the core of any nuclear weapon contains ^{235}U or ^{239}Pu. Current nuclear arsenals do not employ ^{233}U, but it remains a possibility for weapon designs.[142] ^{235}U is obtained from natural uranium via a lengthy enrichment process, while ^{239}Pu must be created artificially through transmutation processes. Historically, nuclear weapon States mainly used so-called graphite moderated reactors to produce fissile material.[143] Graphite, a specific form of carbon, is employed to slow down the neutrons produced in the fission process of the reactor fuel. Nuclear weapons States have also opted for the utilisation of heavy-water moderated reactors to produce their fissile material.[144] Heavy water (D_2O) is water in which the hydrogen isotope deuterium (D) replaces the regular hydrogen (H) of H_2O.

Within these reactors, natural or depleted[145] uranium is irradiated by neutrons in order to produce plutonium. However, this production methods leads to a caveat, namely the trade-off between the quality and quantity of the produced plutonium. It should be noted that the irradiation of uranium does not only lead to the desired isotope ^{239}Pu, but also to other isotopes of plutonium such as ^{238}Pu, ^{240}Pu and ^{242}Pu. While the latter three

Volume II – Verification and Compliance, The Hague: T.M.C. Asser Press 2016, 187–212.

142 W. K. Woods, LRL interest in U-233 (1966), Douglas United Nuclear, Inc., Richland, WA (United States).

143 *David Albright/Frans Berkhout/William Walker*, Plutonium and Highly Enriched Uranium 1996 – World Inventories, Capabilities and Policies, Stockholm: SIPRI 1997, at 31.

144 Ibid, at 31.

145 Depleted means that the percentage of U-235 is below the natural weight fraction of 0.7 %.

isotopes can be utilised to a certain extent in nuclear weapons, they limit the overall usability of the produced plutonium.[146] The longer uranium gets irradiated, the more of the undesired isotopes are produced. Conversely, the shorter the irradiation time, the less amount of plutonium in total is produced.[147] This inherent limitation in the process leads to a constrained production of weapon-grade plutonium per year, amount of uranium and reactor by fission technology.

For instance, France's first plutonium producing reactor, the Marcoule G1, had a capacity of producing 12 kg of plutonium from approximately 100 t of uranium per year.[148] The Hanford-N reactor, one of the United States's two plutonium facilities during the Cold War, had a capacity of turning 380 t of uranium into 580 kg of plutonium per year.[149] What these numbers show is that tons of uranium are necessary in order to produce kilograms of plutonium from a fission facility.

Apart from military production, plutonium is also produced in a limited capacity in commercial nuclear power plants. In these facilities, the production of plutonium occurs as an by-product, which changes the energy output of the plant. Notably a single commercial pressurised water fission reactor, the most common type of nuclear reactor,[150] produces around 250 kg of plutonium each year.[151] Given the primary design objective of such a reactor is optimised for energy output rather than fissile material production, the quality of the plutonium produced is inherently limited.[152]

5.1.3 From Fertile to Fissile Material with Fusion

Fusion is a technology which – from the perspective of physics – allows to produce fissile material from fertile material significantly more efficiently than fission.

To recall, the most promising fusion reaction for commercial power plants is considered to be the D-T cycle, i.e., the fusion of the hydrogen

146 *Englert/Harrington* (n 141), at 193.
147 Ibid, at 192 f.
148 *Albright/Berkhout/Walker* (n 143), at 68 f.
149 *Englert/Harrington* (n 141), at 194.
150 *International Atomic Energy Agency*, Nuclear Power Reactors in the World, Vienna: IAEA 2021.
151 *Englert/Harrington* (n 141), at 194.
152 Ibid, at 194 f.

isotopes deuterium D and tritium T to release energy, a neutron and to form the most common helium isotope ^4He:

$$D + T \rightarrow {}^4He + n + 17.6\,MeV \quad (12)$$

Of the 17.6 MeV of energy released, the neutron carries 14.1 MeV.[153] Around these energies, the capture cross-section of fertile material to capture a neutron is in a range which allows for a significant amount of plutonium to take place, while fission events remain rare at these energies.[154] A high cross-section indicates a high probability of a reaction between these two particles. The neutron from a fusion process can be captured by an atomic nucleus of ^{238}U or ^{232}Th.

There are several options for incorporating uranium or thorium into a fusion device in order to produce fissile material. Neutron fluxes are their highest the closer one is to the reactor core. The plasma core itself is not suitable for the production of fissile material as the introduction of other materials into the plasma would prevent fusion reactions.[155] The subsequent layers of a fusion power plant are the wall and the coolant.

Consequently, one option would be to construct a wall containing uranium dioxide UO_2.[156] Neutron-wall interactions will not only be used for tritium breeding, but they might also be beneficial for proliferators. During a certain duration of operation, uranium gets transmuted into ^{239}Pu. The wall material would then be replaced and the plutonium-containing material reprocessed to extract the plutonium. Assuming a large-scale fusion reactor with a thermal power output of 3 GW in the core, such a reactor

153 *Thomas J. Dolan*, Nuclear Fusion, in: Nicholas Tsoulfanidis (ed.), Nuclear Energy, New York, Heidelberg: Springer 2013, 305–342, at 308; *E. Morse*, Nuclear Fusion, Heidelberg: Springer International Publishing 2018, at 29.

154 *Bruce Cameron Reed*, Producing Fissile Material, in: Bruce Cameron Reed (ed.), The Physics of the Manhattan Project, Cham: Springer International Publishing 2021, 119–144 (120). It must be noted that at 14 MeV the capture cross-section is about two magnitudes lower than the fission cross-section. This means that the majority of neutrons would lead to a fission event of U-238 instead of transmuting the nucleus into Pu-239. However, neutrons slow down, allowing for more neutron capture events.

155 The larger the Z of an ion, the higher the plasma energy losses by Bremsstrahlung and line radiation are. Uranium and thorium are heavy elements. On this, see *Alexander Piel*, Plasma Physics – An Introduction to Laboratory, Space, and Fusion Plasmas, Kiel, Heidelberg: Springer 2017, at 103.

156 *F. Faghihi/H. Havasi/M. Amin-Mozafari*, Plutonium-239 Production Rate Study Using a Typical Fusion Reactor, Annals of Nuclear Energy 35 (2008), 759–766.

could produce quantities in the order of magnitude of 10 kg of plutonium annually.[157] Similar to this option, the introduction of fertile material to into the tritium breeding blanket is a theoretical possibility.[158] Depending on the configuration, simulations indicate the potential of up to several hundreds of kilograms in a large-scale facility (5.5 GW thermal power) designed for the production of fissile material or a clandestine production of about one critical mass per year.[159]

An alternative option would be to dissolve uranium within the coolant of the fusion reactor.[160] The underlying principle of D-T fusion power plants is the generation of heat, which is then transported by the coolant to power a steam turbine, which in turn produces electricity. The coolant flows in close proximity to the reactor and its first wall in order to function properly. Such an approach is limited by the low solvability of uranium.[161] However, this issue might be overcome by using a technology called TRISO, tristructural-isotropic particles. These are small particles which consist of a uranium or thorium core, which is coated by several layers of lead. These TRISO particles could be introduced into the coolant and later extracted by a filtration system.[162] Simulation studies indicate that a large-sized fusion power plant (i.e., 2.5 GW of thermal power) would be capable of producing 20 kg of ^{239}Pu or 20 kg of ^{233}U per week.[163] Another study estimates that a small sized fusion power plant (500 MW of thermal power) would be able to convert roughly one metric ton of ^{238}U into ^{239}Pu within a year.[164]

157 Ibid.

158 *Fabian Sievert/Daniel Johnson*, Creating Suns on Earth, The Nonproliferation Review 17 (2010), 323–346; *Giorgio Franceschini/Matthias Englert/Wolfgang Liebert*, Nuclear Fusion Power for Weapons Purposes, The Nonproliferation Review 20 (2013), 525–544, at 542.

159 *Franceschini/Englert/Liebert* (n 158), at 542 f.

160 *Alexander Glaser/Robert J. Goldston*, Proliferation Risks of Magnetic Fusion Energy: Clandestine Production, Covert Production and Breakout, Nuclear Fusion 52 (2012), 043004.

161 Ibid.

162 *Y. Wu/S. Zheng/X. Zhu et al.*, Conceptual Design of the Fusion-Driven Subcritical System FDS-I, Fusion Engineering and Design 81 (2006), 1305–1311.

163 *Glaser/Goldston* (n 160).

164 *John L. Ball/Ethan E. Peterson/R. Scott Kemp et al.*, Assessing the risk of proliferation via fissile breeding in ARC-class fusion power plants, Nuclear Fusion 65 (2025), 036038.

5.1.4 Advantages of Fusion for Plutonium Breeding

There are key advantages of fusion for a nuclear weapons programme with regard to the quality and quantity of the fertile material. Primarily, the transmutation rate is significantly higher with simulations indicating that as little as 220 kg of natural uranium introduced in the blanket would be sufficient to produce 4 kg of plutonium in a single year.[165] In comparison with fission, the production of kilograms of plutonium does not require tons[166] but only hundreds of kilograms of uranium, a difference of an entire order of magnitude. Under specific conditions, a fusion reactor could be configured to convert tens of tons of uranium into several tons of plutonium, further advancing fusion's appeal for nuclear weapons applications.[167] Consequently, either less fertile material is required or more fertile material can be produced from the same amount of fissile material than with fission. The high transmutation rate further enhances the percentage of plutonium within the uranium-plutonium mixture, thereby simplifying the reprocessing procedure.[168]

To put these numbers into perspective: The IAEA defines a significant quantity (SQ) of plutonium as 8 kg.[169] A significant quantity is "the amount of nuclear material for which the possibility of manufacturing a nuclear explosive device cannot be excluded."[170] Depending on the technology and the validity of the simulation studies, a single fusion power plant could produce enough plutonium for dozens of nuclear weapons each year. To provide a ballpark estimate, assuming that roughly 10% of the neutrons are used for plutonium breeding, a fusion power plant could produce one SQ per year per 10 MW of time-averaged power.

A second benefit is the quality of the plutonium.[171] While fission reactors have to find a balance between quality and quantity of plutonium, the specific spectrum of neutron fluxes from fusion reactions lead to plutonium

165 *Englert/Harrington* (n 141), at 198.

166 A 1 GW_e Light Water Reactor consumes roughly 20 t of low enriched uranium and produces 250 kg of plutonium per year.

167 Ibid, at 198.

168 Ibid, at 198.

169 *International Atomic Energy Agency* (n 137), at 31.

170 Ibid, at 30.

171 On the differentiation between MOX(mixed-oxide)-grade, reactor-grade, weapons-grade and super-grade plutonium, depending on the isotopic composition, see *J. Carson Mark/Frank von Hippel/Edward Lyman*, Explosive Properties of Reactor-Grade Plutonium, Science & Global Security 17 (2009), 170–185.

of higher quality, as plutonium isotopes other than ^{239}Pu are not often produced. As a consequence, plutonium from fusion reactors will always be weapon-grade material.[172] This characteristic renders fusion potentially attractive for proliferators as it simplifies the reprocessing process.

5.1.5 Limitations of Fusion as a Plutonium Provider

The following discussion will present several limitations of fusion as a provider of fissile material for nuclear weapons purposes. These limitations include clandestinity, reprocessing and the impact on the operation of a fusion power plant.

Clandestinity

In the context of the potential for a State to covertly utilise fusion for plutonium breeding for military purposes, two distinct scenarios can be delineated: Firstly, there is the possibility that a civilian facility may be utilised covertly to produce nuclear weapons material. Secondly, a State may undertake the clandestine construction of fusion devices for a covert nuclear weapons programme. It is important to note that safeguards are typically limited to verify the former, while the IAEA safeguards regime possesses only a very limited ability to detect clandestine facilities.[173] Historically, national intelligence services[174] or other international bodies[175] have played a significant role in detecting clandestine facilities. The issue of the application of safeguards to such fusion facilities is addressed in Chapter 3. Regarding a clandestine fusion facility producing nuclear weapons material, such a scenario is considered to be highly unlikely.[176] Primarily, fusion facilities are large facilities as witnessed by ITER with its 180-hectare site and is visible on publicly available satellite imagery. Secondly, firing

172 *Englert/Harrington* (n 141), at 198.

173 This is only possible when the State has concluded an Additional Protocol. On this, see Chapter 3, Section 1.3.2.

174 A historic overview is given by *Keith Hansen*, Intelligence and Nuclear Proliferation: Lessons Learned, Paris: Ifri 2011. See also *Thomas Fingar*, The Role of Intelligence in Countering Illicit Nuclear-Related Procurement, in: Matthew Bunn/Martin B. Malin/William C. Potter/Leonard S. Spector (eds.), Preventing Black Market Trade in Nuclear Technology, Cambridge: Cambridge University Press 2018, 48–78.

175 In Iraq, UNSCOM, a subsidiary organ of the UN Security Council, played a major role, *Trevor Findlay*, The Lessons of UNSCOM and UNMOVIC, in: VERTIC (ed.), Verification Yearbook 2004, London: VERTIC 2004, 65–86.

176 *Glaser/Goldston* (n 160).

up a fusion reactor requires substantial amounts of energy, including the infrastructure of supply lines and power conversion buildings to support it. These two factors serve to impede the clandestine construction and operation of a nuclear weapons programme based on fusion facilities. There is, however, the possibility that future generations of fusion power plants might become smaller and thus easier to hide.

Reprocessing

The second limitation derives from the necessity of reprocessing. High neutron fluxes, observed in both fission and modified fusion reactors, result in the transformation of a small percentage of uranium into plutonium. Consequently, the final product is a composite of different materials. To utilise the fissile material for further nuclear weapons purposes, the plutonium has to be separated from the uranium and other materials in reprocessing procedures. Reprocessing is a complicated chemical process,[177] typically requiring large-scale facilities. There are only around a dozen operational reprocessing plants located in five countries (China, France, India, Pakistan and Russia). Reprocessing plants exist for both for military and civilian applications, the latter also in non-nuclear weapon States.[178] The construction of reprocessing plants is a lengthy process, for instance, the construction of a current Japanese project is delayed by 25 years.[179] In addition, radioactive material needs to be transported to such a reprocessing facility, providing an opportunity to detect clandestine activities. However, a State committed to quickly produce nuclear weapons might opt for expedited ways to quickly build a small reprocessing plant for small quantities of plutonium separation.

177 The standard procedure is the so-called PUREX process. On PUREX, see *L.B. Lanham/T.C. Runion*, PUREX Process for Plutonium and Uranium Recovery (1949), Oak Ridge National Laboratory; *F. Baumgärtner/D. Ertel*, The Modern Purex Process and its Analytical Requirements, Journal of Radioanalytical and Nuclear Chemistry 58 (1980), 11–28.

178 Germany operated a reprocessing plant from 1971 to 1990, see https://um.baden-wuerttemberg.de/de/umwelt-natur/kernenergie/kerntechnische-anlagen/sonstige-kerntechnische-anlagen/kerntechnische-entsorgung-karlsruhe-gmbh-kte/wiederaufarbeitungsanlage-karlsruhe-mit-verglasungseinrichtung, last accessed 25 February 2025. Japan currently constructs a reprocessing plant in Rokkasho, see *Tatsujiro Suzuki*, Rokkasho Redux: Japan's Never-Ending Reprocessing Saga in: Bulletin of the Atomic Scientists, https://thebulletin.org/2023/12/rokkasho-redux-japans-never-ending-reprocessing-saga/, last accessed 17 July 2025.

179 *Suzuki* (n 178).

Impact on Tritium and Energy Production

The utilisation a fusion reactor for the purpose producing fissile material requires neutrons. Neutrons from the fusion reactions are not merely a by-product, they are used for two purposes: The deposition of energy into the coolant for energy production and the production of tritium. In the event that these neutrons are directed towards the transmutation of fertile material into fissile material, they become unavailable for their intended purpose within the facility, resulting in a change in energy output and/or tritium production. This leads to a possibility to detect the use of fusion for military purposes. Once fusion power plants are available on a commercial scale, both the standard demand of blanket material and power output should be known. However, as long as fusion remains in a research-and-development or early deployment stage, there will be a degree of uncertainty regarding precise numbers.

Fission Where No Fission Should Be

It is important to note that the neutrons produced in the fusion processes have an additional effect on uranium that extends beyond simply converting it into weapon-grade plutonium: Specifically, neutrons can induce the nuclear fission of ^{238}U. In this case, the neutron is not captured by the nucleus, but divides it into smaller nuclei. Depending on the energy of the neutron, the probability for inducing a fission reaction changes.[180] Fission events, in turn, lead to radiation and fission products in a surrounding where – under purely civilian circumstances – fission events are practically[181] non-existent. It is possible to detect these fission events, which is of particular relevance in the context of discussing potential safeguards approaches to fusion facilities.[182]

5.1.6 Safeguarding ITER

The issue of safeguarding fusion has been actively discussed when ITER was in its design process. Concerning the ITER project specifically, this risk

180 *Reed* (n 154).

181 If beryllium is used as neutron multiplier of the tritium breeding wall, then there might be some traces of uranium within the wall as natural beryllium contains traces of uranium.

182 See Chapter 5.

that the fusion machine could be used for military purposes is considered to be negligible.[183] Primarily, the dimension of the machine, the operational time and the total fusion energy produced limit the neutron flux and thus the potential amount of fissile material that could be bred. It is anticipated that it would be difficult to produce even one significant quantity of fertile material within the lifetime of ITER.[184] Secondly, the international nature of the collaboration, with the presence and supervision of representatives from all the countries involved,[185] reduces the possibility of clandestine plutonium production. However, while both the limited production of neutrons and the international oversight reduce the proliferation potential significantly, there is still the potential to gain important insights into the understanding of proliferation relevant information. For example, if an ITER Member State decided to put fertile material into test blanket modules, they could learn about breeding fissile material. While ITER is located within a nuclear weapons State (France) and other nuclear weapons States are members of the consortium (India, China, United States and Russia), the other States are non-nuclear weapon States (26 Euratom Member States excluding France, as well as South Korea and Japan). ITER itself will not be used for nuclear weapons material production. However it has been pointed out that the knowledge gained from ITER might support future developments.[186] Concerns have also been raised with regard to a potential nuclear arms race initiated by China or India where the knowledge gained from ITER might be beneficial.[187] This scenario, however, seems rather unlikely as both countries already possess the capacity to produce large amounts of fissile material from existing fission-based infrastructure.

5.1.7 Fusion without Transmutation Potential?

The D-T reaction is not the only fusion reaction feasible for fusion power plants. The European roadmap as well as the majority of fusion start-ups focus on this reaction, as it has the lowest triple product requirements and the highest power density (at a given pressure). In contrast, some start-ups

---

183 *IAEA*, Report of the Consultancy Meeting on "Non-Proliferation Challenges in Connection with Magnetic Fusion Power Plants" (2013), IAEA.

184 Ibid; *Englert/Harrington* (n 141), at 190.

185 They are the United States, Russia, Euratom Member States, India, Japan, South Korea, China.

186 *Franceschini/Englert/Liebert* (n 158), at 532 f.

187 Ibid.

pursue a different path to avoid the use of tritium given its supply problems, the need to breed it in the fusion machine's blanket and the radiological issues associated with tritium's radioactivity. Also, they try to avoid the irradiation capabilities of neutrons, potentially leading to proliferation resistant fusion facilities.

As mentioned above, any atom lighter than iron can undergo nuclear fusion. One such example is pursued by the start-up *Helion Energy*, which plans to fuse the helium isotope ^3He with deuterium D resulting in ^3He and regular hydrogen ^1H, while also releasing energy:

$$D + {}^3He \rightarrow {}^4He + {}^1H + 18.3\ MeV. \quad (13)$$

This reaction does not produce any neutrons and is therefore termed an *aneutronic fusion reaction.* This reaction has a key benefit as it does not require the transformation of fusion energy first into heat and then into electricity, since charged particles (protons) are released rather than neutral particles (neutrons). Electricity is nothing but a stream of charged particles.

On the downside, ^3He does not occur naturally on Earth, as it is an exceedingly rare isotope with a relative abundance to helium's standard isotope ^4He of about one in ten thousand, making natural resources on our planet inaccessible. Only the Moon has significant reserves of ^3He.[188] Presently, the primary source of ^3He is the decay of tritium with its own proliferation potential as outlined below. In theory, there are abundant resources on the Moon, yet harvesting ^3He on an extraterrestrial body is outstandingly difficult.[189] *Helion Energy*, next to using ^3He as decay product from tritium, has proposed to produce their ^3He from the fusion of two deuterium nuclei within a closed fuel-cycle:[190]

---

188 On the relevance of moon mining for fusion see: *L. A. Taylor/G. L. Kulcinski*, Helium-3 on the Moon for Fusion Energy: the Persian Gulf of the 21st Century, Solar System Research 33 (1999), 338; *Thomas Simko/Matthew Gray*, Lunar Helium-3 Fuel for Nuclear Fusion:Technology, Economics, and Resources, World Futures Review 6 (2014), 158–171. On the legal implications see: *Richard B. Bilder*, A Legal Regime for the Mining of Helium-3 on the Moon: U.S. Policy Options, Fordham International Law Journal 33 (2009), 243–299.

189 Harvesting the moon would lead to different legal issues. Article 11 of the 1979 Moon Agreement declares the Moon as a common heritage of mankind and requires the establishment of an international regime to govern the exploitation of the moon. However, only a hand full of States have ratified the treaty.

190 https://www.helionenergy.com/articles/explaining-helions-fusion-fuel-choice-d-he-3/, last accessed 25 February 2025.

$$D + D \rightarrow {}^{3}He + n + 3.3\,MeV \quad (14)$$

This reaction between two deuterium nuclei results in a ^{3}He nucleus, energy and, important for proliferation concerns, also neutrons, although with a lower energy of 2.45 MeV compared to 14 MeV from a D-T reaction. Neutrons at these energies are also capable of transmuting fertile material to fissile material.[191] In other words, there is no aneutronic fusion fuel cycle without proliferation concerns. As a consequence, fusion always poses a proliferation concern to some extent, as intense neutron source regardless of the fusion process.

5.2 Tritium and the Hydrogen Bomb

Tritium represents one of the major technological challenges to be solved in order to commercialise fusion.[192] At the same time, it also serves as a critical component in modern nuclear weapons arsenals.[193] Today, almost every nuclear weapon uses tritium.[194] Thus, the development of tritium producing technology as well as an increased availability of tritium pose key proliferation concerns of fusion.

5.2.1 Tritium Boosting of Fission Weapon

Adding tritium to a fission-based nuclear weapon significantly increases its yield. Two to three grammes of tritium are sufficient to increase the yield

191 *Reed* (n 154).

192 *Pearson/Antoniazzi/Nuttall* (n 103).; *G. Federici/W. Biel/M. R. Gilbert et al.*, European DEMO Design Strategy and Consequences for Materials, Nuclear Fusion 57 (2017), 092002; *M. Kovari/M. Coleman/I. Cristescu et al.*, Tritium Resources Available for Fusion Reactors, Nuclear Fusion 58 (2018), 026010.

193 *Martin Kalinowski*, International Control of Tritium for Nuclear Nonproliferation and Disarmament, Boca Raton: CRC Press 2004, at 8 ff.; *Andre Gsponer/Jean-Pierre Hurni*, ITER: The International Thermonuclear Experimental Reactor and the Nuclear Weapons Proliferation Implications of Thermonuclear-Fusion Energy Systems, 2004, at 24.

194 *Robert E. Kelley*, Starve Nuclear Weapons to Death with a Tritium Freeze (*Stockholm International Peace Research Institute*, 2020), https://www.sipri.org/commentary/topical-backgrounder/2020/starve-nuclear-weapons-death-tritium-freeze, last accessed 17 July 2025.

by a factor of 10 to 100.[195] This increase in yield is due to fusion reactions increasing the percentage of fission material burnt in the bomb. Firstly, the fusion processes provide neutrons that drive the fission processes, and secondly, they compress the fission material to higher densities.[196] More neutrons result in more reactions, leading to a higher release of energy. Higher densities lead to higher probabilities that a neutron initiates a fission reaction. These two effects make the use of the fissile material more efficient and increase the yield of the bomb. By changing the amount of tritium within the primary, it is possible to have one weapon design with a variable yield. Tritium also allows for more compact weapons designs for modern delivery systems.[197]

5.2.2 Tritium in Multi-Stage Devices

Today, most modern nuclear weapons are multi-stage thermonuclear weapons, or short: hydrogen bombs since they use the fusion energy from the hydrogen isotopes deuterium and tritium. These weapons typically contain two stages, a fission primary stage and a fusion secondary stage. The energy produced by the fission bomb is transported by radiation to the fusion secondary, where it induces fusion reactions of deuterium and tritium. The energy released by these reactions further increases the yield of the weapon. A significant number of weapons designs include a third step, producing tritium in-situ from lithium-deuteride. As tritium is a radioactive gas, it decays, requiring regular maintenance as the amount of tritium within the weapon decreases. This reaction is not only of significance to nuclear weapons, but also in the production of tritium in future fusion power plants.

$$^{6}\mathrm{LiD} + \mathrm{n} \rightarrow {}^{4}\mathrm{He} + \mathrm{T} + \mathrm{D} \qquad (15)$$

Neutrons from the fission primary transform the lithium-deuteride into helium (which is irrelevant for the explosion), tritium and deuterium. In other terms: ^{6}Li is transformed into tritium. While this process takes place in the breeding blanket of a fusion reactor, it is also a stage of a mod-

195 *Kalinowski* (n 193), at 8 ff.; *Gsponer/Hurni* (n 193), at 24.

196 *Andre Gsponer/Jean-Pierre Hurni*, The Physics of Thermonuclear Explosives, Inertial Confinement Fusion, and the Quest for Fourth Generation Nuclear Weapons, INESAP Tech. Rep. No. 1 1997, at 11 ff.

197 *Sievert/Johnson* (n 158), at 338.

ern thermonuclear weapon. Given the importance of tritium, proliferators quickly jump to using tritium.

5.2.3 Tritium in Military Programmes and Civilian Nuclear Fuel Cycle

Tritium is a radioactive isotope with a half-life of 12.3 years. As a consequence, nuclear weapons programmes require the constant production of tritium to uphold their inventories as they reduce annually by about 5.5 %. Military programmes employ nuclear fission reactors to produce tritium, utilising heavy-water (D_2O) moderated reactors produce tritium when a deuterium nucleus captures a neutron. The US Stockpile Stewardship Program – the programme charged with maintaining the US nuclear arsenal – for instance, produces 2800 g of tritium within an 18-months period.[198] Civilian reactors also produce tritium, with the CANDU type reactor, which produces approximately 130 g of tritium per reactor per year.[199] The total civilian production amounts to less than 2000 g per year.[200] In CANDU reactors the tritium must be removed from the moderator to prevent its release into the environment; in military reactors tritium needs to be separated for the use in weapons. The removal process is a complex and costly process.[201] Currently, there are only two civilian tritium removal facilities, with a third under construction.[202] Even the separation capacities of nuclear weapon States are limited. For instance, the US military programme uses the Savannah River Site, which is the sole military tritium extraction facility in the United States. The small quantities produced per year result in tritium being the single most expensive material in the world with prices of around USD 30–35,000 per gram.[203]

---

198 *U.S. Department of Defense/U.S. Department of Energy*, Memorandum for Members of the Nuclear Weapons Council – Nuclear Weapons Council Strategic Plan for Fiscal Years 2017–2042 (2016).

199 *Pearson/Antoniazzi/Nuttall* (n 103).

200 Ibid.

201 On the complex development process of tritium extraction technologies for fusion, see *D. Demange/R. Antunes/O. Borisevich et al.*, Tritium Extraction Technologies and DEMO Requirements, Fusion Engineering and Design 109–111 (2016), 912–916.

202 There is the Darlington Tritium Removal Facility in Canada and the Wolsong Tritium Removal Facility in Korea. Currently, the Cernavoda Tritium Removal Facility is built in Romania.

203 *Richard J. Pearson/Olivia Comsa/Liviu Stefan et al.*, Romanian Tritium for Nuclear Fusion, Fusion Science and Technology 71 (2017), 610–615; *Daniel Clery*, Out of Gas, Science 376 (2022), 1372–1376.

Assuming that Russian tritium production facilities are comparable to those of the United States and that the other nuclear weapon States produce tritium relative to their significantly lower nuclear arsenals, the total tritium production per year – both civilian and military combined – is in the range of five kilograms.

5.2.4 Tritium and Fusion Energy

Tritium is essential for fusion power plants, with the vast majority of concepts running on D-T fusion, but also for modern nuclear weapons.

Fusion will significantly increase the production and storage of tritium and thus also the risk of the material's diversion to use in nuclear weapons. While a single nuclear weapon requires just a few grams of tritium, one fusion facility will usually produce and consume amounts of tritium in the range of tens to hundreds of kilograms. ITER's tritium inventory is expected to be in the range of 2–3 kg,[204] and DEMO's annual tritium production is expected to be around 100 kg[205]. This underscores potential of fusion and its tritium with regard of the proliferation of nuclear weapons.

Furthermore, with respect to DEMO and other fusion power plant concepts, it is envisioned that the reactor itself both produces and consumes its own tritium.[206] Tritium is produced by a reaction between a neutron released in a D-T reaction and the lithium isotope ^6Li, which is placed in the wall of the reactor:

$$^6Li + n \rightarrow T + {}^4He \quad (16)$$

This principle is also known from the second stage of thermonuclear weapons, where instead of using the gaseous and radioactive tritium in the

204 *M. Glugla/A. Antipenkov/S. Beloglazov et al.*, The ITER Tritium Systems, Fusion Engineering and Design 82 (2007), 472–487; *I. R. Cristescu/I. Cristescu/L. Doerr et al.*, Tritium Inventories and Tritium Safety Design Principles for the Fuel Cycle of ITER, Nuclear Fusion 47 (2007), 458.

205 *G. Federici/C. Bachmann/L. Barucca et al.*, Overview of the DEMO Staged Design Approach in Europe, Nuclear Fusion 59 (2019), 066013; *Glugla/Antipenkov/Beloglazov et al.* (n 204).

206 *Rachel Lawless/Barry Butler/Anthony Hollingsworth et al.*, Tritium Plant Technology Development for a DEMO Power Plant, Fusion Science and Technology 71 (2017), 679–686; *M. Coleman/Y. Hörstensmeyer/F. Cismondi*, DEMO Tritium Fuel Cycle: Performance, Parameter Explorations, and Design Space Constraints, Fusion Engineering and Design 141 (2019), 79–90.

secondary, ^{6}Li is incorporated into the weapon to produce tritium during the explosion, as seen above in Equation 15.[207]

Such an in-situ production presents two risks with regard to non-proliferation. Firstly, research on the breeding-blankets of fusion devices – which is a main area of research on the way to commercialising fusion[208] – is tightly closed to processes that take place in the second stage of thermonuclear weapons. The question of breeding tritium within the operation of a fusion device is so complex that even ITER will only be equipped with test blanket modules. Knowledge acquired from this research may hold significance for military programmes on thermonuclear weapons.

Secondly, this method is associated with a risk of diversion. Although in-situ breeding method reduces the risk of tritium diversion in the delivery process, fusion reactors have to produce more tritium than is needed for the fusion processes themselves. This is in order to account for calculation uncertainties, radioactive decay, permeation into the facility's equipment and the start-up of the next fusion reactor or power plant.[209] Current estimates indicate that the so-called tritium breeding-ratio (TBR), defined as the ratio between the amount of tritium produced and the amount of tritium consumed, is in the range of approximately 1.1 to 1.2.[210] This means that the fusion reactor needs to produce ten to twenty percent more tritium than it consumes. For instance, DEMO's excess tritium production is estimated to be in the range of ten to twenty kilograms per year.[211] This is enough to boost ten thousand nuclear weapons. To put that number into context: The *Stockholm International Peace Research Institute* (SIPRI)

207 *David Kramer*, DOE Prepares Major Upgrade of its Lithium-6 Operations, Physics Today 71 (2018), 29–31; *Ralph E. Lapp*, Nuclear Weapons: Past and Present, Bulletin of the Atomic Scientists 26 (1970), 103–106; *Thomas B. Cochran/William M. Arkin/Robert S. Norris*, U.S. Nuclear Weapons Production: An Overview, Bulletin of the Atomic Scientists 44 (1988), 12–16.

208 On the design of the tritium breeding blanket for DEMO, see *Ion Cristescu/F. Priester/D. Rapisarda et al.*, Overview of the Tritium Technologies for the EU DEMO Breeding Blanket, Fusion Science and Technology 76 (2020), 446–457.

209 *Neill Taylor/Pierre Cortes*, Lessons Learnt From ITER Safety & Licensing for DEMO and Future Nuclear Fusion Facilities, Fusion Engineering and Design 89 (2014), 1995–2000.

210 *Didier Perrault*, Safety Issues to Be Taken Into Account in Designing Future Nuclear Fusion Facilities, Fusion Engineering and Design 109–111 (2016), 1733–1738; *Coleman/Hörstensmeyer/Cismondi* (n 206); *J. Lion/J. C. Anglès/L. Bonauer et al.*, Stellaris: A High-Field Quasi-Isodynamic Stellarator for a Prototypical Fusion Power Plant, Fusion Engineering and Design 214 (2025), 114868.

211 Based on DEMO's 100 kg annual tritium production, see above n 205.

estimates that there are about 12,000 nuclear weapons in the world.[212] Consequently, if each weapon contains one to three grams of tritium, the excess production from a single large fusion power plant could be sufficient to boost almost every nuclear weapon in existence.

Consequently, the excess production of tritium represents a serious risk for proliferation. As noted above, the excess is intended to address various issues, with the result that, in theory, each tritium nucleus is used only for energy production. However, these issues create the potential for proliferators to use this tritium to boost fission weapons or to use it in a hydrogen bomb.

In summary, tritium's involvement in fusion poses a risk for proliferation. It can be used to increase the sophistication of a nuclear weapon (vertical proliferation) and to support the efforts to build a hydrogen bomb (both vertical and horizontal). It should be noted that the availability of tritium alone is not sufficient to build a nuclear weapon or any other explosive device. It is only in combination with fissile material and the knowledge and mastering of the complex physics behind a hydrogen bomb that tritium poses a proliferation concern.

5.3 Inertial Confinement Fusion

Inertial confinement fusion (ICF), also referred to as laser fusion as it is the most common form of ICF, has given rise to another concern of nuclear proliferation. ICF replicates processes that are essential for hydrogen weapons. This technology involves heating small pellets made of fusionable material using extremely powerful lasers. The heat causes the outer part of the pellet to expand outwards. In accordance with Newton's Third Law *actio est reactio,* the centre of the pellet is compressed. This compression may create the physical conditions necessary for fusion to occur. To this date, only one fusion facility has produced more energy than was put into the fusion process itself:[213] The National Ignition Facility (NIF), located at the Lawrence Livermore National Laboratory in California, USA. Interestingly,

212 *Hans M. Kristensen/Matt Korda*, World Nuclear Forces, in: Stockholm International Peace Research Institute (ed.), SIPRI Yearbook 2022, Stockholm, Oxford: Oxford University Press 2022, 341–432, at 342.

213 The NNSA calls this ignition. It must be noted that the fusion processes produced more energy than the laser light contained which went into cylindrical hohlraum capsule containing the fuel.

in terms of proliferation, the press release on the first ignition addresses not only on the benefits of fusion for energy production, but puts its potential for the United States's nuclear weapons arsenal at the beginning:

> *"The U.S. Department of Energy (DOE) and DOE's* ***National Nuclear Security Administration (NNSA)*** *today announced the achievement of fusion ignition at Lawrence Livermore National Laboratory (LLNL)—a major scientific breakthrough decades in the making that* ***will pave the way for advancements in national defense*** *and the future of clean power. [...] This historic, first-of-its kind achievement will provide* ***unprecedented capability to support NNSA's Stockpile Stewardship Program*** *and will provide invaluable insights into the prospects of clean fusion energy."*[214]

Indeed, NIF was not constructed with the intention of paving the way to a fusion power plant, rather it was aimed to develop computer codes for hydrogen bombs in order to replace nuclear testing.[215] It thereby serves the Stockpile Stewardship Program, which aims to keep the United States's nuclear arsenal operational. The National Nuclear Security Administration (NNSA) is mandated to maintain and enhance safety, reliability and performance of the US nuclear weapons stockpile.[216]

Some even compare inertial confinement fusion with a miniature version of a hydrogen bomb.[217] While the two largest laser fusion facilities - NIF and the Laser Mégajoule in France - are located in nuclear weapons States and serve military purposes, several start-up companies are endeavouring to use inertial confinement fusion in a power plant design.[218] In addition to that, both state and non-state actors in non-nuclear weapon States such as Japan (Gekko XII - a public entity) and Germany (Marvel Fusion, Focused Energy - private entities) are also focusing on laser fusion. As the development of inertial confinement fusion accelerates, particularly among

---

214 Emphasis added. *U.S. Department of Energy*, DOE National Laboratory Makes History by Achieving Fusion Ignition (2022), https://www.energy.gov/articles/doe-national-laboratory-makes-history-achieving-fusion-ignition, last accessed 17 July 2025.

215 *B. G. Logan*, Use of the National Ignition Facility for Defense, Energy, and Basic Research Science (1994), Lawrence Livermore National Laboratory.

216 50 U.S. Code § 2401.

217 *Garry McCracken/Peter Stott*, Chapter 7 – Inertial-Confinement Fusion, in: Garry McCracken/Peter Stott (eds.), Fusion (Second Edition), Boston: Academic Press 2013, 67–81, at 67.

218 Examples for private companies engaged in inertial confinement fusion are *tea* and *Longview Fusion* (both based in the United States), *General Fusion* (based in Canada), *Marvel Fusion* and *Focused Energy* (both based in Germany).

private entities, the risk of knowledge being diverted to the construction of hydrogen bombs increases substantially.

When NIF was constructed, the US Department of Energy reviewed the proliferation potential of ICF facilities. The study concluded that insights from the facility could provide information for advanced proliferators pursuing secondary designs, given the insights in X-ray transport, the equation of state and thermonuclear reactions. However, it was also stated that "without access to data from nuclear tests, ICF or unclassified NIF data would be of very limited utility to proliferators."[219] These appeasing remarks have been criticised.[220]

As with magnetic confinement fusion, the proliferation potential of ICF depends on the precise technology used. As mentioned above, ICF functions by heating small pellets of fusion fuel with lasers. The aspect of ICF that renders it valuable for the purposes of nuclear weapons research is the transfer of energy from the laser to the fusion fuel. While a direct transfer of energy could work for energy purposes (so-called direct-drive targets)[221], military research facilities prefer an indirect transfer (so-called indirect-drive targets). While the direct-drive fusion bears only distant resemblance to thermonuclear weapons,[222] indirect-drive fusion is of particular interest for weapons research. In this case, the lasers are first absorbed by a surrounding material (so-called *hohlraum*) which then emits X-ray radiation that drives the implosion of the fusion fuel.[223] It is this energy transfer that is of interest for the design of a hydrogen bomb as this transfer is

219 *U.S. Department of Energy*, The National Ignition Facility (NIF) and the Issue of Nonproliferation (NN-40), 1995, especially at 29.

220 *Robert J. Goldston/Alexander Glaser*, Inertial Confinement Fusion Energy R&D and Nuclear Proliferation: The Need for Direct and Transparent Review, Bulletin of the Atomic Scientists 67 (2011), 59–66.

221 For an overview of the direct-drive approach, see *R. S. Craxton/K. S. Anderson/T. R. Boehly et al.*, Direct-Drive Inertial Confinement Fusion: A Review, Physics of Plasmas 22 (2015), 110501. On its future, see *E. M. Campbell/T. C. Sangster/V. N. Goncharov et al.*, Direct-Drive Laser Fusion: Status, Plans and Future, Philosophical Transactions of the Royal Society A: Mathematical, Physical and Engineering Sciences 379 (2021), 20200011.

222 *National Research Council*, Assessment of Inertial Confinement Fusion Targets, Washington DC: The National Academies Press 2013, at 37.

223 *John Lindl*, Development of the Indirect-Drive Approach to Inertial Confinement Fusion and the Target Physics Basis for Ignition and Gain, Physics of Plasmas 2 (1995), 3933–4024.

necessary in multi-stage devices.[224] Rather than materials, the proliferation concern with inertial confinement fusion lays with the potential knowledge gain. Given that literature on the physics of these weapons is classified, it is difficult to quantify the proliferation potential.

Again, it is imperative to acknowledge that the mere existence of an ICF facility does not inherently result in the development of nuclear weapons. The knowledge that could be gained from ICF fusion experiments is one of numerous factors contributing to the construction of thermonuclear weapons. Even the knowledge of indirect energy transfer is, in isolation, not sufficient to build such a weapon.

5.4 Fusion-Fission-Hybrid Systems

During the decades of fusion research, scientists have discussed the feasibility of fission-fusion hybrid systems. The idea is somewhat similar to principles behind thermonuclear weapons: The neutrons generated in the fusion reactions could be used to increase the amount of fission events.[225] The ideas went as far as using waste from regular fission power plants in such hybrid systems.[226] These States could use such hybrid systems as source of tritium and pure plutonium.

Concepts for these hybrid systems were prominently supported by the German-American physicist and Nobel Laureate Hans Bethe in the 1970s.[227] The United States also pursued a concept to use the knowledge gained from NIF to develop a hybrid fusion-fission plant called *LIFE*,[228] but

224 Goldston and Glaser note that a restriction to direct-driven ICF facilities could easily be overcome since the lasers could still be used for an indirect drive, *Goldston/Glaser* (n 220).

225 *B. R. Leonard Jr*, A Review of Fusion-Fission (Hybrid) Concepts, Nuclear Technology 20 (1973), 161–178.

226 *T. A. Mehlhorn/B. B. Cipiti/C. L. Olson et al.*, Fusion–fission Hybrids for Nuclear Waste Transmutation: A Synergistic Step Between Gen-IV Fission and Fusion Reactors, Fusion Engineering and Design 83 (2008), 948–953.

227 *Hans Bethe*, The Fusion Hybrid, Physics Today 32 (1979), 44–51.

228 LIFE is an abbreviation for Laser Ignition Fusion Energy. On the hybrid system see *Kevin J. Kramer/Massimiliano Fratoni/Jeffery F. Latkowski et al.*, Fusion-Fission Blanket Options for the LIFE Engine, Fusion Science and Technology 60 (2011), 72–77.

the project has since been discontinued.[229] In recent times, both Russia[230] and China[231] have pursued hybrid concepts.

However, as fusion itself is a technology that has not yet been sufficiently mastered to generate energy, it is even more difficult to realise a fusion-fission hybrid concept. The concepts currently pursued are far from a commercial dimension. Government-backed research is far from the scale of pure fusion technology, which is demonstrated for instance in ITER or the European DEMO project. Especially the private sector, which plays an important role in transforming a technology from research labs to a commercial scale, does not show any real interest in this technology. Consequently, these hybrid concepts are excluded from this research.

Furthermore, the safeguards dimension of these systems has already been discussed.[232] Such systems would be covered by the existing legal framework as they are to characterise as *nuclear facilities* that operate with *nuclear material*.[233]

5.5 Fundamental Differences Between Fusion and Fission

At this juncture, it is important to underscore the key differences between the proliferation potentials of fusion and fission.

A nuclear fission power plants operates with fissile material. A country that possesses a full nuclear fuel cycle infrastructure is a "virtual nuclear weapon State" as the former IAEA Director General ElBaradei once warned.[234] The process of enriching uranium to a level used in energy production and research is the same physical process as enriching uranium to a level necessary for nuclear weapons. The omnipresence of dual-use

229 *David Kramer*, Livermore Ends LIFE, Physics Today 67 (2014), 26–27.

230 See for example *B. V. Kuteev/P. R. Goncharov*, Fusion–Fission Hybrid Systems: Yesterday, Today, and Tomorrow, Fusion Science and Technology 76 (2020), 836–847.

231 *Maosheng Li/Rong Liu/Xueming Shi et al.*, The Project of Fusion-Fission Hybrid Energy Reactor in China, Fusion Science and Technology 61 (2012), 195–199.

232 *Sievert/Johnson*; *Ralph W. Moir/Wally Manheimer*, Fusion–Fission Hybrid Reactors, in: Thomas J. Dolan (ed.), Magnetic Fusion Technology, London: Springer 2013, 699–742, at 733 ff.

233 On the importance of these notions for fusion, see Chapter 3.

234 *Julian Borger*, Mohamed ElBaradei Warns of New Nuclear Age in: https://www.theguardian.com/world/2009/may/14/elbaradei-nuclear-weapons-states-un, last accessed 17 July 2025.

material gives rise to the proliferation potential of fission, a concept that is frequently termed *nuclear latency* or *nuclear threshold States:*[235] States possessing the technological capability to develop nuclear weapons as a result of their civilian nuclear programmes. These states include Germany, Japan, Canada, Australia, South Africa, South Korea, Taiwan and Iran.[236]

In contrast, in fusion, the proliferation potential is more indirect. Tritium alone does not suffice to build a nuclear weapon. The knowledge gained from ICF alone does not suffice to build a nuclear weapon. Both options still require access to fissile material. Fissile material is not used in a fusion power plant, but could theoretically be produced by fusion reactor. Consequently, fusion can be a puzzle piece within a broader nuclear weapons programme, rather than the starting point as fission is.

5.6 Summary

Nuclear fusion carries both horizontal and vertical proliferation risks due to the release of neutrons, the use of tritium, and the research into ICF. Highly energetic neutrons, released by DT fusion, are intended to breed tritium from ^{6}Li, but can also potentially be used to breed nuclear weapons-grade plutonium or uranium. Tritium and ^{6}Li are used as boosters of fission-based nuclear weapons but are also the essential part of a fusion fuel cycle. Inertial confinement fusion research is based on understanding the physics of hydrogen bombs.

Notwithstanding, fusion has a lower proliferation potential than fission, especially when safeguards are in place: Fusion only complements fission, while fission remains the core part of a weapon, and there are significant technological limitations of fusion's contribution to a nuclear weapons programme. While any potential risk alone is not sufficient to build or increase the yield of nuclear weapons, fusion technology has the capacity to function as a component within the broader context of a nuclear weapons programme which is still based on fission. In light of the immense consequences for humanity and the planet, it is important to explore a

235 See e.g. Joseph Pilat (ed.), Nuclear Latency and Hedging: Concepts, History, and Issues, Washington DC: Woodrow Wilson International Center for Scholars 2019; *Maria Rost Rublee*, The Nuclear Threshold States, The Nonproliferation Review 17 (2010), 49–70.

236 On empirical data on threshold states, see *Matthew Fuhrmann/Benjamin Tkach*, Almost Nuclear: Introducing the Nuclear Latency Dataset, Conflict Management and Peace Science 32 (2015), 443–461.

response in international law to address this non-zero probability of fusion, a technology capable to contribute in combatting the climate crisis, being misused for military purposes. Such a legal response will be explored in the next chapters.

Chapter 2: The Legal Framework of Nuclear Weapons

As demonstrated in the preceding chapter, the development of nuclear fusion as a clean and sustainable energy source has implications for nuclear weapons. This chapter provides a comprehensive overview of the existing international and European legal framework of nuclear weapons as it is of relevance for fusion. It starts by examining the political logic of this legal regime (1). The chapter proceeds to analyse the pillars of nuclear weapons law of nuclear non-proliferation (2) and nuclear disarmament (3). The law is presented with a view to the framework's historic background to better understand the feasibility of the approaches presented in the next chapters. The chapter further explores the limitations of law in the broader context of nuclear ambitions and varying interests among actors (4).

1 Political Logic of Nuclear Weapons Law

The regime of nuclear weapons law is of paramount importance for peace and security, as nuclear weapons and the corresponding regime is at the centre of the international order. The invention of no other weapon has transformed the international security architecture as extensively as nuclear weapons did. When nuclear weapons were first developed in the Manhattan Project during World War II, many thought the invention of the atomic bomb might end all wars, as nuclear war could not be won.[237] A nuclear war could lead to the destruction of the world.[238] The use of nuclear weapons in Hiroshima and Nagasaki on 6 and 9 August 1945, and the

237 Winston Churchill shared this thought in his last major speech in the UK Parliament: "It may be that we shall by a process of sublime irony have reached a stage in this story where safety will be the sturdy child of terror, and survival the twin brother of annihilation", Hansard, 5th Series, Volume 537, cc 1893. On this nuclear peace hypothesis, see *Robert Rauchhaus*, Evaluating the Nuclear Peace Hypothesis: A Quantitative Approach, The Journal of Conflict Resolution 53 (2009), 258–277.

238 *Leo Sartori*, Effects of Nuclear Weapons, Physics Today 36 (1983), 32–41; *R. P. Turco/O. B. Toon/T. P. Ackerman et al.*, Nuclear Winter: Global Consequences of Multiple Nuclear Explosions, Science 222 (1983), 1283–1292; *A. Robock/L. Oman/G. L. Stenchikov et al.*, Climatic Consequences of Regional Nuclear Conflicts, Atmospheric Chemistry and Physics 7 (2007), 2003–2012.

thousands of nuclear weapons tests that have followed, have demonstrated the destructive potential of this weapon. Nuclear weapons have also led to major shifts in the way in which superpowers deal with their rivals.[239] This section will examine the political logic of nuclear weapons that frame the international nuclear legal regime. First, it will analyse the use of nuclear weapons for deterrence and coercion (1.1). Second, it will focus on the conflict between security and the economy (1.2).

1.1 Nuclear Weapons as a Tool for Deterrence and Coercion

The political power of a nuclear weapon stems from the fact that its possession is synonymous with having great power. From a nuclear-weapon State perspective, the fear of nuclear retaliation not only keeps it safe from both conventional and nuclear armed attacks (so-called nuclear deterrence[240]), but also leverages the State's position in negotiations and world politics (so-called nuclear coercion or nuclear blackmail[241]). Thus, the possession

---

239 *Robert Jervis*, The Political Effects of Nuclear Weapons: A Comment, International Security 13 (1988), 80–90; *Richard K. Betts*, Nuclear Peace and Conventional War, Journal of Strategic Studies 11 (1988), 79–95; *Harald Müller*, Looking at Nuclear Rivalry: The Role of Nuclear Deterrence, Strategic Analysis 38 (2014), 464–475.

240 On the theory of nuclear deterrence in political science, see *Robert Powell*, Nuclear Deterrence Theory: The Search for Credibility, Cambridge: Cambridge University Press 1990. On its legality under international law, see the contributions by Nigel D. White, Monique Cormier and Jonathan L. Black-Branch in Jonathan L. Black-Branch/Dieter Fleck (eds.), Nuclear Non-Proliferation in International Law, vol V – Legal Challenges for Nuclear Security and Deterrence, Asser Press 2020; *Stuart Casey-Maslen*, The Status of Nuclear Deterrence Under International Law in Light of the Treaty on the Prohibition of Nuclear Weapons, in: Terry D. Gill/Robin Geiß/Heike Krieger/Christophe Paulussen (eds.), Yearbook of International Humanitarian Law, Volume 21 (2018), The Hague: T.M.C. Asser Press 2020, 23–57; *Daniel J. Arbess/Simeon A. Sahaydachny*, Nuclear Deterrence and International Law: Some Steps toward Observance, Alternatives 12 (1987), 83–111.

241 On this concept, see *Todd S. Sechser/Matthew Fuhrmann*, Nuclear Weapons and Coercive Diplomacy, Cambridge: Cambridge University Press 2017; *Jeff McMahan*, Nuclear Blackmail, in: Nigel Blake/Kay Pole (eds.), Dangers of Deterrence, Oxford, New York: Routledge 1983, 84–111.

of nuclear weapons has been[242] and still is[243] very attractive for many countries. Conversely, States already in possession of nuclear weapons have an interest in maintaining their privileged position and to prevent other States from acquiring nuclear weapons. Keeping the nuclear advantage is a core interest of nuclear weapon States which they maintain by exercising hegemony in shaping the legal framework.[244]

States pursue nuclear capabilities either by acquiring them (horizontal proliferation) or by expanding existing arsenals (vertical proliferation), using a variety of pathways. While some States openly develop nuclear weapons, others follow more opaque strategies. For example, some pursue covert development, as is widely attributed to Israel, which has never officially confirmed its nuclear arsenal. Others engage in nuclear hedging, exemplified by Iran.

Hedging refers to the deliberate development of the technological and industrial capacity to produce nuclear weapons – such as enrichment facilities or other technical expertise – without committing to actually building a bomb.[245] It reflects a strategic posture of ambiguity, maintaining a position of "maybe" that can quickly shift to a "yes" depending on political circumstances.[246]

242 Historic examples are South Africa and Sweden. South Africa built three nuclear warheads but destroyed them subsequently. On the South African nuclear programme, see *Waldo Stumpf*, South Africa's Nuclear Weapons Program: From Deterrance to Dismantlement, Arms Control Today 25 (1995), 3–8 Sweden followed an ambitious nuclear programme after World War II until its accession to the NPT in 1968, *Thomas B. Johansson*, Sweden's Abortive Nuclear Weapons Project, Bulletin of the Atomic Scientists 42 (1986), 31–34. Even Germany had ambitions to develop a federal-German nuclear weapon in the late 1950s and early 1960s. On German Chancellor Adenauer's vision of nuclear weapons, see *Dennis Romberg*, Atomgeschäfte – Die Nuklearpolitik der Bundesrepublik Deutschland 1970–1979, Paderborn: Ferdinand Schöningh 2020, at 55.

243 Iran's nuclear programme is a prominent example. On the state of the programme, see *Paul K. Kerr*, Iran and Nuclear Weapons Production, Washington DC: Congressional Research Service 2024.

244 *Dimitris Bourantonis*, The Negotiation of the Non-Proliferation Treaty, 1965–1968: A Note, The International History Review 19 (1997), 347–357; *Nick Ritchie*, A Hegemonic Nuclear Order: Understanding the Ban Treaty and the Power Politics of Nuclear Weapons, Contemporary Security Policy 40 (2019), 409–434. See also *Rebecca Davis Gibbons*, American Hegemony and the Politics of the Nuclear Nonproliferation Regime, Washington DC: Georgetown University 2016.

245 *Vipin Narang*, Strategies of Nuclear Proliferation – How States Pursue the Bomb, International Security 41 (2016), 110–150.

246 Ibid, at 117 ff.

Nuclear weapons are closely related to the identity of a State.[247] Nuclear weapons are often a sign of national pride, as seen in the French *dissuasion nucléaire* under de Gaulle or in North Korea under the Juche ideology.[248] It gives a State the perception of super power status and provides it with a feeling of control in international relations as they are able to act autonomously without the support of other States.[249] Further reasons for why States pursue or do not pursue nuclear weapons lay within domestic policies and the strength of international norms.[250]

Nuclear deterrence is based on a paradox:[251] The possession of the deadliest weapon ever created by mankind, capable of erasing the entire world several times over, makes the world a safer place by preventing wars. For instance, many attribute the fact that the Cold War never escalated to a direct military conflict between the United States and the Soviet Union to the deterring effects of nuclear weapons.[252] Nuclear weapons are designed not to be used in combat, but to prevent the combat from happening altogether. Some even go as far as arguing that there would not be any bilateral conflict if all nations were nuclear armed.[253] For (neo-)realist scholars, as this stream of political science is called, nuclear deterrence avoids war as the consequences of the use of nuclear weapons are catastrophically.[254] However, history has shown that nuclear deterrence does not avoid military confrontation with a nuclear power. Not only were there proxy wars between the United States and the Soviet Union during the Cold War, military conflicts of the 2020s disprove nuclear deterrence.

---

247 *Jacques E. C. Hymans*, The Psychology of Nuclear Proliferation: Identity, Emotions and Foreign Policy, Cambridge: Cambridge University Press 2006; *Scott D. Sagan*, Why Do States Build Nuclear Weapons?: Three Models in Search of a Bomb, International Security 21 (1996), 54–86.

248 See below, Sections 4.2.1.4 and 4.2.2.

249 *Hymans* (n 247), at 32 ff.

250 *Sagan* (n 247).

251 *Scott D. Sagan*, The Perils of Proliferation: Organization Theory, Deterrence Theory, and the Spread of Nuclear Weapons, International Security 18 (1994), 66–107, at 66.

252 Ibid.

253 *Bruce Bueno de Mesquita/William H. Riker*, An Assessment of the Merits of Selective Nuclear Proliferation, Journal of Conflict Resolution 26 (1982), 283–306, at 283.

254 *Kenneth N. Waltz*, The Spread of Nuclear Weapons: More May Be Better: Introduction, The Adelphi Papers 21 (1981), 1–32; *Kenneth N. Waltz*, Nuclear Myths and Political Realities, The American Political Science Review 84 (1990), 731–745; *Krieger Zanvyl/Ariel Ilan Roth*, Nuclear Weapons in Neo-Realist Theory, International Studies Review 9 (2007), 369–384.

Russia is unable to conquer Ukraine despite Russia's giant nuclear weapons arsenal and even suffered occupation and attacks within its own borders. Russia's nuclear weapons did not deter Ukraine to defend itself, even on Russian territory. Similarly, the nuclear armed States of Pakistan and India have had a minor military conflict in 2025. In addition, Iran has attacked the nuclear armed State of Israel with ballistic missiles in 2024 and 2025. None of these involvements of nuclear weapon States has led to the use of a nuclear weapon. As a consequence, some characterise nuclear deterrence as a myth.[255] For constructivists, the meaning of nuclear weapons is not given by its abstract capability to destroy the opponent, but is constructed within a social context. For them, a changing social context also changes the importance of nuclear weapons.[256] Critical towards nuclear weapons is also a third school of international relations, liberalists, which believe in mitigating the proliferation of nuclear weapons through international cooperation, especially treaties and international organisations.[257]

Nuclear coercion is based on a similar premise as nuclear deterrence. The destructive consequences of the use of a nuclear weapon guide the behaviour of another State. While nuclear deterrence focuses more on defensive action of a nuclear weapon State, nuclear coercion is based on the premise of a nuclear first-use. To prevent such nuclear first-use, States often cope to the demands of a nuclear weapon State. For example, the end of the Korean War has been partially attributed to nuclear coercion.[258]

---

255 *Ward Wilson*, The Myth of Nuclear Deterrence, The Nonproliferation Review 15 (2008), 421–439. Critical: *Derrin Culp*, Part I: A Critical Examination of "The Myth of Nuclear Deterrence", The Nonproliferation Review 19 (2012), 51–68. Critical towards the role of deterrence is *Vipin Narang*, What Does It Take to Deter? Regional Power Nuclear Postures and International Conflict, Journal of Conflict Resolution 57 (2013), 478–508.

256 See for example *Nina Tannenwald*, The Nuclear Taboo: The United States and the Non-Use of Nuclear Weapons Since 1945, Cambridge: Cambridge University Press 2007; *T.V. Paul*, The Tradition of Non-Usa of Nuclear Weapons, Stanford: Stanford University Press 2009.

257 *Elizabeth N. Saunders*, The Domestic Politics of Nuclear Choices—A Review Essay, International Security 44 (2019), 146–184; *Robert E. Kelly*, Liberal Norms or Coercive Counterproliferation: The American Response to Potential South Korean Nuclearization, Pacific Focus 40 (2025), 69–99; Harald Müller/Carmen Wunderlich (eds.), Norm Dynamics in Multilateral Arms Control: Interests, Conflicts, and Justice, Athens: University of Georgia Press 2013.

258 *Rosemary J. Foot*, Nuclear Coercion and the Ending of the Korean Conflict, International Security 13 (1988), 92–112; *Edward Friedman*, Nuclear Blackmail and the End of the Korean War, Modern China 1 (1975), 75–91.

Paradoxically, the division of Korea eventually led to North Korea's nuclear programme and the use of nuclear coercion by that State.[259] There are also examples where nuclear coercion was proven wrong. Nuclear coercion was a tool by Russia in the years leading up to the full-scale invasion starting in 2022.[260] The relevance of nuclear weapons as a tool of coercion has thus been challenged.[261]

The legality of both doctrines revolves around the question of the legality of the threat and use of nuclear weapons which has been the subject of an advisory opinion rendered by the International Court of Justice (ICJ) in 1996.[262] If the use of a nuclear weapons is illegal, then a signalled intention to use such a weapon is also illegal.[263] In the advisory opinion, the Court stated that the threat or use of nuclear weapons is not *per se* illegal under international law: From a *jus contra bellum* perspective, its legality is questionable vis-à-vis the necessity and proportionality requirements of Article 51 of the UN Charter.[264] From a *jus in bello* perspective, the possibility to distinct between military and civilian targets is doubtful, which is the core principle of international humanitarian law.[265] Nevertheless, the Court could not come to a definitive conclusion whether the "fundamental right of every State to survival" might – in extreme circumstances – warrant the use of nuclear weapons.[266] In addition, the Court explicitly did not denounce the policy of nuclear deterrence.[267]

The ICJ's advisory opinion has been heavily criticised, both from within and outside the Court. From within, five judges added a declaration, three a separate opinion and six judges a dissenting opinion. Especially the finding that the Court could not definitively conclude whether the threat or use of nuclear weapons in extreme cases where the State's survival is at stake,

---

259 More on this below, Section 4.2.2.

260 *Anna Clara Arndt/Liviu Horovitz/Michal Onderco*, Russia's Failed Nuclear Coercion Against Ukraine, The Washington Quarterly 46 (2023), 167–184; *Foot* (n 258), *Friedman* (n 258).

261 *Sechser/Fuhrmann* (n 241). The reduced role of nuclear superiority is analysed by *David C. Logan*, The Nuclear Balance Is What States Make of It, International Security 46 (2022), 172–215.

262 *International Court of Justice*, Legality of the Threat or Use of Nuclear Weapons, Advisory Opinion of 8 July 1996, ICJ Reports 1996, p. 226.

263 Ibid, para. 47.

264 Ibid, paras 37 ff.

265 Ibid, paras 90 ff.

266 Ibid, para. 96 f.

267 Ibid, para. 67.

was split by a 7–7 decision with the President's casting vote deciding. From outside, the advisory opinion has resulted in a wealth of scholarly contributions.[268] Many authors join the dissenting judges in their opinion that the effects of the use of nuclear weapons cannot be justified under any circumstances and are always in violation of international law,[269] thus also leading to the illegality of the doctrines of nuclear deterrence and nuclear coercion.

Despite the critiques, nuclear deterrence and nuclear coercion are still guiding the interests of nuclear weapon States.[270]

1.2 Conflict between Security and Economy

The international rules regulating nuclear weapons are a matter giving rise to a conflict between political and economic interests. There is a global interest that no further country acquires nuclear weapons. Nuclear weapon States want to maintain their elevated status and non-nuclear weapon States do not want to see an increased threat of nuclear war rising from an increased number of nuclear weapon States. However, as long as countries exploit the atomic nucleus for energy purposes, due to the dual-use characteristics of nuclear energy, there is always an underlying risk that countries use the technology for nuclear weapons. Consequently, any measure aiming to prevent the proliferation of nuclear weapons might impede the use of nuclear material for peaceful applications. It is important to acknowledge the substantial economic benefits offered by nuclear energy to numerous

---

268 A search of "ICJ Advisory Opinion Nuclear Weapons" on Google Scholar leads to about 37,600 results. See for example Laurence Boisson de Chazournes/Philippe Sands (eds.), International Law, the International Court of Justice and Nuclear Weapons, Cambridge: Cambridge University Press 1999; *Mariano J. Aznar-Gomez*, The 1996 Nuclear Weapons Advisory Opinion and Non Liquet in International Law, International and Comparative Law Quarterly 48 (1999), 3–19; Special Issue, International Review of the Red Cross, No 316.

269 From the ICJ: Dissenting opinions of Vice-President Schwebel, Judge Shahabuddeen, Judge Weeramantry and Judge Koroma. From the literature, see for example *Eric David*, The Opinion of the International Court of Justice on the Legality of the Use of Nuclear Weapons, International Review of the Red Cross 316 (1997), 21–34; *Michael Greenwood*, Jus ad bellum and jus in bello in the Nuclear Weapons Advisory Opinion, in: Laurence Boisson de Chazournes/Philippe Sands (eds.), International Law, the International Court of Justice and Nuclear Weapons, Cambridge: Cambridge University Press 1999, 247–265.

270 On the various interests, see below Section 4.2.

countries by providing them with a stable supply of cheap energy. The oil crisis of the 1970s as well as the recent energy crisis in Europe following the targeted sanctions against Russia underscore the economic and political significance of affordable energy. Peaks in energy costs can have far-reaching political and societal ramifications.[271] The political impacts of the *Fridays for Future*[272] or *Gilets Jaunes*[273] movement are examples of this political dimension of the transition towards greenhouse gas-free sources of energy. In addition, the heightened awareness of the climate crisis has led to a growing emphasis on nuclear energy, which plays an essential role for many countries in transitioning their energy production to greenhouse gas-free sources of energy, as for instance recognised by many States during COP28.[274] The heightened attention towards nuclear energy is evident in both industrialised nations such as the United States, the United Kingdom or Poland, as well as countries in the Global South, including African nations.[275] Energy is a matter of paramount importance to the sovereignty of a State.[276] Any external interference, thus, is typically met with a degree of scepticism, being accepted only for reasons of equal importance, such as national security in the context of the proliferation of nuclear weapons.

In principle, the most effective strategy for ensuring the highest level of non-proliferation would be to impose a complete prohibition on nuclear

271 *Kenneth E. Boulding*, The Social System and the Energy Crisis, Science 184 (1974), 255–257; *Daniel Faber*, Trump's Election Victory, the Climate Crisis, and the Working Class: What Does this Mean for the Future?, Capitalism Nature Socialism 35 (2024), 1–18; *Jonathan Federle/Cathrin Mohr/Moritz Schularick*, Inflation Surprises and Election Outcomes, Kiel Working Paper 2278 (2024), 1–31.

272 *Marc Fabel/Matthias Flückinger/Markus Ludwig et al.*, The Power of Youth: Political Impacts of the "Fridays for Future" Movement, CESifo Working Paper 9742 (2022), 1–47.

273 *Pierre C. Boyer/Thomas Delemotte/Germain Gauthier et al.*, Les déterminants de la mobilisation des Gilets jaunes, Revue économique 71 (2020), 109–138.

274 See for example the Declaration Recognizing the Key Role of Nuclear Energy In Keeping Within Reach the Goal of Limiting Temperature Rise to 1.5 Degree Celsius, signed during COP28 in Dubai by 26 States. It is available at https://www.energy.gov/articles/cop28-countries-launch-declaration-triple-nuclear-energy-capacity-2050-recognizing-key, last accessed 25 February 2025.

275 *Joseph Maina*, Africa Explores Nuclear Energy as Climate-Friendly Way to Ease Power Shortfalls (2022); *Laura Gil*, Is Africa Ready for Nuclear Energy? (2018), International Atomic Energy Agency.

276 *Jorge E. Viñuales*, Energy in International Law, Cambridge: Cambridge University Press 2022, 45 ff.; *Magnus Abraham-Dukuma*, Sovereignty, Trade, and Legislation: The Evolution of Energy Law in a Changing Climate, Energy Research & Social Science 59 (2020), 101305; Principle 2 of the Rio Declaration on Environment and Development, A/CONF.151/26.

energy, potentially leading to significant impacts on domestic development. Conversely, the least effective strategy would be to implement no international control whatsoever, and giving nuclear energy no restraints in its development and deployment. Consequently, the non-proliferation regime aims to find a middle ground that offers the greatest benefits for both international security and domestic development.

Another dimension pertains to the financial implications of ensuring that non-nuclear weapon States remain nuclear weapons-free. The system of verification, termed *safeguards*, incurs various costs, both domestically and internationally. At the domestic level, safeguards impose costs on operators and exporters. Operating all verification systems and providing access to international inspectors lead to limitations in the operation of a power plant, thus leading to costs for operators.[277] Exporters must follow strict export control laws, leading to additional costs and potentially facing a prohibition to export nuclear material to a specific country. Granting international inspectors access to information and facilities increases the risk of industrial espionage.[278] More safeguards lead to more interference and more work for nuclear operators, increasing the cost and impacts of safeguards on their nuclear industries.[279]

At the international level, the implementation of a safeguards system leads to costs for the inspecting organisation, most notably the International Atomic Energy Agency (IAEA). In accordance with numerous international organisations,[280] the IAEA's budget has been subject of a zero growth policy for many years.[281] Any increase of the Agency's budget is limited to a price adjustment following inflation. The IAEA has an operational regular budget of $ 390.2 million, with 39 % allocated to nuclear verification, by

277 *David Fischer*, Innovations in IAEA Safeguards ot Meet the Challenges of the 1990s, in: David Fischer/Ben Sanders/Lawrence Scheinman/George Bunn (eds.), A New Nuclear Triade: The Non-Proliferation of Nuclear Weapons, International Verification and the International Atomic Energy Agency, Southampton: The Mountbatten Centre for International Studies, University of Southampton 1992, 27–43, at 28.

278 Ibid.

279 Ibid. Especially Germany was quite hesitant to accept strengthened safeguards and took a leading role of a critical block in the negotiations, *Oliver Meyer*, A Civilian Power Caught Between the Lines: Germany and Nuclear Non-Proliferation, Trier: 1998.

280 Examples are the International Organization for Migration or the UNFCCC Secretariat.

281 *Trevor Findlay*, Unleashing the Nuclear Watchdog – Strengthening and Reform of the IAEA (2012), Centre for International Governance Innovation.

far the largest item of the budget.[282] This underscores that any modification or evolution of the safeguards system gives rise to questions regarding costs. Do countries accept potential economic losses for their operators and exporters? Do countries accept to increase the budget of the IAEA? Most often the answer is no.

2 The Law of Nuclear Non-Proliferation

The law of nuclear non-proliferation contains of various legal sources on the international and European level. The regime tries to comprehensively prevent the further spread of nuclear weapons and consists of four elements:[283] Commitments by non-nuclear-weapon States not to develop and build nuclear weapons, deterring measures to prevent the dissemination of means to build nuclear weapons, verification of compliance, and enforcement.

International law provides only limited means of enforcement. As the failure to comply with the regime of nuclear weapons has far-reaching consequences to the international security architecture, nuclear weapons law includes methods of ensuring compliance which are more impactful than most other regimes. The field of nuclear non-proliferation law has developed two methods to verify compliance: safeguards and export controls. Safeguards focus on the verification of the amount, use and location of nuclear material within a country, while export controls impose restrictions on access to material and technologies necessary for nuclear weapons production.

Safeguards are typically categorised by their focus: Material-based safeguards focus on material, its location, use and deposition. Facility-based safeguards focus on facilities, how they are designed and operated as well as how they handle material. For the development of nuclear weapons, both facilities and materials are important. Without material, there is no bomb, but without facilities there is no possibility to enrich or produce the material required for the bomb.

---

282 International Atomic Energy Agency, *The Agency's Programme and Budget 2022–2023,* GC(65)/2, at 11.

283 *Ben Sanders*, IAEA Safeguards: A Short Historical Background, in: David Fischer/Ben Sanders/Lawrence Scheinman/George Bunn (eds.), A New Nuclear Triad: The Non-Proliferation of Nuclear Weapons, International Verification and the International Atomic Energy Agency, Southampton: Mountbatten Centre for International Studies, University of Southampton 1992, 1–13.

In the decade following the invention of the atomic bomb, there were only limited international instruments to ensure nuclear non-proliferation (2.1). It was not until 1957 with the establishment of the International Atomic Energy Agency (IAEA) that an international organisation was created with a significant level of authority (2.2). This institution is charged with ensuring compliance with the Nuclear Non-Proliferation Treaty (2.3) and safeguards agreements (2.4). In Europe, safeguards are further implemented by Euratom institutions and regulations (2.5). Beyond the realm of safeguards, export controls play a significant role in ensuring nuclear non-proliferation (2.6).

2.1 Non-Proliferation Predating the IAEA

The non-proliferation regime is a highly political regime that consists of a web of legal sources. While it emerged as a fragmented system in 1945 and remained so for decades, a standard level of safeguards converged into an almost universal system by the end of the 20th century. Historically, the genesis of the regime can be traced back to the United States' desire to maintain its monopoly of nuclear weapons following the Trinity Test in 1945, while also benefiting from exporting civilian nuclear technology.[284] Consequently, the first non-proliferation measures were codified in US domestic law and bilateral treaties between the United States and an importing State. Prior to the establishment of the IAEA and Euratom in 1957, specialists of the US Atomic Energy Commission (AEC) verified the use of exported nuclear goods.[285] During this time, the United States proposed in the so-called Baruch Plan the creation of an International Atomic Development Authority which would have had a global monopoly on the mining of nuclear material and on the operation of nuclear power plants, while also establishing and operating a safeguards mechanism.[286] Also, the United

284 *Grégoire Mallard*, Fallout: Nuclear Diplomacy in an Age of Global Fracture, Chicago: The University of Chicago Press 2014, 120 f.

285 The plan was based on the earlier Acheson-Lilienthal report which was mainly drafted by Dean Acheson (then Undersecretary of State), David E. Lilienthal (then director of the Tennessee Valley Authority) and J. Robert Oppenheimer (Leader of the Manhattan Project). The Baruch Plan was presented by Bernard Baruch, representative of the United States to the UN Atomic Energy Commission, to this commission on 14 June 1946.

286 *Elisabeth Röhrlich*, Inspectors for Peace, Baltimore: John Hopkins University Press 2022, at 24.

States pledged to decommission their nuclear weapons in the process. This plan was quickly rejected by the Soviet Union due to a lack of trust – since the United States had tested nuclear weapons secretly in 1945, there was a perceived possibility of it doing so again – and the fear of the United States prolonging its nuclear monopoly.[287] The first international safeguards system was established in a cooperation treaty between the United States and Euratom.[288]

2.2 The IAEA Statute

The International Atomic Energy Agency (IAEA) is widely regarded as the world's nuclear watchdog.[289] While the IAEA's powers are limited in relation to other areas of nuclear law such as nuclear safety and security,[290] it is in the domain of non-proliferation that the watchdog has teeth[291] and where it has significant authority.

2.2.1 The IAEA's Authority as Nuclear Watchdog

Limiting the proliferation of nuclear weapons stands at the very heart of the International Atomic Energy Agency. The IAEA was founded in 1957

287 *Mallard* (n 284), at 67–72.

288 Articles XI and XII of the Agreement For Cooperation Between The Government Of The United States Of America And The European Atomic Energy Community (Euratom) Concerning Peaceful Uses Of Atomic Energy of 8 November 1958.

289 See for example *Findlay* (n 281); *Tobias Weise*, The Involuntary Watchdog: Legitimating the International Atomic Energy Agency, in: Klaus Dingwerth/Antonia Witt/Ina Lehmann/Ellen Reichel/Tobias Weise (eds.), International Organizations under Pressure – Legitimating Global Governance in Challenging Times, Oxford: Oxford University Press 2019, 130–160; *Mohamed ElBaradei*, Nuclear Power – an Evolving Scenario, IAEA Bulletin 46 (2004), 4–8.

290 Nuclear safety describes the area of nuclear law which aims at preventing accident, mitigating accident consequences and protecting workers, the public and the environment from undue radiation risks. Nuclear security aims at preventing, detecting and responding to criminal or intentional unauthorised acts involving or directed at radioactive material or nuclear facilities. On this, see *International Atomic Energy Agency*, IAEA Nuclear Safety and Security Glossary, Vienna: IAEA 2022, at 139 f.

291 *Wolfram Tonhauser*, The International Atomic Energy Ageny as the "Watchdog" over the Safe and Peaceful Use of Nuclear Energy?, in: Kerstin Odendahl (ed.), Internationales und europäisches Atomrecht, Berlin: Duncker & Humblot 2013, 167–184.

following US President Eisenhower's proposal of an international organisation at the UN General Assembly in his famous *Atoms for Peace* speech.[292] He envisaged an international organisation that possesses and distributes nuclear material supplied by both the United States and the Soviet Union. His idea was to limit the Soviet Union's capacity to build a nuclear weapon by ensuring that the Soviet Union would supply so much uranium to this international pool that their remaining resources would not suffice to build a weapon.[293] While Eisenhower underestimated the available resources of uranium, the very foundation of the IAEA was shaped by the global interest to limit the proliferation of nuclear weapons.

The IAEA is headquartered at the Vienna International Center, sharing its offices with the United Nations Office in Vienna. It is not a UN specialised agency, but the two organisations are linked by a Relationship Agreement.[294] 178 States have ratified its Statute. It has a typical structure of an international organisation with an assembly of all Member States, a General Conference, a Board of Governors as an executive organ, and a bureaucratic body of international public servants led by a Director General. The General Conference and the Board of Governors make up the policy-making bodies of the IAEA. The General Conference convenes once per year and each country has one single vote. This body decides with a simple majority of votes except for financial questions, amendments of the Statute and the suspension of voting rights in which cases a two-thirds majority is required.[295] In practise, the General Conferences adopts decision by consensus.[296] The Board of Governors currently consists of 35 Member States, including the "most advanced countries in the technology of atomic energy" and additional representatives from specific regions of the world.[297]

292 The transcript of the speech is available at https://www.iaea.org/about/history/atoms-for-peace-speech, last accessed 25 February 2025.

293 *Röhrlich* (n 286), at 41.

294 Agreement Governing the Relationship Between the United Nations and the International Atomic Energy Agency, published as INFCIRC/11.

295 This is set out in Article V of the IAEA Statute.

296 *Laura Rockwood*, The International Atomic Energy Agency (IAEA), in: Eric Myer/Thilo Marauhn (eds.), Research Handbook on International Arms Control Law, Cheltenham: Elgar 2022, 503–529, at 509.

297 This is set out in Article VI.A.1 of the IAEA Statute. The Board of Governor currently is composed of Algeria, Argentina, Armenia, Australia, Bangladesh, Belgium, Brazil, Burkina Faso, Canada, China, Colombia, Ecuador, Egypt, France, Georgia, Germany, Ghana, India, Indonesia, Italy, Japan, the Republic of Korea, Luxembourg, Morocco, the Netherlands, Pakistan, Paraguay, Russia, South Africa, Spain, Thailand, Ukraine, the United Kingdom, the United States and Venezuela.

As with the General Conference, each Member State has one vote and the Board usually decides with a simple majority except for budgetary and financial questions where a two-thirds majority is necessary.[298] It is important to note that no country has a veto right in any policy-making body, neither directly like in the UN Security Council,[299] nor indirectly like in the Bretton Woods system[300]. The Director General, currently the Argentinian diplomat *Rafael Mariano Grossi*, is appointed by the Board of Governors with the approval of the General Conference and is the chief of the administrative officers of the IAEA.[301]

The IAEA's extensive authority in the field of nuclear non-proliferation has led to its depiction as *nuclear watchdog*. The next section analyses these powers.

2.2.2 The IAEA's Powers in Nuclear Non-Proliferation

While most of the safeguarding powers are derived from bilateral (or trilateral[302]) agreements, the Statute of the IAEA itself contains the foundation of the IAEA's powers, including the safeguards system. Outlined as a function of the Agency in Article III.A.5 and specified in Article XII, safeguards are a significant field of operation of the IAEA. Article III.A.5 grants the IAEA the authority "to establish and administer safeguards." These safeguards are designed to ensure that "special fissionable and other materials, services, equipment, and information [...] are not used in such a way as to further any military purpose." Furthermore, the Statute authorises the Agency "to apply safeguards, at the request of the Parties, to any bilateral or multilateral arrangement, or at the request of a State, to any of that State's activities in the field of atomic energy." The application of this provision to fusion is a key question that will be addressed in the subsequent chapter.

Article XII of the IAEA Statute envisages a safeguards system that includes equipment and facilities (facility-based approach) next to a pure material-based approach started by US domestic law. This system is further specified in various decisions by the IAEA's Board of Governors.[303] In

298 This is set out in Article VI of the IAEA Statute.
299 Article 27 para. 3 of the UN Charter.
300 Article XII of the IMF Agreement, Article VI of the World Bank Agreement.
301 This is set out in Article VII of the IAEA Statute.
302 In some cases, Euratom is also a Party to the agreement.
303 Especially INFCIRC/26 and INFCIRC/66. On this, see below Section 2.4.1.

accordance with Article XII, the IAEA has specific rights and responsibilities when requested to apply safeguards by the Parties. They include the examination of facility and equipment designs, the verification of the use of source and special fissionable material, requesting data, sending inspectors into countries and to suspend or terminate assistance in the case of non-compliance.

In the event that a State is found to be in non-compliance, the inspectors report to the Director General, who, in turn, reports to the Board of Governors. The Board of Governors reports such a case of non-compliance to all Members of the IAEA, the UN Security Council and the UN General Assembly. Furthermore, it possesses the authority to suspend assistance or even membership rights of the respective country, as outlined in Article XII.C.

The IAEA's main role in safeguards is to implement safeguards, according to Article III.A.5 of the IAEA Statute, when requested by a treaty, such as the Non-Proliferation Treaty.

2.3 The Non-Proliferation Treaty

The most important legal instrument within nuclear weapons law and one of the most adhered to international treaties is the 1968 Treaty on the Non-Proliferation of Nuclear Weapons (NPT).

2.3.1 The Cornerstone of Nuclear Non-Proliferation

The NPT is widely regarded as the cornerstone of the nuclear non-proliferation regime.[304] There is no other treaty regarding nuclear weapons that has as many Member States as the NPT and no other treaty has shaped nuclear non-proliferation as profoundly as the NPT did. Most discussions

304 See e.g. *U.S. Department of State*, The Nuclear Non-Proliferation Review Conference, 2022; *Leonard S. Spector*, Meeting the New Challenges to the NPT, Disarmament Topical Papers 8 (1991), 177–194; *Thomas Graham Jr./Damien J. LaVera*, Cornerstone of Security – Arms Control Treaties in the Nuclear Era, Seatlle, London: Univeristy of Washington Press 2002, at 98 ff. Recently, *Joelien Pretorius* and *Tom Sauer* challenged the NPT's role as cornerstone, *Joelien Pretorius/Tom Sauer*, Ditch the NPT, Survival 63 (2021), 103–124; *Joelien Pretorius/Tom Sauer*, When is it Legitimate to Abandon the NPT? Withdrawal as a Political Tool to Move Nuclear Disarmament Forward, Contemporary Security Policy 43 (2022), 161–185.

concerning nuclear non-proliferation regard the implementation of the NPT.

The treaty was negotiated in the context of the rapid proliferation of nuclear weapons, beginning with the United States' first testing of nuclear weapons in 1945, followed by the Soviet Union's first test in August 1949, the United Kingdom's first test in October 1952, France's first test in February 1960 and China's first test in October 1964. The 1960s were characterised by the widespread fear of further proliferation of nuclear weapons. At that time, several other countries aspired for nuclear weapons, such as, among others, Sweden,[305] Brazil[306] and Germany[307]. South Africa even built a handful of nuclear explosive devices.[308]

To interrupt this momentum of nuclear weapon proliferation, following a proposal by Ireland,[309] the Eighteen Nations Committee on Disarmament (ENDC)[310] undertook negotiations on the NPT between 1965 and 1968. The ENDC followed the Ten Nations Committee on Disarmament, a forum which was founded by the Big Four powers (United States, United Kingdom, France, Soviet Union) in 1960 with the objective of addressing the issue of nuclear disarmament and consisted of five NATO and five Warsaw Pact States.[311] The ENDC added eight non-aligned States to the conversation on disarmament. The negotiations conducted by the conference were based on two identical drafts submitted by the United States

305 *Thomas Jonter/Emma Rosengren*, From Nuclear Weapons Acquisition to Nuclear Disarmament – The Swedish Case, in: Ilkka Taipale (ed.), Nuclear Exits – Countries Foregoing the Nuclear Option, London: Routledge 2016, 46–63.

306 *Matias Spektor*, The Evolution of Brazil's Nuclear Intentions, The Nonproliferation Review 23 (2016), 635–652.

307 *Romberg* (n 242), at 55.

308 *Stumpf* (n 242).

309 The so-called Irish Resolution included a first proposal for the prevention of the wider distribution of nuclear weapons. It is available at https://archives.nato.int/uploads/r/nato-archives-online/7/2/6/7266018483f149bf8190c1673dbbdf09e298829348947eb7f77fc10af7043e1a/1_-_POL_VII_Nuclear_Weapons_Irish_Resolution_To_UN_1961_ENG.pdf, last accessed 25 February 2025.

310 The Committee was established by UN General Assembly Resolution A/RES/16/1722 and was composed of Brazil, Bulgaria, Burma, Canada, Czechoslovakia, Ethiopia, France, India, Italy, Mexico, Nigeria, Poland, Romania, Sweden, Union of Soviet Socialist Republics, United Arab Republic, United Kingdom of Great Britain and Northern Ireland and United States of America.

311 It was composed by Canda, France, United Kingdom, Italy, United States (NATO) and Bulgaria, Czechoslovakia, Poland, Romania, Soviet Union (Warsaw Pact).

and the Soviet Union.[312] Both the forum and the draft show the hegemonic influence of NWS on the NPT. The finalised treaty was referred to the UN General Assembly for adoption, which took place on 12 June 1968 with 95 votes in favour, 21 abstentions[313] and four no[314] votes.[315]

As demonstrated by the result of the vote, approximately 20 % of the Members of the UN General Assembly did not vote in favour of the NPT. In its early days, many States highly criticised the treaty. A central point of critique was the enshrinement of super-power status by the permanent Members of the UN Security Council, while all other States had to renounce nuclear weapons. Some State officials even denounced the discriminatory structure as the establishment of a "super-cartel of the world powers"[316] or nuclear apartheid.[317] Even States that the treaty recognises as NWS were hesitant to join treaty, such as China and France. France hesitated to join the treaty for economic (being able to export nuclear goods freely) and political (escaping the hegemony of the United States and USSR) reasons.[318] China, in support of the Global South, condemned the nuclear monopoly of five NWS and the interference with national nuclear programmes.[319]

Nevertheless, over the subsequent decades, more and more States joined the NPT. Resistance against the treaty fell as the Cold War came to a close. A significant milestone in terms of adherence was reached in 1992 when France and China ratified the treaty. Today, the treaty has 190 Parties. The

312 *United Nations*, Yearbook of the United Nations 1968, New York: United Nations 1968, at 4.

313 Algeria, Argentina, Brazil, Burma, Burundi, Central African Republic, Republic of Congo, France, Gabon, Guinea, India, Malawi, Mali, Mauritania, Niger, Portugal, Rwanda, Saudi Arabia, Sierra Leone, Spain and Uganda.

314 Albania, Cuba, Tanzania and Zambia.

315 A/RES/2373 (XXII).

316 Federal Republic of Germany's Finance Minister Franz Josef Strauß in a letter to Federal Republic of Germany's Chancellor Kurt Georg Kiesinger, 15 February 1967, Archive for Christian-Democratic Policy 01-226-285.

317 India uses this framing, see for instance the comments of government officials *Krishnan Raghunath*, From Nuclear Apartheid to Nuclear Deal: The First Steps, Indian Foreign Affairs Journal 5 (2010), 85–122; *Jaswant Singh*, Against Nuclear Apartheid Essay, Foreign Affairs 77 (1998), 41–52.

318 *Georges-Henri Soutou*, La France et la non-prolifération nucléaire, Revue historique des armées 262 (2011), 35–45; *Bertrand Goldschmidt*, La France et la non-prolifération, Relations internationales (1992), 41–50.

319 *Zachary S. Davis*, China's Nonproliferation and Export Control Policies: Boom or Bust for the NPT Regime?, Asian Survey 35 (1995), 587–603, at 588 f.

only countries outside the treaty are the nuclear weapons possessing States of Pakistan, India, North Korea[320] and Israel, as well as the young and troubled nation of South Sudan.

2.3.2 Legal Framework of the NPT

A fundamental principle of the treaty is the delineation of the world into two distinct categories of States: Nuclear-Weapon States (NWS), the *Haves*, and Non-Nuclear-Weapon States (NNWS), the *Have-nots.* Article IX para. 3 defines NWS as those countries that have successfully conducted a nuclear weapons test prior to 1 January 1967. This criterion is met by the United States, the Soviet Union, the United Kingdom, France and China. NWS are allowed to possess nuclear weapons, Article I, while NNWS are forbidden to possess, manufacture or control nuclear weapons or other nuclear explosive devices[321], Article II. NWS are further not allowed to assist, encourage or induce nuclear weapons programmes in NNWS, Article I. Non-proliferation is verified by a safeguards system and the implementation of export controls, Article III. The majority of States have thus agreed to never obtaining nuclear weapons while accepting that the P5 keep the weapon that has proven to be the most devastating military instrument humankind has ever created. The acceptance of such a discriminatory system required concessions from NWS. Firstly, Articles IV and V stipulate provisions for technical assistance. While NNWS renounce the possession of nuclear weapons, they receive assistance in using the atomic nucleus for peaceful purposes. This assistance includes support in building nuclear power plants as well as the use of radiological technologies in medicine or agriculture.[322] Secondly, Article VI includes a provision on the cessation of the nuclear arms race and sets a pathway to nuclear disarmament, even including the prospect of a treaty on general and complete disarmament.

---

320 There is some ambiguity in North Korea's standing within the NPT, *Masahiko Asada*, International Law of Nuclear Non-Proliferation and Disarmament (Volume 424), The Hague: Brill | Nijhoff 2022, 73–75.

321 Historically, there was a differentiation between nuclear explosive devices used as a weapon and those used for civilian purposes, such as excavating.

322 In 2023, the IAEA spent approximately 130 Million euros in its technical cooperation programme, *International Atomic Energy Agency*, Technical Cooperation Report for 2023, GC(67)/RES/9, Vienna: IAEA 2024.

The objective of the treaty can be outlined as follows: Freezing the status quo of nuclear powers at the moment of negotiation without impeding the deployment of commercial nuclear activities and by promising disarmament. Given that the primary nuclear exporters in the late 1960s were the United States and the Soviet Union,[323] maintaining the status quo and fostering nuclear export follows the clear interest of the hegemonic powers of the Cold War. The treaty provisions of Article VI on nuclear disarmament as well as the prospects of complete and general disarmament was a concession for non-nuclear weapon States to accept the treaty. This hegemonic imbalance in the treaty's power dynamics is further underscored by the language of the provisions. While the articles on freezing the status quo contain legal obligations indicated by clear legal indicators such as "undertakes", "not to transfer", "not [...] to assist, encourage or induce", "not to receive", "not to manufacture or otherwise acquire", "not to seek", "accept" and "not to provide", the language regarding disarmament is significantly weaker. In this case, the obligation is limited to undertakings "to pursue negotiations in good faith."

Every five years, all State Parties of the NPT meet and review the progress of implementing the treaty's provisions in so-called Review Conferences (or RevCons for short), Article VIII.III of the NPT. In the three years leading to a RevCon, State Parties meet in Preparatory Commission (or PrepCom for short) to prepare the upcoming RevCon.

Originally, the nuclear status quo was intended to be provisional: Article X para. 2 of the NPT stipulates a limited duration of 25 years. Despite the end of the Cold War, hegemonic powers succeeded in indefinitely extending the NPT at its Review and Extension Conference of 1995.

These three aspects of the NPT – non-proliferation, technical assistance and nuclear disarmament – are referred to as the three pillars of the NPT.[324] The entire construct of agreeing to a discriminatory treaty for technical

323 On their nuclear export policies, see *Gloria Duffy*, Soviet Nuclear Export, International Security 3 (1978), 83–111; *Michael A. Bauser*, United States Nuclear Export Policy: Developing the Peaceful Atom As a Commodity in International Trade Selected Developments in International Trade and Investment Controls, Harvard International Law Journal 18 (1977), 227–272.

324 *Daniel H. Joyner*, Interpreting the Nuclear Non-Proliferation Treaty, Oxford: Oxford University Press 2011, at 26; *Ingrid Kirsten/Mara Zarka*, Balancing the Three Pillars of the NPT: How Can Promoting Peaceful Uses Help?, Non-Proliferation and Disarmament Papers 79 (2022), 1–18; *Dean Rust*, How We've Come to View the NPT: Three Pillars, in: Henry Sokolski (ed.), Nuclear Rules, Not Just Rights: The NPT Reexamined, Arlington: Nonproliferation Policy Education Center 2017, 37–101.

assistance and the perspective of nuclear disarmament is termed as the *grand bargain*.[325]

For this analysis, the NPT safeguards provisions are important. The NPT itself does not contain any detailed provisions on how the safeguards system looks like. Article III.1 requires all States to accept safeguards which are set forth and negotiated in an agreement with the IAEA. These agreements must be in accordance with the IAEA's Statute and the IAEA's safeguards system. The scope of safeguards is limited to "the exclusive purpose of verification of the fulfilment of its obligations assumed under this Treaty with a view to preventing diversion of nuclear energy from peaceful uses to nuclear weapons." In terms of procedure, they "shall be followed with respect to source or special fissionable material whether it is being produced, processed or used in any principal nuclear facility or is outside any such facility." The NPT further stipulates "that safeguards required by this Article shall be applied on all source or special fissionable material in all peaceful nuclear activities within the territory of such State, under its jurisdiction, or carried out under its control anywhere."

Safeguards obligations are further defined in agreements between the State Parties and the IAEA.

2.4 Safeguards Agreements

Safeguards are the core of the verification regime in nuclear non-proliferation law. The underlying objective of safeguards is twofold: confidence-building and deterrence.[326] On the one hand, safeguards lead to trust among States by demonstrating good behaviour. On the other hand, States are deterred to start a nuclear weapons programme given the high risk of discovery.

Today's conception of safeguards is to focus on nuclear material in civilian facilities with a relatively recent shift to also look comprehensively at nuclear activities in a non-nuclear weapon State as a whole. The objective of safeguards is to monitor the amount, use and location of nuclear material

325 *Leonard Weiss*, Nuclear-Weapon States and the Grand Bargain, Arms Control Today 33 (2003), 21–25; *Phil Twyford*, What Next for the Nuclear "Grand Bargain?", New Zealand International Review 47 (2022), 19–23; *Christian Mölling*, The Grand Bargain in the NPT: Challenges for the EU Beyond 2010, in: Jean Pascal Zanders (ed.), Nuclear Weapons After the 2010 NPT Review Conference, Paris: European Union Institute for Security Studies (EUISS) 2010, 49–70.

326 *Sanders* (n 283).

in order to ensure that such material is only used for peaceful purposes. Nuclear material within a country is monitored and accounted for by the IAEA from its entry until its deposition or exit. These powers of the IAEA are set out in safeguards agreements which have evolved since the IAEA's foundation in 1957.

2.4.1 Structure of Safeguards Agreements

Safeguards agreements are agreements concluded between the IAEA and a State. While each NNWS concludes a safeguards agreement individually, their content is the same for all. In order to ensure that all agreements are identical in content, the development and conclusion of safeguards agreement follows a specific procedure. The Board of Government decides on the content and structure of the agreement. While the Board's decisions on early stages of the safeguards system contained the outline of the content and structures with the precise content to be specified in negotiations with the IAEA Director General, the most recent iteration of safeguards – the Additional Protocol – was adopted by the Board as a template where only the name of the State is added.

During the negotiations of a safeguards agreement, the Board of Government considers the input of committees and the IAEA Secretariat.[327] The adoption of such a template agreement is published in the IAEA's information circular (INFCIRC) series and made available to all Member States. The safeguards system predating the NPT is published in INFCIRC/26 and was expanded by a decision of the Board published in INFCIRC/66, the NPT-mandated comprehensive safeguards agreement is published as INFCIRC/153(Corrected) and the model Additional Protocol is published as INFCIRC/540(Corrected). Following the adoption of a template agreement, the Board of Governors instructs the Director General to conclude and subsequently implement safeguards agreement individually with each non-nuclear weapon State Party of the IAEA.

As the content and structure of the safeguards agreements with each NNWS only translates the decision of the Board of Governors, it is customary to refer to the INFCIRC document containing the decision rather than quoting each individual safeguards agreement. Legally, however, it is important to note that obligations of States and the authority of the IAEA

327 *International Atomic Energy Agency*, IAEA (ed.), The Evolution of IAEA Safeguards, Vienna: IAEA 1998.

only come from the individual safeguards agreement concluded by the State, not from the Board of Governors' decision.

2.4.2 Safeguards Predating the NPT

The first safeguards system administered by the IAEA was established in 1961, four years after the foundation of the Agency and seven years before the adoption of the NPT. This system was established by the IAEA's Board of Governors in a decision which is published in INFCIRC/26,[328] and focused on States receiving technical assistance from the IAEA. The entire safeguards system was based on two provisions within the IAEA's Statute, Articles III.A.5 and XII. It was subsequently expanded in 1965 by the Board of Governors in INFCIRC/66. This safeguards regime is item-specific in contrast to the later developed comprehensive safeguards agreements. This means that agreements concluded following INFCIRC/66 are limited to those facilities specifically listed in the agreement. Item-specific safeguards agreements are still guiding the IAEA's verification activity in States that are Members of the IAEA but not Parties to the NPT. This applies to India, Pakistan and Israel, but they do not update their agreements to include new nuclear facilities, especially those for military use. The limited effects of these agreements are obvious given the fact that these three countries all possess nuclear weapons.

Item-specific safeguards apply to both nuclear material[329] and nuclear facilities[330], as well as non-nuclear material and equipment (defined as items,[331] hence the name). The IAEA's powers include a design review of principal nuclear facilities,[332] review of reports[333] and inspections.[334]

---

328 On pre-NPT safeguards, see *John Carlson/Vladimir Kuchinov/Thomas Shea*, The IAEA Safeguards System Prior to the NPT from 1959 to 1972 (The IAEA's Safeguards System as the Non-Proliferation Treaty's Verification Mechanism, 2020), Nuclear Threat Initiative.

329 Paras 32 ff. of INFCIRC/26; paras 19 ff. of INFCIRC/66.

330 Paras 36 ff. of INFCIRC/26, paras 30 ff. of INFCIRC/66.

331 Para. 31 of INFCIRC/26.

332 Paras 30 ff. of INFCIRC/66.

333 Paras 39 ff. of INFCIRC/66.

334 Paras 45 ff. of INFCIRC/66.

2.4.3 Comprehensive Safeguards Agreements and the Additional Protocol

The adoption of the NPT and especially its Article III led to a significant extension of the safeguarding responsibility of the IAEA upon entering into force in 1970. The IAEA is since is mandated to apply safeguards to all NNWS that had signed the NPT, not only to those States that received technical assistance. Additionally, the safeguards now applied to all source and special fissionable material in all peaceful activities, not only to a limited list of facilities as before.[335] The implementation of the newly extended safeguards mandate was entrusted to the Safeguards Committee, open to all IAEA Member States and included leading experts in the field. However, it were the United States and the Soviet Union, as well as the advanced nuclear States of the Federal Republic of Germany and Japan, that dominated the negotiations.[336]

In 1972, the IAEA's Board of Governors adopted the "Structure and Content of Agreements Between the Agency and States Required in Connection with the Treaty on the Non-Proliferation of Nuclear Weapons" or INFCIRC/153(Corrected), in order to operationalise Article III.1 of the NPT. Based on this document, the IAEA concludes individual Comprehensive Safeguards Agreements (CSA) with each NNWS Party to the NPT. This agreement stipulates the rights and privileges of the IAEA to verify that no nuclear material is diverted from civilian to military purposes. State Parties with no or limited nuclear material have the option to adopt the Small Quantities Protocol which simplifies the safeguards regime by suspending the application of a significant part of the CSA's provisions.[337]

In 116 paragraphs, the CSA sets out a comprehensive and detailed system. The agreement contains both competences and limits of the IAEA. The CSA requires a State to maintain an accounting and reporting mechanism for nuclear material subject to safeguards (paras 7, 31–32, 51–58, 62–67) and to provide the IAEA with information on nuclear material and facilities, including their designs (paras 8, 42–50). Furthermore, States accept IAEA inspectors entering their territories and facilities (paras 9, 70–89). These inspections include both routine and ad-hoc inspections. The agreement

335 *Elisabeth Röhrlich*, Negotiating Verification: International Diplomacy and the Evolution of Nuclear Safeguards, 1945–1972, Diplomacy & Statecraft 29 (2018), 29–50, at 40.

336 Ibid.

337 The implementation of safeguards under the Small Quantities Protocol is explained in detail in *International Atomic Energy Agency*, Safeguards Implementation Guide for States with Small Quantities Protocols, Vienna: IAEA 2013.

defines the objective of safeguards as the "timely detection of diversion of significant quantities of nuclear material from peaceful nuclear activities to the manufacture of nuclear weapons" (para. 28). In addition, the agreement contains a long list of definitions (paras 98–116). The implementation of safeguards must be designed in a manner to avoid "hampering the economic and technological development", "undue interference in the State's peaceful nuclear activities", and to protect commercial and industrial secrets and to ensure optimum cost-effectiveness (paras 4–6). The question whether these provisions apply to fusionable material and fusion facilities will be addressed in the next chapter.

Despite the comprehensive nature of the agreement, subsequent events have demonstrated the limited authority of the IAEA in key domains. The discovery of clandestine nuclear activities by Iraq in 1991 led to the adoption of the "Model Protocol Additional to the Agreement(s) Between State(s) and the International Atomic Energy Agency for the Application of Safeguards"[338] in 1997.[339] The IAEA has since implemented Additional Protocols (AP) with 141 States,[340] thereby extending the IAEA's competences significantly. The AP obliges the State Party to inform the IAEA about *all nuclear activities*[341] and extends the IAEA's rights to access all relevant locations throughout the nuclear fuel cycle,[342] including extensive competences of environmental sampling.[343] The Additional Protocol fundamentally changed the approach to safeguards. While the IAEA Statute, the NPT and the CSA all focus on nuclear material mainly in nuclear facilities – specific material at specific locations –, the AP explicitly extends the safeguards to a broader list of facilities and – due to the explicit mentioning of environmental sampling – even outside declared locations. While under the CSA the IAEA also had the right to implement safeguards with a view of detecting undeclared facilities,[344] such requests by the IAEA were quite

338 INFCIRC/540(Corrected).

339 *Laura Rockwood*, The IAEA's Strengthened Safeguards System, Journal of Conflict and Security Law 7 (2002), 123–136; *Richard Hooper*, The System of Strengthened Safeguards, IAEA Bulletin 39/4 (1997), 26–30.

340 https://www.iaea.org/sites/default/files/20/01/sg-ap-status.pdf, last accessed 25 February 2025.

341 Article 2 of INFCIRC/540 (Corrected).

342 Article 5 of INFCIRC/540 (Corrected).

343 Article 6 of INFCIRC/540 (Corrected).

344 See paras 19, 76, 78–82 of INFCIRC/153 and the interpretation presented by *Laura Rockwood*, IAEA Safeguards: Correctness and Completeness of States' Safeguards Declarations, in: International Atomic Energy Agency (ed.), Nuclear Law: The

rare.[345] The AP further provides the IAEA with the right to complementary access.[346] While the CSA provides the IAEA with the right to *special inspections*[347], the notion itself implied circumstances of extraordinary concern, thus leading to the introduction of *complementary access* in the AP.[348] Safeguards under the CSA focus primarily on a facility-by-facility basis to verify declared nuclear material at declared nuclear facilities,[349] while the Additional Protocol aims to verify nuclear activities by a State as a whole. Chapter 3 will address the question of whether the IAEA's extended authority under the AP also extends to fusion.

2.4.4 Voluntary Offer Agreements

The NPT requires safeguards exclusively for NNWS. However, due to criticism from NNWS and concerns regarding the commercial disadvantage of operators who have to accept safeguards, the NWS accepted safeguards for their civilian infrastructure during the 1970s and 1980s.[350] The five NWS under the NPT have concluded Voluntary Offer Agreements (VOA) with the IAEA.[351] These cover source and special fissionable material in specifically selected civilian nuclear facilities from which the IAEA can select those in which it verifies that the nuclear material in these facilities remains in peaceful activities. The NWS itself decides which facilities it opens for IAEA safeguards and it retains the right to remove any facility

---

Global Debate, The Hague: T.M.C. Asser Press 2022, 205–222. This is also reflected in decisions by the IAEA's Board of Governors, GOV/OR.776 paras 48, 83 f. and GOV/2636.

345 *George Bunn*, Nuclear Safeguards – How Far Can Inspectors Go?, IAEA Bulletin 48-2 (2007), 49–55.

346 Articles 4–6 of INFCIRC/540(Corrected).

347 Para. 73 of INFCIRC/153(Corrected).

348 *Theodore Hirsch*, The IAEA Additional Protocol: What It Is and Why It Matters, The Nonproliferation Review 11 (2004), 140–166, at 117.

349 *Rockwood* (n 344).

350 *Adolf von Baekmann*, IAEA Safeguards in Nuclear-Weapon States, IAEA Bulletin 30-1 (1988), 22–25 (22).

351 United States: INFCIRC/288 of 18 November 1977; United Kingdom: originally a tri-partite agreement between the United Kingdom, Euratom and the IAEA, INFCIRC/263 of 6 September 1976, which was replaced by INFCIRC/951 of 12 January 2021 due to Brexit with no change to the content; France: INFCIRC/290; Russia: INFCIRC/327 of 21 February 1985; China: INFCIRC/369 of 20 September 1988.

from its list.[352] The specific extent of the applied safeguards differs from NWS to NWS.[353] Following the adoption of the Additional Protocol to the CSA for NNWS, all NWS have adopted additional protocols to their VOA, extending the authority of the IAEA and approaching the level of safeguards in NNWS.[354] It is important to note that the additional protocol is unique for each NWS and differs from those for NNWS.[355] None of the VOA's extended safeguards are as far-reaching as those for NNWS. For example, no NWS accepts environmental sampling. While the Additional Protocol to the CSA intended to increase the IAEA's capacity to detect undisclosed nuclear activities and other violations of the NPT, this is not the objective in NWS. In these countries, the VOAs' additional protocols serve to assist to the IAEA in developing more effective procedures, tools and techniques for safeguarding activities in NNWS.[356] They also aim to encourage the acceptance of NNWS to accept the exercise of authority by the IAEA.[357]

2.5 Euratom Safeguards

Historically, European States pursued a path independent from the IAEA. In the same year as the IAEA was founded, the Euratom Treaty was signed by France, Federal Republic of Germany, Italy, Belgium, the Netherlands and Luxembourg.[358] Today, all 27 EU Member States are Members of Euratom. In addition, Switzerland and the United Kingdom are associated

352 This is set out in Article 1 b) of each agreement. The United States limits the removal to associations with "activities of direct national security significance", the United Kingdom "for national security reasons", while France, Russia and China have not included limitations.

353 *von Baekmann* (n 350), at 23.

354 United States: INFCIRC/288/Add.1 of 9 March 2009; United Kingdom: INFCIRC/263/Add.1 of 24 February 2005 and replaced by INFCIRC/951/Add.1 of 12 January 2021; France: INFCIRC/290/Add.1 of 24 February 2005; Russia: INFCIRC/327/Add.1 of 8 January 2008; China: INFCIRC/369/Add.1 of 22 April 2002.

355 The differences are highlighted in *James Martin Center for Nonproliferation Studies*, Additional Protocol (Inventory of International Nonproliferation Organizations and Regimes, 2015).

356 Letter from Ambassador Kenneth Brill to the IAEA Director General, 30 April 2002, United States Senate Treaty Document 107–7, at 6.

357 *Frank S. Houck*, The Voluntary Safeguards Offer of the United States – A Review of its History and Implementation, IAEA Bulletin 27 (1985), 13–18.

358 The Euratom Treaty is one of the two Treaties of Rome, signed on 25 March 1957.

Members.[359] Euratom is governed by the same institutions as the European Union.[360] The Commission is the institution which assumes the safeguarding powers within Euratom.

This section first gives an overview of the historic development of the question of nuclear weapons under Euratom (2.5.1), before focussing on the safeguards regime under the Euratom Treaty (2.5.2).

2.5.1 The European Route

Euratom has played an essential role in the development of today's non-proliferation regime for several reasons. A core objective of the organisation is securing and providing Europe with nuclear material (Article 2(d) Euratom Treaty), thereby fostering the civilian development of nuclear energy. Apart from this civilian dimension, there are also indications that Euratom was intended to serve another purpose: A common Western European nuclear deterrence in Europe driven by France, Federal Republic of Germany and Italy.[361] It is important to note that in the mid and late 1950s only the United States, the Soviet Union and the United Kingdom possessed nuclear weapons with numerous countries around the world having nuclear ambitions. Nuclear weapons played of pivotal role in Western Europe, as *Bernard Baruch* – Presidential Advisor and US Representative to the United Nations Atomic Energy Commission and author of the aforementioned Baruch plan – stated: "The only thing that stands in the way of the over-running of Europe today is the atom bomb."[362] At the same time, the rearmament of the Federal Republic of Germany, particularly with regard to nuclear weapons, was a highly debated topic in the 1950s. Ultimately, mainly pushed by *Charles de Gaulle*, France decided to unilaterally develop nuclear weapons and to abandon any European military nuclear cooper-

359 The United Kingdom is associated by the UK-EU Trade and Cooperation Agreement, Switzerland has a Cooperation Agreement in place since 1978. Association with Euratom is possible following Article 206 of the Euratom Treaty.

360 The institutions merged with the Treaty establishing a single Council and a single Commission of the European Communities, signed on 8 April 1965 in Brussels.

361 *Mallard* (n 284), at 117 ff. with further references. France, Federal Republic of Germany and Italy entered into a secret Tripartite Agreement in military nuclear cooperation discussing a potential use of Euratom for common nuclear weapons purposes.

362 Baruch 1948 (October 5), Letter to John Foster Dulles, cited after ibid, at 68.

ation.[363] In 1960, France conducted its first nuclear weapons test in the Algerian desert. This led to an unanticipated scenario: Euratom provides its Member States with nuclear material, yet one of its Member States had become an NWS.

This situation has led to a distinctive characteristic of the Euratom safeguards regime: Rather than verifying that certain material is not diverted from peaceful to military purposes, the regime's objective is to verify that "ores, source materials and special fissile materials are not diverted from their intended uses", Article 77(a). Moreover, the scope of Euratom's safeguarding powers extend to verify that Member States are in accordance with safeguarding obligations assumed by Euratom under an agreement with an international organisation, Article 77(b).

The establishment of this specific safeguards regime gave rise to a considerable disagreement between Euratom Member States and the IAEA in the late 1960s and early 1970s. At the time the NPT was concluded, Euratom had already ten years of experience in administering safeguards. Consequently, the six Member States were reluctant to accept IAEA safeguards out of fear of giving up a functional safeguards system[364] and the potential for industrial espionage by non-European inspectors.[365] Another dispute emerged from a conflict between the NPT and existing treaties, with both the Euratom Treaty and the US-Euratom agreement being incompatible with the NPT safeguards system. The most significant conflict stemmed from the fact that within Euratom, a supranational organisation is responsible for all nuclear material.[366] Acting in compliance with the NPT would necessitate the exercise of sovereignty in an area where sovereignty has already been delegated to a supranational organisation. However, Euratom was unable to join the NPT as intergovernmental organisation to an interstate treaty. Especially the Federal Republic of Germany was opposed to establishing official relations between Euratom and the IAEA as it feared that too many powers by the IAEA could undermine the legitimacy of Euratom controls.[367] Thirdly, the discriminatory treatment between

363 Ibid, at 175.

364 *H. W. Schleicher*, Nuclear Safeguards in the European Community – A Regional Approach, IAEA Bulletin 22 (1980), 45–50.

365 *Fischer* (n 277), at 28.

366 Article 52 Euratom Treaty.

367 Memorandum of F. Cancellario D'Alena, from the Foreign Relations Department of Euratom. EC, BAC 086/1982–29, cited after *Mallard* (n 284).

Euratom Members – France as NWS and all other Euratom Member States as NNWS – was deemed unacceptable.[368]

In order to resolve the dispute, the IAEA and Euratom reached an agreement in 1973.[369] This agreement provides for a cooperative application of safeguards by both the IAEA and Euratom. For example, Euratom carries out preliminary checks and analysis.[370] The design of facilities is examined jointly and inspections of IAEA and Euratom are closely coordinated.[371] This agreement pathed the way to the accession of all Euratom NNWS to the NPT in 1975, and subsequently France's accession in 1992.

2.5.2 Safeguards in Europe

The Euratom Treaty includes an entire chapter (Chapter 7) on safeguards, with Article 77 introducing two avenues to apply safeguards, different to the safeguards regime introduced by the IAEA Statute and later the NPT. Firstly, as Euratom verifies that "ores, source material and special fissile materials are not diverted from their intended uses as declared by the users", Article 77(a), there is a slightly different wording than the application of IAEA safeguards to source and special fissionable material. Another difference to IAEA safeguards is the application regardless of status as NWS or NNWS. Given the fact that the Euratom Treaty also applies to France and applied to the United Kingdom for decades as NWS, Euratom only focuses on verifying the declared use of that material, while the IAEA also verifies the absence of undeclared material.

The second pillar is the application of international safeguards agreements, Article 77(b). As mentioned above, Euratom and IAEA safeguards were in competition in the 1950s and 1960s, resulting today in a cooperative approach by both international organisations, which is based on an agreement pursuant Article 77(b).

368 Notes à la Commission de Cancelario d'Alena sur les répercussions du contrôle dans le Traité, Notes de la Commission sur le projet de l'URSS d'article n.3 du Traité et sur l'aide-mémoire américain à ce sujet, cited after *Mallard* (n 284).

369 Agreement between Euratom and the IAEA in Implementation of the Treaty on the Non-Proliferation of Nuclear Weapons of 1973.

370 *David Fischer*, IAEA/Euratom Agreement – An Explanation, IAEA Bulletin 15 (1973), 11–16.

371 Ibid.

Article 78 imposes an obligation to declare basic technical characteristics for facilities that work with source and special fissile materials to the Commission to facilitate its safeguarding operations.

Safeguards procedures under the Euratom Treaty encompass the verification of records (Articles 79, 82) and the right to access all places and data (Article 81). In the event of non-compliance, the Commission is authorised to issue sanctions, starting with a warning, the withdrawal of financial or technical assistance and extends as far as placing the undertaking under administration of the Commission or withdrawal of the material (Article 83). All sanctions are subject to review by the Court of Justice of the European Union. Safeguards under the Euratom Treaty, however, are limited by the dual nature of its Member States as the treaty applies to both NWS and NNWS: Safeguards may not extend to materials intended to meet defence requirements, Article 84.[372]

The detailed application of these safeguards is further delineated in Commission Regulation (Euratom) 302/2005 and in Commission Recommendation of 11 February 2009 on the implementation of a nuclear material accountancy and control system by operators of nuclear installations.

In accordance with Article 77(b) of the Euratom Treaty, Euratom has also adopted an Additional Protocol and verifies the Member States' compliance jointly with the IAEA.[373]

2.6 Export Controls

Complimentary to safeguards, export controls play an essential role in preventing the proliferation of nuclear weapons by regulating the conditions of the supply of both nuclear material and dual-use technology to a State. Supplier States only provide another State with such a material or technology if certain conditions are met. Unlike mandatory safeguards, the requirements of export controls also apply to all NPT Member States, both NWS and NNWS, via Article III.2 of the NPT.

---

372 The competences of the European Commission with regards to safeguards have been characterized as "extraordinary rights", *Wolfgang Kilb*, The Nuclear Safeguards Regime of EURATOM: A Regional Cornerstone of the Verification of Non-Proliferation Obligations in the European Union, in: Jonathan L. Black-Branch/Dieter Fleck (eds.), Nuclear Non-Proliferation in International Law: Volume II – Verification and Compliance, The Hague: T.M.C. Asser Press 2016, 151–165, at 154.

373 Additional Protocol 1999/188/Euratom.

This treaty provision prohibits to provide source or special fissionable material or equipment or material especially designed or prepared for the processing, use or production of special fissionable material, to an NNWS for peaceful purposes, unless the source or special fissionable material is subject to safeguards. This treaty provision left open the question of when equipment or material is especially designed or prepared, as neither the NPT nor any other treaty includes a definition.

The NPT contains two mechanisms to ensure compliance: Safeguards and export controls. While Article III.1 of the NPT mandates the IAEA to apply safeguards and requires NNWS to conclude safeguards agreements with the IAEA, Article III.2 of the NPT leaves the implementation of export controls up to the Member States. The IAEA harmonises the application of safeguards to all NNWS, but there is no mandate within the NPT for an international organisation to harmonise export controls.

In order to establish a common understanding of definitions and procedures to specify the NPT's obligation with regard to export controls, nuclear exporting States have set up two informal groups: The Zangger Committee and the Nuclear Suppliers Group (NSG).

There are many similarities between the Zangger Committee and the NSG. Both are informal intergovernmental discussion groups that produce legally unbinding documents which serve as a basis for the harmonisation of the understanding and procedure of nuclear export controls.[374] Also, there is a significant overlap of their Members. All 39 Member States of the Zangger Committee are also Members of the NSG, while the NSG has nine more Member States.[375] Furthermore, both groups observe the work of and coordinate with the respective other group.[376] Additionally, both groups work on an informal basis and rely on consensus-based rule-making.

2.6.1 Zangger Committee

The Zangger Committee was established in 1971 with the aim of harmonising the interpretation of Article III.2 of the NPT. It functions as an inter-

374 *Fritz W. Schmidt*, The Zangger Committee: Its History and Future Role, The Nonproliferation Review 2 (1994), 38–44, at 38 f.; *Fritz W. Schmidt*, NPT Export Controls and the Zangger Committee, The Nonproliferation Review 7 (2000), 136–145, at 138.

375 Brazil, Cyprus, Estonia, Iceland, Latvia, Lithuania, Malta, Mexico, Serbia.

376 *Schmidt*, The Zangger Committee (n 374), at 42 ff.

governmental forum to discuss export controls and to coordinate them. It is not a formal body of the NPT, nor an international organisation, but an informal intergovernmental forum for discussion.

Originally, 15 nuclear exporting States held informal meetings chaired by the Swiss diplomat *Claude Zangger*, hence the name. The primary objective of this committee is to find a common interpretation of Article III.2 of the NPT and to develop procedures for nuclear exports among participating governments.[377] The committee, now comprising 39 Member States, maintains a Trigger list which stipulates the criteria that must be met for a State to export nuclear material.[378] The consensual understanding of nuclear exporting States is that they may only export material listed on the Trigger List, if it is guaranteed that: Nuclear material must not be diverted to nuclear weapons, material and equipment has to be placed under IAEA safeguards, and re-exporting to a third State is only allowed under the same conditions as the first export.[379]

Decisions by the Zangger Committee, including the Trigger List, are legally non-binding and are limited to serve as a basis for harmonised unilateral policy declarations.[380] Formally, they are adopted by an exchange of notes among the members of the Zangger Committee, unilaterally declaring that these understandings would be implemented through domestic export control and by sending letters to the Director General of the IAEA informing the Agency that the State intends to act in conformity with the understandings reached in the Zangger Committee.[381] The Trigger List as well as any subsequent updates are published by the IAEA in its Information Circular (INFCIRC) series as INFCIRC/209.

While decisions by the Zangger Committee itself are legally non-binding, they have legal implications. Subsequent agreements regarding the interpretation of a treaty or the application of its provisions and subsequent practise in the application of the treaty have to be taken into account according to the general rule of interpretation, enshrined in Article 31 para. 3 of the Vienna Convention on the Law of Treaties (VCLT). As the decisions taken by the Zangger Committee are non-binding, they do not constitute an

377 Ibid.

378 The most current version is from 2020, published as INFCIRC/209/Rev.5.

379 INFCIRC/209/Rev.5, para. 3.

380 *Schmidt*, The Zangger Committee (n 374), at 38.

381 NPT/CONF.2010/WP.1, para. 10.

agreement in the sense of Article 31 para. 3(a) VCLT.[382] They can, however, constitute subsequent practise establishing the agreement of the Parties regarding the interpretation of Article III.2 of the NPT, according to Article 31 para. 3(b) VCLT. As the majority of nuclear exporting State Parties to the NPT agree on the interpretation of Article III.2 of the NPT and act accordingly, the decisions by the Zangger Committee have to be taken into account in interpreting Article III.2 of the NPT. In addition, several documents of the NPT Review Conferences referred to the Zangger Committee's activity, some even underlying the contribution the Committee has in strengthening the implementation of Article III.2 of the NPT.[383] Thus, the Trigger List and other decisions by the Zangger Committee have legal implications as they have to be taken into account in the interpretation of the NPT's export control obligations.

2.6.2 Nuclear Suppliers Group

The Indian nuclear test of 1974 showcased that there were gaps within the Zangger Committee regime. As response, nuclear exporting States, including France which has not been a Party to the NPT until 1992, met in London[384] in 1974 to address the deficiencies. The NSG has a membership that extends beyond that of the Zangger Committee, and includes nine further States, totalling 48 Member States with relevant nuclear infrastructure. As the Zangger Committee, the NSG is an informal intergovernmental forum which takes no legally binding decisions. NSG Member States inform the IAEA Director General about their intent to apply the NSG Guidelines in their domestic legal order when considering the export of nuclear material, equipment or technology. The NSG Guidelines are also published by the

382 *Matthias Herdegen*, Interpretation in International Law, in: Anne Peters/Rüdiger Wolfrum (eds.), Max Planck Encyclopedia of Public International Law, Heidelberg, Oxford: Oxford University Press 2020, at para. 35.

383 An overview is given in Annex I of NPT/CONF.2010/WP.1, para. 10.

384 As a consequence, the NSG is sometimes referred to as "London Club", see e.g. *Louis Reitmann*, Reforming the 'London Club': How transparency and outreach can benefit the Nuclear Suppliers Group (2023), European Leadership Network; *Sarah Bidgood*, The Establishment of the London Club and Nuclear-Export Controls, Adelphi series 56 (2016), 135–162.

IAEA as INFCIRC/254. As with the Zangger Committee, the NSG Guidelines have to be translated into domestic law.[385]

The NSG bases its work on the Zangger Lists, but expands them in two key ways. First, it extends the list content-wise, by including important areas such as heavy water production items, which is not required by the NPT. Secondly, it introduces a procedural requirement for the recipient to assure the implementation of IAEA safeguards.[386]

The NSG Guidelines *de facto* specify and, in certain instances even exceed the export control regime required by Article III.2 of the NPT. Within the NSG, national governments establish rules and procedure for the export of nuclear material. These guidelines are divided into two parts. The first part – the so-called Trigger List[387] – includes materials whose main purpose is to be used in nuclear technology. The second part – the so-called Dual Use List[388] – contains materials, equipment and software that could contribute significantly to the development and/or construction of nuclear explosive devices, but which also have peaceful applications.

The NSG Guidelines require States to apply export controls if they intend to export material, equipment or software listed in either one of the lists. The specific export control procedure depends on the specific list. In the event that a given material, equipment or component is included on the Trigger List, the export State should require the recipient State to provide formal assurances that certain stipulated conditions are met: the material will not be used for "nuclear explosive activities", the material should be placed under physical protection, and the material will only be transferred to NNWS under the condition that the material is subject to IAEA safeguards.[389] Material listed on the Trigger List includes enriched uranium, natural uranium exceeding a certain threshold, and specific nuclear reactor components. For dual use items, the procedure is more lenient. If a recipient State wishes to receive an item on the Dual-Use List, the export may only be made to a NNWS if a CSA is in place with the IAEA, if there is no unacceptable risk of diversion to nuclear-weapons purposes, and if there is no unacceptable risk of diversion to acts of nuclear terrorism. Items

385 In the European Union Regulation (EU) 2021/821 of the European Parliament and of the Council of 20 May 2021 following Article 207 para. 1 TFEU incorporates the Guidelines of the Nuclear Suppliers Group.

386 On the history of the NSG, see *Tadeusz Strulak*, The Nuclear Suppliers Group, The Nonproliferation Review 1 (1993), 2–10.

387 INFCIRC/254, Part 1.

388 INFCIRC/254, Part 2.

389 INFCIRC/254, Part 1, para. 4.

on the Dual Use list include inter alia specific lasers, certain software, and equipment related to heavy water production.

As the NSG Guidelines do not constitute an agreement in the sense of Article 31 para. 3(a) VCLT, similar to the Zangger List, they are not subsequent agreements on the interpretation of the NPT provision. While the Zangger List has to be taken into account in interpreting Article III. 2 of the NPT as subsequent practise in the application of the NPT, the situation for the NSG Guidelines is different. First, the NSG extends export controls beyond to what is required by Article III.2 of the NPT. This indicates that the practise of applying export controls on certain goods is not *in application of the treaty,* as required by Article 31 para. 3(b) VCLT. Second, the NSG Guidelines show no indication that they are intended to be used in the application of the NPT. Where the NPT is mentioned, the reference is limited to encourage technology transfer following Article IV of the NPT[390] or to define categories of procedural requirements for importing States.[391]

The NSG Guidelines, in addition, do not constitute customary international law. This would require both a general practise (*consuetudo*) and the acceptance as law (*opinion iuris*).[392] There are doubts with regard to both elements that the NSG Guidelines constitute customary international law. First, the existence of a general and consistent practise is doubtful. On the one hand, the membership of the NSG is limited to only 48 States and excludes the majority of States.[393] While it is not necessary that each and every State follows a certain practise, it has to be *sufficiently widespread and representative.*[394] With regard to the NSG, this depends especially on whether or not all major nuclear exporting States follow the practise of implementing the NSG Guidelines. The NSG Member States include all nuclear exporting States that are Party to the NPT, however non-NPT States such as India and Pakistan export nuclear goods without following the NSG Guidelines. In addition, even those States that are part of the NSG do not always implement the guidelines, as there are plenty of exam-

390 INFCIRC/254, Part 1, paras 7 and 12.

391 INFCIRC/254, Part 2, para. 4.

392 Article 38 (1)(b) ICJ Statute, *Permanent Court of International Justice*, Lotus Case, PCJ (1927) Series A No. 10, at 28; *International Court of Justice,* North Sea Continental Shelf (Federal Republic of Germany v. The Netherlands), Judgment, ICJ Reports 1969, p. 3, at para. 77.

393 *Andrea Viski*, The Status of Nuclear Export Control Regimes in International Law, Tilburg Law Review 15 (2010), 183–204, at 201.

394 *International Law Commission*, Draft Conclusions on Identification of Customary International Law, New York: United Nations 2018, Conclusion 8.

ples where States do not follow the procedures, such as the United States exporting nuclear goods to India as a non-State Party to the NPT. A varying practise usually indicates the absence of a custom.[395] Thus, the existence of practise as first constitutive element of customary law is doubtful.[396]

Second, States have to undertake the practise with a sense of legal right or obligation.[397] On the one hand, NSG Member States inform the IAEA about their intent to implement the NSG Guidelines in their domestic legislations via a note verbal, indicating a sense of legal obligation. On the other hand, States are persistent in highlighting that the NSG is only an informal forum for discussing export controls and that the Guidelines are non-binding, Thus, there is no clear evidence for an *opinion juris* as second constitutive element. As a consequence, the NSG Guidelines do not reflect international customary law.

Thus, NSG Guidelines are legally non-binding, intended to harmonise national export control procedures without a legal obligation.

While the NSG has been regarded as a successful forum for promoting nuclear non-proliferation,[398] the group has been subject to controversies and cannot escape current geopolitical tensions. While the Cold War had no effect on the work of the NSG, as both the United States and the Soviet Union cooperated productively,[399] the topic of India has left its mark on the group. While being the reason for the formation in 1974, the United States has been advocating for years for exporting its nuclear goods to India despite the State's non-adherence to the NPT and refusal of comprehensive safeguards as it possesses nuclear weapons.[400] There are further allegations that Russia and China have not respected NSG Guidelines in bilateral nuclear cooperation relationships as well.[401] A further controversy within the

395 Ibid, Conclusion 7.

396 Similar, *Viski* (n 393).

397 *International Law Commission* (n 394), Conclusion 9.

398 *Mark Hibbs*, The Nuclear Suppliers Group and Geostrategic Politics, Strategic Trade Review 3 (2017), 5–24; *Fred McGoldrick*, The Road Ahead for Export Controls: Challenges for the Nuclear Suppliers Group, Arms Control Today 41 (2011), 30–36.

399 *Hibbs* (n 398).

400 *Leonard Weiss*, U.S.-India Nuclear Cooperation, The Nonproliferation Review 14 (2007), 429–457; *Mario E. Carranza*, From Non-Proliferation to Post-Proliferation: Explaining the US–India Nuclear Deal, Contemporary Security Policy 28 (2007), 464–493; *Oliver Meier*, The US–India Nuclear Deal: The End of Universal Non-Proliferation Efforts?, Internationale Politik und Gesellschaft (2006), 28–43.

401 *McGoldrick* (n 398); *Sibylle Bauer*, Developments in the Nuclear Suppliers Group, in: Bates Gill/Ian Anthony/D.A. Cruickshank (eds.), SIPRI Yearbook 2011, Stockholm: SIPRI 2011, 376–386, at 384 f.; *Hibbs* (n 398).

NSG is whether to extend its export requirements from the implementation of a CSA to also require the implementation of the Additional Protocol.[402]

Chapter 3 will address the question of whether the export control regime finds an answer to fusion's proliferation potential.

2.7 The Limited Success Story of the Non-Proliferation Regime

This section analyses the limited success story of the NPT regime. While there are a lot of achievements attributable to the regime (2.7.1), there are also significant shortcomings (2.7.2), highlighting the highly political nature of the regime. This analysis allows to understand the feasibility of approaches developed in the next chapters in order to apply the regime to fusion.

2.7.1 Achievements

The NPT is by many regarded as the cornerstone of nuclear non-proliferation as there are significant achievements attributable to the regime. They include the establishment of an international norm and the prevention of nuclear proliferation. These achievements will be analysed in the following section.

2.7.1.1 Setting an International Norm

One of the NPT's achievements is the establishment of an international norm on nuclear non-proliferation. This is, firstly, evidenced by the significant number of States that have joined the treaty. The NPT has 190 State Parties, a number surpassed by only a few other treaties.[403] Some characterise the treaty as "the most inclusive security treaty in the world."[404] Despite being negotiated during the Cold War, States from both East and

402 *Hibbs* (n 398), at 22; *McGoldrick* (n 398).

403 There are only 26 treaties with a higher number of State Parties. Examples are the UN Charter, the UN Framework Convention on Climate Change, the Convention on the Rights of the Child or the Chemical Weapons Convention.

404 *Maria Rost Rublee/Carmen Wunderlich*, The Vitality of the NPT After 50, Contemporary Security Policy 43 (2022), 5–23.

West as well as non-aligned States quickly joined the treaty. In its fifty-five years of existence, the NPT has established a near universal international norm against nuclear proliferation.[405]

This success is further underscored by the fact that the NPT has enabled the IAEA's characterisation as nuclear watchdog. As Article III.1 of the NPT requires NNWS to conclude Comprehensive Safeguards Agreements with the IAEA, all 185 non-nuclear weapon State Parties to the NPT have concluded these agreements, giving the IAEA extensive verification and monitoring rights. The regime has set up a detailed framework with a unique level of authority of an international organisation.[406]

The international norm is not only set for the present, but also for the future. While the treaty was created with a limited duration of 25 years, it has been indefinitely extended by the 1995 Review and Extension Conference. Consequently, the prohibition on the proliferation of nuclear weapons, in conjunction with the accompanying safeguards system, is set to remain indefinitely. The perpetual character of the norm is further supported by the requirements to withdraw from the regime. According to Article X.1 of the NPT, a withdrawal is only possible if a State "decides that extraordinary events, related to the subject matter of this Treaty, have jeopardized the supreme interests of its country." Despite numerous wars and tensions in the last decades, also including the involvement of NWS and even threats to use nuclear weapons against NNWS,[407] there has only been one withdrawal, by North Korea, in 2003.[408]

Furthermore, States tried to act within the broader NPT framework even in times of crisis. For example, the NPT framework was operationalised to stop the Iranian nuclear weapons programme with the Joint Comprehensive Plan of Action (JCPoA) in 2015. The JCPoA was intended to guide a path for Iran to full compliance with the NPT, while at the same time

405 *Nobuyasu Abe*, The NPT at Fifty: Successes and Failures, Journal for Peace and Nuclear Disarmament 3 (2020), 224–233, at 4. *Spurgeon M. Keeny Jr.*, The NPT: A Global Success Story, Arms Control Today 25 (1995), 3–7 speaks of a "norm of international behavior".

406 On this, see above Section 2.2.1.

407 A recent example are Russia's threats to use nuclear weapons in Ukraine. On this, see *Tom Sauer*, How Useful Are Nuclear Weapons in Practice? Case-Study: The War in Ukraine, Journal for Peace and Nuclear Disarmament 7 (2024), 194–210.

408 On North Korea's withdrawal, see *Assia Dosseva*, North Korea and the Non-Proliferation Treaty Recent Developments, Yale Journal of International Law 31 (2006), 265–286; *Masahiko Asada*, Arms Control Law in Crisis? A Study of the North Korean Nuclear Issue, Journal of Conflict and Security Law 9 (2004), 331–355.

lifting sanctions against the Islamic Republic. The JCPoA included clear references to the NPT as the cornerstone of the nuclear non-proliferation regime,[409] and the IAEA was mandated to monitor and verify compliance.[410] The protocol contains clear references to Iran's Comprehensive Safeguards Agreements as well as the Additional Protocol.[411] Despite the risk of a breach of the NPT, States tried to find an answer within the regime to ensure further compliance with the treaty. While the JCPoA failed in the end, this is not due to shortcomings of the NPT and its regime, but due to a political decision of the first Trump administration.[412] Enforcing compliance with the NPT through sanctions is a strong lever in international politics. A similar strategy has been followed with regard to North Korea following its withdrawal from the NPT in 2003 during the so-called six-party talks.[413] Similarly to the JCPoA, the objective of these talks was to encourage North Korea to rejoin the NPT regime in exchange for the lifting of sanctions. However, these talks ultimately failed due to North Korea withdrawing from the talks and resuming its nuclear weapons programme.

These examples illustrate the NPT's role in establishing an international norm against nuclear proliferation, something that no other international instrument has achieved.

2.7.1.2 Stopping Nuclear Weapons Programmes

In addition, the NPT has led to the cessation of several nuclear weapons programmes. Sweden has pursued nuclear weapons, but dismantled its programme after acceding to the NPT.[414] Similar developments were observed in South Korea,[415] Argentina and Brazil.[416] It also kept threshold States,

409 Preamble and General Provisions para. vii.
410 Preamble and General Provisions para. x.
411 E.g. paras 1 and 13.
412 *Mark Fitzpatrick*, Assessing the JCPOA, Adelphi series 57 (2017), 19–60, at 51 ff.
413 Five rounds of talks took place from 2003 to 2007. The six parties were China, Japan, North Korea, South Korea, Russia and the United States. A comprehensive overview of the talks is given by *Leszek Buszynski*, Negotiating with North Korea – The Six Party Talks and the Nuclear Issue, London: Routledge 2013.
414 *Jonter/Rosengren* (n 305).
415 *Abe* (n 405), at 3.
416 *Julio C. Carasales*, The Argentine-Brazilian Nuclear Rapprochement, The Nonproliferation Review 2 (1995), 39–48; *José Goldemberg/Carlos Feu Alvim/Olga Y. Mafra*,

i.e. States that have the technological capacity to develop nuclear weapons relatively quickly, such as Germany and Japan, despite early critics,[417] from acquiring nuclear weapons. The decades before the adoption of the NPT were characterised by a rapid proliferation of nuclear weapons. This development has been slowed down by the adoption of the NPT. The success becomes even more apparent when compared with the proliferation of nuclear energy. Since the adoption of the NPT, the number of fission power reactors has more than quadrupled.[418] Also, the number of States with nuclear reactors increased significantly. In 1968, the year of the adoption of the NPT, there where eleven countries with nuclear reactors.[419] Today, there are 30 countries operating nuclear power plants and 20 additional countries with past or future programmes.[420] At the same time, the number of States possessing nuclear weapons has less than doubled.

Moreover, the NPT framework enabled two States possessing nuclear weapons to abandon them while joining the treaty. South Africa developed nuclear weapons during the time of the apartheid regime but dismantled them prior to acceding to the NPT in 1991.[421] Ukraine decided to give up the nuclear weapons stored in its territory after the end of the Soviet Union and joined the NPT as a non-nuclear weapon State.[422]

2.7.2 Shortcomings

The NPT is not only a success story, but also suffers from significant shortcomings. These shortcomings include the lack of universality of the NPT, its retroactive rather than proactive nature of dealing with the proliferation of nuclear weapons and the lack of consensus on fundamental questions of

---

The Denuclearization of Brazil and Argentina, Journal for Peace and Nuclear Disarmament 1 (2018), 383–403.

417 *Romberg* (n 242), at 55; *George H. Quester*, Japan and the Nuclear Non-Proliferation Treaty, Asian Survey 10 (1970), 765–778.

418 *Mark Ho/Edward Obbard/Patrick A. Burr et al.*, A Review on the Development of Nuclear Power Reactors, Energy Procedia 160 (2019), 459–466.

419 These countries are United States (1942), Canada (1945), Soviet Union (1946), France (1948), United Kingdom (1956), India (1956), West-Germany (1957), East-Germany (1957), China (late 1950s), Japan (1963), Italy (1964) and Spain (1968).

420 *International Atomic Energy Agency*, Nuclear Power Reactors in the World, Vienna: IAEA 2024.

421 *Stumpf* (n 242).

422 *Mariana Budjeryn*, The Power of the NPT: International Norms and Ukraine's Nuclear Disarmament, The Nonproliferation Review 22 (2015), 203–237.

the treaty regime. These shortcomings have led to some authors questioning the future of the regime altogether.[423]

2.7.2.1 Lack of Universality

The most evident shortcoming of the treaty is its lack of universality. Since 1968 – the year in which the NPT was adopted – nuclear weapons have been proliferated. The treaty is not universal. Israel, India, Pakistan and North Korea all possess nuclear weapons and have either never signed or have left the treaty. South Africa also possessed nuclear weapons in the 1970s. The treaty has thus failed to achieve what it was created for: maintain the nuclear status quo of the 1960s.[424] Iran is on the brink of developing its first nuclear weapon.[425] Once Iran succeeds in acquiring a nuclear weapon, other countries in the Middle East might follow, especially Saudi Arabia, despite the treaty's obligations.[426] With each new NWS outside the NPT, support for NPT among NNWS diminishes.[427] For instance, in recent years, Türkiye's President Erdogan has openly criticised the NPT's asymmetry in the UN General Assembly.[428] Ukraine has put the option of a re-nuclearisation on the table.[429] Even voices in the European Union called for a breach of the NPT.[430] In the current geopolitical climate, the future of the entire treaty regime is uncertain.

---

423 *Pretorius/Sauer*; *Pretorius/Sauer*; *Richard Leaver*, The Failing NPT: The Case for Institutional Reform, Australian Journal of International Affairs 59 (2005), 417–424; *Michael Wesley*, It's Time to Scrap the NPT, Australian Journal of International Affairs 59 (2005), 283–299.

424 *Pretorius/Sauer*, Ditch the NPT (n 423), at 105.

425 *Jennifer Hansler/Kylie Atwood*, Blinken Says Iran's Nuclear Weapon Breakout Time is Probably Down to 1–2 Weeks (*CNN*, 2024), https://www.cnn.com/2024/07/19/politics/blinken-nuclear-weapon-breakout-time/index.html, last accessed 17 July 2025.

426 On Saudi Arabia's nuclear ambitions *Norman Cigar*, Saudi Arabia and Nuclear Weapons – How Do Countries Think About The Bomb?, London: Routledge 2016.

427 *Pretorius/Sauer*, Ditch the NPT (n 423), at 117.

428 https://www.reuters.com/article/us-turkey-nuclear-erdogan-idUSKCN1VP2QN, last accessed 25 February 2025.

429 *Alexander K. Bollfrass*, Are Nuclear Weapons an Option for Ukraine? (2025), IISS.

430 *Philipp Sauter*, European Nuclear Weapons – Europe's Nuclear Ambitions and the Constraints of International Law (2024), in: Verfassungsblog, https://verfassungsblog.de/nuclear-weapons/, last accessed 25 February 2025.

2.7.2.2 Reactivity Instead of Proactivity

The second crucial shortcoming is the reactivity of the non-proliferation regime, which is only strengthened after countries have either succeeded in building a nuclear weapon or have had advanced programmes which remained undiscovered for a long time. This is primarily due to shortcomings within the verification regime.

The reactive character of the non-proliferation regime is evident throughout history. The issue of nuclear weapons was first raised on the international stage during the First UN General Assembly, several months *after* the first use of nuclear weapons. As the 1950s and 1960s have demonstrated, the mandate of the IAEA without comprehensive safeguarding powers proved inadequate in preventing the proliferation of nuclear weapons. By the mid-1960s, prior to the adoption of the NPT, all five permanent Members of the UN Security Council had conducted nuclear weapons tests.[431] In the 1970s, India, South Africa and Israel followed. Especially the Indian test shocked both the world and the IAEA given that IAEA inspectors were present in India on the day of the test unaware of the State's capacity to construct a nuclear explosive device.[432] This incident highlighted the inadequacy of the then existing legal safeguards framework with limited competences,[433] and how it was insufficient in addressing the potential of diverting nuclear material from peaceful to military[434] purposes. One fact especially caught the attention of many States: India was able to build their nuclear explosive device *Smiling Buddha* with Western nuclear technology.[435] To prevent any further circumvention of nuclear material, States with a nuclear infrastructure founded the NSG, *after* the previous export control regime of the Zangger Committee proved insufficient.

When the biggest step in strengthening safeguards happened in the early 1970s with the adoption of the CSA, there were already several States

431 The first tests from each country were: United States 1945, Soviet Union 1949, United Kingdom 1952, France 1960, China 1964.

432 *Röhrlich* (n 286), at 1 ff.

433 This regime is set out in INFCIRC/26 and INFCIRC/66.

434 It must be noted that India declared to have tested a so-called Peaceful Nuclear Device. However, it is impossible to distinguish peaceful nuclear devices from unpeaceful nuclear devices. On peaceful nuclear explosions, *Frederick Reines*, The Peaceful Nuclear Explosion, Bulletin of the Atomic Scientists 15 (1959), 118–122.

435 *Röhrlich* (n 286), at 136; *Susanna Schrafstetter*, Preventing the 'Smiling Buddha': British-Indian Nuclear Relations and the Commonwealth Nuclear Force, 1964–68, Journal of Strategic Studies 25 (2002), 87–108, at 90.

that had either nuclear weapons or advanced development programmes. The next step of strengthening the system, the adoption of the Additional Protocol in 1997, was also a response to failures of the system. The 93+2 programme, which led to the adoption of the protocol, was a reaction to the detection of Iraq's clandestine nuclear programme – not by the IAEA, but by UN inspectors.[436] The non-proliferation system has always been strengthened only after its shortcomings were presented by breaches of the regime.

2.7.2.3 Lack of Consensus on Fundamental Questions

The third shortcoming of the NPT regime is the lack of consensus on a manifold of fundamental questions related to the operation of the regime. As the treaty has tried to maintain the status quo of the late 1960s, progress on numerous aspects has been either slow or completely halted. These fundamental questions encompass the implementation of Article VI, the legality of nuclear sharing and specific forms of nuclear cooperation, the implementation of the 1995 extension deal, and the review of the treaty itself.

2.7.2.3.1 Implementation of Article VI

The first point of contention relates to the implementation of the disarmament provision in Article VI, which stipulates that "[e]ach of the Parties to the Treaty undertakes to pursue negotiations in good faith on effective measures relating to cessation of the nuclear arms race at an early date and to nuclear disarmament, and on a treaty on general and complete disarmament under strict and effective international control."

Despite this obligation, nuclear weapon States are not only opposed to nuclear disarmament, but are also actively perpetuating the nuclear arms race. Although the NPT entered into force in 1970, the number of nuclear weapons has increased significantly during the Cold War. While this number decreased in the decade following the fall of the Iron Curtain, the reduction has halted in the last decade. The number of nuclear warheads

436 It must be reiterated that the IAEA is *not* a UN specialised agency.

has remained within the range of 13,000 to 15,000 for years.[437] In recent years, there has been the first increase of the number of nuclear weapons in decades,[438] primarily attributable to China's intentions to massively build up its nuclear arsenal.[439] The *Stockholm International Peace Research Institute* (SIPRI) anticipates that China will be soon on level with the United States or Russia with respect to intercontinental ballistic missiles (ICBMs).[440] Similarly, the United Kingdom is on its path to increase its number of nuclear weapons from 225 to 260 warheads.[441] Even those countries that do not increase their number of nuclear warheads are allocating substantial resources towards the modernisation of nuclear weapons.

While many NNWS from the Global South view the Treaty on the Prohibition of Nuclear Weapons (TPNW) as a fulfilment of Article VI's obligation, NWS are rejecting this treaty in a rare case of unanimity, deeming it "simultaneously irrelevant and dangerous"[442], further emphasising a lack of will to implement *all* NPT obligations, including Article VI.

2.7.2.3.2 Legality of Nuclear Sharing

A further point on which consensus is missing pertains to nuclear sharing agreements. Under NATO agreements, the United States deploys nuclear weapons in allied States. Currently, US nuclear weapons are deployed in Belgium, Germany, Italy, the Netherlands, and Turkey.[443] Poland has also

---

437 *Robert S. Norris/Hans M. Kristensen*, Global Nuclear Weapons Inventories, 1945–2010, Bulletin of the Atomic Scientists 66 (2010), 77–83.

438 *Hans M. Kristensen/Matt Korda*, World Nuclear Forces, in: Stockholm International Peace Research Institute (ed.), SIPRI Yearbook 2023: Armaments, Disarmament and International Security, Stockholm: Stockholm International Peace Research Institute 2023, 247–336.

439 Ibid, at 284 ff.

440 Ibid.

441 *UK Government*, Global Britain in a Competitive Age – The Integrated Review of Security, Defence, Development and Foreign Policy (2021).

442 Statement by France on behalf of the P5, IAEA General Conference, 23 September 2020.

443 *Hans M. Kristensen/Matt Korda/Eliana Johns et al.*, Nuclear Weapons Sharing, 2023, Bulletin of the Atomic Scientists 79 (2023), 393–406; *Alexander Mattelaer*, Nuclear Sharing and NATO as a Nuclear Alliance, in: Stephan Frühling/Andrew O'Neil (eds.), Alliances, Nuclear Weapons and Escalation, Canberra: ANU Press 2021, 123–131, at 124 f.

expressed interest in hosting US nuclear weapons.[444] Recently, Russia and Belarus entered into a similar agreement with the stationing of Russian nuclear weapons in Belarus.[445] Moreover, South Korea has recently signalled its interest in hosting US nuclear weapons in the country in the wake of heightened tensions with its nuclear weapons possessing neighbour North Korea.[446]

NATO countries[447] and some scholars[448] argue that nuclear sharing is legal under the NPT, as these agreements predate the NPT. The United States is further of the opinion that the NPT would no longer be applicable in case of a nuclear war in order to justify the transfer of control of a nuclear weapon in the case of war, despite Article I NPT.[449] However, other States and some scholars[450] contest this interpretation and the legality of nuclear sharing under the NPT. Mexico questioned the legality of nuclear sharing agreements during a session of the 1995 RevCon.[451] During both

---

444 *Julian Borger*, Poland Suggests Hosting US Nuclear Weapons Amid Growing Fears of Putin's Threats in: The Guardian, https://www.theguardian.com/world/2022/oct/05/poland-us-nuclear-wars-russia-putin-ukraine, last accessed 17 July 2025.

445 *Kristensen/Korda/Johns et al.* (n 443).

446 *Jean Mackenzie/Barbara Plett Usher*, US and South Korea Agree Key Nuclear Weapons Deal in: BBC News, (25 February 2025) https://www.bbc.com/news/world-us-canada-65404805, last accessed 17 July 2025. On the historic dimension, see *Hans M. Kristensen/Robert S. Norris*, A History of US Nuclear Weapons in South Korea, Bulletin of the Atomic Scientists 73 (2017), 349–357.

447 *U.S. Government*, Questions on the Draft Non-Proliferation Treaty Asked by US Allies Together with Answers Given by the United States, 1968; *Mohamed Ibrahim Shaker*, The Nuclear Non-Proliferation Treaty – Origin and Implementation 1959–1979, Dobbs Ferry: Oceana Publication 1980, at 222 ff.; *NATO*, Factsheet: NATO's Nuclear Sharing Arrangements, 2022; *Wissenschaftlicher Dienst des Deutschen Bundestages*, Kurzinformation: Rechtsfragen zur atomaren Bewaffnung Deutschlands (2020).

448 *Mika Hayashi*, NATO's Nuclear Sharing Arrangements Revisited in Light of the NPT and the TPNW, Journal of Conflict and Security Law 26 (2021), 471–491; *Shaker* (n 447), at 235 ff.; *Kate Deere*, The Obligations of Nuclear-Weapon States Not to Transfer Nuclear Weapons and Devices (Article I NPT), in: Jonathan L. Black-Branch/Dieter Fleck (eds.), Nuclear Non-Proliferation in International Law – Volume I, The Hague: T.M.C. Asser Press 2014, 23–45, at 27.

449 The United States shared this point of view during the NPT negotiations in *U.S. Government* (n 447). The excerpt is printed in *Shaker* (n 447), at 234. See also *Hayashi* (n 448), at 482 ff. with further references.

450 *Bernd Hahnfeld*, Nukleare Teilhabe ist völkerrechtswidrig – Ein Widerspruch zur anderslautenden Behauptung der Bundesregierung, Wissenschaft und Frieden (W+F) 46 (2020), 46–48.

451 NPT/CONF.1995/32 (Part III), at 244.

the 2015 Review Conference and the 2019 Preparatory Commission,[452] Russia stated that nuclear sharing agreements contradicted the NPT.[453] China also regularly calls for ending nuclear sharing agreements.[454] The failure to reach a consensus on this important question further weakens the NPT regime.

2.7.2.3.3 Legality of Nuclear Cooperation

Another lack of consensus is evident in the context of civilian nuclear cooperation, particularly with regard to the US-India Civil Nuclear Cooperation. Since 2005, India has received support from the United States for a civilian nuclear energy programme. While this cooperation led to India placing its civilian nuclear infrastructure under IAEA safeguards, these safeguards are not comprehensive and do not apply to *any principal nuclear facility* in the sense of Article III.1 NPT. The safeguards applied to Indian nuclear facilities are not based on INFCIRC/153, the full-scope safeguards, but rather on pre-NPT safeguards based on INFCIRC/66, so-called item-specific safeguards, where the State decides which facilities to declare to the IAEA. However, as a State Party to the NPT, the United States is not permitted to provide States with this type of infrastructure, as long as the recipient country does not consent to comprehensive safeguards, Article III.2 of the NPT. Additionally, the nuclear deal provides India with uranium, which in turn frees up India's own uranium resources for its nuclear weapons programme.[455] This can be interpreted as assisting any NWS outside the NPT to manufacture or otherwise acquire nuclear weapons, which would constitute a violation of Article I of the NPT.[456] This cooperation between the United States and India does not only violate the spirit of the NPT,[457] but also its letter.[458] The United States justifies this nuclear cooperation by

452 Two Preparatory Conferences are held in the two years prior to a Review Conference.

453 NPT/CONF.2020/PC.III/WP.6, at para. 15; Statement by Russia, NPT Review Conference (27 April 2015), at 10, available at https://www.un.org/en/conf/npt/2015/statements/pdf/RU_en.pdf, last accessed 25 February 2025.

454 NPT/CONF.2020/PC.III/WP.40, para. 3; NPT/CONF.2010/PC.I/WP.46, Recommendations 6–9.

455 *Carranza* (n 400), at 474.

456 Similarly, ibid.

457 *Meier* (n 400).

458 The legality is also questioned by *Weiss* (n 400).

arguing that this deal strengthens the global non-proliferation regime by placing all of India's civilian nuclear facilities under IAEA safeguards.[459]

2.7.2.3.4 Implementation of 1995 Extension Deal

Another lack of consensus is shown with regard to the implementation of the 1995 Extension Deal. Originally, the NPT was intended to last for 25 years. When the 25-year period elapsed in 1995, States discussed the future of the treaty. While many NNWS from the South were in favour of only a limited extension,[460] especially due to the shortcomings with respect to Article VI, States from the Global North succeeded in convincing the international community to unanimously extend the NPT indefinitely.[461] This was achieved by promising three aspects which, thirty years later, are still not fulfilled.

The first promise was to establish a nuclear-weapons-free zone in the Middle East.[462] Still today, the Middle East continues to be a major concern with regard to nuclear security with Israel as a NWS outside the NPT, Iran being close to having nuclear weapons, and Saudi-Arabia potentially ready to develop nuclear weapons once Iran acquires them. However, thirty years later, there is no substantial progress in this regard. Several conferences have taken place, yet no consensus has been reached.[463] The current rise of tensions in the Middle East following the Hamas attacks on Israel on 7

459 Ibid.

460 *George Bunn/John B. Rhinelander*, Extending the NPT: What are the Options?, Arms Control Today 25 (1995), 8–10; *Harald Müller*, The NPT Review Conferences, in: Emily B. Landau/Azriel Bermant (eds.), The Nuclear Nonproliferation Regime at a Crossroads, Tel Aviv: Institute for National Security Studies 2014, 17–26, at 20.

461 NPT/CONF.1995/32 (Part I), Annex, Decision 3.

462 Ibid, Decision 2, para. 5. On a nuclear weapons-free zone in the Middle East, see *Konstantinos D. Magliveras*, The Conference on the Establishment of a Middle East Zone Free of Nuclear Weapons and Other Weapons of Mass Destruction: Too Little, Too Late?, in: Jonathan L. Black-Branch/Dieter Fleck (eds.), Nuclear Non-Proliferation in International Law – Volume VI: Nuclear Disarmament and Security at Risk – Legal Challenges in a Shifting Nuclear World, The Hague: T.M.C. Asser Press 2021, 113–133 (optimistic view); *Claudia Baumgart/Harald Müller*, A Nuclear Weapons-Free Zone in the Middle East: A Pie in the Sky?, The Washington Quarterly 28 (2004), 45–58 (pessimistic view).

463 The Conference on the Establishment of a Middle East Zone Free of Nuclear Weapons and Other Weapons of Mass Destruction have been held annually (except in 2020) since 2019, following A/RES/73/546.

October 2023 and Israel's military response to Iran's nuclear programme casts a shadow over the prospects of any imminent progress.

Second, the NWS promised to bring into force the Comprehensive Test Ban Treaty (CTBT).[464] More than 2000 nuclear weapons tests have been conducted since the Trinity Test in 1945, with the vast majority of tests between the 1950s and 1980s. In earlier times, most tests were conducted above ground, with a shift to underground testing occurring from the 1960s on. Above-ground nuclear testing led to consequences for the atmosphere. Not only does a nuclear explosion lead to nuclear fallout, radioactive dust produced by the weapon gets spread over hundreds, if not thousands, of kilometres. Above-ground test also caused an increase in radioisotopes in the atmosphere.[465] The ecological and health concerns caused by the then around 500 overground tests[466] led to the adoption of the Partial Nuclear Test Ban Treaty in 1963 (PTBT). This treaty, which is signed by the United States, the United Kingdom, the Soviet Union, India, Pakistan, and Israel, but not by China and France, prohibits nuclear testing in the atmosphere, in outer space, or under water. Under this treaty, only underground testing is allowed. Such underground tests were continued during the decades following the adoption of the PTBT.

In order to ban all testing, the Global South pushed for the adoption of the CTBT. With formal negotiations beginning in 1993 and a push from both the 1995 RevCon and civil society, the CTBT was adopted in 1996. The CTBT extends the provisions of the PTBT to prohibit *any nuclear weapon test explosion* […] *at any place* (Article I.1). Unlike the PTBT, the CTBT also includes a verification mechanism. To this end, a new international organisation, the Comprehensive Nuclear-Test-Ban Treaty Organiza-

464 Decision 2, para. 4a, NPT/CONF.1995/32 (Part I), Annex. On the failure of the CTBT, see *Daryl Kimball*, What Went Wrong: Repairing the Damage to the CTBT, Arms Control Today 29 (1999), 3–9; *Keith Hansen*, CTBT: Forecasting the Future, Bulletin of the Atomic Scientists 61 (2005), 50–57; *Christophe Danielo*, Quel avenir pour le Traité d'interdiction complète des essais nucléaires?, DSI (Défense et Sécurité Internationale) (2014), 52–55.

465 This anthropogenic increase of radionuclides has even been considered for the characterisation of a new geological era, the Anthropocene: *Alexandra Witze*, This Quiet Lake Could Mark the Start of a New Anthropocene Epoch in: Nature, https://www.nature.com/articles/d41586-023-02234-z, last accessed 17 July 2025; *Paul Voosen*, Pond Mud Proposed as Anthropocene's 'Golden Spike,' Defining Human-Altered Geological Age in: Science, https://www.science.org/content/article/pond-mud-proposed-anthropocene-s-golden-spike-defining-human-altered-geological-age, last accessed 17 July 2025.

466 *Daryl Kimball*, The Nuclear Testing Tally (2022), Arms Control Association.

tion (CTBTO), was established. This organisation, which shares the very same building with the IAEA, has a wide range of authority to verify the comprehensive nuclear test ban. Hundreds of monitoring stations in tens of laboratories cross 90 countries are established and would allow for detecting clandestine tests through a range of technologies.[467] However, the treaty never entered into force. Entry into force requires the ratification of the treaty by countries listed in Annex 2 to the treaty, Article XIV.[468] These countries include, among others, all States possessing nuclear weapons. However, neither the United States, nor China, nor Pakistan, nor India, nor Israel, nor North Korea have ratified the treaty. Despite regular calls by the UN Security Council[469] and different countries,[470] the entry into force of the CTBT seems out of reach. Russia's recent move to de-ratify the treaty further diminishes the likelihood of the CTBT's entry into force.[471]

Third, a treaty focusing on fissile material was promised.[472] The idea behind a fissile material treaty is simple: If no new fissile material is produced, no new nuclear weapons (apart from recycling material in existing weapons) can be built. Called for by the UN General Assembly in 1993[473] and mandated by the Conference of Disarmament in 1995,[474] negotiations on the treaty were quickly halted, primarily due to a lack of consensus on the mandate. While some countries advocate for negotiations leading

---

467 On the role of the CTBTO in verification, see *Sabine Bauer/Cormac O'Reilly*, The Comprehensive Nuclear-Test-Ban Treaty Organization (CTBTO): Current and Future Role in the Verification Regime of the Nuclear-Test-Ban Treaty, in: Jonathan L. Black-Branch/Dieter Fleck (eds.), Nuclear Non-Proliferation in International Law: Volume II – Verification and Compliance, The Hague: T.M.C. Asser Press 2016, 131–150.

468 On the various problems regarding the entry into force, see *Jenifer Mackby*, The NPT-CTBT Connection, in: Jonathan L. Black-Branch/Dieter Fleck (eds.), Nuclear Non-Proliferation in International Law – Volume V: Legal Challenges for Nuclear Security and Deterrence, The Hague: T.M.C. Asser Press 2020, 31–52, at 46–51.

469 UN Security Council Resolution 2310 (2016).

470 E.g. Germany, Statement of the Federal Republic of Germany on Nuclear Weapon at the UN General Assembly, 77th Session, First Committee, 17th October 2022.

471 *David A. Koplow*, Russia, the CTBT, and International Law, Arms Control Today 53 (2023), 17–17; *Pavel Podvig*, Preserving the Nuclear Test Ban After Russia Revoked its CTBT Ratification, Bulletin of the Atomic Scientists 80 (2024), 75–80.

472 NPT/CONF.1995/32 (Part I), Annex, Decision 2, para. 4b.

473 Resolution A/RES/48/75.

474 The so-called Shannon Mandate established an ad hoc committee to negotiate the FCMT. On the work of that committee, see *Paul Meyer*, Is There Any Fizz Left in the Fissban? Prospects for a Fissile Material Cutoff Treaty, Arms Control Today 37 (2007), 18–22.

to complete nuclear disarmament,[475] other countries favour parallel discussions on preventing an arms race in outer space.[476] Additionally, there is no agreement on the extent of covering fissile material. One stream is a Fissile Material Cut-Off Treaty focusing on the prohibition of producing new material, while another stream is to have a more comprehensive Fissile Material Treaty to cover also existing stockpiles of fissile material.[477] As with the CTBT, the prospects of such a Fissile Material (Cut-Off) Treaty are relatively slim.

Consequently, the very basis of the continued existence of the regime is predicated on unfulfilled promises, which adds to the list of shortcomings of the treaty regime.

2.7.2.3.5 Review of the NPT

Another example of the lack of consensus to fundamental questions of the regime are evidenced by the NPT Review Conferences. Intended to review the operation of the NPT with a view to assuring that the purposes and provisions are being realised,[478] the Review Conferences have largely failed to meet this objective. The last two Review Conferences held in 2015 and 2022 have failed, as both RevCons have not produced an outcome document. The 2015 RevCon was unsuccessful due to the language used with regard to a nuclear-weapons-free zone in the Middle East, which led to vetoes by the United States, the United Kingdom, and Canada.[479] The 2022 RevCon has failed due to a veto by Russia following the mentioning of the Zaporizhzhia Nuclear Power Plant in the war in Ukraine.[480] The failure to reach consensus on the operation of the NPT over the course of ten years highlights the inherent deficiencies of the treaty.

475 *Annette Schaper*, Der Fissile Material (Cutoff) Treaty – ein Vertrag, der niemals kommt?, Sicherheit und Frieden (S+F) / Security and Peace 36 (2018), 86–91.

476 *Meyer* (n 474).

477 Ibid; *Rebecca Johnson*, Little Orphan Fissban, Bulletin of the Atomic Scientists 53 (1997), 4–4.

478 Article VIII.3 of the NPT.

479 *Oliver Meier*, The 2015 NPT Review Conference Failure – Implications for the Nuclear Order (2015), Stiftung Wissenschaft und Politik.

480 https://press.un.org/en/2022/dc3850.doc.htm, last accessed 25 February 2025.

2.7.3 Summary

The NPT has been successful in achieving a number of objectives and continues to be a significant international treaty. However, the treaty also exhibits notable deficiencies and shortcomings, which have the effect of diminishing the effectiveness of the regime, and at times even impeding the achievement of minimal progress. As long as there is no tangible progress in addressing the shortcomings, any change to the NPT regime is hard to imagine. The prospect of developing new safeguards appears highly improbable given the prevailing sentiment of dissatisfaction among many NNWS with the existing regime. This dissatisfaction is further compounded by the reluctance of NNWS to address the majority of the identified shortcomings, thereby creating an impasse within the NPT regime.

3 The Law of Nuclear Disarmament

The second pillar of nuclear weapons law deals with the subject of nuclear disarmament. As with nuclear non-proliferation, fusion will play a role within this part of nuclear weapons law for mainly two reasons. First, fusion technology creates new pathways for the production of nuclear weapons, standing in contrast to the aims of the regime on nuclear disarmament. Second, the treaties on nuclear disarmament contain safeguards provisions separate from the NPT, where the same questions on the applicability of safeguards on fusion arise.

This section first presents nuclear disarmament in the context of the United Nations (3.1). It proceeds to analyse the role of nuclear disarmament within the NPT regime (3.2). It continues to explore the legal basis and functioning of the Treaty on the Prohibition of Nuclear Weapons (3.3), and concludes by investigating the scope and extent of Nuclear-Weapon-Free-Zones (3.4)

3.1 Nuclear Disarmament and the United Nations

The issue of nuclear disarmament has always been an issue at the forefront of activities by the United Nations. The inaugural meeting of the United Nations General Assembly was convened less than six months after the use of the atomic bomb in Hiroshima and Nagasaki. During this inaugural session, the very first resolution of the UN General Assembly raised the topic of nuclear disarmament.[481] Since that time, the abolition of nuclear weapons has been a recurring theme in UN activities, with persistent calls for the prohibition of such weapons.

The UN General Assembly has been at the forefront of UN activities to call for nuclear disarmament, having first called for a treaty to ban nuclear weapons in 1961 with its Resolution 1649 (XVI) and adopted each year resolutions requesting States to conclude such a treaty.[482] Furthermore, the UN General Assembly requested the ICJ to deliver an advisory opinion on the legality of the threat and use of nuclear weapons.[483]

While the UN General Assembly is dominated by countries from the Global South, the UN[484] forum designed to address the issue of disarmament, the Conference on Disarmament (CD), has not yet achieved any progress in nuclear disarmament. The CD is a multilateral disarmament negotiation forum, set up by 65 countries, representing all regions of world. The CD takes its decisions by consensus,[485] each country has effectively a veto right, leading to NWS and their allies impeding any progress towards nuclear disarmament. Despite its role as the successor institution to the ENDC, which negotiated the NPT, as well as the institution's success in abolishing other types of weapons of mass destruction, the CD has not made any progress in the realm nuclear disarmament since 1968.

3.2 Disarmament within the NPT

As part of the grand bargain, disarmament and especially nuclear disarmament was incorporated into the NPT. To recall, Article VI of the NPT includes an obligation to all State Parties to

481 UN General Assembly Resolution 1(I).

482 ICJ, *Nuclear Weapons Advisory Opinion* (n 262), at para. 73.

483 UN General Assembly Resolution 49/75 K.

484 It must be noted that the CD is not a UN organisation or body, yet it is headquartered in the Palais des Nations in Geneva and the Director-General of the United Nations Office at Geneva serves as Secretary-General of the CD. It also submits reports to the UN General Assembly and works on issues recommended by UN General Assembly Resolutions.

485 Rule 18 of the Rules of Procedure of the Conference on Disarmament, CD/8/Rev.5; *Gro Nystuen/Kjølv Egeland/Torbjørn Graff Hugo*, The TPNW: Setting The Record Straight, Norwegian Academy of International Law 2018, at 9.

> *pursue negotiations in good faith on effective measures relating to the cessation of the nuclear arms race at an early date and to nuclear disarmament, and on a treaty on general and complete disarmament under strict and effective international control.*

Despite the vagueness of the language used, the ICJ has recognised that Article VI contains an *obligation* to negotiate in good faith on nuclear disarmament.[486]

As there are still more than 12,000 nuclear weapons in the world[487] and substantial investments in the modernisation of nuclear arsenals are underway[488], this provision is yet to be implemented.

The inclusion of the nuclear disarmament provision has been a tool to convince NNWS to accept the discriminatory nature of the treaty.[489] Combined with the limited duration of the treaty of 25 years, this provision would have ensured the temporary nature of the separation into NWS and NNWS. However, the NPT has been extended indefinitely and NWS consistently refuse to implement nuclear disarmament, while NNWS are left with little leverage.

The failure to implement Article VI of the NPT has resulted in a number of States advocating for nuclear disarmament outside the NPT, which culminated in the adoption of the Treaty on the Prohibition of Nuclear Weapons. The dynamics between Article VI of the NPT and the adoption of the Treaty on the Prohibition of Nuclear Weapons will be of relevance when approaches to newly developed fusion regulation will be discussed in Chapters 4 and 5.

---

486 ICJ, *Nuclear Weapons Advisory Opinion* (n 262), at para. 99.

487 *Kristensen/Korda* (n 438).

488 *Congressional Budget Office*, Approaches for Managing the Costs of U.S. Nuclear Forces, 2017 to 2046, 2017; *Claire Mills/Esme Kirk-Wade*, The Cost of the UK's Strategic Nuclear Deterrent, London: House of Commons Research Briefing 2023; *Julian Cooper*, How Much Does Russia Spend on Nuclear Weapons? in: SIPRI, https://www.sipri.org/commentary/topical-backgrounder/2018/how-much-does-russia-spend-nuclear-weapons, last accessed 17 July 2025.

489 *Paul M. Kiernan*, Disarmament under the NPT: Article VI in the 21st Century, Michigan State University College of Law International Law Review 20 (2011), 381–400, at 384.

3.3 Treaty on the Prohibition of Nuclear Weapons

Following the frustration of the majority of States in the world towards the lack of implementing Article VI of the NPT, and in view of the devastating humanitarian consequences of nuclear warfare, the UN General Assembly adopted the Treaty on the Prohibition of Nuclear Weapons (TPNW) in 2017.[490]

The first attempt to prohibit nuclear weapons in a global treaty was undertaken shortly after the ICJ rendered its Advisory Opinion on the Threat and Use of Nuclear Weapons. In 1997, experts drafted a Model Nuclear Weapons Convention which was submitted by Costa Rica to the United Nations.[491] This draft has been updated in 2007, and Costa Rica submitted it as a working paper to the Preparatory Commission of the 2010 NPT Review Conference.[492] While this treaty has not been adopted, it provided a foundation for the development that has followed.

At the 2010 NPT Review Conference, the International Committee of the Red Cross[493] made a further attempt which led to a focus on "the catastrophic humanitarian consequences of any use of nuclear weapons."[494] In the following preparatory sessions for the 2015 NPT Review Conference, a coalition of States regularly reiterated the humanitarian dimension of nuclear weapons, which resulted in joint statements by the vast majority of countries within the NPT forum[495] and the UN.[496] This humanitarian

490 On the relation between Article VI of the NPT and the TPNW, see *Stefan Kadelbach*, Possible Means to Overcome Tendencies of the Nuclear Weapons Ban Treaty to Erode the NPT, in: Jonathan L. Black-Branch/Dieter Fleck (eds.), Nuclear Non-Proliferation in International Law – Volume V: Legal Challenges for Nuclear Security and Deterrence, The Hague: T.M.C. Asser Press 2020, 305–322, at 312 ff.

491 UN Document A/C.1/52/7.

492 NPT/CONF.2010/PC.I/WP.17.

493 *Jakob Kellenberger*, Bringing the Era of Nuclear Weapons to an End – Statement by Jakob Kellenberger, President of the ICRC, to the Geneva Diplomatic Corps, Geneva, 20 April 2010 (2010), International Committee of the Red Cross. On the ICRC's influence, see also *Elizabeth Minor*, Changing the Discourse on Nuclear Weapons: The Humanitarian Initiative, International Review of the Red Cross 97 (2015), 711–730.

494 NPT/CONF.2010/50 (Vol. I), at 19.

495 The Joint Statement on the Humanitarian Consequences of Nuclear Weapons during the 2015 NPT RevCon was endorsed by 159 States.

496 Joint Statements were presented at the UNGA First Committee's 67th, 68th and 69th sessions and were endorsed by 35 (in 2012), 125 (in 2013) and 155 (in 2014) States, *Minor* (n 493).

initiative then evolved into proper diplomatic conferences in Oslo/Norway (2013), Nayarit/Mexico (2014) and Vienna/Austria (2014). These sessions of conferences culminated in the formulation of the Humanitarian Pledge, which called upon all NPT State Parties "to renew their commitment to [...] Article VI" of the NPT and to "fill the legal gap for the prohibition and elimination of nuclear weapons."[497]

The Humanitarian Pledge eventually resulted in the First Committee of the UN General Assembly to adopt a resolution mandating negotiations for a nuclear ban treaty.[498] Taking place in two sessions in 2017, the conference adopted the TPNW on 7 July 2017 with 122 countries in favour, one abstention (Singapore) and one vote against (Netherlands). It entered into force in 2021 and is the only treaty that prohibits nuclear weapons on a global scale. 94 States signed the treaty and 73 States deposited their ratification instruments.[499] These State Parties to the TPNW are mostly from Africa, South America, Asia and the Pacific region, but also include European countries such as Ireland, Austria and Malta. The TPNW incorporates a comprehensive prohibition of any involvement of a country regarding nuclear weapons, Article 1. Compliance with the TPNW is, inter alia,[500] ensured by a safeguards system, Article 3 and Article 4 para. 3.[501]

Safeguards requirements within the TPNW depend on whether the State is a former NWS or a NNWS. For NNWS, Article 3, the system is based on IAEA safeguards introduced within the NPT framework. These State Parties are required to at least maintain the level of safeguards in effect at the time of accession to the treaty with the possibility of exceeding this level in the future, Article 3 para. 1. All States must have at least a CSA in place, Article 3 para. 2. The Additional Protocol to the CSA is not a requirement within the TPNW,[502] but States that already have an AP in place must keep

497 A/C.1/71/L.24, para. 3. The pledge was endorsed by 107 States.

498 A/C.1/71/L.41.

499 https://treaties.unoda.org/t/tpnw/participants, last accessed 25 February 2025.

500 Former NWS State Parties are also required to submit reports on their progress to the elimination of nuclear weapons, Article 4 para. 5, and to accept safeguards, Article 4 para. 3.

501 Article 4 para. 1 also includes safeguards requirements for a State that has eliminated its nuclear weapons programme between 7 July 2017 and the entry into force of the treaty. The treaty entered into force on 22 January 2021. Since no State had eliminated its nuclear weapons in this period, this provision is of no interest.

502 The exclusion of the AP as safeguards standard has been criticized: *Stuart Casey-Maslen*, The Treaty on the Prohibition of Nuclear Weapons: a Commentary, Oxford: Oxford University Press 2019, Article 3, at paras 3.14 ff. with further references;

it according to its para. 1, while those countries without an AP in place are under no obligation to adopt one.

Former NWS Parties, Article 4 para. 3, once they accede to the treaty, are required to conclude a safeguards agreement with the IAEA "sufficient to provide credible assurance of the non-diversion of declared nuclear material from peaceful nuclear activities and of the absence of undeclared nuclear material or activities." Such a safeguards agreement might exceed the level of Article 3.[503] The prospects of NWS acceding to treaty are slim as, in rare unanimity, NWS regularly reject the TPNW in joint declarations, deeming it "simultaneously irrelevant and dangerous."[504] Similarly, NATO States reject the treaty as well.[505] The majority of State Parties to the TPNW contains of States that already been members of regional nuclear-weapon-free zones.

3.4 NWFZ Treaties

The establishment of regional nuclear-weapon-free zones (NWFZ) has contributed significantly to nuclear non-proliferation and disarmament. In these zones, the development, manufacturing, control, possession, testing, stationing, and transport of nuclear weapons is prohibited.[506] The importance of NWFZ is further emphasised in Article VII of the NPT, which reserves the right of any group of States to enter into such treaties.

The first NWFZ Treaty for Latin America and the Caribbean (Treaty of Tlatelolco) even preceded the NPT. The Member States of these treaties were also the ones who strongly pushed for the adoption of the TPNW.

Newell Highsmith/Mallory Stewart, The Nuclear Ban Treaty: A Legal Analysis, Survival 60 (2018), 129–152, at 135 f.

503 *Casey-Maslen* (n 502), at para. 4.20. Critical with regard to the *travaux préparatoire*, *Adina Carla Loghin*, Which International Authority Should Be Designated for Verifying the Irreversible Elimination of Nuclear Weapons under Article 4 of Nuclear Ban Treaty (TPNW) Scientific, Amsterdam Law Forum 11 (2019), 73–96, at 88 f.

504 Statement by France on behalf of the P5, IAEA General Conference, 23 September 2020.

505 Germany does "not deem the TPNW to be an appropriate framework to make tangible progress on nuclear disarmament and [it] will not accede to it", Statement of the Federal Republic of Germany on Nuclear Weapons at the UN General Assembly, 77th Session, First Committee, October 17th, 2022.

506 UN Report of the Disarmament Commission, A/54/42, at para. 33; Art. 1 Treaty of Tlatelolco; Art. 3 Treaty of Rarotonga; Art. 3 Treaty of Bangkok; Art. 3 Treaty of Pelindaba; Art. 3 Central-Asian Treaty.

Today, the five regional nuclear-weapon-free zone treaties[507] cover more than 50 % of the world's land area and 60 % of all countries on Earth. The regions include Latin America and the Caribbean, the South Pacific (Treaty of Rarotonga), South-East Asia (Treaty of Bangkok), Central Asia (Treaty of Semipalatinsk), and the entire continent of Africa (Treaty of Pelindaba). Moreover, there have been active endeavours to establish a NWFZ in the Middle East for decades.[508] The existing NWFZs include States that have, at one point in history, actively pursued nuclear weapons. Most prominently, South Africa even possessed three nuclear warheads in the 1970s, but later disassembled them.[509] In addition, Brazil and Argentina embarked on a nuclear competition in the 1970s and 1980s.[510] The Central-Asian NWFZ includes former Soviet republics where nuclear weapons were deployed. Furthermore, numerous countries hosted nuclear weapons tests during colonial periods such as Algeria or the Marshall Islands. Moreover, many countries in these zones have nuclear infrastructure, such as Australia in the South Pacific, or intend to build nuclear power plants, such as Thailand in South East Asia or several African States. Consequently, each NWFZ Treaty incorporates its own individual safeguards provisions.

All of these treaties refer to IAEA safeguards to ensure compliance with the obligations set out in the respective treaty.[511] The different levels of safeguards required differ. While all the treaties require a CSA in place with the IAEA, only the Central Asian Treaty requires the conclusion of an

---

507 They are: The Treaty for the Prohibition of Nuclear Weapons in Latin America and the Caribbean of 14 February 1967 (Treaty of Tlatelolco), The South Pacific Nuclear-Free Zone of 6 August 1985 (Treaty of Rarotonga), The Southeast Asian Nuclear-Weapon-Free-Zone Treaty of 15 December 1995 (Treaty of Bangkok), The African Nuclear-Weapon-Free-Zone Treaty of 12 April 1996 (Treaty of Pelindaba), The Treaty on a Nuclear-Weapon-Free Zone in Central Asia of 8 September 2006. On the relevance of NWFZ Treaties, see: Ramesh Thakur (ed.), Nuclear Weapon-Free Zones, Springer 1998.

508 The prospect of a NWFZ in the Middle East was part of the extension deal in 1995, Decision 2, para. 5, NPT/CONF.1995/32 (Part I), Annex. On a nuclear weapons free zone in the Middle East, see *Magliveras* (n 462) (optimistic view); *Baumgart/Müller* (n 462) (pessimistic view).

509 *Stumpf* (n 242).

510 *Spektor* (n 306); *John R. Redick*, Nuclear Illusions: Argentina and Brazil, Washington DC: The Henry L. Stimson Center 1995.

511 Art. 13 Treaty of Tlatelolco, Art. 5 Treaty of Bangkok, Art. 9 Treaty of Pelindaba, Art. 8 Central-Asian Treaty, Art. 8 para. 2 Treaty of Rarotonga.

Additional Protocol.[512] These treaties do not limit themselves to IAEA safeguards to verify compliance, but rather introduce additional instruments and even institutions. These include Councils, Commissions or Committees possessing the authority to demand further information or to conduct special inspections[513] More specifically, reporting and review mechanisms are in place.[514] These mechanisms are coupled with specific powers of regional control bodies that are set up under the respective NWFZ Treaty.[515] The role of fusion under these instruments will be discussed in the next chapter.

4 The Limits of International Law in Preventing Nuclear Proliferation

International legal frameworks, including the NPT and IAEA safeguards, play a critical role in regulating nuclear technology. However, their capacity to prevent proliferation is inherently limited – particularly when a State is politically determined to develop nuclear weapons.

4.1 Limitations of Safeguards

Especially with regard to safeguards, there are significant limitations to what law can achieve. The case of Iran illustrates these limitations. Despite being a party to the NPT and subject to IAEA safeguards, Iran advanced its nuclear program significantly. It was not legal instruments, but diplomatic negotiations culminating in the legally non-binding Joint Comprehensive Plan of Action (JCPoA), that temporarily curtailed its progress. Iran coming close to the nuclear bomb is not necessarily due to a lack of legal

512 Ibid. On the IAEA safeguards in NWFZ Treaties, see *Inout Suseanu*, IAEA Safeguards Under Nuclear-Weapon-Dree Zone Treaties, IAEA Bulletin 62 (2021), 8–9.

513 Articles 15 and 16 Treaty of Tlatelolco, Annex 4 to the Treaty of Rarotonga, Annex to the Treaty of Bangkok, Annex IV to the Treaty of Pelindaba.

514 Art. 14 to 16 Treaty of Tlatelolco, Art. 8 to 10 Treaty of Rarotonga, Art. 10 to 13 Treaty of Bangkok, Art. 12 and 13 Treaty of Pelindaba, Art. 10 Central-Asian Treaty.

515 Art. 7 Treaty of Tlatelolco establishes the Agency for the Prohibition of Nuclear Weapons in Latin America and the Caribbean, Annex 3 to the Treaty of Rarotonga establishes a Consultative Committee, Art. 8 Treaty of Bangkok establishes the Commission for the Southeast Asian Nuclear Weapon-Free Zone, Art. 12 Treaty of Pelindaba establishes the African Commission on Nuclear Energy. The Central-Asian Treaty did not establish a special body.

rules but due to the political will of an individual country. International law can make it more difficult to develop nuclear weapons, especially in a clandestine manner, but it cannot stop a committed State.[516] This has been even acknowledged by the former IAEA Director General Hans Blix during the process of strengthening nuclear safeguards in the 1990s, which ended in the adoption of the Additional Protocol, where he stated:

> "No safeguards system, no matter how extensive the measures, can provide absolute assurance that there has been no diversion of nuclear material or that there are no undeclared nuclear activities in a State."[517]

Similar to Hans Blix, the drafters of the Comprehensive Safeguards Agreement regarded safeguards alone as not being sufficient to prevent nuclear weapons proliferation, instead describing them as confidence-building measures with a deterring effect.[518] International law can decrease the risk of nuclear proliferation significantly, but cannot eliminate it.

A key challenge for safeguards is the dual-use nature of nuclear technology – where the same facilities and materials can be used for both civilian and military purposes. However, this duality is not a fixed characteristic of the technology itself, but rather an assumption underpinning the safeguards regime.[519] In practice, the line between peaceful and military use remains blurred, particularly in threshold states with latent weapons capability. Rather than assuming a clear separation between peaceful and military uses, it may be more accurate to describe nuclear technology as inherently ambivalent.[520] Such ambivalence surrounding nuclear technology,

516 On the limitations of the safeguards regime towards non-cooperative States, see *Gerald Kirchner/Stefan Oeter*, Technical Limits of Verification and Their Implications for Treaty Design, in: Jonathan L. Black-Branch/Dieter Fleck (eds.), Nuclear Non-Proliferation in International Law: Volume II – Verification and Compliance, The Hague: T.M.C. Asser Press 2016, 167–186.

517 Strengthening the Effectiveness and Improving the Efficiency of the Safeguards System – Report by the Director General to the General Conference, GC(39)/17, para. 15.

518 *Röhrlich* (n 286), at 42; *Werner Ungerer/Ryukichi Imai/I. D. Morokhov et al.*, Safeguards: Five Views, IAEA Bulletin 13-3 (1971), 2–13, at 6.

519 *Matthias Englert/Anne Harrington*, Next Generation Nuclear Technologies: New Challenges to the Legal Framework of the IAEA from Intense Neutron Sources, in: Jonathan L. Black-Branch/Dieter Fleck (eds.), Nuclear Non-Proliferation in International Law: Volume II – Verification and Compliance, The Hague: T.M.C. Asser Press 2016, 187–212, at 205.

520 *Wolfgang Liebert/Rainer Rilling/Jürgen Scheffran*, Die Janusköpfigkeit von Forschung und Technik. Zum Problem der zivil-militärischen Ambivalenz, Mar-

specifically with regard to latent nuclear capabilities and the possibility of its discovery, remains with fusion. While safeguards intend to reduce such ambivalence, there is only limited success as safeguards replace ambivalence with a perceived certainty of objectivity by science and verification techniques.[521]

Ultimately, the development of nuclear weapons is shaped by a complex web of factors – including technical expertise, geopolitical tensions, espionage networks, and resource availability.[522] Legal instruments like safeguards obligations and export control regimes are essential, but they function within this broader landscape and cannot, in isolation, prevent the use of fusion for nuclear proliferation. This broader landscape is shaped by political interests which are highly heterogenous.

4.2 Heterogenous Set of Interests

This section presents an overview of the heterogenous set of interests in the realm of nuclear weapons law among the various actors in international law, covering key States, groups of States as well as the IAEA and the EU. These interests stretch from full support to all aspects of nuclear weapons law, to clear opposition.

4.2.1 Nuclear Weapon States Recognised by the NPT

The NPT recognises five nuclear weapon states (NWS): The United States, Russia, the United Kingdom, France and China. While these States rarely share a common interest, it is exceptionally with nuclear non-proliferation and nuclear disarmament where they do.

As they possess an elevated position under the NPT, they have a key interest in maintaining this position. They want to remain the gate keepers to nuclear deterrence and nuclear coercion. These States want to be able

---

burg: BdWi-Verlag 1994; *Itty Abraham*, 'Who's next?' Nuclear Ambivalence and the Contradictions of Non-Proliferation Policy, Economic and Political Weekly 45 (2010), 48–56.

521 *Englert/Harrington* (n 519), at 209.

522 *Sophie Grape/Erik Branger/Vitaly Fedchenko et al.*, Development of Uranium and Plutonium Based Nuclear Weapons – What Impacts the Choice of Fissile Material Route?, Journal of Strategic Trade Control 3 (2025), 1–27.

to use these political advantages of the weapon without seeing another State gaining a similar level of power. As a consequence, they are strictly in favour of maintaining the status quo. They support the non-proliferation regime and push for its implementation.[523] These States are against existing initiatives on nuclear disarmament,[524] but offer negative security assurances to nuclear weapon free zones.[525]

However, their interests differ in details, especially on how they use nuclear coercion, on how large their nuclear stockpiles are and how strict their disapproval of nuclear disarmament is.

4.2.1.1 United States

The United States invented nuclear weapons in 1945 during the Manhattan Project at the height of World War II. Today, the United States possesses 5044 nuclear weapons.[526]

Historically, the United States aimed at limiting the capacity of other States to develop nuclear weapons as they were the only State possessing nuclear weapons between 1945 and 1949. As mentioned above, a key motivator of the United States to suggest the foundation of the International Atomic Energy Agency (IAEA) was to limit other States' capacities to develop nuclear weapons.[527]

The United States is also one of the architects of the NPT. The NPT not only allows the United States to maintain its elevated position; it also enables the United States to export its nuclear technology all around the world. Its exports of nuclear reactors alone amount to roughly half a billion USD per year.[528]

---

523 NPT/CONF.2015/PC.I/12.

524 Statement by France on behalf of the P5 (n 442).

525 Additional Protocols to all NWFZ Treaties except the Treaty of Bangkok are signed by all NWS under the NPT and ratified by all except the US.

526 *Hans M. Kristensen/Matt Korda*, World Nuclear Forces, in: Stockholm International Peace Research Institute (ed.), SIPRI Yearbook 2024: Armaments, Disarmament and International Security, Stockholm: Stockholm International Peace Research Institute 2024, 271–376, at 272.

527 *Röhrlich* (n 286), at 41.

528 *Observatory of Economic Complexity (OEC)*, Nuclear Reactors in the US (2025), https://oec.world/en/profile/bilateral-product/nuclear-reactors/reporter/usa, last accessed 17 July 2025.

The United States usually sees itself as a defender of the non-proliferation system. Bilateral safeguards agreements between the United States and importing States of nuclear technology before the inception of the IAEA were the model of the first IAEA safeguards regime. The United States also constantly advocates for a functioning safeguards system. However, the export of US nuclear technology also facilitated India's development of nuclear weapons and the United States continues to export nuclear technology to India.[529] In addition, the United States has used its interest to prevent the proliferation of nuclear weapons as justification for military action, such as the Iraq War[530] or its attacks on Iranian personnel and nuclear infrastructure in 2020 and 2025.[531]

Nuclear deterrence is crucial to nuclear interests of the United States. The United States perceives its possession of nuclear weapons as insurance for deterring any attack, historically mainly from the Soviet Union or later Russia, but nowadays also from China.[532] The United States and Russia keep their stockpiles at levels sufficient to ensure mutually assure destruction. This follows the neo-realist logic that – as their arsenals are capable to fully destroy the other State –, any conventional or nuclear attack is deterred. The United States extends its nuclear deterrence also to its NATO partners, via Article 5 of the North Atlantic Treaty and nuclear sharing agreements. US nuclear weapons are currently deployed to Belgium, Germany, Italy, the Netherlands and Turkey.[533] In case of a nuclear war, the weapons would be mounted onto the allied country's fighter jets.

Together with the Soviet Union and later Russia, these two States have always maintained the vast majority of nuclear weapons in the world of more than 90 %.[534] Especially during the Cold War but also in the first decade of the 2000s, the United States had an interest in maintaining an equal level of nuclear weapons with the Soviet Union and later Russia. The United States also supported the reduction of both arsenals in several

529 See above n 400.

530 Colin Powell, Remarks to the United Nations Security Council, 2 February 2003.

531 *William Tobey*, Overview: Nuclear Scientists as Assassination Targets in: Bulletin of the Atomic Scientist, https://thebulletin.org/premium/2020-11/overview-nuclear-scientists-as-assassination-targets/, last accessed 17 July 2025; Donald J. Trump, Address to Nation, 22 June 2025.

532 *U.S. Department of Defense*, Nuclear Posture Review, Washington DC: U.S. Government 2022, at III.

533 See above n 443.

534 *Norris/Kristensen* (n 437).

nuclear arms control treaties, such as the SALT Agreements, the Intermediate-Range Nuclear Forces Treaty or the New-START Treaty.

4.2.1.2 Russia

The Soviet Union conducted its first nuclear test in 1949. Today, Russia, as the legal successor of the Soviet Union, possesses 5580 nuclear weapons.[535]

Russia is a proponent of the NPT as well and supports the non-proliferation regime. The Soviet Union was a key architect of the NPT as well, presenting identical drafts to the conference in 1968.[536] To ensure non-proliferation, Russia tried to act as negotiator with North Korea and Iran in their nuclear activities.

During times of the Warsaw Pact, the Soviet Union also extended its nuclear deterrence to allied States. After the dissolution of the Soviet Union, Russia succeeded as NWS and secured its nuclear weapons and materials from former Soviet Union States, such as Ukraine (which used to have the third largest nuclear arsenal), Kazakhstan and Belarus.[537] Following its full-scale invasion of Ukraine, Russia has also engaged in a nuclear sharing agreement with Belarus.[538] This conflict also led to the suspension of the last nuclear arms control treaty in force.[539] Since the 1980s, the Soviet Union and later Russia has had the largest nuclear arsenal in the world.[540]

4.2.1.3 United Kingdom

The United Kingdom tested its first nuclear weapon in 1952 and possesses today 225 nuclear weapons.[541]

The United Kingdom follow a different approach to nuclear weapons compared to the United States or Russia. The United Kingdom possesses

535 *Kristensen/Korda* (n 526), at 272.

536 *United Nations* (n 312), at 4.

537 *Vijai Kumar*, Problems of Succession to the Soviet Nuclear Arsenal and International Law, International Studies 31 (1994), 305–320.

538 See above n 445.

539 *Philipp Sauter*, Russia's Withdrawal from New START – The End of a Cold War Relic, but Not the Beginning of a New Nuclear Arms Race (2023), in: Völkerrechtsblog, https://voelkerrechtsblog.org/russias-withdrawal-from-new-start/.

540 *Norris/Kristensen* (n 437).

541 *Kristensen/Korda* (n 526), at 272.

less than 5 % of the nuclear weapons of either the United States or Russia, following a policy of minimum credible deterrent. While nuclear coercion is also used by the United States or Russia, the United Kingdom's policy is limited to nuclear deterrence. The United Kingdom is also engaged in discussions on nuclear disarmament,[542] but does not support the TPNW.[543] Given its limited nuclear arsenal, the United Kingdom was never part of any arms control regime.

The United Kingdom's nuclear programme is also closely aligned with the United States, as its Trident missiles carrying the nuclear warhead are manufactured and maintained by the United States.[544] In addition, the United Kingdom was a partner in the Manhattan Project.

4.2.1.4 France

France tested its first nuclear weapon in 1960 and today possess 290 nuclear weapons.[545] Historically, nuclear weapons were essential for France's self-understanding of its position in the post-war world order, initially under the presidency of Charles de Gaulle.[546]

Central to France's nuclear weapons policy is its *dissuasion nucléaire* and its independence from other States. It is based on strict sufficiency of having just enough nuclear weapons to deter any aggression against France's vital interests. France controls its nuclear forces entirely nationally with no foreign involvement like the United Kingdom, despite its comparable size of arsenals.

Historically, France used to be critical towards the international non-proliferation regime. Despite being recognised as NWS by the NPT, it only acceded to the treaty in 1992 for political and economic reasons.[547] France has been bound by the Euratom safeguards regime since the community's foundation in 1957. Today, France unequivocally supports the nuclear non-

542 For example, the UK Foreign, Commonwealth & Development Office has hosted three conferences on the topic of irreversibility on nuclear disarmament through 2022 to 2024.

543 Statement by France on behalf of the P5 (n 442).

544 *Hans M. Kristensen/Matt Korda*, United Kingdom Nuclear Weapons, 2021, Bulletin of the Atomic Scientists 77 (2021), 153–158.

545 *Kristensen/Korda* (n 526), at 272.

546 *Bruno Tertrais/Ministère de la Défense*, La France et la dissuasion nucléaire : Concept, moyens, avenir, Paris: La documentation Française 2017, at 79 ff.

547 See above 2.3.1.

proliferation regime set up by the NPT, but it is against the TPNW. In addition, France might extend its nuclear deterrence to European States in the future.[548]

4.2.1.5 China

China tested its first nuclear weapon in 1964 and today possesses 500 nuclear weapons.[549] With this arsenal size, it sits between the smaller arsenals of the United Kingdom and France on the one hand, and the large arsenals of the United States and Russia on the other hand. It follows a path of nuclear armament, intending to increase its nuclear arsenal, but (potentially) not seeking parity with the United States or Russia.[550]

Similar to France, it only joined the NPT in 1992 despite its recognition as NWS after opposing the treaty for decades for political reasons.[551] It supports the non-proliferation regime. They limit their arsenals to deter nuclear attacks, counter nuclear coercion and maintain strategic stability.[552] It does not support the TPNW.[553] China is further a strong criticizer of US nuclear sharing.[554] It further opposes being included in US-Russia arms control talks as long as these States do not significantly reduce their arsenals.[555]

4.2.1.6 Summary

NWS recognised under the NPT share a dislike towards the TPNW, while France, the United Kingdom and China are more open towards nuclear disarmament compared to the United States and Russia. It also those two States that use nuclear weapons not only for deterrence, but also as leverage

548 *Philipp Sauter*, European Nuclear Weapons - Europe's Nuclear Ambitions and the Constraints of International Law (2024), in: Verfassungsblog, https://verfassungsblog.de/nuclear-weapons/, last accessed 25 February 2025.

549 *Kristensen/Korda* (n 526), at 272.

550 *Hans M. Kristensen/Matt Korda/Eliana Johns et al.*, Chinese Nuclear Weapons, 2025, Bulletin of the Atomic Scientists 81 (2025), 135–160.

551 See above 2.3.1.

552 *Kristensen/Korda/Johns et al.* (n 550).

553 Statement by France on behalf of the P5 (n 442).

554 See above n 454.

555 *David Santoro*, Getting Past No: Developing a Nuclear Arms Control Relationship with China, Journal for Peace and Nuclear Disarmament 6 (2023), 68–86.

in international relations. Regarding non-proliferation, all States share an interest in an effective regime in order to maintain the order established by the NPT.

4.2.2 Nuclear Weapon States Outside the NPT

The interests from NWS outside the NPT differ significantly from those within. These States are India, Pakistan, Israel and North Korea.

India's (first test in 1974 and 172 nuclear weapons[556]) and Pakistan's (first test in 1998 and 170 nuclear weapons[557]) possession of nuclear weapons is mainly motivated by regional conflicts. Both countries have been in an ongoing conflict among each other for decades, which from time to time turns military, especially in the Kashmir region.[558] In addition, India has had wars against the nuclear-armed China,[559] further motivating India to possess nuclear weapons. Their stockpiles are limited to a credible minimum deterrence against their rivals to maintain strategic balance. As they are outside the NPT, they do not support the international safeguards regime. Yet, as they have safeguards agreements in place with the IAEA predating the NPT, they have opened up parts of their civilian nuclear infrastructure for IAEA safeguards. They also, in principle, support nuclear disarmament.[560]

Israel has never officially admitted to possess nuclear weapons, while it is one of the worst kept secrets that they do. Experts estimate Israel's arsenal to consist of 90 nuclear weapons.[561] Given the geopolitical situation in which Israel finds itself, nuclear weapons and its deterring factor are seen

556 *Kristensen/Korda* (n 526), at 272.

557 Ibid.

558 *Rajesh M. Basrur*, Nuclear Weapons and India–Pakistan Relations, Strategic Analysis 33 (2009), 336–344.

559 *Kumar Sundaram/M. V. Ramana*, India and the Policy of No First Use of Nuclear Weapons, Journal for Peace and Nuclear Disarmament 1 (2018), 152–168; *Hans M. Kristensen/Matt Korda/Eliana Johns et al.*, Indian Nuclear Weapons, 2024, Bulletin of the Atomic Scientists 80 (2024), 326–342.

560 *Rajesh Basrur*, India and Nuclear Disarmament, Security Challenges 6 (2010), 69–81; *Mohd Amin Mir/Thseen Nazir*, South Asian Perspectives on the Nuclear Weapons Ban: Challenges and Prospects for Disarmament, Peace Review 36 (2024), 256–266.

561 *Kristensen/Korda* (n 526), at 272.

as critical for the survival of the State.[562] In addition, Israel is against the further spread of nuclear weapons in the Middle East. Israel's opposition against nuclear weapons in the region is also enforced by military action against nuclear programmes, as seen in 1981 in Iraq, 2007 in Syria or 2025 in Iran.[563]

North Korea possesses nuclear weapons both for survival but also for nuclear coercion. North Korea first tested nuclear weapons in 2006 and is estimated to possess around 50 nuclear weapons.[564] Nuclear weapons serve as an important tool to protect the Kim regime.[565] North Korea further uses its nuclear arsenal as leverage in diplomacy to gain concessions against its isolation and to force negotiations with other States such as the United States or South Korea,[566] as witnessed by the Six Party Talks.[567]

4.2.3 Non-Nuclear NATO States

Another important group of States are non-nuclear NATO States, meaning all NATO States except the United States, the United Kingdom and France. While these 29 States are still quite heterogenous, they share a quandary: They might be the target for Russian nuclear weapons, yet they do not possess any themselves. Instead, they rely on the nuclear umbrella extended by the United States. Thus, they rely on US nuclear weapons for deterrence.

562 On Israel's nuclear weapons programme in a wider context, see *Shlomo Aronson*, The Politics and Strategy of Nuclear Weapons in the Middle East – Opacity, Theory, and Reality, 1960–1991 -- An Israeli Perspective, Seattle: SUNY Press 2012. For a particularly trenchant statement, see *Louis René Beres*, Where the Shadow Really Falls: Why Israel Must Have Nuclear Weapons, The Brown Journal of World Affairs 4 (1997), 127–138.

563 *Istvan Pogany*, The Destruction of Osirak: A Legal Perspective, The World Today 37 (1981), 413–418; *Ori Wertman/Christian Kaunert*, Operation "Outside the Box": The Securitization of the Syrian Nuclear Reactor, in: Israel: National Security and Securitization: The Role of the United States in Defining What Counts, Cham: Springer International Publishing 2023, 123–148; *Michael N. Schmitt*, Israel's Operation Rising Lion and the Right of Self-Defense in: Lieber Institute Articles of War, https://lieber.westpoint.edu/israels-operation-rising-lion-right-of-self-defense/, last accessed 17 July 2025.

564 *Kristensen/Korda* (n 526), at 272.

565 *Benjamin Habib*, North Korea's Nuclear Weapons Programme and the Maintenance of the Songun System, The Pacific Review 24 (2011), 43–64.

566 *Jonathan D. Pollack*, North Korea's Nuclear Weapons Development – Implications for Future Policy, Proliferation Papers 33 (2010), 7–44.

567 See above n 413.

Yet, as they are NATO Member States, they have to support the nuclear dimension of the alliance, despite strong ressentiments against nuclear weapons in some Member States.[568] As members of the alliance, they are against nuclear disarmament under the current security environment.[569]

There are, however several examples of NATO Member States having a critical stance towards this doctrine. Sweden used to be a strong opponent of nuclear weapons.[570] The Dutch Government refused to participate at the negotiations of the TPNW, but was forced to by a parliamentary vote.[571] Germany participates as an observer to meetings of State Parties of the TPNW, but refuses to join the treaty.[572]

Regarding non-proliferation, they share the goal of universalising the Additional Protocol,[573] pushing for a maximum level of safeguards in the world. Most European NATO States are also part of Euratom, where they adhere to the Euratom safeguards regime. Their stance on non-proliferation is even more important as many NATO members can be considered as threshold States. States such as Germany or Canada have the technological capacity to build nuclear weapons, but they decide actively to use nuclear technology for peaceful uses only. Most States are not able to build nuclear weapons and do not want to build nuclear weapons, while many NATO States would be able, but do not want to build nuclear weapons.

Among non-nuclear NATO States, Germany occupies a specific role. It is an outspoken defender of the nuclear non-proliferation regime, even more than others, as seen in the nuclear talks with Iran in 2014 and 2015. Alongside the permanent members of the UN Security Council (which are also the only States that the NPT recognises as NWS), Germany was the only

568 On the role of Sweden and Finland, see *William Alberque/Benjamin Schreer*, What Kind of NATO Allies Will Finland and Sweden Be?, Survival 64 (2022), 123–136.

569 On the role of NATO being a nuclear alliance, see *Kjølv Egeland*, Spreading the Burden: How NATO Became a 'Nuclear' Alliance, Diplomacy & Statecraft 31 (2020), 143–167.

570 Sweden which funds several institutions such as the Alva Myrdal Center for Nuclear Disarmament at the University of Uppsala, named after the Swedish Nobel Peace Prize Laureate for her support of disarmament, or the Stockholm International Peace Research Institute.

571 *Ekaterina Shirobokova*, The Netherlands and the prohibition of nuclear weapons, The Nonproliferation Review 25 (2018), 37–49.

572 *Katja Astner/Moritz Kütt*, The Treaty on the Prohibition of Nuclear Weapons – Changing Disarmament Discourses in Germany?, in: Ulrich Kühn (ed.), Germany and Nuclear Weapons in the 21st Century – Atomic Zeitenwende?, Oxford: Routledge 2024, 203–229.

573 All NATO States have concluded an Additional Protocol.

non-nuclear weapon State participant to those talks with Iran, underlying Germany's specific interest to defend the non-proliferation regime.[574]

4.2.4 Non-NATO States from the Global North

Another important group of States are non-NATO States from the Global North, mainly Ireland, Austria and Malta. Historically, also Sweden had been an example before its accession to NATO in 2024.

These States unequivocally support both nuclear non-proliferation and nuclear disarmament. For example, the negotiations which led to the NPT were initiated by the so-called Irish Resolution in 1958 where Ireland called for an end of the nuclear arms race at the United Nations.[575] Austria not only hosts the headquarters of the IAEA, but it was at the forefront of negotiating the TPNW.[576] All three States are Member States of the TPNW.

4.2.5 States from the Global South

The Global South is a heterogenous group of States. While there is some diversity in their stance on nuclear non-proliferation, the Global South is united in its opinion on nuclear disarmament.

Regarding nuclear disarmament, they are at the forefront of not only talking about it, but at taking action. With the important exception of NWS outside the NPT and some States in the Middle East, all States which are deemed to belong to the so-called Global South are members of NWFZs. The Treaty of Tlatelolco which established the NWFZ in Latin America and Caribbean even predated the NPT. It was especially the States from this region that also pushed for the adoption of a binding instrument leading towards nuclear disarmament, first with proposals of a model nuclear weapons conventions within the NPT framework, later with the adoption

---

574 On Germany's role in the JCPoA negotiations and implementation, see *Cornelius Adebahr*, Germany's Role in the Success and Failure of the Iran Nuclear Deal, in: Ulrich Kühn (ed.), Germany and Nuclear Weapons in the 21st Century, London: Routledge 2024, 281–301.

575 See above n 309.

576 *Nick Ritchie/Alexander Kmentt*, Universalising the TPNW: Challenges and Opportunities, Journal for Peace and Nuclear Disarmament 4 (2021), 70–93.

of the TPNW. Out of the treaty's 73 parties, all but six parties[577] belong to the Global South.

With regard to nuclear non-proliferation, there is a mixed picture. The majority of States pushes for a high level of safeguards in order to ensure that the objectives of the NPT and other nuclear weapons law instruments are met.[578] A key motivator for them is that as long as States are assured that their neighbours are not pursuing nuclear weapons, there is no need for themselves to pursuing them. However, there is also a group which is quite sceptical towards new instruments of nuclear non-proliferation, including Argentina, Brazil, Egypt, Iran, Syria and Venezuela. They regard the three pillars of the NPT – non-proliferation, technical assistance and disarmament – as equals and are disappointed that NWS refuse to consider nuclear disarmament. As long as NWS do not engage in nuclear disarmament, they see additional safeguards as a sign of mistrust, as they keep their end of bargain, unlike NWS according to their perception.[579] As the NPT had a limited duration of 25 years and was set to expire in 1995, States from the Global South tried to use a potential expiration as leverage to force NWS and other States from the Global North to concessions, which ended up in the 1995 Extension Deal, which – as analysed above – still lacks implementation and further increases the frustration of these States. These are the reasons why some States from the Global North did not conclude an Additional Protocol with the IAEA and why the safeguards standard of the Additional Protocol was not included in the TPNW.[580]

4.2.6 Other States with Particular Interests

There are two States in particular which are difficult to group into another category: Japan and Iran.

577 Austria, Holy See, Ireland, Malta, New Zealand and San Marino are State Parties to the TPNW, but belong to the Global North.

578 More than 100 States from the Global South have concluded an Additional Protocol with the IAEA.

579 See for example Brazil's opposition to the Additional Protocol, *Marcos Valle Machado da Silva*, Brazil and the Refusal to the Additional Protocol: Is It Time to Review this Position?, Carta Internacional 16 (2021), 1–26.

580 *Casey-Maslen* (n 502), Article 3, at paras 3.14 ff.

As Japan has witnessed the devastating effects of nuclear weapons and has lost approximately 200,000 people to nuclear weapons,[581] Japan is one of the most outspoken States against nuclear weapons. Despite its status as a threshold State, Japan stands unequivocally to its three non-nuclear principles: Japan shall not possess nuclear weapons, shall not produce nuclear weapons and shall not permit the introduction of nuclear weapons into its territory.[582] It also a fierce advocate of nuclear disarmament.[583] Nonetheless, it is part of the United States' extended nuclear umbrella and has not signed the TPNW.

Another State with particular interests is Iran. Despite being a Member State of the NPT, it (most likely) actively pursues a nuclear weapons programme.[584] Unlike North Korea, it has not yet decided to withdraw from the treaty, yet it does not act in conformity with its obligations under its Comprehensive Safeguards Agreement it has concluded with the IAEA.[585] It pursues nuclear weapons for mainly two reasons. First, its archenemy Israel possesses nuclear weapons. Iranian nuclear weapons would lead to a strategic level playing field. Iran would also be able to deter both conventional and nuclear attacks as well as to use nuclear coercion towards other States in the region. Second, Iran has used its nuclear programme as diplomatic leverage, leading to the JCPoA, which would have resulted in the lifting of a majority of Western sanctions against the Mullah regime. Following the United States' withdrawal from the JCPoA, Iran has resumed its nuclear programme, which was struck militarily by Israel and the United States in 2025.

581 *Masao Tomonaga*, The Atomic Bombings of Hiroshima and Nagasaki: A Summary of the Human Consequences, 1945–2018, and Lessons for Homo sapiens to End the Nuclear Weapon Age, Journal for Peace and Nuclear Disarmament 2 (2019), 491–517.

582 Statement by Prime Minister Eisako Sato, 11 December 1967.

583 *Yukiya Amano*, A Japanese View on Nuclear Disarmament, The Nonproliferation Review 9 (2002), 132–145; *Jonathon Baron/Rebecca Davis Gibbons/Stephen Herzog*, Japanese Public Opinion, Political Persuasion, and the Treaty on the Prohibition of Nuclear Weapons, Journal for Peace and Nuclear Disarmament 3 (2020), 299–309.

584 Iran has enriched uranium to 60 %, which is significantly above levels for commercial application, GOV/INF/2023/1. On the timeline of the programme, see *Matt FIeld*, A Simple TImeline of Iran's Nuclear Program in: Bulletin of the Atomic Scientists, https://thebulletin.org/2025/06/a-simple-timeline-of-irans-nuclear-program/, last accessed 17 July 2025.

585 IAEA Board of Governors, GOV/2025/38.

4.2.7 European Union and Euratom

The European Union and Euratom have a special role corresponding to specific interests in the regime of nuclear weapons law.

On the one hand, there is Euratom, the European community charged with supplying its Member States with nuclear material and to administer safeguards. Historically, Euratom's role to administer safeguards was the cause for hesitation of European States towards the IAEA's safeguards regime, which was only solved after a compromise delimiting the authorities of both institutions. Regarding non-proliferation, Euratom supports the Additional Protocol and its heightened standard of safeguard. Euratom also continues to improve the effectiveness and efficiency of Euratom safeguards.[586] Given the limited scope of the Euratom Treaty, Euratom does not take a stance on expanding nuclear non-proliferation outside Europe.

Such matters of foreign policy are, however, supported by the European Union under the EU's Common Foreign and Security Policy. The EU takes part at NPT Review Conferences, financially supported the setup of the CTBTO, is a large donor to the IAEA and promotes the universalisation of the Additional Protocol.[587] Regarding nuclear disarmament, the EU finds itself in a difficult situation. EU Member States include France as an NWS, NATO States and non-NATO States, which do not share a common stance on the topic. While the EU funds the EU Non-Proliferation and Disarmament Consortium, a network of European think tanks and research centres,[588] the EU does not engage in negotiations on nuclear disarmament.

4.2.8 IAEA

The IAEA as nuclear watchdog also has a specific interest in the regime of nuclear weapons. As safeguards are at the centre of its activities, the IAEA has an interest in a strong nuclear non-proliferation regime. As the IAEA has the mandate to administer safeguards, it has an interest in having the

586 Council Decision (Euratom) 2025/492 of 18 February 2025 approving a Commission Regulation on the application Euratom safeguards.

587 *Peter Van Ham*, The European Union's WMD Strategy and the CFSP: A Critical Analysis, EU Non-Proliferation Consortium Non-Proliferation Papers 2 (2011), 1–16, at 8.

588 Council Decision (CFSP) 2022/597 of 11 April 2022 promoting the European network of independent non-proliferation and disarmament think tanks.

means of effectively implementing its mandate. The non-detection of Iraq's nuclear weapons programme by the IAEA caused heavy critiques of the organisation and finally led to the adoption of the Additional Protocol.[589] The IAEA's interest to effectively administer safeguards is also complementary to the IAEA's role of promoting nuclear energy and other nuclear technologies. Only if it is effectively guaranteed that the IAEA prevents the proliferation of nuclear weapons rather than supporting nuclear weapons programmes, the IAEA can justify its existence.

In addition, it is the IAEA's interest to remain the hub for dealing with nuclear non-proliferation. Regarding other aspects of nuclear weapons law, the IAEA has remained silent. The IAEA did not oppose the creation of the CTBTO to verify the arms control instrument CTBT, neither did it actively advocate for or lobby against a potential future delegation as competent international authority under the disarmament instrument TPNW. It sees itself as politically neutral, relying on the consensus of its Member States. It also acknowledges the limitations of its Statute which is limited to non-proliferation and does not extend to nuclear disarmament or arms control.

4.2.9 Summary

The interests can be summarised as follows: NWS recognised under the NPT unanimously defend the nuclear order established by the NPT. They support a strong non-proliferation regime while they regard nuclear disarmament as crucial. NATO States typically share this interest, while they are more open towards pathways to nuclear disarmament. NWS outside the NPT possess nuclear weapons mostly as a result of regional tensions as a deterrence against attacks. States from the Global South generally push towards nuclear disarmament, but they do not have a common stance towards a strong regime on nuclear non-proliferation. Some support it, some see a movement towards nuclear disarmament by NWS as prerequisite for it. The European Union promotes a strong non-proliferation regime. The IAEA as nuclear watchdog has a heightened interest of a strong regime as well.

589 See above n 339.

5 Summary

The international regulation of nuclear weapons is characterised by a delicate balance of security, economic, and environmental interests. The ongoing challenges in enforcing non-proliferation while allowing peaceful uses of nuclear technology have led to a complex regime of nuclear weapons law. This regime consists of a wide web of legal sources, covering the areas of nuclear non-proliferation and nuclear disarmament.

The development of the nuclear non-proliferation regime can be traced back to a series of incidents involving States developing nuclear weapons clandestinely, kick-started by the Manhattan Project during World War II. The safeguards system mandated by the NPT and implemented by the IAEA has been identified as the cornerstone of this regime. In executing its mandate, the IAEA exercises a high level of authority on NNWS. The scope of the regime is further set out in different safeguards agreements. The basis for NNWS is the CSA, based on INFCIRC/153(Corrected). Many States have also concluded an Additional Protocol, based on INFCIRC/540(Corrected), further extending the IAEA's safeguards authority. NWS recognised by the NPT have concluded Voluntary Offer Agreements with a limited scope of application. In a similar manner, NWS outside the NPT (India, Pakistan, Israel) have item-specific safeguard agreements with the IAEA, with military facilities excluded, thus limiting the IAEA's authority in safeguards. Moreover, the Euratom Treaty includes a regional European safeguards regime, which deals with the specificity of addressing both NNWS and NWS with one regime. The safeguards regime is further complemented by export control regimes, which are further specified in the intergovernmental fora of the Zangger Committee and the NSG.

In the context of nuclear disarmament, there is an absence of a treaty that can be regarded as a cornerstone. Despite being mandated by Article VI of the NPT, NWS continue to refuse to negotiate or join nuclear disarmament treaties. Despite being at the centre of the international agenda since the inception of the United Nations, there is only limited progress. Nevertheless, there are treaties addressing the prohibition of nuclear weapons: The TPNW on the international level, and NWFZ Treaties on the regional level. These treaties include their individual safeguard regimes for verification, based on the IAEA framework.

International law, while important, has inherent limitations in preventing nuclear proliferation, as determined States can circumvent legal frameworks to develop weapons, highlighting the insufficiency of legal measures alone. The dual-use nature of nuclear technology and the influence of multiple factors beyond legal safeguards further complicate efforts to curb proliferation effectively. This is especially due to a variation of interests among States, State groups and international organisations. Regardless of the law's limitations, the legal framework of nuclear weapons is the foundation of any action against nuclear proliferation.

The next chapter will investigate how this framework is applicable to fusion.

Chapter 3: Fusion in the Existing Legal Framework

Chapter 1 has demonstrated that the development of nuclear fusion as a clean and sustainable energy source has applications in nuclear weapons programmes. Chapter 2 has presented the dynamics, content and limitations of the legal framework which tries to prevent the use of civilian nuclear programmes for military purposes. This chapter now analyses how this legal framework applies to fusion and the technology's role in the existing legal framework of non-proliferation and disarmament.

Firstly, the chapter explores the role of fusion within the most important sub-regime in nuclear weapons law, namely the IAEA's verification regime. In that regard, it focuses on the IAEA's Statute, the NPT and safeguards agreements (1). The chapter proceeds to analyse how export control regimes apply to fusion (2). It continues to explore the applicability of further regimes to fusion, including the ITER Agreement, the Euratom Treaty, the TPNW and NWFZ Treaties (3). The chapter concludes with an evaluation of the role of fusion in the broader regime of nuclear weapons law (4). As this chapter will show, there is a gap between the regime's purpose and intent – which is to limit, deter or prevent the use of nuclear technology for nuclear weapons purposes – and its applicability to fusion, despite the technology's applications in nuclear weapons programmes.

1 Fusion in the IAEA's Safeguards Regime

This section explores the applicability of different instruments of the IAEA's safeguards regime to fusion. As will be shown, ambiguity in the application to fusion characterises this framework. This section starts with analysing the role and mandate of the IAEA with regard to fusion (1.1). It proceeds to examine the applicability of the Nuclear Non-Proliferation Treaty (1.2) and of safeguards agreements (1.3) to fusion.

1.1 IAEA and Fusion

As the IAEA is widely regarded as the nuclear watchdog[590], this section explores the role of the IAEA in the development of fusion energy (1.1.1), with a particular focus on its efforts to ensure the peaceful use of fusion (1.1.2).

1.1.1 Fusion and Atoms for Peace and Development

The IAEA represents the most significant international organisation within the nuclear field, with the stated objective of this organisation to "accelerate and enlarge the contribution of atomic energy to peace, health and prosperity throughout the world."[591] The IAEA itself promotes itself with the motto "atoms for peace and development."[592]

This broad mandate is wide enough to include fusion into the IAEA's undertakings. While the ordinary meaning of 'atomic energy' may suggest a narrow focus on fission – which is currently the only nuclear process used for energy production – this interpretation is not inherently required by the term itself. Nuclear fusion liberates the same force that is liberated in fission reactors, the strong nuclear force. The release of the strong nuclear force translates into a release of energy – the energy of the atomic nucleus or short atomic energy. In addition, subsequent practise warrants an interpretation to include fusion under the wide scope of Article II of the IAEA Statute. Subsequent practise is part of the interpretational canon of Article 31 of the Vienna Convention on the Law of Treaties (VCLT) in the application of the general rule of treaty interpretation.[593] First and foremost, it is the subsequent practise by States which is relevant for interpreting a treaty provision as it is them that have concluded the treaty and have the power over it. In recent times, States have addressed the topic of fusion during the

590 See Chapter 2, Section 2.2.1.

591 Article II of the IAEA Statute.

592 See for example *Yukiya Amano*, Atoms for Peace and Development: Working Towards the Sustainable Development Goals, IAEA Bulletin 59–1 (2018), 1–1; *Arjan Koning/Ian Swainson/Kalliopi Kanaki et al.*, Physics and IAEA: Atoms for Peace and Development, Nuclear Physics News 33 (2023), 10–14.

593 Article 31 para. 3(b); *International Law Commission*, Draft Conclusion on Subsequent Agreements and Subsequent Practice in Relation to the Interpretation of Treaties, in: United Nations (ed.), Yearbook of the International Law Commission, Volume II, Part Two, New York: United Nations 2018, 23–88, Conclusion 3.

IAEA's General Conference,[594] underlying that they consider the IAEA as the competent international organisation for questions relating to fusion. Similarly, there is no other international organisation where States have raised questions of fusion to a similar extent. Thus, the subsequent practise of the States warrants and extensive interpretation of *atomic energy*.

In addition to States' subsequent practise, subsequent practise by the international organisation itself can be of relevance in interpreting its constituent treaty.[595] An international organisation's subsequent practise can either be seen as subsequent practise by its Member States or as autonomous subsequent practise, depending on the degree of involvement of Member States.[596] While the former is directly covered by Article 31 para. 3(b) VCLT, the latter requires further justification under international law.[597] These justifications include explicit or implied powers granted by the States in the Statute of the international organisation. As the IAEA is charged with the promotion of atomic energy and is equipped with several powers to fulfill this mandate,[598] the Statute explicitly mandates the IAEA to act. As the Statute expects practise from the IAEA, it is justified to take into account the subsequent practise of the Agency in order to interpret the term *atomic energy* in Article II of the Statute.

The IAEA has demonstrated subsequent practise regarding fusion, further supporting the interpretation that the Agency's mandate covers fusion. Since 1960, only three years after its creation, the IAEA is the publisher of the academic journal *Nuclear Fusion*, which is one of the leading scientific publications in the field of plasma physics and fusion research. In addition, the IAEA hosts several conferences, workshops and other events with relation to fusion, including the biannual Fusion Energy Conference, which it has hosted since 1961. Moreover, since 2023, the IAEA has been publishing its World Fusion Outlook annually,[599] in which the international organisa-

594 See for example the Statements during the 68th General Meeting by Japan in GC(68)/OR.1 para. 31; Italy in GC(68)/OR.2 para. 114; Spain in GC(68)/OR.3 para. 50 and Australia in GC(68)/OR.11 para. 21.

595 *International Law Commission* (n 593), Conclusion 12.

596 *Christopher Peters*, Praxis Internationaler Organisationen – Vertragswandel und völkerrechtlicher Ordnungsrahmen, Berlin, Heidelberg: Springer 2016, at 182 ff.

597 An overview of argumentative approaches is given by ibid, at 216 ff.

598 Articles VIII to XII.

599 *International Atomic Energy Agency*, IAEA World Fusion Outlook 2023 – Fusion Energy: Present and Future, Vienna: IAEA 2023; *International Atomic Energy Agency*, IAEA World Fusion Outlook 2024, Vienna: IAEA 2024.

tion displays itself as a "hub for fusion research & development."[600] The documents seek to find fusion's role within several international treaties adopted under the IAEA's auspices and where it acts as depositary.[601] Furthermore, the General Conference, i.e. the body of the IAEA where every Member State is represented, has mandated the Secretariat to analyse the legal, institutional, safety and regulatory dimensions of fusion.[602] In addition, the IAEA has started a process in which it analyses safety aspects of fusion.[603] As States participate in these activities or at least do not object them,[604] the IAEA's subsequent practise also reflects the practise of Member States, further allowing for its consideration under Article 31 (3)(b) VCLT. Consequently, fusion energy is part of the IAEA's broader mandate of promoting the atom for peace and development.

1.1.2 Fusion and the Peaceful Use of the Atom

As it is in nuclear weapons law, where the IAEA's characterisation as *nuclear watchdog* comes from, this section examines how far the IAEA's authority extends with its mandate to ensure the peaceful use of the atom. This mandate is delineated in two articles of the Statute. While Article III.A.5 provides the overarching principles of the IAEA's authority with regard to safeguards, Article XII provides the details of the IAEA's competences and powers.

1.1.2.1 Article III.A.5 of the IAEA Statute

The IAEA's motto of promoting atoms for peace and development are materialised in what the Statute calls "functions" of the Agency and are further described in Article III of the Statute. This article provides for a range of aspects under the broader mandate of atoms for peace and development and specifies the extent of the IAEA's authority.

600 *International Atomic Energy Agency*, IAEA World Fusion Outlook 2023 (n 599), at 4.

601 Ibid, at 23 ff.

602 Ibid, at 87.

603 IAEA TECDOC Series 2076, Experiences for Consideration in Fusion Power Plant Design Safety and Safety Assessment.

604 On the role of *acquiescence* of States in interpreting an international organisation's constitutive treaty *Anne Peters*, Das Gründungsdokument internationaler Organisationen als Verfassungsvertrag, Zeitschrift für öffentliches Recht 68 (2013), 1–57, at 48.

With regard to safeguards, according to Article III.A.5 of its Statute, the IAEA has the authority

> *to establish and administer safeguards designed to ensure that special fissionable and other materials, services, equipment, facilities, and information made available by the Agency or at its request [...] are not used in such a ways as to further any military purposes; and to apply safeguards, at the request of the parties, to any bilateral or multilateral arrangement, or at the request of a State, to any of that State's activities in the field of atomic energy.*

Or in short terms, the IAEA has the authority to apply safeguards in two circumstances: Firstly, if the IAEA functions as a supplier of nuclear material, equipment or technology similar to Euratom; and secondly, if States request the IAEA to administer safeguards.

Despite the fact that the IAEA has been envisaged to also function as a global uranium bank and thus as a supplier,[605] the IAEA has never assumed such a role. The IAEA's involvement in this aspect is limited to training and support through its Technical Cooperation Programme,[606] where the IAEA does not provide any material, including material used in fusion. Similarly, the IAEA does not provide States with any detailed information on fusion power plants. Thus, this provision of the IAEA Statute is currently not in use, thus also not applicable to fusion, but this might change in the future. As fusion is covered by the broad mandate of atoms for peace and development, the IAEA would have the powers to act actively in the promotion of fusion, including fusion in its Technical Cooperation Programme or other future support programmes. One such option might be the administration of rare tritium resources as "other materials" in the sense of Article III.A.5 of the Statute, since an external tritium supply is necessary for the first power up of a fusion facility. This provision in the Statute provides the IAEA with the authority to act as a tritium bank in case its Member States request the Agency to take up such a role. Such a scenario then would require the application of safeguards under Article III.A.5.

605 *Elisabeth Röhrlich*, Inspectors for Peace, Baltimore: John Hopkins University Press 2022, at 41.

606 Article III.A.1 of the IAEA Statute. An overview of the IAEA's role in the development of nuclear energy programmes is found at *International Atomic Energy Agency*, Technical Cooperation Report for 2022, GC(67)/INF/5, Vienna: IAEA 2023, at 82 f.

This leaves the second subclause as the only case where the IAEA currently exercises its mandate under Article III.A.5: The request by Parties to apply safeguards following an agreement or a unilateral request. As the Article only requires a request to administer safeguards, this subclause is sufficiently broad to include fusion. In the event that IAEA Member States or an agreement requests the IAEA to administer safeguards on fusionable material and/or fusion facilities, the IAEA has the mandate to do so under Article III.A.5. The most prominent example of an agreement requesting the IAEA to administer safeguards is the NPT, but this also includes the TPNW and NWFZ Treaties. Their application to fusion will be analysed below.

1.1.2.2 Article XII of the IAEA Statute

Once the IAEA applies safeguards following such an agreement or request, Article XII of the Statute defines "rights and responsibilities" of the IAEA. While the application of safeguards on fusion depends on the exact agreement (see below), the Statute already gives some cornerstones to the application of safeguards, with some of these cornerstones applicable to fusion and others not.

Firstly, where the mandate applies to fusion: According to Article XII.A.1, the IAEA has the competence to examine designs of specialised equipment and facilities, including nuclear reactors. The purpose of the paragraph is to ensure that such equipment and facilities "will not further any military purpose" and that it "will permit effective application of safeguards." As the phrasing is not limited to fission, such a design review includes the role of fusion in ensuring that the facility is not supporting military purposes. In addition, according to Article XII.A.4, the IAEA has the right to call for and receive progress reports. As this paragraph does not focus on fission, the IAEA can demand reports on fusionable material and from fusion facilities.

However, the mandate of the IAEA has its limitations. This is due to the fact that many provisions limit themselves to *source or special fissionable material*. The IAEA has the right to require the maintenance and production of records and accounting for *source and special fissionable materials*. In addition, the most important part of IAEA safeguards, sending inspectors into the State territory to access at all times all places and data as well as persons involved in the operations, is limited to account for *source and special fissionable material*. The notion of *source and special fissionable material* is defined in Article XX of the IAEA Statute. The next section analyses whether Article XX of the IAEA Statute covers the application of IAEA safeguards to fusion.

1.1.2.3 Article XX of the IAEA Statute

Article XX of the IAEA Statute defines the key term *source and special fissionable material.*

Source material is defined in Article XX.3 of the IAEA Statute as "uranium containing the mixture of isotopes occurring in nature; uranium depleted in the isotope 235; thorium any of the foregoing in the form of metal, alloy chemical compound, or concentrate; any other material containing one or more of the foregoing in such as the Board of Governors shall from time to time determine; and such other materials as the Board of Governors shall from time to time determine."

Special fissionable material is defined in Article XX.1 of the IAEA Statute as "plutonium-239, uranium-233, uranium enriched in the isotopes 235 or 233, any material containing one or more of the foregoing, and such other fissionable material as the Board of Governors shall from time to time determine." Uranium, thorium and plutonium are atoms that can only undergo fission, not fusion.

Even if one disregards the explicit list of elements, there are other indications why there is no interpretation of *source and special fissionable material* which could include fusionable material. As has been highlighted by both international courts[607] and academia[608], science plays an important role in the interpretation of treaty provisions. In order to determine the ordinary meaning in the sense of the general rule of interpretation, as

607 *International Tribunal for the Law of the Sea*, Advisory Opinion, Request for an Advisory Opinion Submitted by the Commission of Small Island States on Climate Change and International Law, 21 May 2024, Case No. 31; *International Court of Justice*, Whaling in the Antarctic (Australia v. Japan: New Zealand intervening), Judgment, ICJ Reports 2014, p. 226.

608 David Duarte/Pedro Moniz Lopes/Jorge Silva Sampio (eds.), Legal Interpretation and Scientific Knowledge, Heidelberg: Springer 2019. On the increased role of science in international courts, see *Katalin Sulyok*, Science and Judicial Reasoning: The Legitimacy of International Environmental Adjudication, Cambridge: Cambridge University Press 2020.

reflected under customary law[609] and Article 31 para. 1 VCLT, reference to physics is necessary.

The fuels most likely to be used in commercial fusion power plants are tritium and deuterium, with ^{6}Li also playing a role as it is used to produce tritium within the fusion machine. These materials are neither uranium nor thorium nor plutonium; thus, they are not covered by the definition provided by the IAEA Statute. These materials are lighter than iron. As illustrated in Figure (1) in Chapter 1, there is a clear physical distinction between fusionable and fissionable material. Atoms that are heavier than iron undergo fission, while only those atoms lighter than iron undergo fusion. Each atom can be divided into distinct blocks of either being fissionable or fusionable. Given this clear difference, fusionable material, such as deuterium or tritium, cannot be considered fissionable material. Deuterium and tritium can only undergo nuclear fusion, not fission. Consequently, these materials are not fissionable material. The ordinary meaning in the sense of the general rule of interpretation (Article 31 para. 1 VCLT) is limited to the enumerated material of specific uranium and thorium isotopes.

Other interpretative methods do not allow for an inclusion of fusionable material under the term of fissionable material as well. The purpose of the provision is to prevent the specific dual use nature inherent in fissionable material. As highlighted in Chapter 1, the connection between a fission power plant and a nuclear weapon is close given the physics involved. This is in contrast to fusion, where the material only plays more of a secondary role within a broader nuclear weapons programme. Similarly, the historical application of the treaty provisions is limited to the materials explicitly listed in Article XX, or at least other fissionable materials.

Given the focus on source and special fissionable material and its narrow definition in Article XX, fusionable material is outside the scope of the provisions of the Statute that refer to source or special fissionable material.

609 *International Court of Justice*, Case Concerning the Arbitral Award of 31 July 1989 (Guinea-Bissau v. Senegal), Judgment, ICJ Reports 1991, p. 53, para. 48; *Anthony Aust/Oliver Dörr*, Vienna Convention on the Law of Treaties (1969), in: Anne Peters/Rüdiger Wolfrum (eds.), Max Planck Encyclopedia of Public International Law, Heidelberg, Oxford: Oxford University Press 2023, at paras 14 ff.; *Oliver Dörr*, Article 31, in: Oliver Dörr/Kirsten Schmalenbach (eds.), Vienna Convention on the Law of Treaties – A Commentary, Heidelberg: Springer 2018, 559–616, at paras 6 ff.; *Matthias Herdegen*, Interpretation in International Law, in: Anne Peters/Rüdiger Wolfrum (eds.), Max Planck Encyclopedia of Public International Law, Heidelberg, Oxford: Oxford University Press 2020, at para. 7 with further references. Wherever the VCLT is used for interpretation, the findings presented in this chapter are equally valid under the customary rule.

Despite the use or occurrence of deuterium and tritium in the fission cycle, these materials are not covered by the scope of IAEA safeguards.

This limitation does not mean that inspecting fusion facilities would be outside the IAEA's mandate. Yet, the default safeguarding authority by the IAEA created by the request by States or agreements to apply safeguards would not suffice to apply the same safeguards to fusion as the IAEA currently applies to fission, as this authority is limited to fissionable material. Only if a State or treaty specifically demands the IAEA to apply safeguards to fusion, the IAEA has the authority to extend its safeguarding activities to fusionable material and the fusion fuel cycle.

1.1.3 Summary

The IAEA's mandate to promote atoms for peace and development includes promoting fusion. The IAEA's authority to administer safeguards, however, is constrained by the system's focus on *source and special fissionable material*, not including fusion technology in IAEA safeguards unless another treaty explicitly mandates the IAEA to apply safeguards on fusion technology. Without such an explicit referral by Parties or Treaties, the extent to which safeguards are described in the Statute limits the scope of application of safeguards to fusion to a general level, exempting large parts of the IAEA's verification activities.

1.2 Fusion and the NPT

While the NPT is not a treaty under the auspices of the IAEA, rather a treaty created under the UN regime, the treaty mandates the IAEA to implement measures to verify the compliance of NNWS with the obligation not to acquire nuclear weapons, a possibility opened by Article III.A.5 of the IAEA Statute. This section analyses the extent and limitations to which the NPT applies to fusion.

1.2.1 Article I NPT

Article I NPT allows NWS to possess nuclear weapons. The term *nuclear weapon* is commonly defined, both by academia[610] and jurisprudence[611], as "explosives that derive their destructive force from either fission or fusion of atomic nuclides." The inclusion of fusion weapons within this definition is supported by a historic argument: Research on thermonuclear weapons began as early as in 1949, with numerous tests in the following decade. Thus, following an interpretation according to Articles 31 para. 1 and 32 of the VCLT, a weapon using fusion processes is a nuclear weapon in the sense of the NPT. As nuclear weapons include both fission and fusion driven nuclear weapons, the NPT allows NWS to use nuclear fusion research and reactors for military purposes. Fusion is relevant for both the miniaturisation of nuclear warheads and the increase of the yield for strategic nuclear weapons, thus there is a specific relevance for vertical proliferation. The NPT only prohibits horizontal proliferation, not vertical.[612] Consequently, NWS are permitted by the NPT to utilise fusion processes and fusion research in their nuclear weapons programmes.

1.2.2 Article II NPT

Article II NPT is what makes the NPT the non-proliferation treaty: Non-nuclear weapon States are obliged to maintain their non-nuclear status and are prohibited from receiving the transfer of, manufacturing or any other acquisition of nuclear weapons under any circumstances. The application of this norm to fusion is unambiguous. If a NNWS uses fusion research to

610 *Stefan Kadelbach*, Nuclear Weapons and Warfare, in: Anne Peters/Rüdiger Wolfrum (eds.), Max Planck Encyclopedia of Public International Law, Heidelberg, Oxford: Oxford University Press 2019; *Stuart Casey-Maslen*, The Impact of the TPNW on the Nuclear Non-Proliferation Regime, in: Jonathan L. Black-Branch/Dieter Fleck (eds.), Nuclear Non-Proliferation in International Law – Volume VI: Nuclear Disarmament and Security at Risk – Legal Challenges in a Shifting Nuclear World, The Hague: T.M.C. Asser Press 2021, 385–409, at 388.

611 *International Court of Justice*, Legality of the Threat and Use of Nuclear Weapons, Advisory Opinion, Reports 1996, p. 226, at para. 35.

612 On the critique of vertical proliferation being outside the NPT, see *Tarja Cronberg*, For Survival, the NPT Has to Be Renegotiated in: European Leadership Network, https://www.europeanleadershipnetwork.org/commentary/for-survival-the-npt-has-to-be-renegotiated/, last accessed 17 July 2025.

develop a nuclear weapon, that State is in violation of its obligations under the NPT.

These considerations are especially true for two of the three above-mentioned proliferation risks. In the event of a fusion facility in a NNWS producing plutonium for use in a weapon, the State is in violation of Article II of the NPT. Similarly, if a NNWS uses inertial confinement research to build a hydrogen bomb, the manufacturing and later possession of that weapon is a violation of Article II of the NPT. Regarding the use of tritium, the role of Article II is not clear. If a NNWS uses tritium produced in a fusion facility to boost a nuclear weapon, the possession of the nuclear weapon itself is the violation of Article II of the NPT. It is debatable if the mere act of boosting an existent weapon constitutes a separate violation of Article II of the NPT, as the original act of acquiring a nuclear weapon already constitutes a violation.

1.2.3 Safeguards: Article III.1 NPT

Article III.1 of the NPT is of fundamental importance to the safeguards system, as it introduces mandatory safeguards for NNWS. Following this article, all NNWS are required to enter into a safeguards agreement with the IAEA. Article III.A.5 of the IAEA's Statute expressly extends the safeguarding authority to any bi- or multilateral arrangement upon request by the relevant Parties. This system aims to prevent the diversion of nuclear energy to nuclear weapons or other nuclear explosive devices.[613] Fusion is of relevance for the non-proliferation framework as it plays a role under both Articles I and II of the NPT. While compliance of NNWS with Article II is ensured by the safeguards system, this section shows that the scope of the NPT's safeguards provision does not extend to fusion.

1.2.3.1 Objective of Article III.1 NPT

Article III.1 of the NPT introduces the connection between the NNWS' obligation not to possess nuclear weapons and the implementation of this obligation by mandating nuclear safeguards. NNWS are required to accept

613 Art. III. 1 of the NPT. The distinction between nuclear weapons and other nuclear explosive devices stems from plans by some States to use nuclear explosions for civilian purposes such as excavation.

the discriminatory nature of the NPT and they have to accept the exercise of authority by the IAEA in verifying the State's compliance with its obligations assumed under the NPT. Given the significance of fusion within Article II NPT, verifying a State's compliance is necessary with regard to fusion.

The objective of NPT safeguards would include fusion. According to Article III.1 cl. 1, the goal of the inspection is the "verification of the fulfilment of [the NNWS's] obligations assumed under this Treaty, with a view of prevention diversion of nuclear energy from peaceful uses to nuclear weapons." It is evident that the NPT does not limit the purpose of its inspections to nuclear fission, rather it looks at *nuclear energy* at its entirety.[614] As argued above, fusion energy is a specific form of nuclear energy, also in the sense of the NPT.

While the objective of Article III.1 would include verifying fusion, the scope of the safeguards required by Article III.1 of the NPT is constrained by two core requirements that must be met in order for safeguards to apply: The presence of *source or special fissionable material* being produced, processed or used in or outside a *principal nuclear facility*. In this section, interpretative methods are applied to show that this article does not cover the application of NPT safeguards to fusion.

1.2.3.2 Source or Special Fissionable Material

Safeguards under the NPT are mainly material-based, meaning that Article III.1 of the NPT mandates safeguards to control the use, amounts and location of this specific kind of material. Notably, unlike other international agreements on nuclear non-proliferation and disarmament, the NPT does not contain a definition of the term *source or special fissionable material.* However, the Statute of the IAEA, as mentioned above, contains such definition of source or special fissionable material.

The question arises whether the interpretation of *fissionable material* of Article XX of the IAEA Statute is identical to *fissionable material* in the sense of the NPT. The first indication of this is the exact same wording. The second indication is the context of the provision. The treaty makes reference to source and special fissionable material in Article III, wherein the two verification mechanisms are introduced: safeguards and export

614 *George Bunn*, Nuclear Safeguards – How Far Can Inspectors Go?, IAEA Bulletin 48–2 (2007), 49–55.

controls. Article III.1 mandates the IAEA to apply its safeguards system in accordance with its Statute, thereby strongly indicating an understanding of fissionable material in the sense of the IAEA Statute. Otherwise, there could be a collision between the required safeguards by the NPT and the IAEA Statute and thus, the treaty would not bring its intended effects. In accordance with Article 31 para. 2 VCLT, the preamble is also relevant in exploring the context of a treaty provision and thus in the application of the general rule of interpretation. According to the preamble of the NPT, the Parties to the Treaty undertake to cooperate in facilitating the application of IAEA safeguards on peaceful nuclear activities. In addition, they express their support to further the application of effectively safeguarding the flow of source and special fissionable material within the framework of the IAEA safeguards system given pre-existing safeguards. Accordingly, the meaning of *fissionable material* in the sense of the NPT is to be interpreted in the sense of Article XX of the IAEA Statute.

The only application of this notion to fusion is in the context of the first proliferation potential mentioned above, i.e. using a fusion reactor to produce nuclear weapons material. If a proliferator uses fusion processes as an intense neutron source to produce plutonium from uranium, the material in question is specifically listed in Article XX.1 of the IAEA Statute. However, as a civilian fusion facility does not customarily handle fissionable material, the IAEA would not apply safeguards to such a facility.

Article III.1 is not applicable to the proliferation potential of the use of tritium. As analysed above, fusionable material cannot be understood as fissionable material under Article XX of the IAEA Statute. Consequently, Article III.1 of the NPT seems to not apply to tritium.

This finding that fusionable material is not covered by the scope of Article III.1 is further supported by statements issued by NPT Member States in the context of the negotiations and ratification. The United States articulated during the NPT negotiations its view that the NPT would not affect thermonuclear fusion technology.[615] Germany made reference to the US statement in its depositary note and emphasised that the treaty "may never be interpreted or applied in such way to hamper or inhibit

615 Statement by United States *Ambassador Goldberg*, Security Assurances and the Nonproliferation of Nuclear Weapons, May 15, 1968, Documents on Disarmament 1968, United States Arms Control And Disarmament Agency (1969), 336–345, p. 344.

research and development in this sphere."[616] Although such interpretative declarations are outside the scope of the VCLT,[617] they can nevertheless be taken into account in interpreting a treaty.[618]

Consequently, Article III.1 of the NPT does not apply to fusionable material and is limited to fissionable material.

1.2.3.3 Principal Nuclear Facility

Secondly, safeguards following Article III.1 apply to source or special fissionable material *in- or outside a principal nuclear facility*, thereby establishing a second requirement for the application of the NPT's safeguards provision. In contrast to *source or special fissionable material*, the term *facility* is not defined by the IAEA Statute.

The context (Article 31 para. 1 VLCT) speaks against the inclusion of fusion facilities under the term *nuclear facility* under the NPT. First, the term is used in the context of source and special fissionable material. As safeguards apply to source and special fissionable material inside and outside a nuclear facility, the NPT assumes a facility, which is part of the fission fuel cycle, as the primary location to find source and special fissionable material. This material, as will be shown below, is referred to as *nuclear material* in subsequent agreements and practice (Article 31 para. 2(b) VCLT). Thus, the term nuclear facility is used in the context of nuclear material, while nuclear material is fissionable material. The context, hence, indicates a limitation to fission facilities.

However, the ordinary meaning does not preclude the application to fusion facilities. Fusion processes are nuclear processes, thus a facility where nuclear fusion takes place can – linguistically and scientifically – be considered a nuclear facility. The purpose of the term supports this finding. The decision to include nuclear facility was to give the IAEA the freedom to develop a safeguards system that does not solely focus on

616 Germany's Depositary Note is available in UN Treaty Series, volume 729, at 267 ff., with a reference to fusion on p. 268.

617 *Malgosia Fitzmaurice*, Treaties, in: Anne Peters/Rüdiger Wolfrum (eds.), Max Planck Encyclopedia of Public International Law, Heidelberg, Oxford: Oxford University Press 2021, at para. 73.

618 Article 4.7.1 of the ILC Guide to Practice on Reservations to Treaties (2011); *D. M. McRae*, The Legal Effect of Interpretative Declarations, British Yearbook of International Law 49 (1979), 155–173, at 169.

nuclear material.[619] While the focus of this article is on material, such material is referenced in relation to a nuclear facility. The combination of material and facility under the NPT has historic reasons. Pre-NPT safeguards under INFCIRC/66 included safeguards for nuclear materials *and* principal nuclear facilities.[620] The language of safeguarding material inside and outside any principal nuclear facility was a compromise to leave it open to the IAEA on how material-focused (meaning safeguards to primarily apply on nuclear material) or facility-focused (meaning safeguards to apply primarily on nuclear facilities) the safeguards system should be.[621] Thus, the purpose of the term "principal nuclear facility" is to extend the IAEA's flexibility in implementing safeguards agreements. Such a flexibility speaks against a narrow interpretation which only focuses on fission facilities. Furthermore, a teleological interpretation,[622] i.e., giving the definition the greatest possible effect in order to ensure the objective of non-proliferation, leads to the conclusion that any facility where nuclear processes occur and which has the capacity to support nuclear weapons programmes should be considered a principal nuclear facility. This includes a fusion facility.

As the application of the general rule of interpretation leaves some ambiguity, recourse to historic arguments may be made (Article 32(a) VCLT). Historic arguments both speak for and against the inclusion of fusion facilities in the definition of a nuclear facility. The IAEA interprets the term to exclude fusion facilities and does not apply safeguards to fusion facilities.[623] As the IAEA is an international organisation that applies a treaty within

619 *Ben Sanders*, IAEA Safeguards: A Short Historical Background, in: David Fischer/Ben Sanders/Lawrence Scheinman/George Bunn (eds.), A New Nuclear Triad: The Non-Proliferation of Nuclear Weapons, International Verification and the International Atomic Energy Agency, Southampton: Mountbatten Centre for International Studies, University of Southampton 1992, 1–13, at 3 ff.

620 INFCIRC/66/Rev.2, at para. 45.

621 *George Bunn*, Does the NPT Require its Non-Nuclear-Weapon Parties to Permit Inspections by the IAEA of Nuclear Activities that have not been Reported to the IAEA?, in: David Fischer/Ben Sanders/Lawrence Scheinman/George Bunn (eds.), A New Nuclear Triad: The Non-Proliferation of Nuclear Weapons, International Verification and the International Atomic Energy Agency, Southampton: Mountbatten Centre for International Studies, University of Southampton 1992, 44–58, at 52.

622 Teleological interpretation is based on the object and purpose as part of Article 31 para. 1 VCLT's canon, *Herdegen* (n 609), at para. 14.

623 *International Atomic Energy Agency*, IAEA World Fusion Outlook 2023 (n 599), at 25.

its mandate, it has the right to interpret a treaty.[624] Such an interpretation stands next to the interpretation of all other actors, including States and international courts.[625]

What speaks historically for an inclusion of fusion facilities under the term of nuclear facility is the fact that fusion and its role in weapons have been known in 1968 when the NPT was concluded. Nuclear fusion is known since the 1930s, even predating the discovery of nuclear fission.[626] Thermonuclear weapons based on fusion research for military purposes have been proposed during the Manhattan Project in the early 1940s.[627] The first thermonuclear explosion took place in 1951.[628] Major research facilities were established in the 1950s and 1960s, such as the Princeton Plasma Physics Laboratory in 1951, the Max-Planck-Institute for Plasma Physics in 1960 or the Culham Centre for Fusion Energy in 1965. In addition, the aforementioned comments by the United States and Germany during the negotiations and ratification process support the finding that the inclusion of fusion facilities has been considered in the negotiations. The lack of a clarification of the meaning of "principal nuclear facility" indicates – also from a historic argument – that fusion facilities are within the scope of this term.

Apart from Germany and the United States, there are no records of States mentioning fusion in the non-proliferation context. Furthermore, there are no records of States requiring the IAEA to apply safeguards to fusion research facilities. In addition, the IAEA does not regularly inspect

624 *Richard K. Gardiner*, Treaty Interpretation, Oxford: Oxford University Press 2015, at 125; *Paul Reuter*, Introduction to the Law of Treaties, London, New York: Kegan Paul International 1995, at 95; *Dörr* (n 609), at 568 f. The ICJ accepted the UN Security Council's authority to interpret its own resolutions in *International Court of Justice*, Kosovo Unilateral Declaration of Independence, Advisory Opinion, ICJ Reports 404, at 442, para. 94.

625 *Gardiner* (n 624), at 125; *Reuter* (n 624), at 95; *Dörr* (n 609), at 568 f.

626 Fusion has first been described by *Marcus Laurence Elwin Oliphant/Ernest Rutherford*, Experiments on the Transmutation of Elements by Protons, Proceedings of the Royal Society of London. Series A, Containing Papers of a Mathematical and Physical Character 141 (1933), 259–281, while fission was first described by *Otto Hahn/Fritz Strassmann*, Über den Nachweis und das Verhalten der bei der Bestrahlung des Urans mittels Neutronen entstehenden Erdalkalimetalle, Naturwissenschaften 27 (1939), 11–15 and *Lise Meitner/Otto R. Frisch*, Disintegration of Uranium by Neutrons: a New Type of Nuclear Reaction, Nature 143 (1939), 239–240.

627 *Herbert F. York*, The Advisors: Oppenheimer, Teller, and the Superbomb, Stanford: Stanford University Press 1989, at 62.

628 The so-called Ivy Mike weapon exploded on 1 November 1952 during a test conducted by the United States.

fusion research facilities. Fusion has only been relevant in advanced NWS, but in NNWS has been limited to academic research and experiments, not necessitating the attention of the IAEA or other States under the non-proliferation regime. Whether or not the safeguards system will be applied in the future once fusion power plants exist is a discussion that has just recently started. The historical practise indicates that a fusion facility does not fall within the scope of "principal nuclear facility."

Consequently, it remains an open question whether a fusion facility qualifies as a principal nuclear facility within the meaning of Article III.1 of the NPT, as compelling arguments exist on both sides without a predominating position.

1.2.3.4 Summary

While the purpose of safeguards is to verify compliance of NNWS with their obligations not to possess nuclear weapons assumed under Article II NPT, the mandated safeguards regime of Article III.1 of the NPT largely do not include fusion, or is at least ambiguous in its applicability. As the article focuses on *source and special fissionable material*, safeguards under the NPT do not apply on *fusionable material.* While safeguards have nuclear facilities as starting point for its application, it is ambiguous whether a fusion facility would fall under the scope of the provision. Ambiguity remains whether a fusion facility can be considered a *principal nuclear facility.*

1.2.4 Export Controls: Article III.2 NPT

Next to safeguards, export controls are the second verification mechanism of the NPT as mandated by Article III.2 NPT. However, the application of export controls on fusion faces the same obstacle as the safeguards provision: The restriction to *source and special fissionable material,* as set out in the IAEA Statute and Article III.1 NPT. Article III.2 NPT contains the same limitation for the application of export controls. State Parties are under the obligation not to provide source or special fissionable material or equipment or material especially designed or prepared for the processing, use or production of such material, unless that material is subject to safeguards. Export controls are based on *source or special fissionable material* or technology with a direct link to such material. As a consequence, the NPT does not mandate export controls for a fusion fuel cycle.

1.2.5 Summary

The application of the NPT to fusion shows gaps and is in parts ambiguous. NWS are allowed to use fusion technology for their nuclear weapons, while the prohibition for NNWS to use nuclear technology for the development of nuclear weapons extends to both fission and fusion. However, Article III, which introduces the verification mechanisms of safeguards and export controls to ensure the compliance of NNWS, does not apply to a large extent to fusion. Both safeguards and export controls mandated under the NPT limit themselves to *source and special fissionable material* or technology related to such material, thereby excluding its application to fusion.

1.3 Fusion and Safeguards Agreements

This section analyses the applicability of various types of safeguards agreements to fusion. There are two fundamental questions regarding their application to fusion: Firstly, do safeguards apply to fusionable material – especially deuterium, tritium and ^{6}Li? Secondly, do safeguards apply to a fusion facility, regardless of whether the material present is fissionable or fusionable?

To recall, there are different types of safeguards agreements. NNWS under the NPT have Comprehensive Safeguards Agreements (CSAs) in place. The majority of them also have concluded an Additional Protocol (AP). NWS outside the NPT have concluded so-called item-specific safeguards agreements, based on INFCIRC/26 and INFCIRC/66. NWS recognised by the NPT have concluded Voluntary Offer Agreements. In all these cases, safeguards agreements are concluded bilaterally with the IAEA.

1.3.1 Comprehensive Safeguards Agreements

Comprehensive Safeguards Agreements put in place the safeguards that are mandated by Article III.1 of the NPT. Within these agreements, the States specify the rights and privileges of the IAEA with regard to the verification of the non-diversion of nuclear material from civilian to military purposes.

There is a notable difference between the CSAs and the NPT: CSAs use a different wording compared to the NPT's safeguards mandate of Article III.1. These agreements use the term *nuclear material* instead of *source and special fissionable material* and refer to *facilities* instead of *principal nuclear facilities*. This section explores whether the use of different wordings allows for the application of CSAs to fusion.

1.3.1.1 Nuclear Material

Wherever obligations of States and procedures are described, the agreement uses the term "nuclear material"[629] or "*nuclear material* subject to safeguards."[630] The ordinary meaning of the term would allow fusionable material to be covered, as fusionable material can undergo nuclear fusion which is a nuclear process. However, paragraph 112 of the CSA refers to the definition of nuclear material in Article XX of the IAEA Statute. As analysed above, it is not possible to include fusionable material within the definition of Article XX of the IAEA Statute. Therefore, the safeguards regime circumscribed by the CSA is limited to fissionable material and does not include fusionable material.

1.3.1.2 Facility

While the CSA does not allow the IAEA to inspect fusionable material, there would still be a benefit if a fusion facility falls under the CSA. One proliferation potential of fusion comes from the technology's capability to transform uranium into plutonium. As both these materials are *source or special fissionable material*, and thus fall under the scope of nuclear material, inspecting fusion facilities for the absence of nuclear material would still be a key measure in addressing at least one of fusion's proliferation potential.

The CSA uses the term *facility* in a general sense, in contrast to the NPT, which refers to *principal nuclear facility*. According to para. 106 of the CSA, a facility is defined as "a reactor, a critical facility, a conversion plant, a fabrication plant, a reprocessing plant, an isotope separation plant or a separate storage installation" or "any location where nuclear material in amounts greater than one effective kilogram is customarily used." This section analyses whether a fusion fuel cycle will include facilities that might be put under one of these elements of the definition, allowing the IAEA to inspect them.

629 See for example paras 4–8, 11–14.
630 Ibid.

Critical Facility

A critical facility is a facility where criticality can be reached, meaning to sustain a chain reaction of fission events.[631] A fusion facility is not a critical facility as criticality is exclusively associated with sustaining a chain reaction of fission events.[632] Fusion does not include chain reactions as, unlike in fission, it is not the previous reaction that induces the following reaction. Conversely, the energy production in fusion is maintained by constant external influence, such as magnetic fields or lasers (depending on the confinement method of the fusion reactor), heat and fuel supply.

Conversion Plant

A conversion plant is a facility where the chemical composition of nuclear material is converted with the purpose for facilitating its use or processing.[633] The IAEA Safeguards Glossary lists the conversion of uranium ore into uranium hexafluoride (UF_6) as an example. Such a conversion is necessary for the enrichment process of fission fuel. Another example is the conversion from UF_6 into uranium dioxide (UO_2), a process used in the fuel production for fission reactors. These processes are specific for fission. In fusion, no enrichment is necessary, thus, there is no chemical conversion similar to fission prior the use of the fuel. Furthermore, since the fuel is simply hydrogen gas (both in magnetic confinement and inertial confinement[634]), there is no conversion necessary for the fuel production. Consequently, the fusion fuel cycle does not include a conversion plant.

Fabrication Plant

A fuel fabrication plant is limited to plants that manufacture fuel elements or other reactor components containing nuclear material.[635] Examples of fuel elements include the fuel rod or fuel pellet elements. In fusion, it depends on the confinement method if one could speak of fuel elements.

---

631 *International Atomic Energy Agency*, IAEA Safeguards Glossary, Vienna: IAEA 2022, at para. 4.55.

632 See for example ibid, at para. 4.55; *David Hafemeister*, Physics of Societal Issues: Calculations on National Security, Environment, and Energy, Springer 2016, at 8 ff.

633 *International Atomic Energy Agency* (n 631), at para. 4.56.

634 The only difference between magnetic and inertial confinement is that in ICF the gas is inside a spherical shell, see *Garry McCracken/Peter Stott*, Chapter 7 – Inertial-Confinement Fusion, in: Garry McCracken/Peter Stott (eds.), Fusion (Second Edition), Boston: Academic Press 2013, 67–81, at 67.

635 *International Atomic Energy Agency* (n 631), at para. 4.57.

Inertial confinement fusion uses fuel pellets, which contain the fusionable material, and these are manufactured in a dedicated facility. However, as these fusion pellets fabrication plants do not involve the handling of nuclear material in the sense of the CSA, they do not fall under the classification of a fuel fabrication plant. In the case of magnetic confinement fusion, it is even clearer as the fuel is simply gas that is introduced into the fusion device. One could then focus on the plant that produces the fusionable material, e.g. deuterium and tritium. Deuterium is produced in heavy water production plants and is then separated from oxygen through electrolysis. Heavy water plants are only of limited interest under current IAEA safeguards.[636] Tritium will be produced on site of the fusion facility, not requiring a facility on a separate site. As a consequence, the fusion fuel cycle does not include a fabrication plant in the sense of the CSA. Plants to fabricate the blanket for fusion facilities come close to a fabrication plant in fission, however they also do not use nuclear material.

Reprocessing Plan

A reprocessing plant is a facility that undertakes the reprocessing of nuclear material.[637] Reprocessing is the separation of nuclear material from fission products in irradiated nuclear material.[638] While waste from fusion facilities will contain irradiated material, fusion waste will not be treated in conventionally defined reprocessing plants as they do not intend to separate nuclear material from the waste.

Isotope Separation Plant

An isotope separation facility is an enrichment plant.[639] The typical example is a plant in which uranium gets enriched in its isotope U-235. This process is specific to fission and has no relevance for the fusion fuel cycle. However, the definition is not limited to specific isotopes. Fusion requires isotope separation, mainly for ^{6}Li, opening the door for some parts of the fusion fuel cycle to being covered by existing definitions.

636 They are limited to the provision of a description of the scale of operations and only for those States that have ratified the Additional Protocol, Article 2.a.iv and Annex I para. xi Additional Protocol. The Additional Protocol refers to deuterium as "non-nuclear material for reactors." The application of safeguards to heavy water is extremely limited, *Martin Kalinowski*, International Control of Tritium for Nuclear Nonproliferation and Disarmament, Boca Raton: CRC Press 2004, at 195.

637 *International Atomic Energy Agency* (n 631), at para. 4.58.

638 Ibid, at para. 4.22.

639 Ibid, at para. 4.59.

Separate Storage Installation

A separate storage facility is defined as any installation which stores or is specifically designed to store nuclear material generated or to be used by another installation.[640] In the context of fusion, deuterium as material is produced in separate facilities. Tritium is both produced and consumed by the fusion reactor itself. The separation and storage of the tritium takes places on the site of the fusion power plant. An exception might occur for the start-up of a fusion plant. The start-up of a fusion facility requires a certain amount of tritium which might be stored in a separate storage facility. Moreover, given ICF uses specifically produced targets, it is conceivable that the target production will be outsourced from the actual plant installation, thereby necessitating separate storage facilities. However, as the CSA links separate storage facilities to *nuclear material* in the sense of fissionable material, there is no storage facility including nuclear material in the fusion fuel cycle.

Facility where nuclear material of at least one effective kilogram is customarily used

Furthermore, a fusion facility is not a facility where nuclear material of at least one effective kilogram is handled. An effective kilogram is either the weight of the material itself or the weight multiplied by an enrichment factor.[641] An effective kilogram is defined with reference to plutonium and uranium, thus not a material that is used in a fusion facility. Even if one would consider one effective kilogram of tritium or deuterium to equal one kilogram of its material, many fusion facilities would not exceed the threshold of handling one kilogram customarily. Fusion power plants will customarily handle only grams of materials at any given time; kilograms of tritium and deuterium are enough to power a power plant for an entire year or even longer. Due to the constant need of refuelling and the constant production of tritium with the fusion device itself, an effective kilogram is not a suitable order of magnitude for fusion.[642] Consequently, no such facility is part of a fusion fuel cycle.

640 Ibid, at para. 4.60.

641 Para. 104 of INFCIRC/153.

642 *Kalinowski* (n 636), at 130 ff. proposes a significant quantity of one gram for tritium, showing the vast difference of orders of magnitude.

Reactor

The term *reactor* requires interpretation. Scientifically speaking, a reactor is any device where reactions take place. The term *reactor* is also used in the context of fusion to describe a machine that produces a net-energy output.[643] In fission, the production of energy requires a self-sustaining fission reaction, while in fusion this requires that the fusion processes produce more energy than the initiation of the process – mainly heating to hundreds of millions of degrees – and maintaining the fusion reactions require. The ordinary meaning of the term would allow for an inclusion of fusion under the term *reactor*. However, the context indicates that fusion reactors would not be included. A reactor is listed as one of eight subtypes of facilities while all seven others clearly do not include fusion and are focused on a fission fuel cycle. In addition, in light of the objective and purpose defined in para. 1 of INFCIRC/153, which is "in accordance with Article III.1 of the Treaty on the Non-Proliferation of Nuclear Weapons [...] to accept safeguards [...] on all source or special fissionable material in all peaceful nuclear activities", there are strong indications to not include fusion. The CSA sees peaceful nuclear activities as involving fissionable material, indicating that a *reactor* is also a fission reactor. A further indication is the IAEA Safeguards Glossary, which defines a nuclear reactor as any device in which a controlled, self-sustaining fission reaction can be maintained,[644] thus excluding fusion reactors. However, as the wording is wide enough and as will be shown below, the Board of Governors could extend the authority of the IAEA to fusion reactors by broadening the term's interpretation.

1.3.2 Additional Protocol to the CSA

While fusion largely falls outside the scope of the CSA, the Additional Protocol offers some aspects where the existing regime grants the IAEA the authority to apply safeguards to fusion. The Additional Protocol allows for the implementation of some procedures and verification mechanisms in order to verify the absence of nuclear material within fusion facilities, addressing the proliferation concern of breeding nuclear weapons material.

643 See for example *Paul-Henri Rebut*, ITER: The First Experimental Fusion Reactor, Fusion Engineering and Design 30 (1995), 85–118; *Tetsuo Tanabe*, Introduction of a Nuclear Fusion Reactor, in: Tetsuo Tanabe (ed.), Tritium: Fuel of Fusion Reactors, Tokyo: Springer Japan 2017, 3–25.

644 *International Atomic Energy Agency* (n 631), at para. 4.53.

This section analyses the extent to which the AP and its mechanisms, including *complementary access* and *environmental sampling*, applies to fusion.

The Additional Protocol uses mostly the same definitions as the CSA. Article 18(h) of the Model Additional Protocol refers to Article XX of the IAEA Statute in its definition of nuclear material, thus also excluding fusionable material. Similarly, the CSA uses the term "facility" and defines it identically to the CSA in Article 18(i). There is, however, a key difference: In contrast to the CSA, the AP refers explicitly to fission reactors in its Annex.[645] In Annex II, the AP lists equipment which requires reporting of exports and imports according to Article 2.a.(ix) of the AP. There, it lists *complete nuclear reactors* and defines them as "[n]uclear reactors capable of operation so as to maintain a controlled self-sustaining fission chain reaction." In addition, other reactor components and fuels are defined with reference to fission reactors, indicating that a *reactor* is limited to fission reactors. This difference in wording between the Additional Protocol and the CSA further raises doubts regarding the applicability of safeguards to fusion facilities.

In contrast to the focus on facilities, the Additional Protocol extends the IAEA's authority to other locations. The IAEA can access *locations not involving nuclear material*, can demand *complementary access* and conduct *environmental sampling.*

Regarding *locations not involving nuclear material*: According to its Article 2.a.(i), the State has to provide a "general description of and information specifying the location of *nuclear fuel cycle-related research and development* activities not involving *nuclear material* carried out anywhere that are funded, specifically authorized or controlled by, or carried out on behalf of" the State. The explicit exclusion of nuclear material, on the first glance, indicates that activities in fusion need to be reported to the IAEA, especially as fusion would be considered as nuclear research and development. However, the scope of *nuclear fuel cycle-related research and development* is defined in Article 18.a, which also limits research and development on processes related to *nuclear material*, i.e. *source and special fissionable material*, not including fusion.

Nevertheless, the AP includes a provision that allows the IAEA to apply safeguards to fusion to some extent: complementary access. The AP

645 Annex II (List of Specified Equipment and Non-Nuclear Material for the Reporting of Exports and Imports According to Article 2.a.(ix)), at para. 1 of INFCIRC/540(Corrected).

provides the IAEA with the authority to complementary access without focussing on *nuclear material*, a tool allowing the IAEA to access locations outside the regular scope of inspections under the CSA. This provision encompasses the right to access any place on a site, any location identified under Article 2.a.(v)-(viii) or any decommissioned facility or decommissioned location where nuclear material was customarily used (Article 5.a). The locations identified under Article 2.a.(v)-(viii) are uranium mines, concentration plants, locations where source material or small quantities are handled and locations of high-level waste containing plutonium, high enriched uranium or ^{233}U. A site is defined as a delimited area for a facility (Article 18.b), while a fusion facility is currently not considered by the IAEA as a facility in the sense of the CSA or the AP (see above). A fusion facility is also not a location identified under Article 2.a.(v)-(viii), nor is it a location where nuclear material in the sense of the Additional Protocol is customarily used. IAEA inspectors can, however, require complementary access by demanding to verify uranium beds in which tritium is stored. Complementary access can not only help to assure the absence of nuclear material such as uranium, but also the absence of nuclear activities, such as tritium breeding or enrichment of lithium.

In addition, the IAEA can also demand complementary access for environmental sampling, Articles 5.c and 9.Environmental sampling allows the IAEA to detect clandestine nuclear activities. While there was some limited authority already under the CSA,[646] it is only with the adoption of the Additional Protocol that environmental sampling is conducted on a regular basis.[647] Fissile materials leave a characteristic environmental signature, indicating nuclear activities.[648] Consequently, if environmental samples show such a signature in the vicinity of fusion facilities, there would be an indication for a breakout scenario and hint at the production of fissile material in a fusion reactor.

646 *Laura Rockwood*, IAEA Safeguards: Correctness and Completeness of States' Safeguards Declarations, in: International Atomic Energy Agency (ed.), Nuclear Law: The Global Debate, The Hague: T.M.C. Asser Press 2022, 205–222, at 209 f.

647 *David L. Donohue*, Strengthening IAEA Safeguards Through Environmental Sampling and Analysis, Journal of Alloys and Compounds 271–273 (1998), 11–18.

648 *Paula Cable-Dunlap/Lee Trowbridge/Debra Bostick et al.*, Comparison of Active and Passive Environmental Sampling for Safeguards Applications, Journal of Radioanalytical and Nuclear Chemistry 296 (2013), 943–949; *A. Axelsson/D. M. Fischer/M. V. Peńkin*, Use of Data From Environmental Sampling for IAEA Safeguards. Case Study: Uranium With Near-Natural 235U Abundance, Journal of Radioanalytical and Nuclear Chemistry 282 (2009), 725–729.

The Additional Protocol differentiates between *location-specific* environmental sampling, Article 5.c, and *wide-area* environmental sampling, Article 9. Location-specific environmental sampling is permitted in any location specified by the IAEA. Thus, the IAEA has the possibility to select specific locations to carry out inspections in order to ensure that no undeclared nuclear material is present.[649] Such a location would also be a fusion facility, providing the IAEA with possibilities for deploying safeguards inspectors to access fusion facilities or close-by areas to carry out environmental sampling. However, since the IAEA does not have the authority to demand design information, it is difficult for inspectors to decide where exactly in the facility they should take the samples. Furthermore, in cases where the samples cause questions or are inconsistent with the reporting of the State, the IAEA has the right to visually observe the location, carry out radiation detection and measurements as well as "other objective measures", Article 6.d. Thus, location-specific environmental sampling allows the IAEA to address the proliferation concern of producing nuclear weapons material with a fusion facility.

A second tool which allows the IAEA to address this proliferation concern is wide-area environmental sampling. In the event that a State uses a fusion facility to irradiate ^{238}U to produce plutonium for nuclear weapons, the result is a mixture of several isotopes. In order to use that plutonium for nuclear weapons, the material has to be reprocessed at a separate facility, which in turn produces traces in the environment. In such a scenario, the implementation of wide-area environmental sampling increases the level of assurance that no clandestine nuclear weapons programmes supported by fusion exist. The extraction of plutonium from the resulting alloy is a complicated chemical process which requires a plutonium extraction facility. Environmental sampling and atmospheric measurements assist in detecting clandestine plutonium extraction facilities.[650] In these activities, the IAEA can collect environmental samples at a set of locations in order

649 Article 18 (f) AP. On environmental sampling, see *Martin B. Kalinowski/Johann Feichter/Mika Nikkinen et al.*, Environmental Sample Analysis, in: Rudolf Avenhaus/Nicholas Kyriakopoulos/Michel Richard/Gotthard Stein (eds.), Berlin, Heidelberg: Springer 2006, 367–387; *Laura Rockwood*, The IAEA's Strengthened Safeguards System, Journal of Conflict and Security Law 7 (2002), 123–136, at 132 f.

650 *Michael Schoeppner/Alexander Glaser/Mark. E Walker*, Detecting Clandestine Plutonium Separation Activities With Krypton-85 (2015), INMM 56th Annual Meeting Proceedings.

to get a more comprehensive overview over a wide area.[651] What limits the IAEA's authority to conduct wide-area environmental sampling are procedural requirements set out in Article 9 AP, which requires pre-approval by the Board of Governors after consultations with the concerned State. The Board of Governors has never authorized wide-area environmental sampling.

To summarise, the Additional Protocol provides the IAEA with the authority of location-specific environmental sampling accompanied with complementary access to these location under the Additional Protocol and further supported by wide-area environmental sampling to address one proliferation potential associated with fusion: the clandestine production of nuclear weapons material. Other proliferation potentials such as the abundance of tritium or the military dimension of ICF research is not addressed by the Additional Protocol.

1.3.3 Item-Specific Safeguards Agreements

INFCIRC/66, which is an evolution from the original safeguards system contained in INFCIRC/26, forms the basis for item-specific safeguards agreements for State Parties outside the NPT. Item-specific safeguards apply to *nuclear material* in *principal nuclear facilities* in India, Pakistan and Israel. This section analyses the application of these agreements to a fusion fuel cycle.

1.3.3.1 Nuclear Material

Fusion material cannot be considered *nuclear material* under INFCIRC/66 safeguards, albeit a first observation would suggest otherwise.

Safeguards based on INFCIRC/66 predate NPT safeguards and their implementation with CSAs. While the NPT and the IAEA Statute explicitly refer to *source and special fissionable material*, INFCIRC/66 instead uses

651 Article 18 (g) AP. On wide-area environmental sampling, see *Ephraim Asculai*, Verification Revisited: The Nuclear Case, Washington DC: Institute for Science and International Security Press 2002, at 101–111; *Ned A. Wogman*, Prospects for the Introduction of Wide Area Monitoring Using Environmental Sampling for Proliferation Detection, Journal of Radioanalytical and Nuclear Chemistry 296 (2013), 1071–1077.

the broader term *nuclear material* without a definition. The term *nuclear material* is also found in CSAs, however there the agreements define the term. Interpreted in light of Article 31(1) of the VCLT – which considers the ordinary meaning as well as the object and purpose of a treaty – this broader terminology could support an interpretation that includes fusionable material. Further, INFCIRC/66 distinguishes between nuclear material and the two categories of fissionable material – source and special.[652] This differentiation suggests that "nuclear material" may be intended as a broader category, within which fissionable material is only one subset. Such an interpretation could allow for the inclusion of other substances involved in nuclear processes, such as fusionable material.

However, several factors weigh against this broader reading. First, INFCIRC/66 includes exemptions for small quantities of specific materials[653] – plutonium, uranium, and thorium – which all fall under the category of source or special fissionable material.[654] The explicit mention of these substances, and the absence of others, indicates an intention to exhaustively define nuclear material in line with the categories established in the IAEA Statute.

Second, the historical lineage of INFCIRC/66 reinforces this narrow scope. It directly builds on INFCIRC/26, which is cited in its preamble. INFCIRC/26 explicitly defines nuclear material by reference to Article XX of the IAEA Statute, which limits the term to source and special fissionable material. No provision is made for fusionable materials, which remain outside the definitional scope of these foundational instruments.

Taken together, the context, historical evolution, and specific material references in INFCIRC/66 support a restrictive interpretation. Despite the initial appearance of a broader term, the item-specific safeguards under INFCIRC/66 do not extend to fusionable material.

1.3.3.2 Principal Nuclear Facility

Furthermore, item-specific safeguards do not apply to fusion facilities. Firstly, safeguards are limited to declared facilities by the country with such

652 See paras 21–24.

653 See para. 21 of INFCIRC/66.

654 On the application of the CSA to States with a Small Quantities Protocol see: *International Atomic Energy Agency*, Safeguards Implementation Guide for States with Small Quantities Protocols, Vienna: IAEA 2013.

an agreement in place. Neither India, nor Pakistan, nor Israel have any relevant fusion facilities that they could declare under their safeguards agreements concluded in the type of INFCIRC/66. Additionally, INFCIRC/66 itself refers to *principal nuclear facilities*, which is defined in INFCIRC/26 as "reactor facilities, plants for processing special fissionable or irradiated source material, plants for separating the isotopes of uranium or isotopes of plutonium an such other facilities or plants which may be designated by the Board."[655] A reactor facility in turn is also limited to fission reactions.[656] Without the designation of the Board of Governors, a fusion facility would be outside the scope of INFCIRC/26 and INFCIRC/66.

Consequently, item-specific safeguards do not apply to fusion facilities, excluding its application on fusion technology.

1.3.4 Voluntary Offer Agreements

The current Voluntary Offer Agreements (VOAs) – safeguards agreements with NWS recognised by the NPT – do not apply to fusion for three reasons. Firstly, they are limited to source and special fissionable material. Secondly, their application is limited to declared facilities, which do not include a fusion facility. Thirdly, some fusion research institutions in these countries are part of dedicated military programmes, such as the National Ignition Facility in the United States or Laser Mégajoule in France, and are thus excluded, as VOAs are limited to civilian facilities.

1.3.5 Summary

Fusion falls mostly outside the various safeguards agreements. They are either focused on material and technology related to *source and special fissionable material* in fission facilities, or they are explicitly not listed where the agreements only apply to pre-defined facilities. It is only in States that have adopted an Additional Protocol where the IAEA has some authority by demanding complementary access and conducting environmental sampling, partly addressing the proliferation concern of using fusion facilities to produce nuclear weapons material. The proliferation potential of the use

655 Para. 15 of INFCIRC/26.
656 Paras 13 and 14 of INFCIRC/26.

of tritium as well as the risks associated with inertial confinement fusion are outside the scope of any safeguards agreement.

1.4 Summary

Fusion falls under the broader mandate of the IAEA to promote the atom for peace and development. However, when addressing the proliferation potential of fusion, there are significant lacks in the legal framework. The IAEA's safeguards system is focused on *source and special fissionable material*, excluding its application on fusion. While the NPT prohibits NNWS from using fusion in developing nuclear weapons, the mandated verification mechanisms do not apply to fusion technology. As the verification is further specified in safeguards agreements, they also widely do not include fusion given their equal focus on *source and special fissionable material* as well as on fission facilities. The IAEA's authority to address the proliferation potential of fusion is thus limited, with only the Additional Protocol providing a partial solution to this issue by allowing for environmental sampling and complementary access.

2 Export Control Regimes

As analysed in the previous chapter, export controls are the second important verification mechanism next to safeguards. While the NPT does not mandate export controls for fusion technology, this section analyses the application of the existing export control regimes to fusion in order to analyse if export controls limit the non-proliferation potential of fusion. To recall from the last chapter, States have established two nuclear export control fora: the Zangger Committee and the Nuclear Suppliers Group. This section will show that both export control regimes apply to a certain extent to fusion, with the export control lists including material and equipment used within a fusion facility. However, as this section will show, the required procedures limit their application to fusion.

This section firstly explores the scope of the two regimes with regard to fusion (2.1). It then proceeds to apply the regimes both with regard to content (2.2) and procedure (2.3) to fusion.

2.1 Scope of Export Control Groups

The two fora for nuclear export controls are not international organisations, as they do not have a constituent treaty, rather they are intergovernmental groups without their own legal personality.[657]

As analysed in the previous chapter, the two groups have much in common: The content of their Trigger lists and their procedures are quite similar, and there is an overlap in membership. However, the scope of the two groups are different.

Governments established the Zangger Committee with the mission to find a common understanding on the interpretation of the term "equipment and material especially designed or prepared for the processing, use or production of special fissile material" in Article III.2 NPT. As the Zangger Committee is not an international organisation and does not possess a separate legal personality, the Committee refers to a "mission" rather than a "mandate."[658] The export of such equipment and material is only allowed under the NPT, if the source or special fissionable material is subject to safeguards under Article III.1 NPT. This is where the direct link between the proliferation potential of fission and the dual-use characteristics becomes apparent. Export controls seek to limit proliferation by ensuring that auxiliary equipment and other materials that could be used to support a nuclear weapons programme are used only for peaceful purposes. As shown above, fusion is outside the scope of Article III.2 NPT and the NPT's mandate on export controls. The mission and *raison d'être* of the Zangger Committee therefore indicate that the Zangger regime is not applicable to fusion. However, as the regime applies once an item is on its list, the regime is applicable even in cases where material or equipment relevant for fusion is listed.

Unlike the Zangger Committee, the aim pursued by governments participating in the NSG is not limited to the common goal of finding an interpretation of a provision of the NPT. As the NSG is not an international organisation or a body thereof and does not possess any legal personality, but rather acts as a discussion forum, the NSG uses the term "aim" rather

657 On the definition of an international organisation, see Article 2(a) of the ILC's Draft Articles on the Responsibility of International Organizations. On the ILC's definition, see *Stephen Bouwhuis*, The International Law Commission's Definition of International Organizations, International Organizations Law Review 9 (2012), 451–465.

658 https://zanggercommittee.org/our-mission.html, last accessed 6 June 2025.

than "mandate." According to its self-understanding, the NSG "is a group of nuclear supplier countries of nuclear material, equipment and technology and nuclear-related dual-use equipment, material, software and related technology, which seek to contribute to the non-proliferation of nuclear weapons."[659] The group further describes the aim of its guidelines as "to ensure that nuclear trade for peaceful purposes does not contribute to the proliferation of nuclear weapons and other nuclear explosive devices."[660] The NSG's purpose is thus much broader than that of the Zangger Committee. As the focus of the NSG is on preventing the proliferation of nuclear weapons by establishing rules for nuclear trade, there is not an exclusive focus on fission as there is in the Zangger Committee. As fusion technology might play an auxiliary role in nuclear weapons, the aim of the NSG includes fusion.

2.2 Material Application of the Guidelines

The Trigger Lists of the NSG and the Zangger Committee are specifically designed to address the proliferation potential of the fuel of fission power plants and places them under export controls: source and special fissionable material as defined in Article XX of the IAEA Statute and related material and equipment.[661] Fissionable material is not intended to be used in a fusion facility. Thus, fusion is not covered by the main provision of the NSG and Zangger Trigger Lists. However, the Trigger Lists also include both deuterium (exceeding 200 kg per year)[662] and plants for the production of deuterium;[663] a material which play an important role in fusion technology. However, as 200 kg of deuterium will be sufficient to operate a single fusion power plant for several years, export controls would only be triggered in the rare case of acquiring deuterium for a large fleet of fusion power plants.

---

659 The Nuclear Suppliers Group: Its Guidelines, Origins, Structure, and Role, INFCIRC/539/Revision 8, at 1.

660 Ibid.

661 INFCIRC/254/Rev.14/Part 1, at p. 12 (NSG); INFCIRC/209/Rev.5 at p. 1 (Zangger).

662 A single 1 GW_e sized fusion power plant is expected to consume around 125 kg of deuterium per year, *Beom Seok Kim/Suk-Ho Hong/Keeman Kim*, Preliminary assessment of the safety factors in K-DEMO for fusion compatible regulatory framework, Scientific Reports 12 (2022), 8276.

663 INFCIRC/254/Rev.14/Part 1, at p. 13, 19, 51 ff. (NSG); INFCIRC/209/Rev.5 at p. 5, 35 ff. (Zangger).

In addition, some of the equipment used in nuclear (fission) power plants will also be used in fusion power plants as well. This is particularly true for the production of electricity. A fission power plant is – oversimplified – a giant water kettle. The nuclear reactions release heat, this heat is converted into steam by a heat exchanger (listed in para. 1.9 of both Trigger Lists), then the steam drives a turbine and a generator which produces electrical energy. A fusion power plant only changes the type of nuclear reaction at the very beginning of the process, while the remaining technology remains mostly the same. Electricity generation is indifferent to the nuclear processes involved in the heat production. Similarly, the measurement of neutron fluxes is relevant to the operation of any nuclear power plant (para. 1.10 on both Trigger Lists).

As mentioned above, fusion is outside the mission of the Zangger Committee. This exclusion is also reflected in a clarification of the definition of "nuclear reactors and especially designed or prepared equipment and components thereof."[664] This clarification specifically excludes fusion: "This entry does not control fusion reactors." As a result, the export of entire fusion reactors as well as heat exchangers and neutron detectors for fusion reactors falls outside the scope of the Zangger Trigger List. As the Zangger List is relevant for the interpretation of Article III.2 of the NPT, this clarification further supports the result of interpretation in Section 1.2.4 above.

As the NSG's aim is broader than harmonising the interpretation of Article III.2 of the NPT, the NSG's Dual Use List contains more fusion-related material: Firstly, similar to the heat exchangers on the Trigger Lists, some materials and equipment already proven in the nuclear industry will be used in fusion plants. This is particularly true for industrial equipment (para. 1 on the Dual Use List), such as high-density radiation shielding windows (para. 1.A.1), cameras (para. 1.A.2), robots for maintenance (para. 1.A.3), machines and tools with high precision (paras 1.B.2 and 1.B.3) as well as software to operate these machines (para. 1.D).

Secondly, materials and equipment with an auxiliary character in fission are of essential use in fusion. This is particularly the case for the material which is central to fusion's proliferation potential: tritium. The list contains tritium as a material (para. 2.C.17), tritium facilities (2.B.1) and methods to separate tritium from coolants (2.A.2). While tritium in fission power

664 Para. 1 of the Annex to Memorandum B of the Zangger List.

plants is produced only as a by-product,[665] an essential part of a fusion power plant will be its tritium production and recovery. Similarly, beryllium as a material (para. 2.C.2) and lithium isotope separation equipment (para. 2.B.2) play a role in the tritium production. Irradiation of ^{6}Li results in the production of tritium, while the rare isotope of ^{6}Li first has to be separated from the significantly more abundant ^{7}Li. In addition, beryllium can be used as a neutron multiplier to increase production.[666] Furthermore, ^{3}He is listed on the Dual Use List (para. 2.C.18); a material which some start-ups consider as a fuel for their fusion power plants.

2.3 Procedural Application of the Guidelines

Although a significant amount of material and equipment used for fusion is either listed on a Trigger List or the Dual Use List, procedural limitations significantly reduce the effect of limiting the proliferation potential. There are four reasons for this limited effect. They stem from the safeguards requirement for exports, the limited use of exports, the requirement to assess whether an export presents an unacceptable risk of diversion, and the legal character of the regime.

First, all exports of items listed on either a Trigger or the Dual Use list require the application of IAEA safeguards.[667] Countries export such material and equipment despite the potential risk of diversion with the assurance in mind that the application of safeguards significantly reduces that risk of diversion. Exporting countries trust that the IAEA would detect the use of such material and equipment in a nuclear weapons programme. However, the export control regime is based on Article III.2 of the NPT – which does not apply to fusion – and require IAEA safeguards – which do not apply to fusion, in particular to fusion facilities. This procedure with regard to fusion defeats the whole purpose of allowing the export of

665 In CANDU reactors, neutrons from the fission process sometimes interact with the deuterium as part of its heavy water coolant, forming a tritium atom: *Richard J. Pearson/Armando B. Antoniazzi/William J. Nuttall*, Tritium Supply and Use: a Key Issue for the Development of Nuclear Fusion Energy, Fusion Engineering and Design 136 (2018), 1140–1148.

666 *Satoshi Shimakawa/Hisashi Sagawa/Toshimasa Kuroda et al.*, Estimation of the Tritium Production and Inventory in Beryllium, Fusion Engineering and Design 28 (1995), 215–219.

667 Para. 3 Memorandum B of Zangger List; para. 4 of the NSG-Trigger List Guidelines, para. 2 of the NSG Dual-Use Guidelines.

nuclear material and equipment while not securing their end-use through the application of safeguards.

Second, even if export controls applied, they would only apply to exports. Any material or equipment produced within a country's borders is outside the scope of export controls. Export controls can by principle not effectively control the risk of nuclear proliferation in isolation, they can only complement other international verification mechanisms that apply to domestic fuel cycles such as safeguards. This limitation applies in particular to tritium, a material with proliferation potential in fusion. It is unlikely that tritium will be transferred between countries during the operation of a fusion power plant.[668] Because of its high price and the huge quantities required, it is intended to be bred within the fusion vessel itself from ^{6}Li. The only point to apply export controls is the export of lithium, especially enriched in this isotope, or of separation equipment for lithium. However, lithium has a wide range of applications. An export could be denied if there is an unacceptable risk of diversion. The wide range of application makes it is difficult to assess whether the supply of lithium or lithium isotope separation equipment poses an unacceptable risk of diversion in any particular situation.

Third, with regard to the NSG Dual-Use list, the guidelines do not provide a definition of an unacceptable risk of diversion. In the absence of such a definition, it is left to the discretion of each individual nuclear supplier State whether it considers the above-mentioned risks to be acceptable or unacceptable.[669] In the absence of definitions and binding rules, States have historically tended to favour political and economic benefits over proliferation concerns.[670]

Fourth and finally, the export control regimes are *soft law* instruments. The NSG system, in particular, has come under criticism, as there are a number of Member States suspected to ignoring these provisions. The United States supplies India with material on the Trigger List even though India has not accepted comprehensive safeguards and is not a member State of

668 An exception must be made for the start-up of a fusion power plant. The neutrons from fusion reactions allow for the in-situ production of tritium. However, to start the fusion reactions, a start-up quantity of tritium is required.

669 *Abram Chayes/Antonia H. Chayes*, Regime Architecture: Elements and Principles, in: Janne E. Nolan (ed.), Global Engagement: Cooperation and Security in the 21st Century, Washington DC: Brookings Institution 1994, 65–130.

670 Ibid.

the NPT.[671] Similar allegations of violating the NSG procedures have been made against Russia and China.[672] As there is no legal obligation to follow the rules and in the absence of any enforcement mechanism, the readiness of the regime to address fusion's proliferation potential is questionable.

To summarise, given the constraints in the procedure, export control regimes currently do not adequately address the proliferation potential of fusion.

2.4 Summary

The Trigger List drafted by the Zangger Committee is of no relevance for fusion as its mission is limited to interpret Article III.2 of the NPT, which in turn is not applicable to fusion. However, the NSG Guidelines include materials and equipment relevant to fusion, yet their effectiveness is limited. The NSG's broader aim covers fusion-related materials, such as deuterium, tritium, and lithium isotope separation equipment, but its guidelines do not explicitly address fusion reactors or components. In addition, the NSG Guidelines allow for export controls when a procedure is followed, while the procedure has limited effects in addressing fusion's proliferation potential: IAEA safeguards do not apply to fusion, export controls are limited to international trade (not domestic production), and decisions are often based on political considerations. Additionally, the non-binding nature of these guidelines limit their effectiveness. Overall, current export control regimes do not adequately address fusion's proliferation risks.

3 Further Regimes

Preventing the use of nuclear technology for nuclear weapons programmes is also the objective of treaty regimes outside the IAEA regime and export

671 *Oliver Meier*, The US–India Nuclear Deal: The End of Universal Non-Proliferation Efforts?, Internationale Politik und Gesellschaft (2006), 28–43; *Leonard Weiss*, U.S.-India Nuclear Cooperation, The Nonproliferation Review 14 (2007), 429–457.

672 *Fred McGoldrick*, The Road Ahead for Export Controls: Challenges for the Nuclear Suppliers Group, Arms Control Today 41 (2011), 30–36; *Sibylle Bauer*, Developments in the Nuclear Suppliers Group, in: Bates Gill/Ian Anthony/D.A. Cruickshank (eds.), SIPRI Yearbook 2011, Stockholm: SIPRI 2011, 376–386, at 384 f.; *Mark Hibbs*, The Nuclear Suppliers Group and Geostrategic Politics, Strategic Trade Review 3 (2017), 5–24.

controls regimes This section analyses the extent to which these regimes apply to fusion technology. It begins with an analysis of the ITER Agreement, which is the basis for the ITER project, the world's largest fusion research project (3.1). It proceeds to analyse the applicability of Euratom safeguards to fusion (3.2). This is followed by an examination of the verification regimes of the Treaty on the Prohibition of Nuclear Weapons (3.3) and Nuclear Weapon Free Zone treaties (3.4) with a view to their applicability to fusion.

3.1 ITER Agreement

The ITER Agreement is the only international treaty that directly addresses the link between fusion and non-proliferation. The Agreement was signed in 2006 by the seven ITER Members: Euratom, the United States, China, Russia, India, Japan and South Korea. It establishes the ITER Organization as the institution responsible for the ITER project, the largest fusion research facility ever built. ITER in unique in that both NWS and NNWS are working together to build and operate a fusion research facility. In addition, ITER is located in St Paul-lez-Durance, France, thus in an NWS. Nuclear infrastructure in France is in principle not subject to safeguards. Only those facilities where France agrees to are safeguarded by the IAEA under a voluntary offer agreement.[673] However, the ITER project is not a French nuclear installation.[674] According to Article 5 of the ITER Agreement, the ITER Organization has its own international legal personality, separate from its Member States. The ITER Organization itself is responsible for the ITER project. As an international organisation, it is not bound by the NPT or any other safeguards instruments. However, the ITER Agreement itself addresses non-proliferation. According to its Article 20, any material, equipment or technology shall be used solely for peaceful purposes (para. 1) and shall not be transferred to any third party to manufacture or otherwise acquire nuclear weapons (para. 2). Unlike the NPT, the ITER Agreement

673 Accord conclu le 27 juillet 1978 entre la France, la Communauté Européenne de l'Energie Atomique et l'Agence Internationale de l'Energie Atomique relatif à l'application de garanties en France, available as INFCIRC/290.

674 For regulatory purposes, ITER is regulated under the French nuclear code as a nuclear installation, see *Lina Rodriguez-Rodrigo/Joëlle Elbez-Uzan/Carlos Alejaldre*, ITER Licensing Process from Design and Construction to Dismantling, Fusion Science and Technology 56 (2009), 809–813.

does not require a safeguards system. The compliance mechanisms with the agreement are very limited. The only provisions in the agreement stipulate "appropriate measures" to be taken by both the organisation and the members, combined with mandating the ITER Council to "interface with appropriate international fora and establish a policy supporting peaceful uses and non-proliferation." There are no plans to apply IAEA safeguards to ITER.[675] This provision shows that the State Parties to the ITER Agreement have recognised a non-proliferation dimension, while not including any safeguards provisions. This implies that these States regard the proliferation potential as limited, at least in the context of a fusion experiment carried out by an international organisation.

3.2 Fusion in the Euratom Treaty

The role of fusion in the Euratom Treaty is comparable to the situation under the IAEA Statute. While both organisations' broader mandates to promote nuclear technology and research are wide enough to cover fusion, the treaties' safeguards provisions of the Treaties are not applicable to fusion.

Euratom is a major player in the field of fusion research. It funds EUROfusion, a consortium of 28 fusion research institutions in 26 EU Member States, with around 580 million Euros over a five-year period, representing 55 % of the consortium's budget.[676] Euratom is also one of the signatories of the ITER Agreement and provides 45 % of the funding of the ITER project through its joint undertaking Fusion For Energy.[677] According to Article 4 Euratom Treaty, Euratom shall promote and facilitate research in the field of nuclear energy. Annex I of the Treaty specifically lists fusion research

675 Anna Taylor and Laetitia Grammatico, Legal Advisors for ITER, during the 2023 Fusion For Energy Round Table.

676 European Commission – Directorate-General for Research and Innovation, *Euratom Research and Training Programme 2021–2025*, Publications Office, 2021, https://data.europa.eu/doi/10.2777/200656, last accessed 25 February 2025. The remaining 45 % come from the Member States in which the research institution is located.

677 European Commission: Directorate-General for Budget, *The EU's 2021–2027 Long-Term Budget and NextGenerationEU – Facts and Figures*, Publications Office of the European Union, 2021, https://data.europa.eu/doi/10.2761/808559, last accessed 25 February 2025. Fusion For Energy was established following Article 45 Euratom Treaty by Council Decision of 27 March 2007, 2007/198/Euratom.

as an area covered by the mandate of Article 4.[678] Thus, the Euratom Treaty allows the Community to take a role in fusion and to develop legal approaches.

Euratom's important role in fusion research does not come with safeguards. To recall, the central safeguards provision of the Euratom Treaty is that the Commission shall satisfy itself that ores, source materials and special fissile materials are not diverted from their intended uses as declared (Article 77 (a)) and that safeguarding obligations assumed under an agreement with an international organisation (Article 77 (b)) are complied with.

As far as Article 77 (b) is concerned, the same considerations as presented for the IAEA safeguards regime, apply to Euratom. Under this article, the compliance with IAEA safeguards obligations does not require safeguarding fusion facilities.

Concerning Article 77 (a), the other pillar of Euratom safeguards does also not apply to fusion either. The mandate of the Commission is limited to "ores, source material and special fissionable material." Article 197 defines these terms in a similar way to Article XX of the IAEA Statute. Special fissionable materials are defined as certain uranium isotopes or enriched material, while source material is (mainly) natural or depleted uranium. Thus, fusion falls outside the scope of the safeguards system established by Euratom.

Moreover, Euratom's focus on source and special fissionable material is not just a feature of the safeguards regime, but is inherent in the way Euratom operates. One *raison d'être* of Euratom is to have a common European stock of nuclear materials and reactor fuel.[679] Within Europe, it is not the operator or a country that purchases nuclear material on the market, but Euratom with its own Supply Agency. Also, ownership of the material remains with Euratom.[680] The safeguards system is designed in the context that Euratom supplies the material to the individual States and

678 Annex I, para. II.1(e).

679 Articles 2(d) and 52 ff. Euratom Treaty. See also *Pierre Mathijsen*, Some Legal Aspects of Euratom, Common Market Law Review 3 (1966), 326–343.

680 This is set out in Chapter 8 of the Euratom Treaty. On the role of ownership in the broader context of Euratom, see *Peter Böhm*, Ownership of Nuclear Materials in Euratom, The American Journal of Comparative Law 11 (1962), 167–183; *Andre Bouquet*, How Current Are Euratom Provisions on Nuclear Supply and Ownership in View of the European Union's Enlargement?, Nuclear Law Bulletin 68 (2001), 7–38; *Jürgen Grunwald*, Peaceful Uses of Nuclear Energy Under EURATOM Law, in: Jonathan L. Black-Branch/Dieter Fleck (eds.), Nuclear Non-Proliferation in International Law – Volume III: Legal Aspects of the Use of Nuclear Energy for Peaceful Purposes, The Hague: T.M.C. Asser Press 2016, 171–213.

users. However, Euratom only supplies countries with material for their nuclear fission fuel cycle. The exclusion of fusion is therefore a consequence of Euratom's overall focus on a European fission fuel cycle.

As a consequence, the Euratom Treaty does not provide the Commission with adequate tools to address the proliferation potential of fusion. The possibility of including fusion in a broader context of Euratom's procurement and control system is discussed in the next chapter.

3.3 Fusion and the TPNW

Within the TPNW, there are various rules for verifying compliance with the provisions of the treaty: on the one hand, verifying that a former NWS has irreversibly eliminated its nuclear weapons programme (Article 4) and on the other hand, that all Member States remain nuclear-weapons-free (Article 3).

The above findings of limited applicability of the IAEA's safeguards regime have direct implications for the TPNW. For NNWS, the TPNW sets out a safeguards regime in its Article 3. These safeguards are based on a fission-based approach. According to Article 3.2 of the TPNW, the minimum level of safeguards required is that of the CSA. As shown above, the safeguards provisions of the CSA as part of the NPT safeguards system largely do not include fusion from its scope of application. Furthermore, while the Additional Protocol closes some gaps in the regime, its adoption is not required under the TPNW. For NNWS, the TPNW does not fill the gaps in the application of safeguards to fusion.

For NWS, Article 4 of the TPNW provides a procedure towards the complete elimination of nuclear weapons. This article requires the conclusion of a safeguards agreement with the IAEA. Such an agreement must be "sufficient to provide credible assurance of the non-diversion of declared nuclear material from peaceful nuclear activities and the absence of undeclared nuclear material or activities in the State as a whole." While Article III.1 of the NPT mandates safeguards to verify nuclear non-proliferation, Article 4 of the TPNW mandates safeguards to verify nuclear disarmament.

A closer look at this provision leads to several observations. First, such a safeguards agreement is *prima facie* independent of existing safeguards instruments such as INFCIRC/66, a CSA or a VOA. While these instruments could serve as basis,[681] the language is explicitly open to safeguards that go beyond the existing instruments.

Second, similar to other safeguards agreements, an Article 4 TPNW agreement focuses on *nuclear material.* The language of the treaty itself does not define *nuclear material* and goes beyond both the NPT and the IAEA Statute which focus on *special fissionable* or *source material.*[682] Moreover, while both the CSA and its Additional Protocol also use the term *nuclear material,* the TPNW stops short of defining this term, unlike the IAEA instruments, which define nuclear material in accordance with Article XX of the IAEA Statute. By applying a teleological interpretation supported by the preamble of the Treaty (Article 31 para. 1 VCLT) – both with the aim of achieving final and irreversible nuclear disarmament[683] – this definition must be understood more broadly, to include special *fusionable material.* This is supported by historical observations (Article 32 VCLT): The TPNW is influenced by the work on the (Model) Nuclear Weapons Convention.[684] This convention defined nuclear material as "any source or special fissionable or fusionable material as defined in this Convention."[685] There has been an explicit inclusion of fusionable material. Fusionable material was defined as "any isotope capable of undergoing fusion with the same kind of nuclide or with any other nuclide by applying sufficient conditions (pressure, temperature and inclusion time) with technical means."[686] This includes deuterium and tritium as well as any other fusion fuel, as the context indicates a broader understanding of the term.

---

681 *Stuart Casey-Maslen,* The Treaty on the Prohibition of Nuclear Weapons: a Commentary, Oxford: Oxford University Press 2019, at 193.

682 It should be noted that the NPT refers to nuclear material in its Article III.3 on international exchange.

683 Para. 14 of the Preamble of the TPNW. On the role of fusion in irreversibility of nuclear disarmament, see *Philipp Sauter,* The Emergence of Nuclear Fusion Energy: A New Nuclear Technology, a New Chance for Nuclear Disarmament?, in: Wilfred Wan/Vladislav Chernavskikh (eds.), Expanding Perspectives on Nuclear Disarmament, Uppsala: SIPRI/Alva Myrdal Centre for Nuclear Disarmament 2023, 160–171.

684 *Jonathan L. Black-Branch,* The Treaty on the Prohibition of Nuclear Weapons. Legal Challenges for Military Doctrines and Deterrence Policies, 2021, at 13 f.; *Christopher P. Evans,* Questioning the Status of the Treaty on the Prohibition of Nuclear Weapons as a 'Humanitarian Disarmament' Agreement, Utrecht Journal of International and European Law (2021), 52–74.

685 NPT/CONF.2010/PC.I/WP.17, at para. II. 14; UN document A/C.1/52/7, at para. II.14.

686 UN document A/C.1/52/7, at para. II.17.

Thus, the issue of safeguarding fusionable material would become relevant once the NWS acceded to the TPNW. The development of specific verification mechanisms for former NWS would need to include provisions focusing on fusion. This is particularly relevant to the proliferation concerns associated with inertial confinement fusion: These facilities currently exist only as part of military programmes. Such a mechanism would also need to focus on tritium and its role in nuclear weapons. However, in view of the unanimous rejection of the treaty,[687] which is also supported by the partner States,[688] this does not appear to be likely in the foreseeable future.

3.4 Fusion in Nuclear Weapon Free Zone Treaties

As analysed above, NWFZ Treaties play an important role in ensuring non-proliferation and nuclear disarmament at the regional level.[689] Similar to the IAEA's safeguards system, there are shortcomings in the regional verification systems with regard to fusion. The gap between the objective of a regime and the implementation of its verification regime extends to NWFZ Treaties as well.

3.4.1 Treaty of Tlatelolco

The South and Latin American NWFZ, which is the oldest NWFZ and predates the NPT, establishes an international organisation with structures and authority reminiscent of the IAEA. Article 7 of the Treaty of Tlatelolco establishes the Agency for the Prohibition of Nuclear Weapons in Latin America and mandates its General Conference to "establish procedures for the control system", Article 9 para. 2b. The objective of the verification is to ensure the exclusive use of nuclear material and facilities for peaceful

687 See for example the P5 Joint Statement on the Treaty of Non-Proliferation of Nuclear Weapons of 24 October 2018, available at https://www.gov.uk/government/news/p5-joint-statement-on-the-treaty-on-the-non-proliferation-of-nuclear-weapons, last accessed 25 February 2025.

688 In the case of Germany as a NATO country, see the statement of the German government in the publication of the German parliament Bundestag Drucksache 20/2268 of 10 June 2022. On the consequences for NATO, see *Mika Hayashi*, NATO's Nuclear Sharing Arrangements Revisited in Light of the NPT and the TPNW, Journal of Conflict and Security Law 26 (2021), 471–491.

689 See above, Chapter 2, Section 3.4.

purposes.[690] A particular focus of the control system is to verify that "devices, services and facilities intended for peaceful uses of nuclear energy are not used in the testing or manufacture of nuclear weapons."[691] The term "nuclear material" itself is applicable to both fission and fusion as long as there is no definition limiting the scope to source and special fissionable material as in the CSA. Furthermore, fusion facilities are not excluded from the scope of verification in view of the potential of fusion to develop or support nuclear weapons programmes. However, there is a lack in the design of the control system. The control system comprises of IAEA safeguards (Article 13), semi-annual reports of the Parties (Article 14) and the possibility of special reports and special inspections (Articles 15 and 16). The IAEA carries out regular inspections. As analysed above, mandating the IAEA to apply safeguards does not include the application to fusion as long as there is no clear reference to fusion.

Furthermore, Article 13 requires the States to apply safeguards to their *nuclear activities* without further definition. Given the purpose of the treaty, which is the military denuclearisation of Latin America and constituting a significant contribution towards preventing the proliferation of nuclear weapons[692] as well as its broad obligation to "undertake to use exclusively for peaceful purposes the nuclear material and facilities",[693] *fusion activities* would fall within the scope of *nuclear activities* under Article 13. As a consequence, once Latin American States engage in fusion activities, they would have to negotiate an agreement with the IAEA to apply safeguards to these activities.

As will be shown next, the other NWFZ Treaties were concluded after the adoption of the NPT. Hence, they follow a more fissile material-based approach by the NPT and specifically mention source and special fissionable material. These treaties also refer to specific IAEA safeguards instruments that do not include fusion.

3.4.2 Treaty of Rarotonga

While the South Pacific NWFZ Treaty also renounces the manufacturing or otherwise acquisition of nuclear weapons (Article 3), the undertaking

690 Articles 12 and 1 of the Treaty of Tlatelolco.
691 Article 12 para. 2a.
692 Para. 17 of the Preamble.
693 Article 1.

vis-à-vis peaceful nuclear activities focuses on rules for providing source or special fissionable material or material for its processing, use or production (Article 4). Such material can only be provided to a NNWS if safeguards following Article III.1 NPT apply or to a NWS under a VOA. The control system then focuses on compliance with all obligations from the treaty, including the renunciation of nuclear weapons and peaceful nuclear activities. The objective of Article 3 is broad enough to include fusion. However, the control system does not reflect fusion's proliferation risk. This system is limited to reports to the Director of the South Pacific Bureau for Economic Co-operation, consultations, a complaints procedure and the application of IAEA safeguards to peaceful nuclear activities (Article 8). The IAEA safeguards are further detailed in Annex 2. They are applied on all source or special fissionable material in all peaceful nuclear activities, based on the CSA. While the purpose of these safeguards is to verify the non-diversion of *nuclear material* – which would allow for an inclusion of fusion – CSA-based safeguards apply only to source and special fissionable material. This does not include the application of safeguards to fusion.

3.4.3 Treaty of Bangkok

Similar to all NWFZ Treaties, the South-East Asian NWFZ Treaty prohibits any form of acquisition, development or control of nuclear weapons (Article 3). With regard to the civilian use of nuclear weapons, States shall use nuclear material and facilities exclusively for peaceful purposes (Article 4 para. 2a). Similar to the Treaty of Rarotonga, providing source and special fissionable material to other countries is prohibited without safeguards agreements in place for the recipient State. While the provisions on the use of nuclear energy for civilian purposes focus only on nuclear material – thus allowing for the inclusion of fusionable material –, the verification process is also not adapted to fusion. While the objective of the system includes fusion, its application does not. The verification system consists of reports and the application of IAEA safeguards (Article 10). The safeguards are further described in Article 5 as full-scope safeguards, which is synonymous with the standard introduced in the CSA.[694] As analysed above, fusion is outside the scope of this safeguards regime and thus outside from the Treaty of Bangkok as well.

694 *International Atomic Energy Agency* (n 631), at 4, 11.

3.4.4 Treaty of Pelindaba

The African NWFZ Treaty prohibits any kind of possession or control of nuclear weapons as well (Article 3). Peaceful uses of nuclear energy are to be carried out under strict non-proliferation measures to provide assurance of exclusively peaceful uses (Article 9a). In this respect, the conclusion of a CSA with the IAEA is required (Article 9b). Similar to the other NWFZ Treaties, the provision of a country with source or special fissionable material requires safeguards agreements as well (Article 9c). The verification mechanism includes reports to the African Commission on Nuclear Energy and the implementation of IAEA safeguards (Article 12 and Annex II). While the purpose of safeguards is to verify the non-diversion of nuclear material from peaceful nuclear activities to nuclear explosive devices (Annex II para. 3), the safeguards are limited to source or special fissionable material, thus excluding fusion. Unlike the other NWFZ Treaties, the Treaty of Pelindaba contains its own definitions. It defines nuclear material (Article 1.f) in the sense of Article XX of the IAEA Statute, thus only source and special fissionable material are to be considered nuclear material, thereby excluding fusionable material. It contains a definition of nuclear installation, which includes nuclear-power reactors and nuclear research reactors (Article 1.e). In the absence of any further specification, these terms are broad enough to include fusion powered reactors or fusion research reactors alongside fission reactors.

3.4.5 Treaty of Semipalatinsk

Similar to the other NWFZ Treaties, any form of control or possession of nuclear weapons is prohibited in the Central Asian NWFZ (Article 3). In addition, only the exclusively peaceful use of nuclear material and facilities is permitted. Providing NNWS with nuclear material or related equipment is limited to those NNWS that have both a CSA and an Additional Protocol in place, while there are no requirements for NWS. As in some NWFZ treaties, the treaty's definition of *nuclear material* (Article 1.d) refers to Article XX of the IAEA Statute and the definition of *facility* (Article 1.f) is similar to that of the CSA, limiting the applicability of the treaty to fission. However, there is a difference to the other NWFZ Treaties in terms of verification: The Central Asian NWFZ is the only zone without the establishment of a separate international organisation. Verification is ensured through consultative meetings (Article 10) and the application of IAEA safeguards (Article 8). In contrast to the other treaties, the level of safeguards is not only at the level of the CSA, but also includes the Additional Protocol. As the AP applies to some extent to fusion as well, the Treaty of Semipalatinsk includes the limited possibility of applying safeguards to fusion.

3.4.6 Summary

While the rules regarding the peaceful use of nuclear weapons are open enough to include fusion, there is a gap in verification. Since all NWFZ rely primarily on IAEA safeguards to verify compliance with the respective treaty provisions, these mechanisms do not apply to fusion. NWFZ Treaties do not effectively reduce the gap in the regime between the treaties' objectives of preventing a nuclearisation of their respective regions and their verification mechanisms regarding fusion technology.

3.5 Summary

As with the IAEA's verification regime and the nuclear export control regime, further regimes show gaps in their application to fusion. All the regimes examined- the ITER Agreement, the Euratom Treaty, the TPNW and NWFZ Treaties – aim to prevent the use of fusion technology for nuclear weapons. However, these regimes lack verification mechanisms to ensure that fusion remains exclusively in the peaceful domain.

4 Evaluation of the Applicability of the Framework on Fusion

To conclude this chapter, it is analysed that, despite the gap between the objective of preventing the use of fusion technology to develop nuclear weapons in NNWS and the applicability of the various verification regimes on fusion technology, the regime does not contain an obligation for States to support the development of an effective non-proliferation regime (4.1). The chapter then summarises the findings in order to set the stage for the next chapter, which discusses approaches to adapting the legal framework (4.2).

4.1 A Sprit but not an Obligation to Strengthen the Safeguards Regime

Various international legal instruments contain the spirit of strengthening the safeguards regime. However, in most cases they fall short of a legal obligation.

The NPT as the cornerstone of the non-proliferation regime is a pertinent example. Despite the objective to verify compliance of NNWS with the prohibition to seek nuclear weapons under Article II, the limited scope of application of the verification mechanisms of Article III does not include an obligation to conclude safeguards agreements covering fusion. With the conclusion of a CSA and the implementation of export controls on fission technology, NNWS fulfil their obligations under the NPT to verify that they maintain their nuclear-weapon-free status. The desire to strengthen the safeguards system is only contained in the Preamble, which does not contain legally binding obligations. The Preamble includes the "[u]ndertaking to co-operate in facilitating the application of International Atomic Energy safeguards on peaceful activities" as well as the State Parties "[e]xpressing their support for research development and other efforts to further the application" of IAEA safeguards. While the spirit to strengthening safeguards is clear, the NPT stops short of obliging States to actually taking action to strengthen the regime.

In addition, United Nations Security Council Resolution (UNSCR) 1540 expresses the desire to strengthen the safeguards regime, while at the same time also stopping short of imposing an obligation. Despite the resolution being adopted under Chapter VII of the UN Charter and, thus being legally binding for all Member States, the Security Council does not use an operator that indicates a legally binding obligation. Para. 8 of the resolution *calls upon* all States to "promote [...] where necessary, strengthening of multilateral treaties to which they are parties, whose aim is to prevent the proliferation of nuclear [...] weapons." While there is some room for interpretation as to whether a strengthening is necessary, such an argument can be made. The implementation of Article II of the NPT is affected by fusion technology, while the verification mechanisms do not address this issue. In addition, it *calls upon* all States to "fulfil their commitment to multilateral cooperation, in particular within the framework of the International Atomic Energy Agency [...] as important means of pursuing and achieving their common objectives in the area of non-proliferation." However, the legal operator *calls upon* is the weakest operator used by the UN Security

Council and usually indicates recommendations rather than obligations.[695] When the Security Council intends to impose a legal obligation, it uses operators such as *decides* or *requests*.[696] UNSCR 1540 also distinguishes between clear obligations, such as its *decisions* to take effective measures against non-state actors and weapons of mass destruction, and the *calls* to strengthen the safeguards system.[697]

Where UNSCR 1540 imposes obligations, these are limited to national regimes and do not extend to international frameworks. In the context of export controls, para. 3 of the resolution *requires* States to strengthen their domestic controls to prevent the proliferation of nuclear weapons, including through effective regulation of related materials. This includes reviewing national export control legislation. Since international export regimes do not cover fusion-related materials, they may not align with UNSCR 1540. However, the resolution places obligations solely on States to act within their national systems, not to coordinate through international bodies like the Zangger Committee or the Nuclear Suppliers Group.

Another legal instrument that recommends, rather than obliges, States to adapt the system is the NSG Guidelines. Para. 14 of the Trigger Lists states:

> "Similarly, they should make every effort to support the IAEA in increasing further the adequacy of safeguards in the light of technical developments and the rapidly growing number of nuclear facilities, and to support appropriate initiatives aimed at improving the effectiveness of IAEA safeguards."

Fusion is perhaps the best example of technical developments that challenge the adequacy of safeguards, where the NSG Member States should support the inclusion of fusion in the IAEA's safeguards regime. However, as these guidelines are non-binding soft law, there is no legal obligation.[698]

695 *Michael Wood/Eran Sthoeger*, The UN Security Council and International Law, Cambridge: Cambridge University Press 2022, at 39 f.; *Justin S. Gruenberg*, An Analysis of United Nations Security Council Resolutions: Are All Countries Treated Equally?, Case Western Reserve Journal of International Law 41 (2009), 469–511, at 487.

696 Ibid.

697 See paras 1–3.

698 On soft law, see *Alan Boyle*, Soft Law in International Law-Making, in: Malcolm Evans (ed.), International Law, Oxford: Oxford University Press 2018, 118–136. Critical towards soft law is *Jan Klabbers*, The Redundancy of Soft Law, Nordic Journal of International Law 65 (1996), 167–182.

There are few exceptions, however, where treaties contain clear obligations for States to work towards the strengthening of the legal regime of nuclear weapons, namely two NWFZ Treaties. The Treaties of Bangkok and Rarotonga contain a specific obligation of their Member States "to support the continued effectiveness of the international non-proliferation system based on the NPT and the IAEA safeguards system."[699] Since effectiveness of the system is limited with regard to fusion, at least the twenty-three Member States of these two NWFZs combined would have to actively support an inclusion of fusion into the safeguards systems, either through the exercise of authority under the existing regime or through treaty changes.

Since there is no legal obligation for most States to actively reform nuclear weapons law to include a verification mechanism for fusion technology, there is a clear gap between the objective of the regime and its application, as well as the spirit to actively work towards the strengthening of the regime. The next chapter will develop approaches to closing the gap between the proliferation potential of fusion and the lack of legal regimes.

4.2 Summary of the Findings

As presented in Chapter 1, fusion has potential applications in nuclear weapons as the technology can be used to support nuclear weapons programmes. The legal framework of nuclear weapons law, which is designed to prevent the use of nuclear technology for nuclear weapons by NNWS, applies to fusion only to a limited extent. There is a gap between the provisions prohibiting the use of nuclear energy, materials and facilities for non-peaceful purposes and the verification regime when it comes to fusion. As the statement of the IAEA's former Director General Blix is true, that "[n]o safeguards system, no matter how extensive the measures, can provide absolute assurance that there has been no diversion of nuclear material or that there are no undeclared nuclear activities in a State,"[700] the existing safeguards regime provides only very limited, and in parts highly ambiguous, assurance with respect to fusion. While the Additional Protocol allows for environmental sampling to address one proliferation potential of fusion, this is not universally applicable as the AP is limited to 141 NNWS and Euratom. Neither instruments or regimes on the international

699 Article 4 para. 2(b) Treaty of Bangkok, Article 4(b) Treaty of Rarotonga.

700 Strengthening the Effectiveness and Improving the Efficiency of Agency Safeguards: Report by the Director General to the General Conference, GC(39)/17, para. 15.

level – the IAEA's safeguards system – nor regional approaches – Euratom and NWFZs – are comprehensively applicable to fusion. Where there are regimes that include the proliferation potential of fusion to a certain extent – the ITER Agreement and export control regimes –, there are no effective procedures to verify that fusion is not being used for nuclear weapons purposes. The next chapter explores interpretative, doctrinal and treaty-making approaches to closing the gap between the existing proliferation potential and the legal regime of nuclear.

Chapter 4: Adapting the Legal Framework

The previous chapter has shown that the existing framework of nuclear weapons law is characterised by gaps and ambiguity with regard to its application to fusion. While the regime prohibits NNWS from using fusion for applications in nuclear weapons programmes, the majority of rules and procedures of the verification regime do not apply to fusion. The few rules that apply do not cover all aspects of fusion's proliferation potential. The existing framework has been developed with a fission fuel chain in mind, leading to rules that do not adequately address fusion's role in nuclear weapons despite the goals of the nuclear non-proliferation and disarmament regime.

This chapter explores possibilites on how to adapt the legal framework in order for it to apply to fusion. The first section undertakes an analysis of the constraints that exist when adapting the framework in its application to fusion (1). The chapter proceeds with the application of evolutionary interpretation on the legal instruments and analyses to which extent this interpretative approach allows for the application of the existing regime to fusion (2). The third section examines how different international organisations and other institutions can extend the scope of verification measures in non-proliferation to fusion (3). The chapter proceeds with an analysis where treaty changes are required in order to allow for the verification of fusion (4). The chapter concludes with an overview of the benefits and disadvantages of the different approaches (5).

1 Constraints to Adapt the Framework

Making changes to the international legal framework of nuclear weapons law is an outstandingly difficult task. This is due both to financial and commercial interests tied to international oversight and control (1.1), and to the political interests of the various actors involved (1.2).

1.1 Financial and Commercial Interests

As analysed in Chapter 2, there is a trade-off between security and development, making any changes to the safeguards regime outstandingly difficult.

This trade-off materialises especially in the allocation of resources within the IAEA, given the Member States' zero-growth budget policy.[701] Any strengthening of the safeguards system, especially for a completely different technology such as fusion, would result in financial difficulties for the IAEA. At present, the IAEA is underway to reduce its staff by 10 % within two years,[702] while more safeguarding would require more personnel. Either the Agency would need to convince its Member States to increase its budget or relocate resources within the current budget. With respect to the former, discussions surrounding fusion safeguards have become increasingly visible among industry representatives, research institutions, and policymakers. Some publications produced by advocates of fusion energy emphasise the technological and safety differences between fusion and fission and argue that fusion presents comparatively lower proliferation risks.[703] Industry actors have also expressed concern that safeguards obligations, depending on their design, could introduce additional costs, technical constraints, or delays to commercialisation. Linking fusion and proliferation might shed a negative light on fusion and equates a good technology with a terrible use. Referring to the technology as *fusion* rather than as *nuclear fusion* is another example of the public relations dimension of fusion and the attempt to distance fusion from fission technology. These positions may shape how some States view proposals to increase the IAEA's budget if such increases are framed as primarily supporting fusion safeguards. Regarding the latter: Reallocating resources within the budget would most likely hurt the current work within safeguarding fission reactors. As analysed above, fission poses significantly higher proliferation risks than fusion due to its potential direct contributions to a nuclear weapons programme. It is therefore difficult to move resources away from this highly security-relevant part of safeguards.

---

701 *Trevor Findlay*, Unleashing the Nuclear Watchdog – Strengthening and Reform of the IAEA (2012), Centre for International Governance Innovation.

702 International Atomic Energy Agency, *The Agency's Programme and Budget 2022–2023*, GC(65)/2, at 3.

703 *Michael Y. Hua/Sachin S. Desai/Amy C. Roma et al.*, Nonproliferation and Fusion Power Plants, arXiv:2207 14348 (2022), 1–26; *Sachin S. Desai/Michael Y. Hua/Amy C. Roma et al.*, Building a Path Toward Global Deployment of Fusion: Nonproliferation and Export Considerations (2025), Atlantic Council.

Commercial considerations play a pivotal role in the development of fusion energy. The market for fusion energy is estimated to reach approximately USD 840 billion by the year 2040.[704] The deployment of fusion energy is driven by start-up companies, which rely to a large amount on venture capital and also on public funding. Conversely, the regulation of any technology is associated with costs and financial risks. As analysed above, this especially true for safeguards:[705] The designs have to be adapted to allow for the implementation of safeguards. The presence of inspectors can influence the operation of the plant. Inspectors also pose a potential risk of industrial espionage. As in other capital-intensive technology sectors, firms tend to favour regulatory approaches that minimise uncertainty, cost, and operational burden. These general economic incentives help explain why commercial actors express interest in ensuring that any safeguards framework for fusion is efficient, predictable, and proportionate to the assessed proliferation risk.

1.2 Political Interests

Different actors have different political interests in the discussion on adapting the regime to fusion, including individual States, groups of States, the IAEA and the EU.

1.2.1 NWS recognised the NPT

As analysed above in Chapter 2, NWS under the NPT defend the nuclear order as it stands. Consequently, NWS are in favour of strengthening the safeguards regime where ever it is possible. From their perspective, the stronger the safeguards regime, the less likely the further proliferation of nuclear weapons becomes and the easier it is to maintain the nuclear order. As mentioned above, economic interests, however, serve as a counter interest to this political interest. This is especially true for the United States as home of the majority of fusion start-ups and the biggest contributor to

704 *Allied Market Research*, Fusion Energy Market Size, Share, Competitive Landscape and Trend Analysis Report, by Technology, by Fuels: Global Opportunity Analysis and Industry Forecast, 2030–2040 (2023).

705 Chapter 2, Section 1.2.

the IAEA.[706] NWS accept economic consequences of safeguards, at least to an extent where the deployment of the technology is still feasible. As a consequence, NWS have a political interest in safeguarding fusion as long as it does not hinder their domestic fusion industries to develop.

Among NWS recognised by the NPT are also other leading States in the development of fusion energy. For example, until Brexit all of these States used to be part of ITER and all States except the United Kingdom remain committed to ITER. In addition, there are important research activities in all and start-up activity in most of these States. As a consequence, these States also have a leverage to promote their interest of safeguarding fusion: Exporting fusion technology under the condition that the importing State accepts fusion safeguards.

Given their hesitation towards nuclear disarmament, their interest is mainly focused on strengthening the non-proliferation regime, while a materialisation of Article VI of the NPT and pathways to nuclear disarmament is not in their interest. In addition, any connection between the introduction of new safeguards and clear steps towards nuclear disarmament is against the political interest of NWS under the NPT.

1.2.2 NWS outside the NPT

NWS outside the NPT have no interest of strengthening the safeguards regime. As they are already outside the regime, any modification of the existing regime is of no interest for them. This is also a limitation for a safeguards regime for fusion: Any safeguards instrument to be developed for fusion would not include those States that already possess nuclear weapons and are outside the regime. While these States might already use thermonuclear weapons, meaning a combination of fission and fusion, the deployment of fusion technology still has benefits for these States.

Still, the current non-proliferation regime has indirect effects on these States: Export controls mandated under Article III.2 of the NPT prohibit exports of nuclear goods to these States. Similar limitations are found in the export control lists of the Zangger Committee and the NSG. NWS outside the NPT have an interest of deploying fusion while preventing similar indirect effects which might limit their capacity in using fusion technology for their stockpiles.

706 The United States contributes 25 % to the IAEA's regular budget, followed by China with about 15 %, Japan with about 8 % and Germany with about 6 %, GC(66)/11.

1.2.3 NNWS from the Global North

States from the Global North share several interests with NWS under the NPT. They have an interest in a strong non-proliferation regime that also encompasses fusion. While the motivation might differ between NATO and non-NATO States for having a strong non-proliferation regime, none of these States have an interest that fusion technology is used by a NNWS to develop nuclear weapons.

Within States from the Global North, a distinction between States with a fusion industry and States without a fusion industry has to be drawn. Currently, it is mainly Germany, Canada and Japan which are NNWS with a landscape of several fusion start-ups and other companies involved in a fusion supply chain. These States have an interest in promoting their technologies worldwide, leading to two consequences. First, as security interests collide with economic interests, their interest in promoting safeguards for fusion might be gradually reduced. As they do not defend their own privileged position as it is the case with NWS, this interest is not countered to a similar extent. However, as these States have historically unequivocally supported the non-proliferation despite their fission industry, it is feasible to assume that their economic interest would not limit their commitment to strengthening the safeguards regime and to advocate for fusion safeguards. In addition, given the controversial nature of nuclear technologies, a safeguards regime for fusion might increase social acceptance of fusion technology.

1.2.4 States from the Global South

As shown above in Chapter 2, there are two fractions of States from the Global South with diverging interests in nuclear non-proliferation. There are many States supporting high level of safeguards in order to prevent the acquisition of a nuclear weapons by another State, while there is also a strong group of States which is against any strengthening of the safeguards regime. The latter fraction sees any additional safeguards as a sign of a lack of trust of their commitment towards nuclear non-proliferation as long as there is no progress towards nuclear disarmament from NWS.[707]

707 *Rebecca Gibbons/Todd Robinson*, Twenty-Five Years Safer? Assessing the IAEA's Model Additional Protocol and its Role in International Politics, The Nonprolifer-

Nuclear disarmament, on the other side, is strongly supported by all States from the Global South. These States have an interest in combining a strengthened safeguards regime with clear pathways towards nuclear disarmament.

In addition, States from the Global South also have an interest in gaining access to fusion technology for peaceful applications. As fusion energy will provide a carbon-free source of energy regardless of meteorological or geographic conditions, this technology has transformative potential for their energy sectors as well. As a consequence, this allows for a trade-off between accepting new safeguards in return for getting access to fusion technology.

1.2.5 European Union and Euratom

As argued above in Chapter 2, the European Union is a supporter of a strong non-proliferation regime and typically argues for an extension in its Common Foreign and Security Policy. Therefore, it is likely that the European Union would also be in favour of adapting the regime to cover fusion. The EU's position would mirror the position of its Member States, which would in general support safeguards for fusion.

Euratom's position, however, is not entirely clear as it is charged with safeguards in two scenarios. First, where Euratom provides a Member State with nuclear material, and second, where it implements IAEA safeguards, Article 77 Euratom Treaty. Currently, there is no indication that Euratom has an interest in acting as a fusion material supplier similar to its role with fission material. Regarding the application of IAEA safeguards, Euratom acts rather neutral as the extent of IAEA safeguards depends on IAEA Member States. If IAEA safeguards are adapted to fusion, then Euratom would follow suit. If Euratom Member States require the European Commission to apply safeguards to fusion, Euratom would follow suit as well.

ation Review 29 (2022), 1–22; *Matias Spektor/Togzhan Kassenova/Lucas Perez Florentino*, Brazil's Nuclear Posture Under Bolsonaro, Arms Control Today 49 (2019), 12–17.

1.2.6 IAEA

As highlighted above, an effective safeguards regime is at the core of the IAEA's reason to exist. This existential interest also extends to fusion technology. Fusion falls under the wider mandate of the IAEA to promote atoms for peace and development.[708] In addition, the IAEA intends to define itself as the international organisation charged with not only fission, but fusion technology as well.[709] As the idea behind the IAEA's mandate to promote nuclear energy only works effectively if this promotion is paired with effective safeguards to prevent its use in nuclear weapons, the IAEA has an interest to apply safeguards to fusion facilities as well.

However, as analysed above, the IAEA suffers from a lack of proper funding. Instead of increasing its staff in order to address new technological challenges, the IAEA is on its way to reduce staff. The interest of the IAEA to extent its safeguards regime to fusion is therefore accompanied with a strong interest of increasing its funding as it would otherwise risk to reduce its safeguards activities with fission. As fission's proliferation potential is significantly higher than fusion's proliferation potential, shifting resources from fission safeguards to fusion safeguards would be against the IAEA's interest. Additionally, there might be differing views within the IAEA, with the Department of Safeguards on the one side, and the other departments promoting fusion energy on the other.

1.2.7 Summary

All NPT Member States share an interest in preventing fusion technology from being used for the development of nuclear weapons by NNWS. Most States share an interest in adapting the non-proliferation regime, with some State also having an economic interest that fusion safeguards do not harm the prospects of commercialising the technology. However, there is a significant number of States in the Global South which oppose an expansion of the safeguards regime as long as there is no tangible progress towards nuclear disarmament. This, in turn, is against the interest of the NWS recognised under the NPT. The IAEA has an interest in applying safeguards to fusion as long as such an extension of the safeguards system would not be detrimental for fission safeguards.

---

708 See above Chapter 3, Section 1.1.

709 Ibid.

2 Evolutionary Interpretation

This section explores the potential of evolutionary interpretation in the application of the existing regime to fusion and how it can contribute to bridging the gap between the objective of the regime and its means of verification. The section first investigates the doctrinal background of evolutionary interpretation (2.1), before applying this interpretative method to the IAEA's safeguards regime (2.2) and its implications to NWFZ Treaties and the TPNW (2.3). The section continues to interpret the Euratom Treaty evolutionary (2.4), before taking stock of the applicability of the nuclear weapons law regime to fusion (2.5).

2.1 Doctrinal Background

Evolutionary interpretation – also termed evolutive or dynamic interpretation[710] – is an interpretation method that emerged in the jurisprudence of human rights courts[711] and tends to become acknowledged as an interpretatitive method in all areas of international law.[712] While it is disputed whether this method fits within the classical canon of interpretation enshrined in Articles 31 to 33 VCLT[713] or whether it is a complementary

710 See *Christian Djeffal*, Static and Evolutive Treaty Interpretation: A Functional Reconstruction, Cambridge: Cambridge University Press 2018; *Sondre Torp Helmersen*, Evolutive Treaty Interpretation: Legality, Semantics and Distinctions, European Journal of Legal Studies 6 (2013), 127–148.

711 Human Rights Courts often refer to Human Rights Treaties as *Living Instruments*. It was first introduced in the landmark judgement *European Court of Human Rights*, Tyrer vs. United Kingdom, Application No. 5856/72, Judgement of 25 April 1978, at para. 31. On the *Living Instruments Doctrine* as evolutionary interpretation, see *Eirik Bjorge*, Evolutionary Interpretation: 'The Convention is a Living Instrument', in: Domestic Application of the ECHR: Courts as Faithful Trustees, Oxford: Oxford University Press 2015, 131–154.

712 *International Court of Justice*, Dispute Regarding Navigational and Related Rights (Costa Rica v. Nicaragua), Judgement, ICJ Reports 2009, p. 213; *Eirik Bjorge*, The Evolutionary Interpretation of Treaties, Oxford: Oxford University Press 2014.

713 *Helmersen* (n 710), at 146 ff.; *Geir Ulfstein*, Evolutive Interpretation in the Light of Other International Instruments: Law and Legitimacy, in: Anne van Aaken/Iulia Motoc (eds.), The European Convention on Human Rights and General International Law, Oxford: Oxford University Press 2018, 83–94.

method outside the VCLT,[714] evolutionary interpretation is gaining increasing acceptance. This method faces the predicament that a treaty provision, due to its wording, would not apply to an instance simply because that situation did not exist when the treaty was drafted. Interpretation is based on the presumption that the text of a treaty is the "authentic expression of the intentions of the parties"[715], while the text itself is, as Max Huber framed it, "sauf de rares exceptions, la seule et la plus récente expression de la volonté commune des parties", as the only and most recent expression of the common will of the Parties, with a few rare exceptions.[716] As treaties tend to be static and amendments are rare, the reality under which the treaty operates evolves over time, especially with regard to technology.[717] Evolutionary interpretation tries to "determine the precise meaning of a rule"[718] without changing its meaning, while also recognising the fact that the reality in which the rule finds itself changes over time. Evolutionary interpretation needs to be applied restrictively to avoid reconstructing the treaty,[719] which would violate the sovereignty of the States bound by the treaty. For this reason, the use of the method itself is – not only, but especially outside human rights conventions – criticised.[720]

For interpreters, evolutionary interpretation is an attractive tool to expand the meaning of an expression beyond its original (textualist) meaning. This is especially true for courts – where the concept of evolutionary interpretation has been developed –, but also for international organisations, such as the IAEA. However, this also represents a shift of power within

714 Similarly, *Georg Nolte*, Subsequent Agreements and Subsequent Practice in Relation to the Interpretation of Treaties, A/CN.4/660, Geneva: International Law Commission 2013, at paras 54 ff.

715 *International Law Commission*, Draft Articles on the Law of Treaties With Commentaries, New York: United Nations 1966, at 220.

716 *Institut de droit interational*, Annuaires – Tome 44 (I) 1952 Travaux Préparatoires, Basel: Verlag für Recht und Gesellschaft 1952, at 199.

717 *Helmersen* (n 710), at 129.

718 Boundary Dispute Between Argentina and Chile Concerning the Frontier Line Between Boundary Post 62 and Mount Fitzroy (1994), XXII Reports of International Arbitral Awards 3, at para. 75.

719 *Permanent Court of International Justice*, Polish Nationality Case, PCJ (1923) Series B No 7, at para. 41.

720 *Rudolf Bernhardt*, Evolutive Treaty Interpretation, Especially of the European Convention on Human Rights Focus Section: The Law of International Treaties in the 21st Century, German Yearbook of International Law 42 (1999), 11–25; *Bruno Simma*, Mainstreaming Human Rights: The Contribution of the International Court of Justice, Journal of International Dispute Settlement 3 (2012), 7–29, at 26.

the actors of international law. For example, one of the most prominent critiques of the European Court of Human Rights is what is perceived as an overreach from Strasbourg as the court engages heavily in evolutionary interpretation.[721] While the text of the treaty is decided on by States, evolutionary interpretation is applied by courts or international organisations. Thus, there is a risk of losing power over the meaning of a treaty provision to the detriment of States,[722] while courts or international organisations increase their interpretative authority. As a consequence, States often perceive evolutionary interpretation as problematic.

The ICJ has applied evolutionary interpretation on several occasions.[723] Within its jurisprudence, two cumulative requirements for the application of said method have been identified: The use of a 'generic' term and a temporal element.[724] Once these requirements are met, the intention of the treaty drafters to interpret an expression evolutively is presumed.[725] While the treaty interpretation following the rules contained in the VCLT is primarily text-based,[726] the ICJ requires a subjective element and limits evolutionary interpretation to cases where the Parties had the explicit or implicit intention that the meaning of a term could evolve.[727] The combination of these two requirements tries to find a balance between the sovereignty of States and the practical necessity to adapt treaty provisions to a world in flux.

721 *Peter Hilpold*, Challenging Strasbourg – The May 2025 Letter and the Pushback Against the European Court of Human Rights (2025), in: Verfassungsblog, https://verfassungsblog.de/may-2025-letter-and-the-pushback-against-the-european-court-of-human-rights/, last accessed 3 June 2025.

722 Ibid.

723 The most prominent cases are *International Court of Justice*, Legal Consequences for States of the Continued Presence of South Africa in Namibia (South West Africa) notwithstanding Security Council Resolution 276 (1970), Advisory Opinion, ICJ Reports 1971, p. 16, at para. 53; Aegan Sea Continental Shelf (Greece v. Turkey), Judgment, ICJ Reports 1978, p. 3, at para. 77; Navigational Rights (n 712), at paras 64–66; North Sea Continental Shelf (Federal Republic of Germany v. The Netherlands), Judgment, ICJ Reports 1969, p. 3.

724 *Helmersen* (n 710), at 136; *ICJ*, Navigational Rights (n 712), at para. 66.

725 *ICJ*, Navigational Rights (n 712), at para. 66.

726 *Fuad Zarbiyev*, The 'Cash Value' of the Rules of Treaty Interpretation, Leiden Journal of International Law 32 (2019), 33–45, at 36; *International Law Commission* (n 715), at 220.

727 *Helmersen* (n 710), at 138 with vast examples of case law.

To consider a term generic, the term has to have a meaning that evolves over time.[728] The ICJ requires that the Parties to a treaty had been aware of the likeliness of such an evolution of the meaning.[729] From a temporal point of view, the ICJ requires that the treaty "has been entered into force for a very long time or is of continuing duration."[730]

2.2 The IAEA's Safeguards System

As analysed before, in its current understanding, the IAEA's safeguards system based on the NPT, the CSA, and the Additional Protocol, is largely not applicable to fusion since the scope of material and facility is too narrow. The safeguarded material is fissionable material, nuclear facilities are fission facilities. This section applies evolutionary interpretation to the key terms of the IAEA safeguards system found in the IAEA Statute and the NPT – *source and special fissionable material* and *nuclear facility* – in order to analyse, whether this allows for an application of the system to fusion and to overcome the gaps in the system.

2.2.1 Source and Special Fissionable Material

The first question is whether evolutionary interpretation would allow for fusionable material in general or at least specific fusionable materials to be covered by the term *source and special fissionable material.* The materials of specific relevance for evolutionary interpretation are the two main fusion fuels, tritium and deuterium, as well as lithium enriched in ^{6}Li, the material necessary to produce tritium within a fusion facility.

The temporal element necessary for evolutionary interpretation is unarguably fulfilled. The NPT entered into force more than 50 years ago, and the IAEA Statute is even older. However, the other requirement for evolutionary interpretation – the use of a generic term – is more difficult to argue. Firstly, it was likely in 1957 when the IAEA Statute was adopted or in 1968 when the NPT was adopted, that scientists and engineers would find other materials that can undergo fission and are potentially usable for

728 Ibid, at 136; *ICJ*, Navigational Rights (n 712), at para. 67.
729 *ICJ*, Navigational Rights (n 712), at para. 66.
730 Ibid.

nuclear weapons. For that reason, Article XX of the IAEA Statute includes a provision for the Board of Governors to determine *other fissionable* material from time to time. This provision limits the possibility for evolutionary interpretation, since the precise will of the treaty authors was to let the Board of Governors as a specific body decide, which material it considers to be potentially usable for nuclear weapons instead of other interpreters. Secondly, it is unlikely that the treaty authors expected the term *fissionable* to include *fusionable*. When the IAEA Statute was adopted in 1957, the United States, the Soviet Union and the United Kingdom had already conducted hydrogen bomb testing. In 1968, when the NPT was adopted, China had also tested its first hydrogen bomb.[731] Also, boosting of fission weapons with tritium was known.[732] Nuclear fusion was even discovered earlier than nuclear fission.[733] Fusion processes for nuclear bombs as well as the use of tritium were in the mind of the treaty authors. This is also supported by the earlier mentioned comments made by the United States during the NPT negotations to exclude fusion from the framework, as well as by the depositary note of Germany, which includes an interpretative note that the NPT would not affect the development of fusion technology.[734] Thus, *fissionable* is not a generic term that can be understood to cover *fusionable*.

As a consequence, even with evolutionary interpretation, fusionable material is not covered by the term *source and special fissionable material* in the sense of Article XX of the IAEA Statute and Art. III.1 NPT. As the CSA refers in its definition of *nuclear material* to Article XX of the IAEA Statute, this safeguards agreement does not apply to fusionable material

731 *Timothy J. Pounds*, A Chronology of Comprehensive Test Ban Proposals, Negotiations, and Debates: 1945–1993, 1994.

732 The first boosted fission weapons were detonated by the United States on 8 May 1951 and by the Soviet Union on 12 August 1953; *Alex Wellerstein/Edward Geist*, The Secret of the Soviet Hydrogen Bomb, AIP Conference Proceedings 1898 (2017), 020008, at 4.

733 Fission was discovered in 1939 by *Otto Hahn/Fritz Strassmann*, Über den Nachweis und das Verhalten der bei der Bestrahlung des Urans mittels Neutronen entstehenden Erdalkalimetalle, Naturwissenschaften 27 (1939), 11–15; fusion was discovered in the early 1930s, *Marcus Laurence Elwin Oliphant/Ernest Rutherford*, Experiments on the Transmutation of Elements by Protons, Proceedings of the Royal Society of London. Series A, Containing Papers of a Mathematical and Physical Character 141 (1933), 259–281.

734 See Chapter 3, Section 1.2.3.2.

as material. Thus, the IAEA safeguards regime based on the NPT cannot apply to tritium, deuterium and ^{6}Li.[735]

2.2.2 Nuclear Facility

In contrast to the terms *nuclear material* or *source and special fissionable material,* the application of the principles of evolutionary interpretation enables the inclusion of fusion facilities under the term *nuclear facility* used by the NPT, CSA and Additional Protocol. As shown in the previous chapter, standard methods of interpretation largely do not allow for the application of these instruments to fusion facilities.[736]

The term *nuclear facility* contains several subsets of facilities, most notably reactors. Safeguards agreements do not apply to fusion facilities as the definition of reactors is limited to devices in which a controlled, self-sustaining fission chain-reaction can be maintained. The definition is included in both item-specific safeguards agreement INFCIRC/26[737] and INFCIRC/66[738], as well as in the Annex of the Additional Protocol.[739]

As the CSAs are based on INFCIRC/153, which was adopted in 1972, and were concluded with each State during the years that followed, the temporal element of evolutionary interpretation is fulfilled. For evolutionary interpretation to apply, it has to be shown that the term *nuclear facility* or *reactor* is a generic term. Technological evolution shapes the understanding of the technical term *nuclear facility.* The CSA attempts to cover different technical components and facilities within the fuel cycle of nuclear energy. As nuclear energy is a sector with a lot of technological development, it must have been on the mind of the States that concepts for reactors could evolve. Since the construction of the first nuclear power reactor in 1942,[740] many different types and concepts of nuclear reactors were developed. They include developments in the material used as moderator (graphite, heavy

735 On the criticism that tritium and breeding-blankets are not included in the safeguards system, see *Noah C. Mayhew/VCDNP*, Reflecting on the Annexes to the Model Additional Protocol in Support of Nuclear Governance, 2022, at 8 ff.

736 Chapter 3, Section 1.3.1.2.

737 Paras 13 and 14.

738 Para. 80.

739 Para. 1.1. of the Annex.

740 The first nuclear reactor was the Chicago Pile-1 reactor as part of the Manhattan Project under the leadership of Enrico Fermi, one of the most important physicists of the 20th century.

water and sodium), in reactions (thermal neutrons or fast-neutrons), in the coolant (boiling water, pressurised water) or size (gigawatt scale, small modular reactors). While these developments were focused on fission, it proves that the term is not static. Developments with regard to reactors happened and they were foreseeable.

Furthermore, the IAEA and safeguards agreements seek to define the term nuclear facility in broad terms. The definition contains a long list of different supporting facilities to cover the entire nuclear fuel cycle on order to avoid loopholes. This demonstrates the objective that regardless of the specific technology used, the definition should be wide enough to prevent any gaps in the safeguards regime.

Additionally, recent developments have demonstrated that fusion can be considered as a nuclear technology. This is shown by the application of the French nuclear code to ITER as a nuclear installation,[741] other national regulatory approaches[742] or the simple fact that the IAEA itself is engaged in the area of fusion.[743] This demonstrates that the term *nuclear facility* is a generic term. Accordingly, evolutionary interpretation enables fusion facility to fall under the term nuclear facility in the sense of the NPT, the CSA and the Additional Protocol.

In summary, evolutionary interpretation would allow for a fusion reactor to be regarded as a nuclear facility under the provisions of the CSA, providing the IAEA with the authority to apply safeguards on fusion facilities. This leads to an important implication: Where the CSA refers to obligations towards facilities, these obligations would extend to fusion facilities. This entails the obligation to provide the IAEA with design information (para. 42), a description of the facility (para. 43), and the authority for the IAEA to conduct routine inspection (para. 80). The IAEA would have the possibility to verify the absence of undeclared source and fissionable material within a fusion facility, addressing one of the key proliferation issues of fusion. The provision under which a State has to provide the IAEA with design information is of particular significance as this would address the concern of plutonium breeding within a fusion facility, given the significant

741 ITER is considered an installation nucléaire de base (INB), which is also the standard category for nuclear fission facilities in France. ITER was declared an INB by the Décret n° 2012–1248 du 9 novembre 2012 autorisant l'Organisation internationale ITER à créer une installation nucléaire de base dénommée « ITER » sur la commune de Saint-Paul-lez-Durance (Bouches-du-Rhône).

742 For example, in the United States the Nuclear Regulatory Commission is the competent authority.

743 See above, Chapter 3, Section 1.1.

modifications required from a standard commercial design. What the IAEA cannot do, however, is to verify fusionable material. As the application of IAEA safeguards, even in fusion facilities, would be limited in verifying the absence of fissionable material in the facility, other proliferation concerns such as the use of tritium for nuclear weapons programmes would not be addressed. Furthermore, the proliferation potential regarding the gaining of knowledge for the functioning of thermonuclear weapons via inertial confinement would not be addressed by expanding the existing regime to fusion facilities by applying evolutionary interpretation.

2.3 Implications to NWFZ and the TPNW

These findings outlined above carry implications for the safeguards regimes of other treaties, including the NWFZ Treaties and the TPNW, as they refer to the IAEA safeguards system. Where these treaties refer to source and special fissionable material or directly quote Article XX of the IAEA Statute, the aforementioned considerations exclude an evolutionary interpretation including fusionable material into the application of safeguards.

With regard to the application to fusion facilities, all but one[744] NWFZ Treaties refer to (at least[745]) the CSA as the baseline for the application of safeguards. As argued above, evolutionary interpretation would allow for a fusion reactor to be considered a nuclear facility in the sense of the CSA. Consequently, the IAEA could exercise its authority to inspect fusion facilities also under the NWFZ regimes, albeit with the aforementioned limitations. This would address one of three aspects in which fusion can play a role in the proliferation of nuclear weapons.

Similarly, the TPNW refers in its Article 3 para. 2 to the CSA as the baseline for safeguards for NNWS. Under the TPNW, NNWS are required to accept IAEA safeguards on the level of the CSA, and, in the event they have adopted an Additional Protocol, to maintain such a heightened level of safeguards. The TPNW's direct reference to IAEA safeguards leads to evolutionary interpretation allowing for the IAEA to apply safeguards

744 As the Treaty of Tlatelolco is older than the NPT and the CSA, there is no reference to it. However, the CSA also serves as basis for safeguards agreements under this Treaty, *Laura Rockwood*, Legal Framework for IAEA Safeguards, Vienna: IAEA 2013, at 12.

745 The Treaty of Semipalatinsk even sets the Additional Protocol as baseline, Article 8(b).

on fusion facilities. It is important to note that, as the TPNW has been adopted in 2017, the temporal element necessary for the application of evolutionary interpretation is missing for the TPNW. However, evolutionary interpretation is not applied to a provision of the TPNW, rather to the IAEA safeguards regime to which the TPNW refers to.

2.4 Euratom Treaty

The application of evolutionary interpretation partially extends the European Commission's authority under the Euratom Treaty to apply safeguards to fusion. To recall, the Euratom safeguards system is based on two pillars: The verification that ores, source materials and special fissile materials are only used for their declared use (Article 77(a)), and the implementation of international agreements (Article 77(b)).

Regarding the implementation of international agreements, the possibility to include fusion facilities into the safeguards activities based on the NPT and the CSA is also true for the Euratom Treaty. Under the Euratom-IAEA Framework, the European Commission applies the CSA, and consequently, the above-mentioned argumentation holds as well: While fusionable material is outside the scope of the safeguards, the European Commission could apply its safeguards to fusion facilities through an evolutionary interpretation of the term *nuclear facility* to the same extent as the IAEA.

However, evolutionary interpretation is not possible for Euratom to extend its own safeguards system to fusion. Extending the meaning of materials is not possible for the same reasons as it is the case with Article XX of the IAEA Statute. Although the temporal requirement is fulfilled as the treaty was signed in 1957, it is not possible to assume the use of a generic term. The Euratom Treaty mentions fusion explicitly,[746] indicating that the drafters of the treaty were aware of fusion as a technology and that leaving out fusion of the safeguards system was a deliberate choice. As the ICJ requires such an evolutive intent of the Parties, the requirement of a *generic term* of evolutionary interpretation is not fulfilled. Regardless of the question on whether such methods of international law are applicable

746 According to Article II.1.(e) of Annex I to the Euratom Treaty, the study of fusion is part of applied theoretical physics to nuclear energy as a field of research concerning nuclear energy referred to in Article 4 of the Euratom treaty.

in interpreting the Euratom Treaty,[747] the European Commission is limited to apply evolutionary interpretation in order to implement the NPT-mandated safeguards system on fusion facilities in Euratom Member States following the CSA between Euratom and the IAEA.

2.5 Stocktaking and Limitations of Evolutionary Interpretation

Before examining the options of exercising authority or treaty changes, it is necessary to take stock to which extent the existing framework – including the application of evolutionary interpretation – applies to fusion. Fusionable material falls outside the scope of safeguards instruments. Consequently, the proliferation potentials of tritium and inertial confinement fusion are not addressed. However, the existing regime can be made applicable to address the proliferation potential of producing fissile material: In States that only have a CSA in place, the IAEA is able to conduct its standard verification procedures by invoking evolutionary interpretation. Where States have concluded an Additional Protocol with the IAEA, the Agency can verify that a fusion facility is not used for breeding nuclear weapons material by environmental sampling and complementary access via a direct application. Given that many other non-proliferation and disarmament instruments refer to the CSA as the baseline for their verification instruments, this finding is also of relevance for the TPNW, NWFZ Treaties and the Euratom Treaty.

However, there are severe limitations of evolutionary interpretation with regard to its application to the safeguards regime and fusion. First, evolutionary interpretation would only address one shortcoming of the regime. It would allow for the fission-based safeguards regime to apply to fusion facilities. The consequence is that one of three aspects of fusion's proliferation potential would be addressed, namely the use of fusion facilities to produce plutonium for nuclear weapons. Evolutionary interpretation would serve to bridge the gap in the NPT System for those 44 States, that have not adopted an Additional Protocol. It also extends the authority to other safeguards

747 The European legal order is an autonomous legal order, which has been established by Court of Justice of the European Union, Judgement of 5 February 1963, *van Gend & Loos*, Case 26–62, ECLI:EU:C:1963:1, at para. 3; Judgment of 15 July 1964, *Costa v. ENEL*, Case 6–64, ECLI:EU:C:1964:66, at 593. On the role of international law in EU law, see also Judgement of 3 September 2008, *Kadi*, ECLI:EU:C:2008:461, joined Cases C-402/05 P and C-415/05 P.

regimes where an Additional Protocol is not necessary, such as the TPNW and NWFZ Treaties. However, evolutionary interpretation does not address the other aspects of the proliferation potential of fusion, namely safeguarding fusionable material and addressing inertial confinement fusion.

Second, States might see the extension of the IAEA's authority via evolutionary interpretation critically. States have been hesitant to extend the Agency's authority with treaty changes to the safeguards system, while an extension via evolutionary interpretation excludes the participation of all States. Such an interpretation would be made either by the Secretariat, where States do not have a direct influence on, the Board of Governors with its limited membership or the General Conference. As both policy-making organs can take decisions by simple majorities, while the introduction of new safeguards agreements would require the consent of the concerned State, the IAEA's authority could be extended without the agreement of a concerned State. Thus, States might perceive evolutionary interpretation as undue interference with their sovereignty.

Third, the application of existing procedures and verification techniques developed for fission to the same extent to fusion would be disproportionate given the different levels of proliferation potential. A fission facility operates with material that has direct use in nuclear weapons programmes, while a fusion facility has no use of such material in a civilian operation. The safeguards system applies to different facilities throughout the fission fuel cycle, while in fusion it is only the reactor where the application of the IAEA safeguards regime addresses a proliferation potential of fusion. Operators of fusion facilities would be burdened with safeguards, while the effects would be limited. As the system has not been designed for the specificities of fusion, such an application would lead to a level of interference disproportionate to the risks posed by fusion.

As a consequence, the next section develops pathways how the exercise of authority under the existing regime opens possibilities to address the proliferation potential of fusion in an adequate manner.

3 Acting under the Existing Regime

This section explores the possibilities of adapting the non-proliferation regime in its application to fusion by exercising authority and acting under the existing framework. The section starts by analysing how two bodies of the IAEA, the Board of Governors (3.1) and the Secretariat (3.2), can exercise authority under the IAEA Statute, established practices and the IAEA safeguards system in order to apply safeguards to fusion. It proceeds by examining the Nuclear Suppliers Group's role to extend export controls to fusion (3.3). This is followed by an analysis of Review Conferences and Meeting of State Parties of the NPT (3.4) and the TPNW (3.5) in their role of developing safeguards for fusion. The section then gives an overview of the role of the United Nations and its possibility in exercising its authority to strengthen the non-proliferation regime for fusion (3.6). The section concludes with an overview of the findings and an analysis of the advantages and disadvantages of the various approaches (3.7).

3.1 Decisions by the Board of Governors

This section analyses the extent to which the IAEA Statute provides the Board of Governors with powers to extend the safeguards regime to fusion. It starts with an analysis of the authority of the Board in general, with a specific focus on the safeguards system, before presenting several decisions that the Board could take.

3.1.1 Authority of the Board of Governors

The IAEA's Board of Governors is the executive organ of the IAEA and is vested with a wide range of powers.

The Board of Governor consists of 35 Member States and changes its composition annually. There are no formal permanent members in the Statute, yet there are *de facto* permanent members. First, it consists of the ten members of the IAEA which are the "most advanced in the technology of nuclear energy", Article VI.A.1 IAEA Statute. Historically, these ten States always composed the United States, the Soviet Union or Russia, the United Kingdom, France, China, (West-)Germany, Canada and Japan. It is the outgoing Board which designates these ten States. The Board is further composed of the most advanced nuclear State of each regional group and of further States elected by the General Conference for a period of two years following a regional distribution, Article VI.A.2 IAEA Statute. It meets five times a year for regular meetings, sometimes more often in case of the request for extraordinary meetings,[748] compared to the General Conference which convenes once per year.[749]

The Board of Governors takes decisions by a simple majority, with the exception of budgetary questions where a two-thirds majority is required, Article VI.E. In practice, decisions by the Board of Governors are adopted by consensus.[750] This "Vienna Spirit" has allowed the IAEA to carry out its work as an independent technical authority and has mostly escaped geopolitical tensions since its foundation in 1957.[751] Following this spirit, States have usually pursued constructive negotiations leading to consensus.[752] In recent times, however, the Vienna Spirit has more and more faded and votes take place more often.[753]

Jointly with the General Conference, the Board is further responsible to approve any new Member State and to appoint the Director General,[754] which heads the Secretariat and is "subject to the control of the Board of Governors."[755]

The Board of Governors has the "authority to carry out the functions of the Agency [...] subject to its responsibilities to the General Conference", Article VI.F IAEA Statute. It submits an annual report to the General Conference and reports to the United Nations if requested, Article VI.J IAEA Statute. While the Statute sets the Board of Governors institutionally under the authority of the General Conference, the IAEA's practice is the opposite.[756] When the General Conference formally takes decisions, they are

748 An example of such an extraordinary meeting was a Board Meeting taking place on 16 June 2025, requested by Russia, following the Israeli attacks on Iranian nuclear facilities.

749 *Laura Rockwood*, The International Atomic Energy Agency (IAEA), in: Eric Myer/Thilo Marauhn (eds.), Research Handbook on International Arms Control Law, Cheltenham: Elgar 2022, 503–529, at 508.

750 Ibid.

751 Ibid; Nuclear Threat Initiative/Center for Energy and Security Studies (eds.), The Future of IAEA Safeguards: Rebuilding the Vienna Spirit through Russian-U.S. Expert Dialogue, Washington DC: Nuclear Threat Initiative 2020.

752 *Kim Fyhr*, Steering the Atoms for Peace and Development: Legal Aspects of the Board of Governors of the International Atomic Energy Agency, AUC IURIDICA 70 (2024), 31–46, at 37.

753 Ibid.

754 Articles IV.B and VII.A IAEA Statute.

755 Article VI.B IAEA Statute.

756 *Fyhr* (n 752), at 36 and 43 f.

most often prepared by the Board.[757] It is the Board which is the forum for agenda-setting, discussions, deal-making and decisions on nuclear issues.[758]

This *de facto* inversion of authority is most obvious in the area of safeguards, where it is the Board of Governors that exercises authority and can sideline the General Conference.[759] While the General Conference may discuss any matter within the scope of the Statute, Article V.D IAEA Statute, its authority ends where the exclusive competence of the Board of Governors starts. Questions on safeguards typically fall under this category of exclusive competences of the Board. The Board of Governors approves safeguards agreements and arrangements, reports any non-compliance of a State's safeguards obligations to the UN General Assembly and UN Security Council, and can recommend the suspension of such a State.[760] For example, it was the Board of Governors that found that Iran was in non-compliance with its obligations under its safeguards agreement.[761] All developments in the IAEA safeguards system were initiated by the Board of Governors. Thus, the role of the General Conference in extending the safeguards regime to fusion is deemed negligible. This section analyses where the Board can take decisions and other actions in order to extend the IAEA's safeguards regime to fusion.

3.1.2 Designate Materials

The Board of Governors has the power to extend the scope of materials under Article XX of the IAEA Statute. However, it lacks the power to include fusionable material into the definition. In accordance with Article XX.1 of the IAEA Statute, the Board of Governors has the authority to extend the list of materials designated as special fissionable material with other fissionable materials. While the Statute permits the Board to add materials to the list, they still have to be *fissionable*, thus excluding material such as deuterium, tritium and ^{6}Li. Similarly, with regard to source material, the Board can include other material into the definition, but only as long as they contain uranium or thorium in a certain concentration. In addition, as specified by para. 112 of INFCIRC/153, any determination by the Board

757 Ibid.
758 Ibid, at 38.
759 Ibid, at 39 f.
760 Articles XII and XIX IAEA Statute.
761 GOV/2025/38.

of Government would additionally require the acceptance by each State in order to be implemented under the CSA.

Lessons on how to expand the definition of nuclear materials can be learnt from processes in the late 1990s, during which the Board of Governors addressed the question on how to handle the proliferation potential of the fissionable materials of neptunium and americium. The Board of Governors considerations followed a report by the IAEA Secretariat indicating that a proliferation potential has evolved.[762] While these materials can be used to build nuclear weapons,[763] no State has yet pursued such a route. At that time, the Secretariat presented to the Board of Governors three options to address the proliferation potential of these materials: designating them as source and special fissionable material in the sense of Article XX of the IAEA Statute, monitoring international transfers and activities at relevant facilities based on voluntary co-operation with the States, or no action at all.[764] The first option would have entailed the implementation of full-scope safeguards on these materials in the same manner as they are applied to uranium and plutonium. As the proliferation potential has been deemed limited, such a step has been regarded as premature.[765] Conversely, not acting at all, could have posed a risk to the credibility of the safeguards system.[766] As a consequence, the Board of Governors opted for the second route of monitoring on a voluntary basis.[767]

While an extension of Article XX to include fusionable material is not possible, such a call for voluntary safeguards on fusionable material similar to neptunium and americium would be a feasible approach. This would allow for a gradual introduction of fusion safeguards without the necessity of treaty amendments. Given the composition of the Board, such a call would lead to a high level of diplomatic pressure.

762 *Laura Rockwood/Viatcheslav Pouchkarev/Jill N. Cooley et al.*, IAEA Implementation of the Board of Governors Decisions on Neptunium and Americium, Vienna: IAEA 2000.

763 *David Albright/Kimberly Kramer*, Neptunium 237 and Americium: World Inventories and Proliferation Concerns, Institute for Science and International Security 6060 (2005), 1–24; *Rockwood/Pouchkarev/Cooley et al.* (n 762).

764 *Rockwood/Pouchkarev/Cooley et al.* (n 762).

765 Ibid.

766 Ibid.

767 *International Atomic Energy Agency*, The Annual Report for 1999, GC(44)/4, Vienna: IAEA 2000, at 97.

3.1.3 Designate Facilities

The Board of Governors could further designate fusion facilities as facilities under safeguards agreements. Which is another limitation of the application of safeguards. Under pre-NPT safeguards, the Board of Governors had the authority to extend the definition of the term *facility*.[768] As argued above, as the documents contain a specific list of what a facility and, especially, a reactor entails, evolutionary interpretation does not allow fusion to be covered. Para. 78 of INFCIRC/66 specifies that "a facility or plant of such other type [...] may be designated by the Board from time to time." This would enable an extension of the definition by a decision of the Board of Governors. However, it must be noted that INFCIRC/66 is only applicable for India, Pakistan and Israel, as the CSA suspends the application of these item-specific safeguards.[769] These three States decide themselves which facilities they open for IAEA inspection. Under the CSA, the Board of Governors has lost the authority to amend the definition of *facility*. This is due to the extension of IAEA safeguards from a facility-by-facility basis – where the interpretation a *facility* is essential – to comprehensive safeguards, intended to cover all nuclear activities of a State and a shift to focus more on nuclear material.[770]

As a legally binding designation is not possible, the Board of Government could issue an interpretative recommendation to tackle the ambiguity. As argued above, the CSA is the only safeguards agreement which does not define a reactor as a fission reactor. The Board of Governors could thus issue a recommendation to either define the term reactor also in the sense of a fusion reactor, or to explicitly exclude it. It issued interpretative recommendations in other cases, such as the definition of the term "any military purposes" of paras 1–2 of INFCIRC/66 in 1974[771] or the term "as early as possible" of para. 42 of INFCIRC/153.[772] Both the IAEA and States can request consultations on questions of interpretation and application of

768 Para. 78 of INFCIRC/66.

769 Para. 24 of INFCIRC/153; *R. Eltayb Hassan Eltayb/I. Tsvetkov*, Past, Current Status and the Future of Safeguards Implementation under INFCIRC/66/Rev.2 (2023), INMM Working Papers, at 3.

770 *Laura Rockwood*, IAEA Safeguards: Correctness and Completeness of States' Safeguards Declarations, in: International Atomic Energy Agency (ed.), Nuclear Law: The Global Debate, The Hague: T.M.C. Asser Press 2022, 205–222, at 207.

771 *Rockwood* (n 744), at 17.

772 Ibid, at 19.; GOV/2554/Att.2/Rev.2.

the treaty, while States can also request the Board of Governors to consider "any question arising out of the interpretation or application" of the CSA.[773] As evolutionary interpretation would allow for an application of safeguards to fusion reactors, there remains some uncertainty regarding the legitimacy of such an interpretation. The legitimacy of such an interpretation would be increased by a decision by the Board of Governors.

3.1.4 Establishing Committees and Advisory Groups

Another path in which the Board of Governors can encourage the development is the establishment of specialised committees. According to Article VI.I of the IAEA Statute, the Board of Governors has the power to establish committees mandated to work on specific topics, especially safeguards. This authority is further enshrined in Rule 57 of the Provisional Rules of Procedure of the Board of Governors. This prerogative was exercised in the preparation of the Additional Protocol in 1996 and 1997,[774] as well as in 2005 to consider ways and means to strengthen the safeguards system.[775] While the mandates of the respective committees have ended, the Board of Governors retains the authority to establish a committee specifically focusing on the question of applying safeguards to fusion. Such a committee could discuss the pathways to apply fusion safeguards. This could include preparatory works for a protocol or agreement specific for fusion safeguards[776] or methods for technical implementation. As the Board of Governors can "establish such committees as it deems advisable"[777] and has the "authority to carry out the functions of the Agency"[778], which include both non-proliferation and the promotion of fusion,[779] there is a wide margin of discretion for the Board to establish fusion safeguards committees.

---

773 Paras 20 and 21 of INFCIRC/153.

774 The so-called Committee 24, consisting of representatives of about 70 Member States, drafted the model text of the Additional Protocol.

775 The Advisory Committee on Safeguards and Verification within the Framework of the IAEA Statute, or short Committee 25, was established on 17 June 2005.

776 See below, Section 4.2.2.

777 Article VI.I of the IAEA Statute.

778 Article VI.F of the IAEA Statute.

779 See Chapter 3, Section 1.1.

3.1.5 Call for Voluntary State Action

Another potential course of action for the Board of Governors is to call upon States for voluntarily submitting their fusion infrastructure and materials comprehensively to IAEA safeguards. Given that the Board of Governors is entrusted with carrying out the functions of the Agency (Article VI.F of the IAEA Statute), including establishing and administering safeguards (Article III.A.5 of the IAEA Statute), such a plea would fall within the competence of the Board.

With respect to NWS, voluntary approaches are the only option to apply safeguards to fusion. According to the NPT, these States are permitted to use all infrastructure for military purposes and to support nuclear weapon programmes. Presently, the five NWS place parts of their infrastructure under Voluntary Offer Agreements. As analysed above, the two Inertial Confinement Fusion Facilities (NIF in the United States and Laser Mégajoule in France) are part of military programmes and thus not part of the United States' or France's Voluntary Offer Agreements under which they voluntarily open their civilian nuclear infrastructure to IAEA safeguards.

As the first commercially feasible fusion power plant could be built either in the United States[780] or the United Kingdom,[781] there is a significant chance that the question of safeguards will arise in NWS first. NWS offered VOAs for two reasons: increasing acceptance and facilitating negotiations.[782] As safeguards lead to additional burdens and costs as well as interference with sovereignty, accepting safeguards voluntarily sets an equal playing ground for both NWS and NNWS without objecting NNWS to a competitive disadvantage. In addition, such a voluntary approach by NWS might facilitate the negotiation of international fusion safeguards. It is at the discretion of each NWS to extend these VOAs to fusion facilities. As these States decide which facilities they declare, their voluntary action is necessary for safeguards to apply to fusion.

---

780 ARC by Commonwealth Fusion Systems (CFS) is the most likely contender and is expected to start its operation in Virginia in the early 2030s.

781 The UK Government currently works on its STEP (Spherical Tokamak for Energy Production) project, which is expected to produce energy for the British energy grid by 2040, *Adam Baker*, The Spherical Tokamak for Energy Production (STEP) in Context: UK Public Sector Approach to Fusion Energy, Philosophical Transactions of the Royal Society A: Mathematical, Physical and Engineering Sciences 382 (2024), 1–8.

782 *Frank S. Houck*, The Voluntary Safeguards Offer of the United States – A Review of its History and Implementation, IAEA Bulletin 27 (1985), 13–18.

For NNWS, there is also a possibility to accept voluntary safeguards. This will be especially of relevance if either a start-up outside a NWS[783] will be the first to deploy fusion power plants or if a NWS-based start-up exports its technology to NNWS. According to Article III.A.5 of the IAEA Statute, the Agency established and administers safeguards at the request of a State. Consequently, in the absence of an international system of fusion safeguards, States entering into fusion have the option to request the IAEA to specifically apply safeguards on their fusion facilities. Similarly, these voluntary safeguards could serve as a template for the development of international safeguards standards to such novel technology.

3.2 Practice by the IAEA Secretariat

While the Board of Governors is the most powerful policy-making organ within the IAEA, it is the Secretariat, specifically its Department of Safeguards as one of six departments, that is responsible to administer and implement safeguards. It is the Secretariat that sends inspectors and analysis the data transferred to Vienna. In addition, it is the Director General as its head which reports the Secretariat's findings to the Board of Governors or the United Nations.

This section analyses whether IAEA's Secretariat has the authority to extend its safeguards activities to fusion.

3.2.1 Authority of the IAEA Secretariat

The IAEA Secretariat is led by the Director General, which in turn is subject to the control of the Board of Governors.[784] It is not a policy-making body, it merely implements the policy set by the Board and the General Conference.

The IAEA Statute is scarce on the authority of the Secretariat. In fact, it only uses the expression *staff* rather than Secretariat. Article VII is limited to declaring that there is staff, led by the Director General. The Secretariat,

783 Germany wants to be the first State in the world to have an operation fusion power plant, *CDU/CSU/SPD*, Verantwortung für Deutschland – Koalitionsvertrag zwischen CDU, CSU und SPD, 21. Legislaturperiode, Berlin: 2025, at 78.

784 Articles VII.A and VII.B.

thus, is composed of the Director General and the staff.[785] The Director General is mentioned several times, giving him the powers to represent the organisation, report to the policy-making bodies and to prepare budget estimates.[786] The Board's Provisional Rules of Procedures further clarify the powers of the Director General and the Secretariat. According to its rule 8(a), the Director General "shall perform his duties in accordance with regulations adopted by the Board and shall be guided by the policy of the Agency". Rule 10 focuses on the Secretariat itself, charging it with administrative duties in support of the Board's work as well with the task to "perform all other work which the Board, its committees and other subsidiary bodies may require". Similarly, the Rules of Procedures of the General Conference charge the Secretariat with administrative duties in support of the General Conference's work and all other work it, its committees or its subsidiary bodies may require.[787]

However, the Secretariat receives authority from the safeguards instruments, where it performs independently its verification activities.[788] For example, the Secretariat decides when, where and to which extent it performs inspections or what information it requests. In exercising its safeguarding activities, the Secretariat has to interpret the relevant provisions, which further provides the Secretariat with a certain degree of interpretative authority.

3.2.2 Advisory Groups

The IAEA Secretariat has a long-standing practice of establishing independent advisory groups to undertake specific tasks. While there is no clear reference in the IAEA Statute granting the Secretariat the authority to establish such groups, this practice has never been criticised neither by the Board of Governors nor the General Conference nor its Member States. On the contrary, the Member States recognise the valuable work of these

785 *Paul C. Szasz*, The Law and Practices of the International Atomic Energy Agency, Vienna: IAEA 1970, at 193.

786 Articles V.A, VII, XII.C, XIV, XVIII.

787 Rule 39.

788 *Pierre Goldschmidt*, The IAEA Safeguards System Moves into the 21st Century, IAEA Bulletin 41 (1999), 1–19, at 2.

independent advisory groups.[789] One of these advisory groups is the Standing Advisory Group on Safeguards Implementation (SAGSI), established in 1975, which comprises 20 experts tasked to advise the IAEA Director General on the implementation of safeguards. Established to facilitate the implementation of the comprehensive safeguards agreements, SAGSI has played a role in developing safeguards design parameters as well as in the development of the Additional Protocol.[790] SAGSI has been instrumental in defining which amount of which material is seen as sufficient for a nuclear weapon (so-called significant quantity).[791] SAGSI is also seen as an important player in updating the annexes of the Additional Protocol, which contain safeguarded activities and lists of equipment and materials for export controls.[792] This advisory group might draw the attention to fusion safeguards and play a role in their development.

Furthermore, in 2013, the IAEA Secretariat organised a Consultative Group regarding the non-proliferation potential of fusion.[793] Technical experts were interviewed on aspects of magnetic fusion and their role in nuclear non-proliferation. The group drafted a report, in which they raised several proliferation concerns, which are analysed in this book's Chapter 1. The IAEA's Secretariat took note of the report, but did not take any immediate action as the time horizon for the necessity of IAEA action was projected to extend over several decades.[794] It is only recently that the commercial sector has shortened the timeline for commercial fusion energy.

The IAEA's Secretariat could use this authority to establish new groups or charge existing groups with developing new approaches to safeguard fusion technology.

---

789 See for example the records of the Board of Governors' 1131st meeting, GOV/OR.1131, especially at para. 28.

790 *John Carlson*, SAGSI: Its Role and Contribution to Safeguards Development, Canberra: Australian Safeguards and Non-Proliferation Office 2007.

791 *Braden Goddard/Alexander Solodov/Vitaly Fedchenko*, IAEA "Significant Quantity" Values: Time for a Closer Look?, The Nonproliferation Review 23 (2016), 677–689, at 677 f.

792 *Laura Rockwood/Noah C. Mayhew/Artem Lazarev et al.*, IAEA Safeguards: Staying Ahead of the Game (2019), Swedish Radiation Safety Authority, Recommendation 9.

793 *IAEA*, Report of the Consultancy Meeting on "Non-Proliferation Challenges in Connection with Magnetic Fusion Power Plants", Vienna: IAEA 2013.

794 Ibid.

3.2.3 Special Inspections

As argued above, environmental sampling under the Additional Protocol allows to verify to a certain degree that a fusion facility is not used for plutonium production. However, the Additional Protocol is only ratified by 141 States and Euratom, leaving 44 NNWS that have only adopted a CSA. Among the States that did not conclude an Additional Protocol are Argentina, Brazil and Egypt; States with nuclear infrastructure that have pursued nuclear ambitions in the past century. For these States, paras 73 and 78 of INFCIRC/153 (the document on which the CSA is based) provide the IAEA's Secretariat with the authority to perform special inspections. The Secretariat can demand special inspections in the case that the information it has received "is not adequate for the Agency to fulfil its responsibilities under the Agreement", para. 73(b). Under special inspections, the Secretariat can demand access to information and locations that are otherwise not covered by the CSA.[795] The IAEA has the responsibility under the CSA to implement safeguards mandated by Article III.1 of the NPT[796] and to apply safeguards on all source or special fissionable material in all peaceful nuclear activities in the territory of the State by verifying that no such material is diverted to nuclear weapons.

These special inspections could be used to apply safeguards to fusion facilities in NNWS that have only adopted a CSA. As existing safeguards methods do not include fusion facilities, the IAEA does not have the information necessary to verify that fusion facilities are not used to produce and later divert source and special fissionable material for nuclear weapons application. Thus, the requirement for the IAEA to demand special inspections would be fulfilled. As the IAEA may, in the course of special inspections, demand access to locations other than those specified in the agreement, the IAEA may demand access to fusion facilities, as well as to locations where the IAEA may take environmental samples.[797] As a consequence, special inspections would allow for a similar approach as the Additional Protocol currently provides.

However, the IAEA has acted restrictively in demanding special inspections and only did so twice in its history: In 1992 to verify plutonium separation experiments in Romania and in 1993 to verify the North Korean

795 Para. 77 of INFCIRC/153.
796 This is explicitly laid out in para. 1 of INFCIRC/153.
797 *Rockwood* (n 770), at 209 f.

nuclear programme.[798] The IAEA's Board of Governors decided that special inspections are limited to rare occasions only.[799] While there is the legal basis for inspecting fusion facilities, the practice of the IAEA Secretariat, as well as the previous decision by the Board of Governors, limits the use of this legal basis to apply safeguards to fusion facilities.

3.2.4 Interpreting the Safeguards Instruments

Another area in which the Secretariat can perform authority is in its interpretation of safeguards agreements. As argued above, the term "reactor" would allow for the application of safeguards on fusion reactors, while current interpretations of the term would not allow to cover fusion. This current interpretation is listed in the IAEA Safeguards Glossary.

The Safeguards Glossary is drafted by the Secretariat to create transparency by defining core terms used in safeguards instruments. The Glossary serves as an important document in the application of safeguards. Although the Glossary itself states that it has "no legal status and is not intended to serve as a basis for adjudicating problems of definitions such as might arise during the negotiation or in the interpretation of safeguards agreements or protocols thereto",[800] it is the go-to document and serves as a primary reference source for definitions in the domain of safeguards.[801] Currently, the IAEA Safeguards Glossary includes the definition of a reactor that is similar to those found in INFCIRC/66 and in Annex II of the Additional Protocol. Clarifying the definition of a reactor would, equally to a decision by the Board of Governors, create some legal clarity by either

798 *Olli Heinonen*, The Case for an Immediate IAEA Special Inspection in Syria, Washington Institute PolicyWatch 1715 (2010), 1–2.

799 *George Bunn*, Nuclear Safeguards – How Far Can Inspectors Go?, IAEA Bulletin 48-2 (2007), 49–55, at 52.

800 *International Atomic Energy Agency*, IAEA Safeguards Glossary, Vienna: IAEA 2022, Foreword.

801 It is referred to for finding a definition for example in *Mark Hibbs*, Iran and the Evolution of Safeguards, in: VERTIC (ed.), Verification & Implementation – A Biennial Collection of Analysis on International Agreements for Security and Development, London: VERTIC 2015, 1–26, at 11; *Laura Rockwood*, The IAEA and International Safeguards, in: Joseph Pilat/Nathan Busch (eds.), Routledge Handbook of Nuclear Proliferation and Policy, London: Routledge 2015, 142–157, at 146; *Renaud Chatelus*, A Little Customs Glossary for IAEA Safeguards: Customs Procedures and Concepts that Matter for the Implementation of Modern Safeguards, Esarada Bulletin 47 (2012), 80–88.

facilitating or explicitly excluding the application of the CSA to fusion reactors. Such a clarification would be the implementation of evolutionary interpretation, as analysed above.

3.2.5 Evaluation of the Authorities of IAEA Bodies

As the Board of Governors is the most important body of the IAEA and given the fundamental change of the safeguards system which an extension to fusion facilities would entail, it is unlikely that the Secretariat would act without either approval or mandate of the Board of Governors. While it has recently intensified its internal considerations on fusion safeguards, especially within SAGSI,[802] the Secretariat does not intend to act without any decision by the Board of Governors. The Secretariat can draft a report to the Board, recommending extensions to the safeguards system, while the final decision to extend the safeguards system to fusion – within the existing authority granted by the NPT and safeguards instruments – would reside within the Board of Governors.

3.3 Nuclear Suppliers Group

The NSG, despite not being an international organisation, exercises authority in the realm of export controls. While the NSG Guidelines are not legally binding, they *de facto* specify the rules and procedures for nuclear equipment and materials, as its Member States – which are the leading nuclear exporting States – publicly announce their adherence and translate them into domestic legislation. In exercising its authority, the NSG has the possibility to address fusion's proliferation potential by adapting its rules and procedures to fusion.

The NSG convenes for plenary meetings once a year, during which potential updates to the export control regime are discussed. Amending the list requires consensus. While the consensus requirement renders a decision difficult, reaching consensus increases the probability that all States translate the NSG soft law into domestic law. The work of the plenary is supported by two sub-bodies: the Consultative Group responsible for holding consultations on topics related to the guidelines and the technical

802 Personal communication to the author.

annexes; and the Information Exchange Meeting where information and developments with relevance to the export control regime are discussed.[803]

3.3.1 Modifying Export Control Procedures

As analysed above, the NSG Guidelines have only limited effect on the proliferation potential, given that the procedures require the application of IAEA safeguards, which, in turn, apply only to fission. There are possibilities to adapt the guidelines in order to address fusion's proliferation concerns by developing new procedural requirements for the export of fusion materials.

An approach might be the requirement of bilateral inspections. Such an approach would be similar to United States export controls prior to the IAEA's foundation. Before international safeguards were established, the United States required other States to accept inspectors from its Atomic Energy Commission (AEC) in bilateral nuclear trade agreements.[804] As there are no proper international fusion safeguards yet, a similar approach might address the proliferation potential of fusion. A State with a fusion industry only allows the export of fusion reactors to another case if they agree on the presence of inspectors sent by the exporting State verifying that the facility is not used for proliferation purposes. The extent of these inspections would be specified in a bilateral treaty as a precondition for the export. Such an approach would be a form of national export controls on fusion technology. As the most advanced fusion start-ups are based in the United States, this would especially require verification by AEC inspectors.

Since NSG export controls try to harmonise the export controls and procedures on an international level, requiring bilateral inspections for fusion facilities could also serve as an example for the NSG regime to address the safeguarding issue for fusion until there is an international treaty-based system.

Requiring specific procedures for tritium could be another approach by the NSG. Currently, both tritium and ^{6}Li are on the Dual-Use list. However, as noted above, the mechanisms of the Dual List are too weak and porous to prevent the proliferation of tritium and tritium breeding technology for boosting nuclear weapons. To strengthen this framework, one option would

803 INFCIRC/539/Rev.8, at para. 42.

804 *Grégoire Mallard*, Fallout: Nuclear Diplomacy in an Age of Global Fracture, Chicago: The University of Chicago Press 2014, at 121.

be to extend the requirements specifically for the export of both tritium and ^{6}Li. While today the conclusion of a CSA between the IAEA and a NNWS is sufficient to allow for exports, this additional requirement could be to provide the NSG with detailed reports on tritium accounting and the end-use of ^{6}Li. Such a combination would allow for an overview of whether tritium from a fusion facility could have been used for military purposes. As tritium itself is extremely expensive, such thorough accounting is done regardless of legal requirements. This modification would not entirely eradicate the proliferation problem, but it is a viable first step given the proliferation risks and timeline of fusion technology development.

These extensions of procedural requirements would fill the gap between the existing recognition of certain materials and technologies relevant for fusion and its lack of procedural requirements designed to verify the peaceful use of such dual-use goods.

3.3.2 Safeguarding Inertial Confinement Fusion

Identifying a legal solution to the proliferation risks of inertial confinement fusion is the most difficult endeavour in addressing fusion's proliferation potential. The technology itself does not produce material that is used in nuclear weapons; rather, it is the knowledge of physics gained in these facilities that may support the development of nuclear weapons.

One approach could be to amend the NSG's Trigger List to include high performance lasers and the components needed to build them. Lasers are critical to inertial confinement fusion, as they are responsible for heating and compressing the fusion plasma while simultaneously providing insights into energy transfer in hydrogen bombs. At present, only lasers and laser systems used for uranium separation and enrichment are listed on the list.[805] Nevertheless, as mentioned above, a procedural condition for exports under the NSG Guidelines to NNWS is this State has accepted IAEA safeguards. While the IAEA safeguards system is limited to verify the use of material and technology, the IAEA cannot inspect or prevent the transfer of knowledge.

Consequently, the incorporation of ICF facilities and components within the export control regime would require new procedures as well. This would entail transparency regarding the design features and configuration,

805 INFCIRC/254/Rev.14/Part 1, at para. 5.7, in particular at 5.7.13.

thereby enabling experts to analyse the similarity to military research. The less the configuration can be modified, the fewer any insights to nuclear weapons there will be. Experimental ICF devices are designed for a wide range of configurations of physical parameters in order to maximise the scientific insights gained. Commercial ICF plants want to maximise the energy output, which will be the case for a specific configuration. Such a limit of configurability allows experts to assess the design of the plant and to determine whether a transfer of knowledge is possible. Such a transparency requirement could be included as procedural requirement within the NSG.

3.3.3 Evaluation of the NSG's Authority

Addressing fusion's proliferation potential within the NSG framework is a likely outcome of current discussions surrounding the topic. Including fusion into the Guidelines has been recommended by several authors as preferred avenue to deal with fusion's proliferation potential.[806] The advantage is that no amendments to international treaties would be necessary and the IAEA could continue to focus on fission safeguards. Furthermore, given that this would require consensus among the largest nuclear exporting States, this could create first experiences on safeguarding fusion, which could – at a later state – translate into a full-scope incorporation of fusion into the IAEA's safeguards regime. However, a key caveat remains with such a solution: Export controls only apply in the case of an export, thus, an advanced State which does not require imports of technology would still be able to use fusion technology for a nuclear weapons programme without the intended international oversight. In addition, export controls are only effectively contributing to non-proliferation when they are accompanied by a strong safeguards regime.

3.4 NPT Review Conferences

Another avenue to apply safeguards on fusion under the existing framework is through the operation of the NPT Review Conferences (RevCons). Un-

806 Wolfram Tonhauser/Karoly Tamas Olajos (eds.), FELEX – Key Issue Report, FELEX 2023, at para. 12; Karoly Tamas Olajos/Fusion For Energy (eds.), Fusion For Energy Roundtable 2024 Proceedings, Barcelona: European Commission 2024, at 62; *Desai/Hua/Roma et al* (n 703).

der Article VIII.3 of the NPT, all State Parties convene every five years to "review the operation of this Treaty with a view to assuring that the purposes of the Preamble and the provisions of the Treaty are being realised." Although these conferences are often slowed down by political divergences that impede consensus[807] – among NWS and NNWS, among Global North and Global South and among East and West – they nonetheless represent a unique institutional mechanism for collectively scrutinising and shaping the evolution of the non-proliferation regime.

From a legal perspective, RevCons do not produce binding obligations;[808] their final documents constitute soft law instruments that primarily guide political expectations. However, their significance should not be underestimated. States dedicate several weeks to intensive negotiations,[809] prepare the conferences for three years in PrepComs and the resulting documents – often extending hundreds of pages – can reinforce or recalibrate expectations of safeguards, thereby indirectly influencing both state practice and the IAEA's operational priorities. This was evident in the 2010 RevCon, which underlined the importance of strengthening safeguards by affirming that "the implementation of measures specified in the model additional protocol provides [...] increased confidence about the absence of undeclared material."[810] While such statements lack direct legal force, they contribute to a normative environment that could facilitate the integration of fusion-related risks into the safeguards discourse.

Given that the proliferation challenges posed by fusion technologies directly engage the aim listed in the NPT's preamble that "the proliferation of nuclear weapons would seriously enhance the danger of nuclear war", as well as the obligations under Articles I and II, addressing this issue is a key concern of RevCons. Yet whether they can effectively operationalise this mandate remains uncertain. The difficulty of achieving consensus outcomes – exacerbated by competing commercial and strategic interests

807 *Sergey Batsanov/Vladislav Chernavskikh/Anton Khlopkov*, 10th NPT Review Conference – The Nonproliferation and Peaceful Uses of Nuclear Energy Pillars, Arms Control Today 52 (2022), 13–19; *Harald Müller*, The NPT Review Conferences, in: Emily B. Landau/Azriel Bermant (eds.), The Nuclear Nonproliferation Regime at a Crossroads, Tel Aviv: Institute for National Security Studies 2014, 17–26; *Manpreet Sethi*, NPT Review: Issues and Challenges, Strategic Analysis 24 (2000), 867–881.

808 One exception was the 1995 Review and Extension Conference, mandated by Article X.2 NPT, which decided to indefinitely extend the duration of the Treaty beyond its inaugural 25-year period.

809 The RevCons typically last 26 days.

810 NPT/CONF.2010/50 (Vol. 1), at 4.

in fusion development – may constrain the capacity of future RevCons to demand robust safeguards measures specific to fusion. Nevertheless, their potential to place fusion explicitly on the NPT agenda makes them a valuable, if imperfect, forum for advancing fusion safeguards.

3.5 TPNW Meeting of State Parties and Review Conferences

In a manner similar to the NPT RevCons, the TPNW establishes a framework of regular conferences of the State Parties to discuss matter relating to the treaty. On a biannual basis, the Meeting of the State Parties convenes in order to consider and take decisions on the implementation and status of the Treaty as well as measures to verify the time-bound and irreversible elimination of nuclear weapons programmes and other matters relating to treaty provisions.[811] Additionally, starting in 2026 and then every six years thereafter, conferences will convene in order to review the operation of the Treaty and the progress in achieving its purposes.[812]

Both of these fora are suitable to establish safeguards for fusion. As stated before, for NNWS the CSA is the standard of safeguards under TPNW, whereas for former NWS acceding to the Treaty, safeguards are yet to be developed. In contrast to the NPT, the interests of Member States to the TPNW are more homogenous. All States share an interest in preventing the use of nuclear technology for nuclear weapons. This shared interest might facilitate the incorporation of fusion safeguards in the TPNW system. While some States disagreed on including the AP as standard for safeguards, their disagreement stems from the role of safeguards under the NPT. Thus, even those States might agree on fusion safeguards which are developed under the TPNW and not under the NPT.

In the case of the application of safeguards to NNWS (which are the only current Member States), these meetings could call on all Member States to voluntarily accept safeguards for their fusion infrastructure and to engage in developing safeguards for fusion. In the hypothetical case of NWS joining the treaty, the Meeting of States Parties could decide on concrete actions

811 Article 8 para. 1 TPNW. There have been Meetings of State Parties in 2022, 2023 and 2025. On their progress, see *Rebecca Davis Gibbons/Stephen Herzog*, The First TPNW Meeting and the Future of the Nuclear Ban Treaty, Arms Control Today 52 (2022), 12–17; *Mackenzie Knight*, TPNW2MSP: Overview And Key Takeaways (*Federation of American Scientists*, 2023), https://fas.org/publication/tpnw2msp-overview-and-key-takeaways/, last accessed 17 July 2025.

812 Article 8 para. 5 TPNW.

to safeguard fusion, including the vertical proliferation potential associated with tritium and inertial confinement fusion.

3.6 United Nations

The United Nations is another actor that could support the development of fusion safeguards. The UN Charter gives a mandate to the United Nations to act in this area of international law via the broader disarmament and regulation of armament provisions,[813] as well as in the context of maintaining international peace and security.[814] The United Nations has been instrumental in developing and strengthening the non-proliferation framework in the past and could take up such a role with regard to fusion as well.

The UN General Assembly called in A/RES/41(I) for the establishment of a verification system for nuclear weapons, predating the establishment of the IAEA by more than a decade. The UN General Assembly has consistently demonstrated its commitment to enhancing non-proliferation and disarmament efforts, as evidenced for example by endorsing the work of the ENDC, in which States negotiated the NPT,[815] and by the work of its First Committee. Furthermore, it was the General Assembly that mandated the negotiations of the TPNW in 2016.[816] As a non-consensus decision-making organ without veto powers, the General Assembly provides flexibility in supporting processes in nuclear non-proliferation and disarmament.[817]

The UN General Assembly is a suitable forum to discuss topics more broadly than within the IAEA context. Its focus is not only on nuclear questions, but more broadly on maintaining international peace and secu-

813 Articles 11 para. 1, 26 and 47 of the UN Charter. On this, see *Daniel H. Joyner*, Non-proliferation Law and the United Nations System: Resolution 1540 and the Limits of the Power of the Security Council, Leiden Journal of International Law 20 (2007), 489–518, at 491.

814 Articles 1 para. 1, 39 of the UN Charter.

815 A/RES/1722 (XVI).

816 A/RES/71/258 para. 8 reads: *Decides* to convene in 2017 a United Nations conference to negotiate a legally binding instrument to prohibit nuclear weapons, leading towards their total elimination.

817 On potential roles of the General Assembly in the future, see *Konstantin Larinov*, Expanding the UN General Assembly's Role in Managing Disarmament and Non-Proliferation Challenges (*European Leadership Network*, 2023), https://europeanleadershipnetwork.org/commentary/expanding-the-un-general-assemblys-role-in-managing-disarmament-and-non-proliferation-challenges/, last accessed 17 July 2025.

rity[818] as well as on promoting its sustainable development goals.[819] This would allow for discussing fusion and its implications to the international order more comprehensively. In addition, given the historic precedents, the UN General Assembly could also initiate for a conference which aims at developing new instruments on safeguarding fusion. However, as resolutions by the UN General Assembly are limited to recommendations without legal bindingness,[820] the General Assembly could not take legally binding decisions which would directly expand the safeguards regime. Its role is limited to facilitate discussions and negotiations.

The Security Council's engagement with non-proliferation, notably through UNSCR 1540, illustrates both the potential and the constraints of this body in shaping safeguards relevant to emerging technologies such as fusion. By acting under Chapter VII, the Security Council imposed binding obligations on all states to strengthen export controls and prevent non-state actors from acquiring nuclear capabilities.

As explored in the previous chapter, UNSCR 1540 does contain provisions of indirect relevance to fusion, by requiring States to establish and maintain effective export controls and domestic measures to prevent non-state actors from acquiring nuclear weapons or related materials. This framework could, in principle, help mitigate the risks of sensitive fusion technologies – particularly inertial confinement fusion, which bears direct parallels to thermonuclear weapons physics – falling into the wrong hands. However, the resolution's primary orientation toward combating terrorism and illicit trafficking means it lacks the technical specificity and sectoral focus necessary to address the proliferation challenges unique to commercial fusion reactors.

In contrast, UNSCR 1887 explicitly underscored the importance of strengthening the global safeguards architecture by urging States to conclude Comprehensive Safeguards Agreements and Additional Protocols with the IAEA, and by calling for adequate resources for the Agency and for an *effective* safeguards system.[821] Yet, because the Council did not invoke Chapter VII, these calls remain legally non-binding.[822] For the context of fusion, this points to a critical gap: while the Security Council has

818 Article 1 para. 1 UN Charter.

819 A/RES/70/1. On the role of fusion under the SDGs, see above Introduction, Chapter 1.

820 Article 10 UN Charter.

821 S/RES/1997, at para. 15b.

822 *Michael Wood*, United Nations, Security Council, in: Anne Peters/Rüdiger Wolfrum (eds.), Max Planck Encyclopedia of Public International Law, Heidelberg, Oxford:

signalled sustained political concern over the robustness of safeguards, it has stopped short of imposing obligations that might directly integrate emerging technologies like fusion into the safeguards regime. This suggests that future Security Council engagement – potentially through similarly worded resolutions – may continue to shape political expectations but is unlikely to substitute for dedicated, technically tailored frameworks necessary to regulate fusion's proliferation-sensitive aspects.

The Security Council's selective activation of its Chapter VII powers – often driven by acute security crises – raises doubts as to whether it would similarly intervene to proactively regulate fusion safeguards, as there is no immediate threat. This suggests that while the UN Charter provides the UN Security Council with the authority to act, its practical utility of the Council's authority for safeguarding fusion may be limited without sustained political will from key permanent members.

3.7 Evaluation and Summary

As this section has shown, various actors have the possibility to establish or implement safeguards for fusion by exercising authority. As these pathways to adapt the regime for fusion do not require treaty changes, they present feasible approaches to address the proliferation potential of fusion. They include the use of existing authorities by the IAEA and its organs, the Nuclear Suppliers Group, review conferences, meetings of State Parties, and the United Nations.

The different approaches offer various advantages and disadvantages. As the IAEA is the most important institution in administering safeguards, actions by the Board of Governors and the IAEA Secretariat are the most relevant. This is particularly salient in the context of majority voting rules or institutional practices, which enable the implementation of these approaches despite the potential objections of individual States, including both NWS and NNWS, but also potentially raising legitimacy concerns by those States. Given the bureaucratic structure of the IAEA, such approaches could be lengthy, but shorter than others such as treaty changes.

Oxford University Press 2008; *Stefan Talmon*, The Security Council as World Legislature, American Journal of International Law 99 (2005), 175–193; *International Criminal Tribunal for the former Yugoslavia*, Prosecutor v. Tadić, Appeal on Jurisdiction, Decision of 2 October 1995, No. IT-94-1-AR27, at para. 44.

While the IAEA Secretariat is the organ which is charged with implementing the safeguards agreements, it seems unlikely that the Secretariat would change the interpretation of these agreements without the consent of the Board of Governors. As it is the Board which adopts the structure and content of safeguards agreements, the Board is the organ of the IAEA which sets the boundaries of the implementation of these agreements. Thus, safeguards activities by the IAEA on fusion technology depends on a decision by the Board of Governors. The Board is dominated by States that represent the most advanced in the technology of atomic energy, while these States are also those most advanced in fusion technology. As a consequence, any action by the IAEA would require the consent of States home to fusion start-ups to apply safeguards on the technology of their promising industries. The probability of such a consent would depend on the perceived proliferation potential of the technology and the scale of interference of fusion safeguards. As the topic of fusion and non-proliferation gains attention within the scientific community, States and international organisations, such a coalition seems possible within the next years or decade.

In contrast, the NSG would offer the possibility to relatively quickly implement new rules. However, as its tools are limited to soft law, their implementation requires all States to support the new measures, requiring consensus and State commitment, as there would be no legal obligation or legal recourse to implement them. Given their non-bindingness and less-intrusive nature compared to safeguards, a modification to export controls regime is the likeliest outcome on addressing fusion's proliferation potential, at least in the near- and mid-term. In addition, export controls are also the preferred approach by start-ups to fusion's proliferation potential.

Given the political character of the implementation of the NPT and its Review Conferences, as well as the opposition by some NNWS to strengthen safeguards as long as there is no progress in nuclear disarmament, decisions by Review Conferences or Meetings of State Parties seem unlikely. In these fora, States cannot agree on universalising the existing safeguards regime, thus any progress in safeguards beyond the status quo seem even more out of reach. Even if States could find consensus, these decisions are also non-binding, and the benefit would be limited. Finally, the United Nations can implement recommendations to develop or apply safeguards on fusion technology, while binding resolutions by the Security Council under Chapter VII of the UN Charter are unlikely. As endorsement of safeguards agreements by the UN were historically tied to existing safeguards agreements, thus, these steps would require first the adoption of new agreement on safeguarding fusion.

These different uses of existing authority would most likely follow each other. Once States hosting start-ups agree within the Board of Governors to expand the safeguards system to fusion, the IAEA Secretariat, supported by SAGSI, would follow suit. Once such an agreement is reached, it is likely that consensus could also be reached among the same States within the NSG to expand the export control procedures to address fusion's proliferation potential. Once these decisions are made, other fora could follow. This could lead to momentum within the NPT Review Conference and the TPNW Meeting of State Parties to recognise and endorse the developments within the IAEA and the NSG. Once agreed upon in these fora, an endorsement by the United Nations bodies could follow. It must be noted, however, that once the topic is discussed outside the IAEA, not only States home to fusion start-ups have to agree, but also States without a fusion industry. Gaining their support without any progress in other areas of nuclear weapons law, either by technical assistance or progress in nuclear disarmament, is unlikely.

As the actors' authority under the existing regime has its limits, the next section analyses the necessity and possible avenues of treaty changes to the regime of nuclear weapons.

4 Treaty Changes

The most complicated approach to address the proliferation potential of fusion is amendments to the existing treaties and agreements.

This chapter has so far demonstrated that some aspects of fusion can be addressed under the application of existing legal instruments, evolutionary interpretation, or the exercise of authority. These approaches allow fusion facilities to be included into the safeguards regime in order to verify that they are not used to produce fissile material for nuclear weapons. In addition, export controls under the NSG can play a role in safeguarding inertial confinement fusion.

What remains outside the scope of these options is the proliferation potential of the substantial quantities of tritium produced. This section analyses how these this aspect could be addressed by new international treaties.

However, it must be noted that treaty changes are most difficult to achieve, especially in the area of nuclear non-proliferation. While States struggle to agree to non-binding outcome documents of the NPT Review Conference, accepting changes to the NPT regime seems even more out of reach. Also, other treaties in the area of nuclear weapons law lack ratification of major States such as the CTBT or the TPNW. The probability of successful negotiations which then turn into the adoption and ratification of a new treaty in nuclear weapons law is very low at the moment. Nevertheless, in order to draw a complete picture of possibilities to adapt the framework and in light of the possibility of changing geopolitical structures, this section analyses the content and procedures of such treaty changes.

4.1 General Considerations on Safeguarding Tritium

The idea of safeguarding tritium is not new. For decades, the proliferation potential of tritium has been raised by academics already in the 1990s,[823] some even proposing the adoption of a tritium freeze treaty.[824] These proposals have consistently been ignored by States. The explanations are manifold. First, the possession of tritium alone is not sufficient to build a weapon, leading to States considering the potential for horizontal proliferation as limited, which is what the entire safeguards system is designed around. This first step in acquiring a nuclear weapon as a NNWS is normally a regular fission-only based nuclear weapon. The question of boosting a weapon or even developing a hydrogen bomb is a secondary one due to the increased degree of technical complexity. For these reasons, it was left out of the Additional Protocol to the CSA.[825] The main proliferation issue of tritium lies within its vertical proliferation potential, which is a core shortcomings of the non-proliferation regime, as it mainly deals with horizontal proliferation.[826] The role of tritium has been predominantly

823 *Martin B. Kalinowski/Lars C. Colschen*, International Control of Tritium to Prevent Horizontal Proliferation and to Foster Nuclear Disarmament, Science & Global Security 5 (1995), 131–203; *Lars C. Colschen/Martin B. Kalinowski*, Can International Safeguards Be Expanded to Cover Tritium?, International Atomic Energy Agency (IAEA): IAEA 1994; *Mayhew/VCDNP* (n 735), at 8 f.

824 *Robert E. Kelley*, Starve Nuclear Weapons to Death with a Tritium Freeze (*Stockholm International Peace Research Institute*, 2020), https://www.sipri.org/commentary/topical-backgrounder/2020/starve-nuclear-weapons-death-tritium-freeze, last accessed 17 July 2025.

825 *Mayhew/VCDNP* (n 735), at 10.

826 On the role of vertical non-proliferation with the NPT, see *Katarzyna Kubiak*, Vertical Proliferation in Light of the Disarmament Commitment, in: Tom Sauer/Jorg

discussed in the context of disarmament.[827] In addition, the safeguarding of tritium has the potential to interfere with commercial interests.[828] When a material is subject to safeguards, civilian and academic actors are burdened with additional expenditures. For instance, tritium is used in a wide range of radioluminescent lamps such as emergency exit lights, as a radioactive tracer in medical diagnostics, and in various scientific research areas such as determining the weight of neutrinos.[829] As a consequence, any amendments which lead to safeguarding tritium might lead to opposition by nuclear exporting States. However, as fusion increases the annual tritium production by many orders of magnitude, this increased availability of fusion might change the opinion of States and can lead to a recognition of the material's proliferation potential.

The next sections analyse to which extent treaty changes can be implemented to include tritium under safeguards regimes.

4.2 Changing the IAEA Safeguards System

As the IAEA is mandated to verify compliance with the cornerstone of nuclear non-proliferation, the NPT, this section analyses options on how to adapt the Agency's safeguards system to include tritium.

4.2.1 Amending the NPT and IAEA Statute

In principle, both the NPT and the IAEA Statute are open to amendment. To amend the NPT, each Party may propose an amendment, which will be

---

Kustermans/Barbara Segaert (eds.), Non-Nuclear Peace: Beyond the Nuclear Ban Treaty, Cham: Springer International Publishing 2020, 59–84. On the interlinkage between nuclear proliferation and disarmament see *Tom Sauer*, Nuclear Proliferation and Nuclear Disarmament – A Complicated Relationship, in: Harsh V. Pant (ed.), Handbook of Nuclear Proliferation, Abingdon: Routledge 2012, 317–326.

827 Kelley (n 824).; *Martin Kalinowski*, International Control of Tritium for Nuclear Nonproliferation and Disarmament, Boca Raton: CRC Press 2004. More on disarmament below.

828 *Mayhew/VCDNP* (n 735), at 10.

829 The most important research project is KATRIN (Karlsruhe Tritium Neutrino Experiment). On that, see *Max Aker/Konrad Altenmüller/Marius Arenz et al.*, First Operation of the KATRIN Experiment with Tritium, The European Physical Journal C 80 (2020), 264.

considered by a conference if requested by one third of the Member States, Article VIII.1. At such a conference, the amendment has to be approved by a majority of Parties, including all NWS and those States that are Members of the IAEA's Board of Governors, Article VIII.2 cl. 1.[830] Such an amendment comes only into effect for those States who ratify the amendment, once a qualified majority has ratified the amendment, Article VIII.2 cl. 2. To date, the NPT has never been amended. As all ten Review Conferences over the last fifty years have shown, it is difficult to reach consensus on this highly political treaty. Keeping the status quo is difficult enough, thus, a treaty change does not seem to be in sight.

Amending the IAEA Statute follows a multi-step process as well. An amendment may be proposed by any Member State, Article XVIII.A of the IAEA Statute. Amendments then need to be approved by two thirds of the General Conference after having considered observations submitted by the Board of Governors, Article XVIII.C.i. However, in contrast to the NPT, amendments to the IAEA Statute bind every Member to the Statute, not only those who ratified the amendment.[831] The only requirement for such an *erga omnes partes* effect is the ratification by two thirds of the Member States, Article XVIII.C.ii. The IAEA Statute has been amended three times in order to change the article on the composition of the Board of Governors, which is Article VI.[832] Since 1999, two amendments are pending (on the composition of the Board of Governors[833] and on budgeting[834]), as they still lack the ratification requirement.

Regardless of the political difficulties in the process of amending these treaties, the content of such an amendment is not trivial either. One possibility would be to change the wording in Article III NPT from "source

830 These are 35 States: Algeria, Argentina, Armenia, Australia, Bangladesh, Brazil, Bulgaria, Burkina Faso, Canada, China, Costa Rica, Denmark, Ecuador, Finland, France, Germany, India, Indonesia, Japan, Kenya, Republic of Korea, Namibia, Netherlands, Paraguay, Qatar, Russian Federation, Saudi Arabia, Singapore, South Africa, Spain, Türkiye, United Kingdom of Great Britain and Northern Ireland, United States of America, Uruguay, and Ukraine.

831 This is in contrast to the *pacta sunt servanda* rule in international law, also enshrined in Article 40 para. 4 VLCT. On this rule, see *Jan Klabbers*, Treaties, Amendment and Revision, in: Anne Peters/Rüdiger Wolfrum (eds.), Max Planck Encyclopedia of Public International Law, Heidelberg, Oxford: Oxford University Press 2006.

832 GC(V)/RES/92; GC(XIV)/RES/272; GC(XXVIII)/RES/422.

833 GC(43)/RES/19.

834 GC(43)/RES/8.

and special fissionable material" to "source, special fissionable and special fusionable material." In addition to that, this term would also need to be defined. As analysed above, the definitions are drawn from Article XX of the IAEA Statute, which suggests that the Statute itself may also require amendments. These revised definitions would need to add tritium as a special fusionable material and lithium enriched in ^{6}Li as source material. In addition to that, the Board of Governors could have the authority to designate other isotopes as special fusionable material, similar to the competence already existing for special fissionable material in Article XX.1 of the IAEA Statute. Instead of listing materials as it is the case with fissionable material, a broader definition of fusionable material could be used. As mentioned above, a definition of "fusionable material" in the context of nuclear non-proliferation and disarmament was first proposed in the context of a Nuclear Weapons Convention in 1997,[835] which was reiterated in the Model Nuclear Weapons Convention in 2007[836]. It was defined as "any isotope capable of undergoing fusion with the same kind of nuclide or with any other nuclide by applying sufficient conditions (pressure, temperature and inclusion time) with technical means."[837] Consequently, these amendments could draw on previous works.

4.2.2 Second Additional Protocol to the CSA

Another option of treaty changes that would not require the amendment of the IAEA Statute or the NPT would be the adoption of a Second Additional Protocol to the Comprehensive Safeguards Agreements.

The adoption and implementation of such a protocol would involve several actors, as evidenced by the existing safeguards agreements. The IAEA Safeguards Committee drafted the CSA, and each Member State was invited to participate. It was then formally adopted by the IAEA Board of Governors. Similarly, the Additional Protocol was drafted in a combined

835 Costa Rica submitted this proposal into the UN General Assembly as UN document A/C.1/52/7. Fusionable material is defined in para. 48.

836 Costa Rica submitted this proposal into the Preparatory Committee for the 2010 NPT Review Conference as conference document NPT/CONF.2010/PC.I/WP.17.

837 Ibid, para. 17.

effort by the IAEA Secretariat and the so-called IAEA Committee 24, where approximately 70 Member States were represented.[838]

Such a Second Addition Protocol could specifically address the proliferation potential of fusion, encompassing specific procedures and methods for fusion, covering all three proliferation aspects of fusion. The protocol could either amend the existing Additional Protocol by adding additional definitions, or be a genuine risk-appropriate new protocol, addressing fusion's proliferation potential based on its different risks compared to fission.

However, two caveats remain: the duration to adopt the protocol and the scope of the protocol.

Firstly, it is a lengthy process for the IAEA to negotiate new protocols with each NNWS. To recall, safeguards instruments are first agreed upon by the Board of Governors, who then instructs the Director General to conclude an agreement with each Member State. While the drafting process of the model of the (First) Additional Protocol started in 1993 and was adopted by a decision of the Board of Governors in 1997, even a decade later, it was only legally binding for less than half of all NNWS.[839] Presently, more than a quarter century later, 141 States and Euratom have concluded an Additional Protocol and brought it into force, 13 more have signed it, with 44 NNWS currently not covered.

Second, this approach would only address the horizontal dimension. While the risk of horizontal proliferation is non-zero – given the potential facilitating effect of an abundant tritium availability – it is significantly lower than the other risks analysed in this chapter. The largest proliferation potential of tritium is of vertical nature and thus mainly relevant for NWS. The NPT stipulates safeguards exclusively for NNWS, and no NWS has concluded a CSA. The five NWS under the NPT have concluded Voluntary Offer Agreements (VOA), which cover specifically selected civilian nuclear facilities, where the IAEA verifies that the nuclear material in these facilities remains in peaceful activities. It is therefore at the discretion of each NWS to decide if and which fusion facilities they open for safeguards. The situation is similar for the NWS outside the NPT. While the NWS under the NPT (United States, United Kingdom, Russia, China, France) adopted protocols that bear a certain resemblance to the Additional Protocol for

838 *Goldschmidt* (n 788); *International Atomic Energy Agency*, IAEA (ed.), The Evolution of IAEA Safeguards, Vienna: IAEA 1998, at 26.

839 https://www.iaea.org/sites/default/files/20/01/sg-ap-status.pdf, last accessed 25 February 2025.

NNWS, the NWS outside the NPT (India, Pakistan, Israel, North Korea) fall short to implement any progress of the safeguards regime.

If States were to agree on a Second Additional Protocol, the soft law instruments analysed in Section 3 of this Chapter could serve as an additional catalyst for the implementation of such a Second Additional Protocol and play a role in allowing the treaty change. One such factor could be a recommendation under Chapter VI of the UN Charter by the UN Security Council, as evidenced in 2009 when it called upon all States to sign, ratify and implement the existing Additional Protocol with UN Security Council Resolution 1887. Another option is within the NPT context. A Review Conference could encourage States to adopt a Second Additional Protocol by the NPT State Parties. In 2010, the Review Conference "noted that the implementation of measures specified in the model additional protocol provides [...] increased confidence about the absence of undeclared material."[840] Authoritative support from bodies such as the UN Security Council or consensus reached at NPT Review Conferences can significantly influence the adoption of a Second Additional Protocol. While not legally binding, such endorsements carry substantial political and normative weight. They can help build momentum among States by signalling consensus and creating diplomatic pressure to conform.

4.3 International Tritium Control System

The introduction of an international control on tritium may not necessarily be limited to only surgical changes to the current framework, but could also follow a new treaty approach outside the framework based on the NPT and implemented by the IAEA. Since the late 1990s, a separate international agreement has been proposed, introducing an International Tritium Control System (ICTS).[841] The primary function of such a system would be to detect and deter illegal diversions of tritium from civilian facilities to military purposes.[842] The proposed system would be governed by four principles: Firstly, tritium produced in civilian facilities is to be

840 NPT/CONF.2010/50 (Vol. 1), at 4.

841 *Kalinowski/Colschen* (n 823); *Colschen/Kalinowski* (n 823); *Lars C. Colschen*, Die Internationalisierung der Tritiumkontrolle als Baustein des Nichtverbreitungsregimes für Kernwaffen: Bedingungen, Einflussfaktoren und Folgen, Aachen: Shaker Verlag 1998.

842 *Kalinowski* (n 827), at 41.

used exclusively for peaceful applications, including NWS. Secondly, the export of tritium to non-Member States is to be prohibited under the ICTS Treaty. Thirdly, the acquisition of tritium is to be permitted exclusively through import or production, subject to accountancy measures, verified by an international agency, and inspections of tritium facilities and stocks. The IAEA would be an obvious candidate to carry out these inspections. Fourthly, a definition of a significant quantity in the range of one gram is introduced, which must be verified for its end use.[843] Such a system, specifically developed for tritium, would allow the highest level of assurance that the tritium produced within the fusion fuel cycle remains in peaceful uses. However, verifying tritium at such low levels is a major technological challenge.

4.4 NWFZ Treaties

Including tritium into the safeguards regimes of NWFZ Treaties would also require treaty changes.[844]

The procedures for changing the treaties differ, but all have in common that each Party may propose an amendment. The Treaties of Bangkok, Rarotonga and Semipalatansk stipulate a consensus requirement for the adoption process, either by all Parties (Semipalatansk) or by the specific treaty body (Bangkok – Commission, Rarotonga – Consultative Committee). The Treaties of Rarotonga and Semipalatansk require ratification by all State Parties for entry into force, while the Bangkok regime requires only seventeen ratifications. In all these treaties, amendments only enter into force for those States that have ratified them. A different approach is followed in Africa, where the Treaty of Pelindaba only requires a two-thirds majority for the adoption of an amendment, and where the ratification of a simple majority suffices for entry into force for all State Parties.

843 Ibid, at 41.

844 Articles on amendments: Art. 19 Treaty of Bangkok, Art. 11 Treaty of Rarotonga, Art. 19 Treaty of Pelindaba, Art. 17 Treaty of Semipalatansk.

4.5 Euratom Treaty

There are two possibilities for adapting the Euratom framework to include tritium. The first is on the basis of Article 77 (b). If the IAEA amends the international regime and Euratom ratifies the respective instruments, then this new framework would automatically apply within Euratom. The second possibility is to change Article 77 (a). Here, amending the article with similar wording such as "special fusionable material" by simultaneously defining it in Article 197, either by listing tritium or by a broader definition as it was included in the Model Nuclear Weapons Convention,[845] could address the proliferation potential caused by tritium.

Within the Euratom Treaty, there are two procedures to amend the powers of the community. First, Article 203 provides for the possibility to provide additional powers to the community if "action by the Community should prove necessary to attain one of the objectives of the Community." Such an ad-hoc competence requires unanimity of the Council on a proposal from the Commission and after consulting the European Parliament. However, unlike the NPT, the non-proliferation of nuclear weapons is not part of the objectives of the Treaty. In contrast, its only objective in that sense is to "make certain [...] that nuclear materials are not diverted to purposes other than those for which they are intended."[846] This objective is considerably narrower than those of the NPT. As Euratom does not provide tritium, this excludes the option of utilising Article 203.

The incorporation of fusion directly into Euratom safeguards would thus necessitate substantial treaty changes, following the procedure of Article 48 TEU.[847] Such an amendment would require consensus among and ratification by all 27 Member States. It is noteworthy that the Euratom Treaty has never been amended in substance.[848]

4.6 Summary

Treaty changes are necessary to address the proliferation risk that is neither covered by the existing framework, nor by possible evolutionary interpre-

845 See above, Section 4.2.1.
846 Article 2(b) Euratom Treaty.
847 Article 48 paras 2 to 5 TEU are applicable via Article 106a para. 1 Euratom Treaty.
848 *Anna Södersten*, Explaining Continuity and Change: The Case of the Euratom Treaty, International Journal of Constitutional Law 20 (2022), 788–817.

tation, nor by actions of international organisation or intergovernmental fora, namely tritium. The potential treaty changes to address tritium and other fusionable material include amendments to the NPT and the IAEA Safeguards System, the adoption of a specific international tritium control system, amendments to NWFZ Treaties and the Euratom Treaty. Caveats remain for approaches involving treaty changes: They require either consensus or qualified majorities, leading to lengthy procedures and the risk of an increased fragmentation of the safeguards system. Nevertheless, treaty changes reflect explicit State consent to these specific changes, which would increase the legitimacy of future fusion safeguards, including secondary measures taken by international organisations and other institutions. As there are no clear political incentives for States to accept fusion safeguards, treaty changes to the regime seem difficult to achieve at the moment.

5 Conclusion

The legal framework of nuclear weapons is situated within a broader economic and political context, constraining the possibilities of adapting the framework in order to apply the regime to fusion. To handle these constraints, an evolutionary interpretation of the IAEA safeguards has been proposed, which would allow for a limited extension of said safeguards regime to fusion facilities under the NPT, CSAs, the Euratom Treaty, the TPNW and NWFZ Treaties. In instances where evolutionary interpretation has its limits, the exercise authority by various actors under the existing regime has been demonstrated to facilitate in bridging the gap between the objective of nuclear non-proliferation and the application of its verification regime. This includes actions undertaken by the IAEA and its bodies, namely the Board of Governors and Secretariat, Review Conferences and Meeting of State Parties under the NPT and TPNW, the NSG, the United Nations.

Where the exercise of authority under the existing regime does not suffice, especially with regard to tritium, there is a necessity for treaty changes, either by amending existing treaties or by adopting new legal instruments. Such changes could include amending the IAEA Statute, the NPT, the TPNW, NWFZ Treaties and the Euratom Treaty. Another approach to create new law for safeguarding fusion could be the adoption of a Second Additional Protocol to the CSA or the establishment of an International Tritium Control System.

While such changes to the system provide for the highest level of legal clarity by defining clear obligations and eliminating ambiguity, their realisation is challenging. The regime of nuclear weapons law faces several challenges, and even the adoption of non-binding documents has recently proven impossible due a convolution of different challenges to the regime. Any changes to the system would necessarily open the Pandora's box, leading to discussions on a wide range of issues within the regime. Furthermore, there are no clear political incentives to strengthen the regime to fusion as this would involve a regulatory burden on a technology that shows great promise in its infancy. The next chapter will address the option of adopting a dedicated treaty on fusion, which could implement fusion safeguards while circumventing the state of crisis of the nuclear weapons regime by offering clear incentives.

Chapter 5: Outlook – The Adoption of a Fusion Treaty

In this chapter, a novel holistic approach to the proliferation potential of fusion is proposed. As the last chapter has shown, approaches to adapt the existing regime are constrained by concerns regarding legitimacy, bindingness, proportionality, and absence of a political incentive to adopt treaty changes. To address these challenges, this chapter proposes the establishment of a new treaty specifically for fusion, as opposed to adapting the existing framework to address the risks of the new technology. The proposed treaty would not only focus on the safeguards dimension of fusion regulation, but also seek to establish a comprehensive international regulatory approach to fusion technology.

This chapter commences with arguing why fusion's proliferation system should be regulated outside the NPT regime (1). It proceeds to set out the structure and content of such a fusion treaty (2) before going into detail on its mechanisms of preventing the proliferation of nuclear weapons aided by fusion technology (3).

1 Regulating Fusion Outside the NPT System

This section explores the benefits of regulating fusion's proliferation risks outside the NPT regime. The rational for this is manifold. The first aspect is the fact that the NPT regime is based on fission, while there are fundamental physical and technological differences between fission and fusion technology (1.1). In addition, as the NPT regime has demonstrated significant shortcomings in recent decades, addressing one issue would open the Pandora's box, quickly stalling any development (1.2). Furthermore, regulating fusion outside the NPT would enable to address aspects of nuclear weapons law that are beyond the scope of the NPT regime, namely vertical proliferation (1.3). Finally, there are precedents where aspects of nuclear weapons law have been deliberately addressed outside the NPT regime (1.4).

1.1 Fusion is not Fission

The most evident reason for regulating fusion's proliferation risks outside the NPT is the fundamental distinction between fusion and fission: Fusion is not fission. The NPT and the entire regime are designed to limit the dual-use characteristics of fission. Those States that customarily handle fissionable material such as uranium and plutonium may also use these materials and the corresponding infrastructure to develop nuclear weapons. As shown in Chapter 1, there are significant differences in the proliferation potential. To simplify, a uranium enrichment facility, for instance, can produce reactor-grade material, or if run long enough and reconfigured, also weapon-grade material. Reprocessing nuclear waste from reactors may result in the recycling of material or the extraction of plutonium for nuclear weapons. These are just two examples where the operation of nuclear fission power plants is closely related to the construction of nuclear weapons.

However, in the case of fusion, there is no direct connection to the bomb comparable to the fission fuel cycle. The basis of any nuclear weapon remains fission. Fusion only has an auxiliary character in the development of nuclear weapons. A State that operates a fusion power plant will not be able to build a nuclear weapon solely based on fusion. Fusion can support a nuclear weapons programme but cannot replace the fission part. Consequently, the proliferation potential is significantly lower compared to the proliferation potential of fission. Thus, it makes only limited sense to include fusion into the regime that is specifically designed and developed for fission.

As the last chapter has shown, a risk-proportionate incorporation of fusion into the regime requires more than mere surgical modifications. Appropriately addressing fusion's proliferation potential within the regime demands fundamental changes to the regime. Rather than fundamentally changing an existing system to include a different technology with different risk characteristics, it would be more rational to initiate a new treaty. This approach would facilitate the development of new approaches to address a different risk profile in a proportionate manner.

1.2 The NPT as Pandora's Box

Moreover, as shown in the previous chapter, including fusion comprehensively into the existing regime would require fundamental changes, including the amendments of the IAEA Statute and the NPT. These amendments are unlikely to occur. As outlined above, preserving the status quo of the NPT is challenging, changes to its foundation are improbable. A full-scope incorporation of fusion into the regime would further require the adoption of new protocols to the existing Safeguards Agreements in order to extend the authority of the IAEA. This process is lengthy and complicated, potentially raising further concerns regarding the entire regime.

As there are many shortcomings to the system, it is unlikely that one single aspect would be addressed while the other shortcomings are ignored. This is especially true with regard to some NNWS not accepting new safeguards as long as there is no progress towards nuclear disarmament. Other shortcomings of the NPT would be brought to the negotiation table. This, in turn, quickly halts any negotiation. While addressing other persistent questions of the regime itself might be beneficial for the system as a whole, this could further delay any progress in adopting the framework for fusion. The allocation of diplomatic resources for safeguarding fusion could be optimised by establishing a dedicated system specifically for fusion outside the NPT regime.

1.3 Vertical Proliferation

Another argument against including fusion into the NPT regime is the fact that essential proliferation risks of fusion are of vertical nature. Fusion will eventually increase the availability of tritium, which is used in multi-staged nuclear weapons and is essential for the miniaturisation of nuclear warheads. Without a fusion boost, there are only gravity bombs with a limited yield and no large-scale strategic nuclear weapons capable of eliminating entire cities nor nuclear warheads for missiles. However, vertical proliferation is largely outside the scope of the NPT. While this assertion is contested by some States[849] and scholars[850], the prevailing

849 See UN/RES/71/371; Statement of the Non-Aligned Movement during the General Debate of the First Session of the Preparatory Committee (PrepComl) for the 2020 Review Conference of the NPT, at para. 10.

850 *Katarzyna Kubiak*, Vertical Proliferation in Light of the Disarmament Commitment, in: Tom Sauer/Jorg Kustermans/Barbara Segaert (eds.), Non-Nuclear Peace: Beyond the Nuclear Ban Treaty, Cham: Springer International Publishing 2020, 59–84; *Vitaly Goldansky*, Connection Between Horizontal and Vertical Proliferation of Nuclear Weapons, in: Joseph Rotblat/Laszlo Valki (eds.), Coexistence, Cooperation

opinion is based on the practise of NWS, which are of the opinion that the NPT allows NWS to freely expand their nuclear arsenals both in number and sophistication; an interpretation which is further substantiated by the *travaux préparatoires*.[851] The disarmament obligation stipulated in Article VI may limit vertical proliferation in severe cases, while a future increased use of fusion technology in nuclear weapons by NWS would not constitute a violation of the NPT. In other words: Fusion's proliferation risks are to a large extent also questions of vertical proliferation, while vertical proliferation remains outside the scope of the NPT. As a consequence, including fusion into the NPT regime would either lead to changes to fundamental principles of the NPT by addressing vertical proliferation issues, which is highly unlikely, or the incorporation of fusion into the regime would have to exclude a significant portion of its proliferation potential.

1.4 Precedents

Dealing with nuclear weapons-related issues outside the NPT regime is nothing new, as evidenced by several precedents. Yet, most treaties were either not even adopted or lack ratification of key States. The first example is the establishment of a separate regime for the verification that no nuclear tests are conducted. States adopted a new treaty, the Comprehensive Test Ban Treaty (CTBT), and established a new international organisation to verify, the CTBTO. Rather than mandating the IAEA to verify that there are no nuclear tests, States opted for a separate international organisation.[852] Moreover, proposals have been made for the establishment of a separate verification system and body for a Fissile Material Cut-Off Treaty.[853]

Arguments against the inclusion of a verification system into the NPT regime are twofold: Firstly, compatibility issues with the existing instru-

---

and Common Security: Annals of Pugwash 1986, London: Palgrave Macmillan UK 1988, 21–36, at 27.

851 *Mohamed Ibrahim Shaker*, The Nuclear Non-Proliferation Treaty – Origin and Implementation 1959–1979, Dobbs Ferry: Oceana Publication 1980, at 926; *Kubiak* (n 850), at 65 f.

852 *Rebecca Johnson*, Unfinished Business – The Negotiation of the CTBT and the End of Nuclear Testing, Geneva: United Nations Institute for Disarmament Research 2009, at 172.

853 *Shannon N. Kile/Robert E. Kelley*, Verifying a Fissile Material Cut-Off Treaty – Technical and Organizational Considerations, SIPRI Policy Paper 33 (2012), 1–42.

ments, and secondly, a lack of experience in verification.[854] Both of these considerations apply to fusion as well. The existing instruments are not compatible with the specific proliferation potential of fusion and the IAEA does not have any experience with verification activities for fusion.

Similarly, the TPNW opted for an approach partially outside the NPT regime. For former NWS, the TPNW intends the adoption of new safeguards agreements outside the NPT, and potentially even the establishment of a new international organisation. Rather than including the verification regime of the elimination of nuclear weapons into the NPT/IAEA system, the TPNW has opted for designating a "competent international authority" to verify the irreversible elimination of nuclear weapons in former NWS.[855] The TPNW's State Parties have yet to designate this competent international authority. This authority might be the IAEA, but there are also discussions to establish a new organisation.[856]

Additionally, the Model Nuclear Weapons Convention (NWC) included a departure from the NPT system and the IAEA. While this proposal failed and was only partially used as a basis for the TPNW, it offers noteworthy insights into the inclusion of fusion into nuclear weapons law outside the NPT regime. The NWC draft explicitly included a reference to fusionable material and the prohibition to use such material for nuclear weapons.[857] It also included the establishment of a new international organisation, the Agency for the Prohibition of Nuclear Weapons.[858] Such an Agency would have been responsible for verifying the compliance with the NWC based on newly concluded safeguards agreements,[859] including those related to fusion.

The reasons for new sub-regimes within the disarmament regime are due to the different requirements for verification.[860] Verifying the elimination of a nuclear weapons programme differs from verifying the absence of

854 Ibid, at 26 ff.

855 Article 4 TPNW.

856 *Stuart Casey-Maslen*, The Treaty on the Prohibition of Nuclear Weapons: a Commentary, Oxford: Oxford University Press 2019, at para. 4.16 ff.; *Adina Carla Loghin*, Which International Authority Should Be Designated for Verifying the Irreversible Elimination of Nuclear Weapons under Article 4 of Nuclear Ban Treaty (TPNW) Scientific, Amsterdam Law Forum 11 (2019), 73–96.

857 Paras II.D.23, 24, 28, 29 of the NWC.

858 Para. VIII.1 of the NWC.

859 Para. XI.A.15 of the NWC.

860 *Jürgen Scheffran*, Verification and Security of Transformation to a Nuclear-Weapon-Free World: The Framework of the Treaty on the Prohibition of Nuclear Weapons, Global Change, Peace & Security 30 (2018), 143–162, at 157 ff.; *Loghin* (n 856), at 87.

undeclared nuclear material, a rationale that extends to fusion. Verifying that fusion technology is not used for military purposes goes beyond the existing safeguards. While there is common ground with respect to verifying that fusion power plants are not used to produce fissile material, verifying that tritium or inertial confinement fusion is not used for military purposes is different from the existing safeguards regime.

2 Structure of a Fusion Treaty

This section explores the structure of the proposed Fusion Treaty. By taking what is good from the NPT and addressing the lessons learnt from the regime, such a Fusion Treaty offers the opportunity to risk-adequately address not only fusion's proliferation potential, but also to harmonise international fusion regulation in other regulatory areas.

The section starts with an analysis of the politics of such a treaty (2.1), continuing with an exploration of the potential scope and context of a Fusion Treaty (2.2). It proceeds with an analysis of the forum for negotiation (2.3) and the institutional framework for this new treaty (2.4).

2.1 Politics of a Fusion Treaty

As already presented in the introduction, fusion has the potential to supply humanity with a virtually unlimited source of clean energy and may play an essential role in the fight against the climate crisis. The climate crisis is an existential threat to humanity, and fusion may play an important role in mitigating such a threat, as analysed in the introduction to this book. Another existential threat to humanity is nuclear weapons, whose destructive potential was demonstrated on 6 and 9 August 1945 in Japan, as well as in numerous tests. While the potential of fusion to mitigate climate change is direct, fusion's potential to be exploited for nuclear weapons programmes is only indirect. Fusion may support existing nuclear weapons programmes, but it does not replace the importance of fission as the basis of nuclear weapons. Adapting and applying the non-proliferation and disarmament regime to fusion must consider both the risks and benefits.

As discussed in the context of safety regulations for fusion,[861] any regulatory response must be risk-appropriate. With regards to nuclear weapons law, this entails two considerations: First, regulation must not overburden a young and promising technology where the risk is limited. Second, as there is a risk, some form of regulation should apply. This is where the international character of the legal framework plays an essential role: Non-proliferation law allows to establish a level playing field among all States by ensuring that there is no competition for the most lenient safeguards, which could potentially endanger international security. States acknowledge the authority exercised by the IAEA to ensure international security, but only as long as there is reciprocity in the legal obligations.

The Fusion Treaty could draw on lessons learnt from the NPT. In order for States to accept the discriminatory nature of the NPT and the exercise of authority by the IAEA, they were offered the incentives of the prospect of nuclear disarmament and technical assistance. In case an international instrument addresses safeguards only, there is no clear political incentive for States to accept such safeguards. As shown in the last chapter, while there are various pathways to address fusion's proliferation risk both under the existing regime and by amending the regime, there are only limited incentives for States to accept new safeguards and to extend the IAEA's authority. The Fusion Treaty has the opportunity to not only address the non-proliferation and disarmament dimension of fusion, but to include multiple aspects of fusion regulation and the promotion of fusion energy throughout the world. The broader the scope of the treaty and the more benefits it includes for NNWS, the more likely the acceptance of new safeguards for fusion is. A broader scope of the treaty, addressing multiple aspects of fusion and the technology's regulation, could serve as such an incentive.

2.2 Incentivising Scope and Content

This section explores the scope and content of the proposed Fusion Treaty. Such a Fusion Treaty could not only include safeguards (see Section 3), but also adopt a holistic approach to fusion and all relevant aspects of the tech-

861 *Matthew Lukacs/Laurence G. Williams*, Nuclear Safety Issues for Fusion Power Plants, Fusion Engineering and Design 150 (2020), 111377; *Neill Taylor/Pierre Cortes*, Lessons Learnt From ITER Safety & Licensing for DEMO and Future Nuclear Fusion Facilities, Fusion Engineering and Design 89 (2014), 1995–2000.

nology's regulation. This comprehensive approach encompasses a range of aspects of nuclear law (2.2.1), a provision offering technical assistance (2.2.2), and the incorporation of disarmament and vertical proliferation components (2.2.3), along with other regulatory aspects (2.2.4).

2.2.1 International Nuclear Law

As mentioned in the introduction, international nuclear law focuses mainly on three pillars – safety, security and safeguards –[862] and encompasses various international treaties and conventions. These include, among others, the Convention on Nuclear Safety, the Convention on the Safety of Spent Fuel Management and on the Safety of Radioactive Waste Management, or the Convention on the Physical Protection of Nuclear Material.

There are ongoing discussions whether and to which extent these conventions apply to fusion.[863] As analysed in the introduction, there is not only ambiguity in the applicability of these instruments, but discussions surround the same question whether the rules, which were developed specifically for fission, should be applicable to fusion as well. While there are safety[864] and security[865] concerns with fusion, these are fundamentally different from those of fission in many aspects.

Instead of addressing the ambiguity and the specific requirements of fusion within several separate frameworks that have all been developed for fission, there are compelling arguments for addressing these concerns within a single separate and specialised treaty for fusion. First, the inclusion

862 Some also consider the aspect of civil liability in case of a nuclear accident as a fourth pillar, see for instance *Rafael Mariano Grossi*, Nuclear Law: The Global Debate, in: Nuclear Law: The Global Debate, The Hague: T.M.C. Asser Press 2022, 1–27, at 2. The question of civil liability is discussed below in Section 2.2.4.

863 *Wolfram Tonhauser/Karoly Tamas Olajos*, Nuclear Fusion: Legal Aspects, Nuclear Law Bulletin 2023/2 (2024), 57–74; *International Atomic Energy Agency*, IAEA World Fusion Outlook 2023 – Fusion Energy: Present and Future, Vienna: IAEA 2023, at 24 ff. On 15 November 2023, the IAEA hosted the First Meeting Focusing on Safety and Regulation of Fusion.

864 *Carley Willis/Joanne Liou*, Safety in Fusion, IAEA Bulletin 62–2 (2021), 14–16; *Lukacs/Williams* (n 861); *M. Nakamura/K. Tobita/W. Gulden et al.*, Study of Safety Features and Accident Scenarios in a Fusion DEMO Reactor, Fusion Engineering and Design 89 (2014), 2028–2032; *Neill Taylor/Dennis Baker/Sergio Ciattaglia et al.*, Updated Safety Analysis of ITER, Fusion Engineering and Design 86 (2011), 619–622.

865 Karoly Tamas Olajos/Fusion For Energy (eds.), Fusion For Energy Roundtable 2024 Proceedings, Barcelona: European Commission 2024, at 63 f.

of fusion technology in a treaty developed for fission technology puts fusion and fission on the same level of perceived risks. However, as this is scientifically inaccurate, such a step could harm the prospects of an emerging technology as this could influence public opinion and investor interests. Second, the creation of a new treaty would allow for the drafting of obligations that are based on the individual risks of fusion, thereby recognising the technological differences between fusion and fission technology.

All aspects of nuclear law – safety, security and safeguards considerations – are relevant for the design of a fusion facility. As many startups are entering the design stage of their power plant concepts, they have an expressed interest in having clarity on the regulation of fusion. Consequently, incorporating all of these aspects in one international treaty regime would be a rational course of action. Adopting a holistic approach to fusion regulation within the framework of a Fusion Treaty would offer the opportunity to use the synergy of addressing all three design-relevant issues (safety, security and safeguards) at the same time, thereby preventing both the creation of gaps and the imposition of overburdening regulation. Addressing this matter on an international level is also the rational choice. Safeguards can only be regulated on an international level, as they pertain to State action. Using the synergies in design requirements for safety, security and safeguards would thus also require an international approach. In addition, harmonizing fusion regulation on an international level would facilitate the timely deployment of fusion energy across several countries in the fight against the clock in tackling the climate crisis, which is in the interest of all States.

2.2.2 Technical Assistance

Another aspect of the proposed Fusion Treaty draws on the NPT: Technical assistance. Accepting the discriminatory nature of the NPT, as well as the safeguarding powers of the IAEA, required a bargain, a *quid pro quo*, between NWS and NNWS. NWS offered the prospect of a cessation of the nuclear arms race as well as technical assistance for civilian nuclear programmes.[866] As the proposed treaty will also include an extension of safeguarding powers by an international organisation,[867] the instrument

866 Articles IV and VI of the NPT.

867 See below, Section 3.

would also have to offer benefits for all States. One incentive would be the inclusion of technical assistance in the development of a fusion energy infrastructure. Either advanced States or the competent international institution[868] could provide technical support for all interested States and foster the deployment in States without the necessary financial or technical means. Such technical assistance could financially be supported by global endeavours on Climate Finance, such as the New Collective Quantified Goal on Climate Finance, which aims to mobilise 1.3 trillion USD annually by 2035.[869]

2.2.3 Vertical Proliferation and Disarmament

Unlike the NPT, the Fusion Treaty could also include obligations towards vertical proliferation and pave a clear way towards nuclear disarmament. Such an inclusion might also be necessary to gain support by NNWS to adhere to a Fusion Treaty that includes new safeguarding obligations. While nuclear disarmament may currently seem out of reach, diplomatic[870] and scholarly[871] efforts remain active to prepare solutions should the geopolitical landscape shift.

Under the NPT, NNWS accept the discriminatory nature of the NPT and the international oversight of the IAEA, in return for technical assistance in civilian nuclear weapons programmes, the promise of a cessation of the nuclear arms race, and the prospect of both nuclear and conventional disarmament. Accepting additional levels of safeguards for fusion would require additional concessions. While including a provision on technical assistance might be a factor, stronger commitments to the goal of Article VI of the NPT with regard to limiting nuclear arsenals would be a necessary requirement, as demonstrated by previous discussions of enhancing the

868 See below, Section 2.3.2.
869 Following Article 9 of the Paris Agreement. The New Collective Quantified Goal on Climate Finance was adopted by Decision -/CMA.6.
870 For example, the British Foreign, Commonwealth and Development Office organised jointly with the Norwegian Ministry of Foreign Affairs a three-year long conference series on irreversibility in nuclear disarmament.
871 See for example Wilfred Wan/Vladislav Chernavskikh (eds.), Expanding Perspectives on Nuclear Disarmament, Uppsala: SIPRI/Alva Myrdal Centre for Nuclear Disarmament 2023.

non-proliferation system.[872] Promising technical assistance in the future for a technology that is not yet commercially available would not serve as sufficient incentive for NNWS to proactively address the proliferation potential of fusion by implementing a new system within the upcoming years. Such a proactive initiative would require a focus on vertical proliferation and nuclear disarmament.

This is especially of relevance given that vertical proliferation lies mostly outside the scope of the NPT regime. The NPT allows NWS to freely expand their nuclear arsenals both in number and sophistication. International law imposes minimal restrictions on vertical proliferation of nuclear weapons within the limits of Article VI.

Addressing the vertical dimension of tritium within a Fusion Treaty could draw on existing proposals to regulate tritium under nuclear weapons law. First, as mentioned above, an international tritium control regime has been proposed.[873] Such a treaty, including tritium safeguards, has been specifically seen in the context of a wider treaty regime also tackling fissile material, not only to strengthen non-proliferation, but to work towards nuclear disarmament.[874] Second, a tritium cut-off treaty has been proposed,[875] with the objective of ceasing the further supply of tritium for military purposes while at the same gradually achieving nuclear disarmament. Given the half-life of tritium of twelve year and its use in a large portion of nuclear warheads, such a treaty would progressively reduce the number of operational nuclear warheads equitably across all nine nuclear arsenals worldwide, ultimately resulting in the number zero. Such a treaty regime would also require verification mechanisms, such as environmental gas-sampling.[876] A focus on fusion safeguards, especially within a Fusion Treaty, might draw on these existing proposals and produce new momentum towards nuclear disarmament. While previous proposals on regulating

872 *Marcos Valle Machado da Silva*, Brazil and the Refusal to the Additional Protocol: Is It Time to Review this Position?, Carta Internacional 16 (2021), 1–26; *Togzhan Kassenova*, Nuclear Safeguards in Brazil and Argentina: 25 Years of ABACC, AIP Conference Proceedings 1898 (2017), 1–6.

873 See Chapter 4, Section 4.2.3.

874 *Martin Kalinowski*, International Control of Tritium for Nuclear Nonproliferation and Disarmament, Boca Raton: CRC Press 2004, at 52, 197.

875 *Robert E. Kelley*, Starve Nuclear Weapons to Death with a Tritium Freeze (*Stockholm International Peace Research Institute*, 2020), https://www.sipri.org/commentary/topical-backgrounder/2020/starve-nuclear-weapons-death-tritium-freeze, last accessed 17 July 2025.

876 Ibid proposes to add tritium detectors to the existing network of gas detectors set up by the Comprehensive Nuclear Test Ban Organization (CTBTO).

tritium were not picked up by States, addressing tritium in a broader framework not limited to the weapons-dimension only might incentivise NNWS to at least consider any kind of international oversight on tritium.

Furthermore, the fact that tritium is rare might further push for nuclear disarmament.[877] ITER is expected to consume all of the world's civilian inventory of tritium.[878] As analysed above, global civilian tritium production of all CANDU reactors is in the range of several kilograms per year, a quantity that a single fusion power plant would consume. While a future fusion power plant will produce in its operation more tritium than it consumes, the tritium quantity required for the startup of the first commercial fusion power plants will be a crucial topic.[879] Such a discrepancy might require the access of military resources of tritium, which are currently stored within nuclear warheads. When the question will be to either maintain nuclear arsenals or to power a solution to climate change, the latter might prevail as a heating world cannot afford a cold war.[880] A potential approach to maintaining a balance of nuclear powers, and making military tritium accessible for fusion energy, is within the framework of a Fusion Treaty.

2.2.4 Further Regulatory Aspects

Another aspect of a Fusion Treaty could be to address the question of civil liability in the case of a nuclear accident, also covered under international nuclear law, where similar considerations as with safety and security are applicable. As nuclear accidents create outstandingly high damages, the nuclear regime includes specific rules of private international law and the application of certain principles to ensure uniform rules of dealing with such damages. Within fusion, the risk of accidents, as well as the extent

877 *Taylor Loy*, Speculating on Tritium Futures – Why Defense Material Should Fuel Fusion Innovation (2023), https://www.newamerica.org/political-reform/briefs/tritium-fuel-futures/, last accessed 17 July 2025.

878 *Richard J. Pearson/Armando B. Antoniazzi/William J. Nuttall*, Tritium Supply and Use: a Key Issue for the Development of Nuclear Fusion Energy, Fusion Engineering and Design 136 (2018), 1140–1148.

879 Ibid; *M. Kovari/M. Coleman/I. Cristescu et al.*, Tritium Resources Available for Fusion Reactors, Nuclear Fusion 58 (2018), 026010.

880 *Mads Christensen*, A Heating World Can't Afford a Cold War in: Greenpeace, https://www.greenpeace.org/international/story/60291/a-heating-world-cant-afford-a-cold-war/, last accessed 17 July 2025.

of damages, is significantly reduced.[881] The existing instruments[882] do not apply to fusion,[883] yet there are ongoing discussions on amending the instruments to fusion.[884] While there is the desire of investors and insurances to have clear rules on the liability in the event of a fusion accident, such a clarification is necessary. However, as the risks differ significantly from those of fission and the existing regimes are designed with fission accidents in mind, addressing fusion in a separate instrument such as the Fusion Treaty would be beneficial.

In addition, other aspects of fusion regulation in a broader term might be included in such a treaty as well. They include questions on intellectual property,[885] rule on public-private partnerships[886] or the handling of supply chains with a focus on trade barriers.[887]

2.2.5 Summary

This section has developed the scope and content of a Fusion Treaty necessary to incentivise States to accept fusion safeguards. The scope of the Treaty is comprehensive, extending to other aspects of nuclear law, especially safety and security aspects, technical assistance in the deployment of fusion technology, an increased commitment to reduce vertical prolifera-

881 *Nakamura/Tobita/Gulden et al.* (n 864).

882 There are two conventions dealing with the topic. Under the auspices of the IAEA, there is the Vienna Convention on Civil Liability for Nuclear Damage. Under the auspices of the OECD, there is the Paris Convention on Third Party Liability in the Field of Nuclear Energy. The application of these two treaty regimes is to some extent harmonised by the Joint Protocol Relation to the Application of the Vienna Convention and the Paris Convention.

883 On this, see the extensive work of *Claire Portier*, Le droit de la responsabilité à l'épreuve des activités de fusion nucléaire, Aix-en-Provence: Aix-Marseille Université 2022. Also, *Tonhauser/Tamas Olajos* (n 863), at 62 f.; *William E. Fork/Charles H. Peterson*, Fusion Energy and Nuclear Liability Considerations, Nuclear Law Bulletin 93 (2014), 43–62.

884 *Exposé des Motifs of the Paris Convention*, NEA/NLC/DOC(2020)1, at 9.

885 *Elias G. Carayannis/John Draper*, The Growth of Intellectual Property Ownership in the Private-Sector Fusion Industry, Fusion Engineering and Design 173 (2021), 112815.

886 *Scott C. Hsu*, U.S. Fusion Energy Development via Public-Private Partnerships, Journal of Fusion Energy 42 (2023), 12; *David Kingham/Mikhail Gryaznevich*, The Spherical Tokamak Path to Fusion Power: Opportunities and Challenges for Development via Public–Private Partnerships, Physics of Plasmas 31 (2024), 1–7.

887 *Richard J. Pearson*, Barriers to Fusion Commercialization: Understanding Innovation, 2020.

tion and to work towards nuclear disarmament, as well as other regulatory aspects.

Such a comprehensive character of the Treaty incentivises wide-spread acceptance of both NNWS and NWS. Regarding NNWS, they would have to accept additional safeguards, yet they receive several benefits in return. First, technical assistance helps them to quickly deploy fusion energy without the cost and time associated with developing their own fusion industry. Second, provisions on vertical and horizontal disarmament would address NNWS' frustration regarding the non-implementation of Article VI of the NPT, which is a pivotal reason why the Additional Protocol has not yet been universally adopted. Third, a harmonisation of fusion regulation would provide assistance for many developing NNWS in creating a regulatory framework for fusion regulation.

Regarding NWS, a Fusion Treaty with a comprehensive scope also provides incentives for them. Safeguards on fusion technology in NNWS give NWS the assurance that this technology is not used in ways that would threaten their nuclear weapons monopoly. In addition, technical assistance would provide these States, which are also at the forefront of fusion development, with a global market for exporting fusion technology. Harmonising other aspects of fusion regulation further facilitates exports as the designs of machines does not have to be adapted to national regulation. These political and economic benefits might also be an incentive for these States to at least engage in negotiations on vertical proliferation and disarmament.

2.3 Forum for Negotiation

As seen with the TPNW,[888] a key question for the success of a treaty is its forum of negotiation. Historic examples may serve as a role model for the negotiation of a Fusion Treaty. The NPT was negotiated under a UN mandate by the Eighteen Nations Committee on Disarmament. Today, this forum has evolved into the Conference on Disarmament (CD), based in Geneva, making it an obvious candidate as forum for negotiation. This forum has been proven to be successful in negotiating the NPT, the Biological Weapons Convention, the Chemical Weapons Convention as well as the

888 *Gro Nystuen/Kjølv Egeland/Torbjørn Graff Hugo*, The TPNW: Setting The Record Straight, Norwegian Academy of International Law 2018, at 6.

CTBT. Nevertheless, the Conference on Disarmament has been labelled as dysfunctional in recent times, mainly due to its limited membership and procedures.[889] The CD consists of only 65 Member States and operates on a consensus basis. These restrictions have led to no progress in negotiations for many years.[890]

Another option could be the context of NPT Review Conferences. Although a Fusion Treaty would ultimately fall outside the NPT regime, its RevCons offer a unique opportunity for nearly all States to come together and to discuss progress on nuclear non-proliferation and disarmament. These discussions are not confined exclusively to the scope of the NPT regime; as drafts of the Nuclear Weapons Convention were proposed within the Review Cycle of the NPT.[891]

Depending on the scope of the Fusion Treaty, another forum could be a separate international conference on this topic. Such a conference could be mandated by a resolution of the UN General Assembly similar to the TPNW in 2016,[892] or initiated by a core group of States. The more such a treaty includes other aspects of fusion in order to develop a comprehensive fusion treaty, the more the treaty negotiations would likely be separated from the nuclear weapons regime.

2.4 Institutional Framework

Another question pertains to the institutional framework, especially with regard to the authority which would be mandated to operationalise and verify the treaty.

An obvious candidate for this role would be the IAEA. The IAEA has more than 70 years of experience in the nuclear sector. It is the international organisation that identifies itself with its motto *Atoms for Peace and Development*. It has 180 State Parties and a functional organisational structure. The IAEA is the depositary of numerous treaties and conventions related to the broader question of nuclear issues, including the Convention

889 *Judith Thorn*, The UN Conference on Disarmament, in: Eric Myer/Thilo Marauhn (eds.), Research Handbook on International Arms Control Law, Cheltenham: Elgar 2022, 77–88, at 78 ff.; *Nystuen/Egeland/Hugo* (n 888), at 6.

890 *Paul Meyer*, Does the Conference of Disarmament Have a Future?, Journal for Peace and Nuclear Disarmament 4 (2021), 287–294.

891 NPT/CONF.2010/PC.I/WP.17.

892 A/RES/71/258.

on Nuclear Safety, the Convention on the Physical Protection of Nuclear Material, and the Vienna Convention on Civil Liability for Nuclear Damage. Given the overlap with fusion, mandating the IAEA with the oversight of a Fusion Treaty would be a logical choice. The IAEA already considers itself as the leading international organisation in the field of fusion.[893] In addition, the IAEA has extensive experience with safeguards and employs around 275 safeguards inspectors.[894] As shown in Chapter 3, the mandate of the IAEA is broad enough to also cover fusion.

However, there are arguments against mandating the IAEA with fusion. First, there is the clear distinction between fusion and fission. Both States and private actors try to keep fusion and fission separate. This is, for example, demonstrated in the use of the expression *fusion* rather than *nuclear fusion* and the intentional omission of the word *nuclear* when talking about fusion technology. This seeks to avoid conflating nuclear fusion with fission, especially to distance fusion from the negative connotations that fission and nuclear energy holds in public discourse. Mandating the institution which is often referred to as nuclear watchdog with fusion could do the contrary.

The second argument against the IAEA is that it has no experience with fusion and vertical proliferation. The IAEA is well-versed in implementing safeguards to prevent proliferation in a fission fuel cycle, the same expertise does not extend to a fusion fuel cycle. As there are fundamental differences between fission and fusion, fusion safeguards would require new know-how and procedures. This is especially true with the vertical proliferation dimension of fusion. The IAEA is experienced in preventing horizontal proliferation, but has no experiences in administering safeguards on preventing vertical proliferation. Given the limited resources in funding and staff of the IAEA, a new international institution might be better suited to apply safeguards to fusion power plants and the fusion fuel cycle.

Thus, the establishment of a new international organisation might be the best approach. Such an International Fusion Energy Agency (IFEA) could draw on the experiences of the IAEA, especially with regard to its organisational structure. Such an IFEA could equally comprise a General Conference, comprising all Member States, a Board of Governors, representing all regions of the world and the most advanced nations in fusion technology, and a Secretariat, comprising different departments focussing

893 *International Atomic Energy Agency* (n 863), at 5.

894 *Rafael Mariano Grossi*, IAEA Safeguards for International Peace and Security, IAEA Bulletin 63–3 (2022), 1–1.

on all aspects of fusion energy. Similar to the CTBTO, setting up the IFEA in Vienna, at the Vienna International Centre alongside the United Nations, IAEA and CTBTO Headquarters, would be a rational choice to maximise collaborative effects. Given the reduced safeguards problematic of fusion compared to fission, the size and costs of the IFEA would be lower than the 430-million-euro regular budget and roughly 2,500 employees of the IAEA.

2.5 Summary

This section has analysed the structure of a Fusion Treaty. Given the risk potential of fusion, it is necessary to develop risk-appropriate approaches to the technology's regulation and to include incentives for States to accept fusion safeguards. A comprehensive regulation of several regulatory aspects of fusion would be such an incentive. In addition, the institutional framework has been discussed, with options of negotiating the treaty in- or outside existing nuclear weapons law fora, as well as the options of creating a new international organisation for fusion.

3 Safeguards Under a Fusion Treaty

The proposed Fusion Treaty is predicated on the incorporation of risk-appropriate safeguards mechanisms to ensure that fusion energy is only used for peaceful applications. The development of a number of these instruments can draw upon existing safeguards for the nuclear fission fuel cycle, while others are newly developed specifically for fusion. This section first explores the possibility of including nuclear weapon States into the regime (3.1). It further addresses the legal architecture of the fusion's safeguards regime (3.2). The section continues to develop approaches for the three different proliferation concerns: the risk of fissile material production (3.3), the substantial availability of tritium (3.4) and the knowledge transfer of inertial confinement fusion (3.5). It concludes with an analysis of the relevance of export control regimes (3.6).

3.1 The Question of Nuclear Weapon States

A fundamental question of a safeguards system under a Fusion Treaty is on how to treat NWS. States have to decide on whether and to which extent the safeguarding measures include fusion facilities within NWS. Fusion facilities may provide NWS with benefits for their nuclear weapons programmes, especially inertial confinement fusion as it is already used in the United States and France for military purposes, as well as a cost-effective source of tritium and an efficient method to produce plutonium. Including the civilian infrastructure in NWS under international fusion safeguards would not only serve to limit vertical proliferation and play a role in disarmament, it would also increase acceptance among NNWS. Under the NPT regime, NWS recognised by the NPT have placed their civilian fusion infrastructure under voluntary safeguards for increasing acceptance.[895]

The extent of the inclusion of NWS depends on how closely the treaty mirrors the NPT. Under the NPT, NWS are free from any safeguarding obligations. However, as argued above, fusion should be regulated outside the NPT. Dealing with safeguards outside the NPT would allow for a more equal treatment of all States and could overcome the discriminatory nature of the NPT regime.

It seems feasible that NWS would accept voluntary safeguards for their civilian fusion infrastructure similar to how they accept voluntary safeguards for their civilian fission infrastructure. Whether obligations go beyond a purely voluntary nature depends on the bargaining power of NNWS. As NNWS are often critiques of new safeguards as long as NWS do not agree on limiting their own nuclear weapons capacities, the acceptance of NNWS of fusion safeguards could depend on obligations of NWS rather than voluntary action only.

3.2 Legal Architecture of Fusion Safeguards

Another question is on how to incorporate fusion safeguards. If the NPT is taken as an example, fusion safeguards could be mandated (either only for NNWS or all States) in general, with further details to be included in safeguards agreements between the States and the competent international authority. Alternatively, the fundamental outline of fusion safeguards,

895 *Frank S. Houck*, The Voluntary Safeguards Offer of the United States – A Review of its History and Implementation, IAEA Bulletin 27 (1985), 13–18.

including the competences of the institution could be incorporated directly into the Fusion Treaty itself.

A balanced consideration of both approaches reveals their respective advantages and disadvantages. In the event that safeguards are specified in further agreements, the competent international authority – to use language from the TPNW – has more leeway on implementing and developing. Especially, should the competent international authority be the IAEA, the basis of the agreement would be a decision by the Board of Governors. As the Board only has limited membership, such a process would not be as inclusive as Treaty negotiations with all Member States. Conversely, safeguards are evolving, particularly in relation to a technology that still exists only in research laboratories. The conceptualisation of fusion power plants at present may differ significantly from those that will be constructed in the future. Setting the safeguards regime in stone in the form of a Treaty might impede future adaptations. As seen with fission, the NPT has remained unchanged, while there have been four iterations of IAEA safeguards on fission.[896] Establishing the foundation in an international treaty, and then subsequently mandating international organisations to develop the framework, has demonstrated to allow for flexibility. This valuable lesson, learnt from the NPT, underscores the need for a dynamic and adaptable safeguards regime.

To find a balance between these advantages and disadvantages, one approach might be to include negotiations on a first set of safeguards into the Treaty conference itself. In order to maintain a level of flexibility for future developments, the Fusion Treat could mandate the competent international authority with the future development of fusion safeguards. Furthermore, the Treaty could include a provision that all future changes to the system will be mandatory for all Parties to the Fusion Treaty. This would avoid the repetition of today's situation, where not all States have adopted the Additional Protocol of 1998, leading to 44 States still having in place safeguards levels that were developed in the early 1970s. Such a scenario would shift power from the States, especially their parliaments, to an international organisation. Today, any modification to the safeguards system requires ratification by each State, thus also the involvement of parliaments. Modifications to the IAEA safeguards system have been drafted in bodies of the IAEA where all States were included, meaning that at least each State's government had the opportunity to influence the modifications

896 INFCIRC/26; INFCIRC/66; INFCIRC/153; INFCIRC/540.

to the system. However, the influence of an individual State in discussions of bodies of international organisations is limited given power structures and the exercise of hegemony, while the requirement of signing and ratifying a new treaty or protocol effectively provides every State with a veto power.

As a consequence, there would have to be an incentive for States to accept such a treaty provision that would take power away and shifts it to an international organisation. An effective safeguards system capable to act proactively rather than reactively is such an incentive. Historic examples have shown that existing safeguards mechanisms often do not suffice to adequately address the proliferation potential of nuclear technology. As there is a shared interest among both NNWS and NWS that no further State acquires nuclear weapons, there is also a shared interest to close loopholes in the system as early and as efficiently as possible.

3.3 Addressing the Risk of Fissile Material Production

A key task of safeguards under a Fusion Treaty is to address the proliferation potential of high-energetic neutrons. As analysed above,[897] neutrons from fusion reactions have the capability to transform fertile materials (such as uranium ore) into fissile material (such as ^{239}Pu). A Fusion Treaty can address this potential by implementing safeguards measures. This section discusses some safeguarding measures that could be implemented, while not providing a comprehensive list. Specific safeguards depend on specificities such as the design and scale of the facility, and have to be developed by technical experts.

3.3.1 Gamma Radiation Detectors

Under peaceful operations of fusion facilities, no fertile or fissile material is present on site. As even the smallest amounts of such material indicate a breakout scenario,[898] a focus on detecting these materials is key to safe-

897 Chapter 1, Section 5.1.3.

898 One limitation might be traces of uranium in the breeding blanket if it is made of beryllium as natural beryllium ore contains some uranium, *B. N. Kolbasov/V. I. Khripunov/A. Yu Biryukov*, On Use of Beryllium in Fusion Reactors: Resources, Impurities and Necessity of Detritiation After Irradiation, Fusion Engineering and

guarding fusion. These materials are detectable through gamma radiation, especially the detection of ^{238}U based on its 1.001 MeV gamma line.[899] Consequently, a key safeguards measure would entail the installation of gamma radiation detectors on-site. These detectors could be remotely observed from the headquarters of the competent international safeguarding authority, such as the IAEA or IFEA. This approach would guarantee a minimally invasive measure while simultaneously providing a high level of certainty that the fusion facility is used solely for peaceful purposes.

3.3.2 Design Review and Monitoring of Energy Output

Another approach to prevent the use of fusion facilities for the production of fissile material is the combined use of a design review and the monitoring of the energy output.

A design review would serve two purposes. First, the designs could be reviewed to assess if the plant has any unusual characteristics that could be used for producing fissile material. As fertile material has to enter the machine at some point and the produced fissile material must be removed, there have to be some technological features that would be recognisable in the design. Second, a design review would allow for estimating the energy output of the facility. Parameters of the fusion device such as heating power, magnetic fields and spatial dimensions of the reactor can be used to determine the power output of the fusion machine.

In fission, States fill out a Design Information Questionnaire (DIQ) and submit it to the IAEA. This questionnaire includes general information about the facility, a description of the types, use and flow of nuclear material, information about handling of nuclear material, accountancy measures as well as protection measures. The IAEA performs a Design Information Verification (DIV) of the facility to verify the correctness and completeness of the design information provided in the DIQ. Implementing DIQ and DIV would be essential for safeguarding fusion facilities.

Design 109–111 (2016), 480–484. On different breeding blanket designs, cf. *G. Federici/L. Boccaccini/F. Cismondi et al.*, An Overview of the EU Breeding Blanket Design Strategy as an Integral Part of the DEMO Design Effort, Fusion Engineering and Design 141 (2019), 30–42.

899 *Alexander Glaser/Robert J. Goldston*, Proliferation Risks of Magnetic Fusion Energy: Clandestine Production, Covert Production and Breakout, Nuclear Fusion 52 (2012), 043004, at 5.

In addition to the design review, the energy output of the fusion machine would be measured. Any neutron that is not used for fusion processes or heat production but rather to produce fertile material is a neutron that does not contribute to the energy production or production of tritium. Using a fusion machine for fertile material production will influence its energy output.[900] Comparing the actual energy output with the estimated output of the fusion reactor could allow to detect discrepancies that might indicate the production of fertile material.

3.3.3 Physical Access to Fusion Facilities and Environmental Sampling

Similar to fission plants, international safeguards inspectors could have the competence to access fusion facilities. These inspections could verify that the detectors proposed above are adequately placed and properly functioning. Also, these visits could verify if the actual design of the plant corresponds to the design reviewed by the competent international authority. Facility access could also be used to take further samples and measurements to ensure that no fissile material has been produced. These inspections could place and check seals to verify that the fusion device has not been opened for adding or replacing a second wall containing uranium for plutonium production.

As under the existing Additional Protocol, physical access and sampling should not only be limited to the facility itself, but could also allow access to random locations on a State's territory in order to take environmental samples. As the handling of fissionable material leads to traces in the environment,[901] such an approach would add another level of certainty. This is especially true with fusion, as the production of fissile material would require the operation of a clandestine plutonium separation plant. The implementation of these safeguards measures would not only enhance fusion safeguards, but also further strengthen fission safeguards.

900 Ibid.

901 *David L. Donohue*, Strengthening IAEA Safeguards Through Environmental Sampling and Analysis, Journal of Alloys and Compounds 271–273 (1998), 11–18.

3.3.4 Satellite Imagery

A further approach to verify the information obtained could be satellite imagery. In the event that a fusion facility was to be used for the breeding of nuclear weapons material, such material would need to be reprocessed, and the facilities used for this process might be detectable from satellite imagery. Furthermore, this approach would address the risk of clandestine fusion facilities, as they are, at least the first generation, large facilities as well.[902] The utilisation of satellite imagery in the broader context of non-proliferation has garnered increased attention,[903] and could further support the verification that fusion facilities remain in peaceful uses only.

3.4 Addressing the Risk of Tritium

Addressing the proliferation potential associated with tritium can be addressed by implementing a tritium accounting system. The proper installation of tritium accountancy devices can be verified by regular visits to the facility, as proposed above. There are, however, various technological challenges in implementing tritium accountancy.

Tritium accountancy is based on plasma measurements, from which the production and consumption of tritium can be calculated. However, as tritium is gaseous, accounting is more difficult than with metals such as uranium and plutonium. Furthermore, tritium is highly reactive and gets absorbed in dust and surfaces. Accounting for tritium is not only a safeguards concern, but a safety and security concern of fusion facilities.[904] Given the value of tritium, currently about USD 30,000–35,000 per

---

902 *Glaser/Goldston* (n 899), at 2.

903 *Irmgard Niemeyer*, Perspectives of Satellite Imagery Analysis for Verifying the Nuclear Non-Proliferation Treaty, in: Gotthard Stein/Bernd Richter/Sven Nussbaum/Irmgard Niemeyer/Bhupendra Jasani (eds.), International Safeguards and Satellite Imagery, Berlin, Heidelberg: Springer Berlin Heidelberg 2009, 35–44; *Frank V. Pabian/Guido Renda/Rainer Jungwirth et al.*, Commercial Satellite Imagery: An Evolving Tool in the Non-proliferation Verification and Monitoring Toolkit, in: Irmgard Niemeyer/Mona Dreicer/Gotthard Stein (eds.), Nuclear Non-Proliferation and Arms Control Verification: Innovative Systems Concepts, Cham: Springer International Publishing 2020, 351–371.

904 *Didier Perrault*, Nuclear Safety Aspects on the Road Towards Fusion Energy, Fusion Engineering and Design 146 (2019), 130–134; *Elahe Alizadeh*, Environmental and Safety Aspects of Using Tritium in Fusion, Journal of Fusion Energy 25 (2006), 47–55.

gram,[905] there is also an economic interest in clear tritium accountancy. Currently, research is being conducted focusing on simulations to account for tritium within the fusion fuel cycle.[906] However, tritium accounting must overcome several difficulties.

Firstly, excess tritium is needed in order to compensate for calculation uncertainties. In other words, it is unclear exactly how much tritium will be consumed by the fusion reactions themselves. The presence of calculation uncertainties makes the implementation of an accounting system difficult.

Secondly, the proliferation potential is increased by the fact that unused tritium will be transferred through a piping system to a tritium processing plant. Not only could tritium escape through microscopic leaks – tritium is, after all, hydrogen, i.e., a gas that tends to escape very easily – but there is also a potential for circumvention due to a potentially covert access to pipes.[907] If a proliferator was to extract some tritium from a small section of a long piping system, it could potentially do so undetected.

Another difficulty for accounting is the question of detecting tritium. The low energy of beta rays emitted from tritium makes detection particularly challenging.[908] ITER foresees daily measurements of the tritium inventory within the fuel cycle, based on several factors including the tritium burn-up rate within the plasma.[909] However, this burn-up rate is difficult to measure and includes significant uncertainties. A 2008 study demonstrated that there is a substantial probability to not detect 100g of tritium diver-

---

905 *Daniel Clery*, Out of Gas, Science 376 (2022), 1372–1376; *Richard J. Pearson/Olivia Comsa/Liviu Stefan et al.*, Romanian Tritium for Nuclear Fusion, Fusion Science and Technology 71 (2017), 610–615.

906 *Samuele Meschini/Sara E. Ferry/Rémi Delaporte-Mathurin et al.*, Modeling and Analysis of the Tritium Fuel Cycle for ARC- and STEP-Class D-T Fusion Power Plants, Nuclear Fusion 63 (2023), 1–34. Also, the UKAEA has recently started its Tritium Inventory Project.

907 *Rachel Lawless/Barry Butler/Anthony Hollingsworth et al.*, Tritium Plant Technology Development for a DEMO Power Plant, Fusion Science and Technology 71 (2017), 679–686; *Tetsuo Tanabe*, Tritium Handling Issues in Fusion Reactor Materials, Journal of Nuclear Materials 417 (2011), 545–550; *Jürgen Raeder/Arthur Weller/Robert Wolf et al.*, Review of the Safety Concept for Fusion Reactor Concepts and Transferability of the Nuclear Fission Regulation to Potential Fusion Power Plants, GRS 2016.

908 *Andrew J. Parker/Michael D. Aspinall/Colin Boxall et al.*, Radiometric Techniques for the Detection and Assessment of Tritium in Aqueous Media – a Review, Progress in Nuclear Energy 162 (2023), 104733; *Kalinowski* (n 874), at 5.

909 *R. Lässer/D. K. Murdoch/M. Glugla*, Tritium Accountancy Issues of the ITER Fuel Cycle, Fusion Science and Technology 48 (2005), 337–342.

sion within an 18-year timespan.[910] However, others argue that there are technical means to introduce a control procedure capable to detect even quantities of 1 gram.[911] The development of verification mechanisms for the use of tritium requires further scientific research.

3.5 Addressing the Risk of Knowledge Transfer in ICF

In contrast to the concerns surrounding the production of fissile material or tritium, the proliferation potential from inertial confinement fusion does not come from the material used in nuclear weapons, but rather from the knowledge gained. Addressing this issue through safeguards measures poses significant challenges. Given the classified nature of many aspects of ICF, it is difficult to quantify the proliferation potential. One potential approach involves a design review, wherein experts from universities and/or NWS could assess whether the facility in question might produce data that could support a nuclear weapons programme. While this approach might risk industrial espionage, procedures could be implemented to mitigate such threats and ensure that the review is confined to the prevention of military knowledge transfer. As the main benefit from ICF for weapons development stems from variations in the experimental set-up, a future ICF power plant will be limited to a specific configuration optimised for power output. Future fusion power plants are designed in one specific configuration to maximise energy output, not to gain insights in nuclear weapon research. The combination of design reviews and limited configurations would ensure that ICF plants are not used for nuclear weapons development. Although limits could come from the protection of intellectual property, transparency in the design stage could be a step to address the proliferation potential. Such a *Safeguards by Design* approach would be minimally invasive, reducing the necessity for safeguards inspections.[912] Another possibility would be to allow NNWS only to import turn-key fusion reactors which are developed in NWS and do not allow for a change of physical parameters. Regulation of ICF could go as far as prohibiting

910 *Jörg Reckers*, Tritiumbilanzierung zur Überprüfung der Nichtweiterverbreitung im Fusionsreaktor ITER, in: DPG (ed.), 72. Jahrestagung der DPG, Berlin: 2008.

911 *Kalinowski* (n 874), at 176 and 197 f.

912 *Jeremy Whitlock*, Safeguards by Design: Designing Nuclear Facilities with Safeguards in Mind, IAEA Bulletin 63 (2022), 22–22. The IAEA has also published seven guidance documents on the Safeguards by Design approach for fission, IAEA Nuclear Energy Series No. NF-T-2.8, 2.9, 3.1, 3.2, 4.7, 4.8 and 4.10.

one type of ICF, indirect-driven ICF, in NNWS, as this technology has the closest resemblance to hydrogen bombs, however such a prohibition would be disproportionately restricting the development and deployment of ICF power plants and would not completely eradicate the proliferation potential.

The dual-use character of ICF is less pronounced than in classical fission or the other two proliferation issues as it is not material but knowledge than can benefit nuclear weapon development. It must further be noted that the information than can be gained from a specific ICF configuration is especially beneficial for States that are already in possession of nuclear weapons.[913] Consequently, this is primarily[914] a vertical proliferation issue. Existing military-used ICF facilities are research facilities designed for a wide range of research, including military research.

3.6 Relevance of Export Control Regimes

Under to Article III.2 NPT, the regime based on fission requires export controls to support the implementation of safeguards. The export of specific dual-use goods is only permitted to States which apply safeguards to these goods.[915] Within a Fusion Treaty, a similar approach could be followed, implementing a lesson learnt from the NPT. As analysed above, export control regimes are relatively easy to adapt to fusion, as they are based on soft-law guidelines. The combination of a mandate to apply safeguards if a country wants to import certain dual-use fusion goods, especially with a focus on tritium and tritium technology as well as ICF-related technology, and soft-law approaches on setting up the details would be an approach to further support a fusion safeguards system. Such a system would serve to complement the verification mechanisms established by an international organisation, thereby enabling other international fora to develop rules and procedures. This, in turn, would serve to maximise the degree of insurance that fusion technology is not used for military purposes.

---

913 Expert statement of Christian Häfner, Fraunhofer Institute for Laser Technology, during a hearing of the German Bundestag, Committee for Education, Research and Technology Assessment, 3 July 2024.

914 *Kalinowski* (n 874), at 39 ff. argues that tritium has a significant horizontal component as well.

915 Article III.2 NPT. On this, see above Chapter 3, Section 2.

3.7 Summary

This section has developed approaches on how to include safeguards into a Fusion Treaty regime. It has discussed the possibility of including nuclear weapon States as equals to non-nuclear-weapons States into the regime. Furthermore, this section has analysed the extent to which safeguards are already defined in the treaty, or is left open for elaboration within an international organisation. The chapter has proposed both technical and legal approaches to address fusion's proliferation concerns within the proposed treaty regime, focussing on all three proliferation aspects of the risk of fissile material production, the abundance of tritium and the knowledge transfer of inertial confinement fusion.

4 Conclusion

This chapter has proposed a novel, holistic approach to addressing the proliferation potential of fusion technology. Rather than adapting the existing non-proliferation framework, which is primarily designed for fission, a new treaty tailored to fusion is advocated. This treaty would encompass not only safeguards but also the comprehensive regulation of fusion on an international level.

Fusion's proliferation risks should be regulated outside the NPT regime. The primary reason is that fusion differs fundamentally from fission, both in its technological characteristics and its proliferation potential. Fusion does not directly contribute to the development of nuclear weapons but can support and enhance existing nuclear weapons programmes. This distinction necessitates a separate regulatory framework. In addition, there is a lack of political incentive to address fusion within the existing regime.

The NPT's successes, such as setting an international norm against nuclear proliferation and stopping several nuclear weapons programmes, are acknowledged. However, its shortcomings, including its lack of universality, retroactive rather than proactive nature, and the absence of consensus on fundamental questions, underscore the need for a new approach for fusion. The NPT's struggles to maintain the nuclear status quo and its limited success in achieving universal adherence further support the argument for a separate fusion treaty.

Adapting the existing NPT framework to include fusion would require extensive changes, including amendments and new protocols, a process that is both lengthy and complicated. Given the challenges in amending the NPT, a more efficient use of diplomatic resources would be to create a new treaty specifically for fusion.

The limited scope of the NPT, which does not adequately address vertical proliferation, is another reason for a separate fusion treaty, as fusion's proliferation potential is to a large extent also of vertical nature.

Precedents for dealing with nuclear weapons-related issues outside the NPT regime, such as the CTBT, proposals for a Fissile Material Cut-Off Treaty and the TPNW, provide a basis for advocating a separate fusion treaty. These precedents demonstrate that creating new international organisations and treaties can be an effective approach to addressing specific proliferation risks.

The structure of the proposed fusion treaty is outlined, emphasizing the need for a holistic approach that includes safety, security, and safeguards considerations. The treaty would address technical assistance, vertical proliferation, and disarmament, as well as other regulatory aspects such as civil liability and intellectual property, in order to serve as an incentive.

The IAEA is considered a potential competent international authority, but the establishment of a new International Fusion Energy Agency (IFEA) is proposed to address the unique requirements of fusion safeguards.

Safeguards mechanisms would be central to a fusion treaty. These mechanisms include gamma radiation detectors, design reviews, energy output monitoring, physical access to fusion facilities, environmental sampling, tritium accountancy systems, and addressing the risk of knowledge transfer in ICF. Export control regimes are another aspect in supporting the implementation of fusion safeguards.

This chapter has presented a pathway toward a new, comprehensive Fusion Treaty, that addresses the proliferation potential of fusion technology in a risk-appropriate way while providing clear incentives in order to adapt the framework to fusion. Such a Treaty would ensure that that both global interests are balanced to an optimal degree: Limiting the risks of the spread of nuclear weapons, while at the same time enabling the development of a new technology to address the climate crisis.

Chapter 6: Conclusion

Fusion energy, the power of stars, has the potential to revolutionise energy production and to play a significant role in combatting the climate crisis. By fusing the atomic nuclei of the hydrogen isotopes deuterium and tritium, future fusion power plants may produce tremendous amounts of energy without the production of greenhouse gases from a virtually unlimited source of energy. As such, fusion might play a significant role in mitigating climate change, the most pressing topic of this century. While fusion has yet to escape research facilities, both government-funded and private-funded projects are underway to achieving the goal of commercially available fusion energy within the next decade or two.

As fusion is a nuclear technology, it has applications in nuclear weapons programmes as it can play an auxiliary role. Fusion's proliferation potential is significantly lower compared to fission, but the risk is non-zero. Fusion can play a role in nuclear weapons programmes in three aspects. Firstly, a State may use a fusion reactor to produce fissile material for the fission part of nuclear weapons. As fusion reactions yield neutrons, which can be used to convert ^{238}U, the most abundant isotope of uranium (which is of no use for fission reactors and weapons), into ^{239}Pu, or the thorium isotope ^{232}Th into ^{233}U. Both materials can be used in nuclear weapons.

Secondly, modern nuclear weapons are multi-staged devices that utilise the energy released by a combination of fission and fusion reactions. The integration of deuterium-tritium fusion reactions in weapons increases the yield significantly and allows for the miniaturisation of weapons, making a variety of deployment systems possible, such as intercontinental missiles. The commercialisation of fusion power plants will increase the annual tritium production by many orders of magnitude, thereby increasing the availability of this crucial component of advanced nuclear weapons.

Thirdly, one specific fusion technology, namely laser-fusion or inertial confinement fusion, is currently only researched in military research facilities. The aim of these facilities is to simulate and to better understand the processes that take place within a thermonuclear weapon. These facilities were constructed with the purpose of replacing nuclear testing. The entry of inertial confinement energy into a commercial scale might lead to the spread of knowledge of the functioning of thermonuclear weapons, thus potentially facilitating the development in NNWS. It is the task of nuclear weapons law to allow for harvesting the benefits of the use of fusion energy, namely the potential to tackling the climate crisis, while at the same time preventing the further proliferation of nuclear weapons.

The international regime of nuclear weapons law intends to prevent or reverse the use of nuclear technology in nuclear weapons. Its sub-regimes of non-proliferation and disarmament comprise a number of institutions, treaties and other international instruments, with the aim of either preventing the further spread of nuclear weapons or prohibiting them. The regime seeks to enable the economic use of nuclear energy while at the same time limiting the risk associated with dual-use technology.

As nuclear weapons have demonstrated their destructive potential in two uses of nuclear weapons in Japan on 6 and 9 August 1945, in addition to the well over two thousand nuclear tests conducted since then, the destructive capacity and the security risks of nuclear weapons are irrefutable. Nevertheless, the possession of nuclear weapons plays a pivotal role in the geopolitical landscape, serving to perpetuate a hegemonic system and to extend the sphere of influence through nuclear coercion and nuclear deterrence.

In light of the threat to peace and security posed by both the possession and the further spread of nuclear weapons, States have almost universally vested a number of institutions with a significant level of authority through various international treaties. At the core of the non-proliferation regime is the 1968 Nuclear Non-Proliferation Treaty (NPT) and the International Atomic Energy Agency (IAEA). The NPT permits five States, namely the United States, the United Kingdom, Russia, France and China, to possess nuclear weapons, while all other non-nuclear weapon states (NNWS) are prohibited from possessing or developing nuclear weapons. In addition, the NPT includes provisions on technical assistance and on nuclear disarmament. The IAEA is entrusted with the responsibility to verify the compliance with the NPT by administering safeguards to nuclear material and nuclear technology. All NNWS have concluded Comprehensive Safeguards Agreements (CSA) with the IAEA, thereby specifying the extent of the Agency's authority. Furthermore, the majority of States has also concluded an Additional Protocol, thereby extending the IAEA's authority further, following the discovery of Iraq's clandestine nuclear weapons programme in the 1990s.

Moreover, there are further regimes specifying obligations with regard to non-proliferation and disarmament. In Europe, Euratom, in its capacity as a common supplier of nuclear material for peaceful uses, is subject to its own non-proliferation obligations and safeguards regime, which acts complementary to the IAEA. In addition, the majority of States, covering the majority of landmass on Earth, signed regional nuclear weapon-free zone (NWFZ) treaties which prohibit nuclear weapons and nuclear weapon related activities. Additionally, the Treaty on the Prohibition of Nuclear Weapons (TPNW) prohibits nuclear weapons for and in all of its State Parties. All of these treaties include a specific verification regime, but they are mostly based on the IAEA system. As all treaties refer to the IAEA's safeguards system, this regime is at the centre of nuclear non-proliferation law.

Safeguards are further complemented by export control regimes. These regimes are based on soft law instruments and are agreed upon in two intergovernmental fora: the Zangger Committee and the Nuclear Suppliers Group.

With regard to fusion, the regime of nuclear weapons law fails to reach its goal as there is a gap in its application to fusion. The regime intends to prevent the use of nuclear technology for nuclear weapons, yet the verification regime is largely inapplicable to fusion technology. As the NPT and the IAEA's safeguards system are focused on source and special fissionable material in fission facilities, the treaty provisions do not apply on verifying fusionable material or fusion facilities. The existing regime only applies to verifying the absence of fissile material in fusion facilities by environmental sampling and complementary access, if a State has adopted the Additional Protocol. As the verification mechanisms for non-nuclear weapon states in nuclear weapon free zones and TPNW Member States do not require the implementation of the Additional Protocol, there are further gaps in these regimes. Furthermore, safeguards under the Euratom Treaty do not apply to fusion as well. While export control regimes cover material used in fusion, the procedures required for exports do not match the intent as they require IAEA safeguards, which are largely not applicable to fusion. There are significant gaps between the regime's objective and its application to fusion.

Given the gap between the objective of the regime and the application of its verification mechanisms, there are several options for adapting the framework for its application to fusion. These approaches vary in terms of their legitimacy, effectiveness and proportionality.

Evolutionary interpretation by the IAEA's Secretariat of the term *facility* allows for the application of existing safeguards to fusion facilities in order to verify the absence of fissionable material, addressing one of three proliferation concerns. However, as the legitimacy of this interpretation might be questioned by States, a path to increased legitimacy are measures by different institutions. They might include decisions and actions by the IAEA's Board of Governors, the IAEA's Secretariat, decisions by NPT and TPNW Review Conferences and Meetings of State Parties, actions by UN organs such as the General Assembly and the Security Council as well as the Nuclear Suppliers Group. Each institution has its own means to further the development of safeguards for fusion.

In instances where such measures are insufficient, treaty changes are necessary to adopt the regime to fusion. Such changes are particularly crucial for incorporating tritium into the safeguards regime. In order to do so, existing legal instruments such as the IAEA Statute or the NPT would require amendments, as well as the Euratom Treaty or NWFZ Treaties. Another approach could be the adoption of a new treaty under an international tritium control system. Furthermore, modifications to the export control guidelines are necessary to ensure alignment between the objectives of export control procedures and the application of export controls.

The incorporation of fusion technology into the existing legal framework governing nuclear weapons law is a complex issue, given the challenges faced by the current legal regime. Firstly, fusion represents a novel technology with significant economic and societal potential, yet its role in nuclear weapons is comparatively limited in comparison to existing nuclear technologies. The integration of fusion into the system could potentially hinder the development of this technology and incur costs for both the operator and the IAEA. Secondly, any modifications to the current framework would fall within the purview of the broader NPT regime, which – despite the treaty's successes – has been subject to considerable criticism and has repeatedly demonstrated its inadequacies over the past several decades. The non-proliferation regime has been largely reactive, rather than proactive, and has been unsuccessful in preventing numerous countries from acquiring nuclear weapons since its inception. Additionally, certain states have disregarded their obligations under the treaty, including nuclear disarmament. The failure of numerous review conferences to even agree on non-binding outcome documents further reinforces the perception that treaty changes are unattainable. Additionally, there is a lack of political incentives for NNWS to accept a further interference with their sovereignty in a field which is as important as energy.

Such an incentive could be the adoption of a comprehensive treaty specifically developed for fusion and encompassing not only the nuclear weapons law dimension, but further aspects of fusion regulation as well. Such a Fusion Treaty could harmonise aspects of nuclear safety and nuclear security on an international level, thereby facilitating the development of commercial fusion technology by reducing regulatory differences between different States. Furthermore, the treaty could develop new approaches for risk-appropriate safeguards measures for a technology with a limited proliferation potential, while implementing lessons learnt from the NPT. A comprehensive Fusion Treaty would help promoting fusion technology and its quick deployment throughout the planet in order to tackle the climate crisis, while at the same time meeting the risk of further proliferation of nuclear weapons.

Yet, law can only do so much, as it is just one of a multitude of reasons why States do or do not engage in nuclear weapons. It is not only the development of a new technology or the legal response that will support a nuclear weapons programme, it is the political will of a State to acquire nuclear weapons which is the most decisive factor whether fusion will only tackle the climate crisis or will also contribute to the further proliferation of nuclear weapons.

To conclude this book, a quote of British physicist Sir Oliver Lodge reminds us of external factors that determine if the commercialisation of fusion, i.e. getting hold of tapping into the energy stored in hydrogen nuclei, will remain solely peaceful:

> *"The atomic weight of hydrogen is not exactly 1, but by careful measurement is found to be 1.0077. Who could imagine that in this slight discrepancy — which indeed needs some explanation to make intelligible — an immense store of possible energy is indicated, which some day, when we have learned how, may become accessible for good or ill to the human race? [...] And if ever the human race get hold of a means of tapping even a small fraction of the energy contained in the atoms of their own planet, the consequences will be beneficent or destructive according to the state of civilization at that time attained."*[916]

916 *Oliver Lodge*, Putting the Atom to Work, Scientific American 130 (1924), 306, 358–359. The mass of atoms is measured in the unified atomic mass unit *u*, which is equal to about 1.66 x 10^{-27} kg. Following Einstein's mass-energy-equivalence $E=mc^2$, mass translates to energy. The deviation of the mass of hydrogen from exactly 1 u corresponds to an enormous amount of energy. In atoms with at least one proton and one neutron, the mass of an atom deviates from the mass of its constituents, as the binding energy between the particles corresponds to a mass which can be measured and – in the form of energy – can be set free.

Bibliography

1 Treaties

Charter of the United Nations (1945)

North Atlantic Treaty (1949), 34 United Nations Treaty Series 243

Treaty establishing the European Atomic Energy Community (EURATOM) (1957)

Statute of the International Atomic Energy Agency (1957), 276 United Nations Treaty Series 3

Treaty for the Prohibition of Nuclear Weapons in Latin America (1967), 634 United Nations Treaty Series 281

Treaty on the Non-Proliferation of Nuclear Weapons (1968), 729 United Nations Treaty Series 161

Vienna Convention on the Law of Treaties (1969), 1155 United Nations Treaty Series 331

Convention on the Prohibition of the Development, Production and Stockpiling of Bacteriological (Biological) and Toxin Weapons and on Their Destruction (1972), 2015 United Nations Treaty Series 163

South Pacific Nuclear Free Zone Treaty (1985), 1445 United Nations Treaty Series 177

United Nations Framework Convention on Climate Change (1992), 1771 United Nations Treaty Series 107

Convention on the Prohibition of the Development, Production, Stockpiling and Use of Chemical Weapons and on their Destruction (1997), 1975 United Nations Treaty Series 45

Treaty on the European Union (1993)

Treaty on the Southeast Asia Nuclear Weapon-Free Zone (1995), 1981 United Nations Treaty Series

African Nuclear-Weapon-Free Zone Treaty (1996)

Convention on the Prohibition of the Use, Stockpiling, Production and Transfer of Anti-Personnel Mines and on their Destruction (1997), 2056 United Nations Treaty Series 211

Treaty on a Nuclear-Weapon-Free Zone in Central Asia (2006), 2970 United Nations Treaty Series

Agreement on the Establishment of the ITER International Fusion Energy Organization for the Joint Implementation of the ITER Project (2007)

Convention on Cluster Munitions (2008), 2688 United Nations Treaty Series 39

Treaty Between the United States of America and the Russian Federation on Measures for the Further Reduction and Limitation of Strategic Offensive Arms (2011)

Paris Agreement (2015), 3156 United Nations Treaty Series 79

Treaty on the Prohibition of Nuclear Weapons (2017), 3370 United Nations Treaty Series

2 Cases

2.1 Permanent Court of International Justice

Permanent Court of International Justice, Lotus Case, PCJ (1927) Series A No. 10

2.2 International Court of Justice

International Court of Justice, North Sea Continental Shelf (Federal Republic of Germany v. The Netherlands), Judgment, ICJ Reports 1969, p. 3.

International Court of Justice, Legal Consequences for States of the Continued Presence of South Africa in Namibia (South West Africa) notwithstanding Security Council Resolution 276 (1970), Advisory Opinion, ICJ Reports 1971, p. 16

International Court of Justice, Aegan Sea Continental Shelf (Greece v. Turkey), Judgment, ICJ Reports 1978, p. 3

International Court of Justice, Case Concerning the Arbitral Award of 31 July 1989 (Guinea-Bissau v. Senegal), Judgment, ICJ Reports 1991, p. 53

International Court of Justice, Legality of the Threat or Use of Nuclear Weapons, Advisory Opinion, ICJ Reports 1996, p. 226.

International Court of Justice, Gabčikovo-Nagymaros Project (Hungary/Slovakia), Judgment, ICJ Reports 1997, p. 7

International Court of Justice, Dispute Regarding Navigational and Related Rights (Costa Rica v. Nicaragua), Judgement, ICJ Reports 2009, p. 213

International Court of Justice, Kosovo Unilateral Declaration of Independence, Advisory Opinion, ICJ Reports 2010, p. 403

International Court of Justice, Whaling in the Antarctiv (Australia v. Japan: New Zealand intervening), Judgment, ICJ Reports 2014, p. 226

International Court of Justice, Obligations concerning Negotiaions relating to Cessation of the Nuclear Arms Race and to Nuclear Disarmament (Marshall Islands v. United Kingdom; Marshall Islands v. India; Marshall Islands c. Pakistan), Judgments, ICJ Reports 2016, pp. 255, 552, 833

2.3 International Tribunal for the Law of the Sea

International Tribunal for the Law of the Sea, Advisory Opinion, Request for an Advisory Opinion Submitted by the Commission of Small Island States on Climate Change and International Law, 21 May 2024, Case No. 31

2.4 Arbitral Awards

Boundary Dispute Between Argentina and Chile Concerning the Frontier Line Between Boundary Post 62 and Mount Fitzroy (1994), XXII Reports of International Arbitral Awards 3

2.5 Court of Justice of the European Union

Judgement of 5 February 1963, *van Gend & Loos*, Case 26–62, ECLI:EU:C:1963:1

Judgment of 15 July 1964, *Costa v. ENEL*, Case 6–64, ECLI:EU:C:1964:66

Judgement of 3 September 2008, *Kadi*, ECLI:EU:C:2008:461, joined Cases C-402/05 P and C-415/05 P

3 Resolutions

United Nations General Assembly Resolution 1 (I)

United Nations General Assembly Resolution 41 (I)

United Nations General Assembly Resolution 1649 (XVI)

United Nations General Assembly Resolution 1722 (XVI)

United Nations General Assembly Resolution 2373 (XXII)

United Nations General Assembly Resolution A/RES/48/75

United Nations General Assembly Resolution A/RES/49/75 K

United Nations General Assembly Resolution A/RES/71/258

United Nations General Assembly Resolution A/RES/73/546

United Nations Security Council Resolution 687

United Nations Security Council Resolution 1373

United Nations Security Council Resolution 1540

United Nations Security Council Resolution 1887

United Nations Security Council Resolution 2310

4 International Documents

4.1 International Atomic Energy Agency

4.1.1 Information Circular

INFCIRC/26
INFCIRC/66
INFCIRC/153(Corrected)
INFCIRC/209
INFCIRC/254
INFCIRC/263
INFCIRC/263/Add.1
INFCIRC/288
INFCIRC/288/Add.1
INFCIRC/290
INFCIRC/290/Add.1
INFCIRC/327
INFCIRC/327/Add.1
INFCIRC/369
INFCIRC/369/Add.1
INFCIRC/539
INFCIRC/540(Corrected)
INFCIRC/951
INFCIRC/951/Add.1

4.1.2 Board of Governors

GOV/OR.776
GOV/OR.1131
GOV/2554/Att.2/Rev.2
GOV/2636
GOV/INF/2023/1
GOV/2025/38

4.1.3 General Conference

GC(V)/RES/92

GC(XIV)/RES/272
GC(XXVIII)/RES/422
GC(39)/17
GC(43)/RES/8
GC(43)/RES/19
GC(65)/2
C(67)/RES/9
GC(68)/OR.1
GC(68)/OR.2
GC(68)/OR.3
GC(68)/OR.11

4.2 United Nations

A/C.1/52/7
A/C.1/71/L.24
A/C.1/71/L.41

4.3 NPT

NPT/CONF.1995/32
NPT/CONF.2010/WP.1
NPT/CONF.2010/PC.I/WP.17
NPT/CONF.2010/PC.I/WP.46
NPT/CONF.2010/50
NPT/CONF.2020/PC.III/WP.6
NPT/CONF.2020/PC.III/WP.40

5 Figures

Figure 1: *Behnaz Nouhi/Nima Darabi/Pooya Sareh et al.*, The Fusion–Fission Optimization (FuFiO) Algorithm, Scientific Reports 12 (2022), 12396

Figure 2: Max-Planck-Institute for Plasma Physics, https://www.ipp.mpg.de/14869/tokamak, last accessed 17 July 2025

Figure 3: Max-Planck-Institute for Plasma Physics, https://www.ipp.mpg.de/4326243/original-1673955102.webp?t=eyJ3aWR0aCI6NjgyLCJmaWxlX2V4dGVuc2lvbiI6IndlYnAiLCJvYmpfaWQiOjQzMjYyNDN9--21888a527ee4a6596ff10bf4dad6b5c56b56dfc1, last accessed 17 July 2025

6 Literature

Itty Abraham, 'Who's next?' Nuclear Ambivalence and the Contradictions of Non-Proliferation Policy, Economic and Political Weekly 45 (2010), 48–56

Magnus Abraham-Dukuma, Sovereignty, Trade, and Legislation: The Evolution of Energy Law in a Changing Climate, Energy Research & Social Science 59 (2020), 101305

Cornelius Adebahr, Germany's Role in the Success and Failure of the Iran Nuclear Deal, in: Ulrich Kühn (ed.), Germany and Nuclear Weapons in the 21st Century, London: Routledge 2024, 281–301

Samina Ahmed, Pakistan's Nuclear Weapons Program: Turning Points and Nuclear Choices, International Security 23 (1999), 178–204

Max Aker/Konrad Altenmüller/Marius Arenz et al., First Operation of the KATRIN Experiment with Tritium, The European Physical Journal C 80 (2020), 264

William Alberque/Benjamin Schreer, What Kind of NATO Allies Will Finland and Sweden Be?, Survival 64 (2022), 123–136

David Albright/Frans Berkhout/William Walker, Plutonium and Highly Enriched Uranium 1996 – World Inventories, Capabilities and Policies, Stockholm: SIPRI 1997

David Albright/Kimberly Kramer, Neptunium 237 and Americium: World Inventories and Proliferation Concerns, Institute for Science and International Security 6060 (2005), 1–24

Stanimir A. Alexandrov, Accepting the Compulsory Jurisdiction of the International Court of Justice with Reservations: An Overview of Practice with a Focus on Recent Trends and Cases, Leiden Journal of International Law 14 (2001), 89–124

Elahe Alizadeh, Environmental and Safety Aspects of Using Tritium in Fusion, Journal of Fusion Energy 25 (2006), 47–55

Allied Market Research, Fusion Energy Market Size, Share, Competitive Landscape and Trend Analysis Report, by Technology, by Fuels: Global Opportunity Analysis and Industry Forecast, 2030–2040 (2023)

Yukiya Amano, A Japanese View on Nuclear Disarmament, The Nonproliferation Review 9 (2002), 132–145

Yukiya Amano, Atoms for Peace and Development: Working Towards the Sustainable Development Goals, IAEA Bulletin 59-1 (2018), 1–1

Ambassador Goldberg, Security Assurances and the Nonproliferation of Nuclear Weapons, May 15, 1968, Documents on Disarmament 1968, United States Arms Control And Disarmament Agency (1969), 336–345

Anguel Anastassov, The Sovereign Right to Peaceful Use of Nuclear Energy and International Environmental Law, in: Jonathan L. Black-Branch/Dieter Fleck (eds.), Nuclear Non-Proliferation in International Law – Volume I, The Hague: T.M.C. Asser Press 2014, 159–197

Daniel J. Arbess/Simeon A. Sahaydachny, Nuclear Deterrence and International Law: Some Steps toward Observance, Alternatives 12 (1987), 83–111

Anna Clara Arndt/Liviu Horovitz/Michal Onderco, Russia's Failed Nuclear Coercion Against Ukraine, The Washington Quarterly 46 (2023), 167–184

Shlomo Aronson, The Politics and Strategy of Nuclear Weapons in the Middle East – Opacity, Theory, and Reality, 1960–1991 – An Israeli Perspective, Seattle: SUNY Press 2012

Masahiko Asada, Arms Control Law in Crisis? A Study of the North Korean Nuclear Issue, Journal of Conflict and Security Law 9 (2004), 331–355

Masahiko Asada, International Law of Nuclear Non-Proliferation and Disarmament (Volume 424), The Hague: Brill | Nijhoff 2022

Ephraim Asculai, Verification Revisited: The Nuclear Case, Washington DC: Institute for Science and International Security Press 2002

Katja Astner/Moritz Kütt, The Treaty on the Prohibition of Nuclear Weapons – Changing Disarmament Discourses in Germany?, in: Ulrich Kühn (ed.), Germany and Nuclear Weapons in the 21st Century – Atomic Zeitenwende?, Oxford: Routledge 2024, 203–229

Anthony Aust/Oliver Dörr, Vienna Convention on the Law of Treaties (1969), in: Anne Peters/Rüdiger Wolfrum (eds.), Max Planck Encyclopedia of Public International Law, Heidelberg, Oxford: Oxford University Press 2023,

A. Axelsson/D. M. Fischer/M. V. Peńkin, Use of Data From Environmental Sampling for IAEA Safeguards. Case Study: Uranium With Near-Natural 235U Abundance, Journal of Radioanalytical and Nuclear Chemistry 282 (2009), 725–729

Mariano J. Aznar-Gomez, The 1996 Nuclear Weapons Advisory Opinion and Non Liquet in International Law, International and Comparative Law Quarterly 48 (1999), 3–19

Adam Baker, The Spherical Tokamak for Energy Production (STEP) in Context: UK Public Sector Approach to Fusion Energy, Philosophical Transactions of the Royal Society A: Mathematical, Physical and Engineering Sciences 382 (2024), 1–8

John L. Ball/Ethan E. Peterson/R. Scott Kemp et al., Assessing the risk of proliferation via fissile breeding in ARC-class fusion power plants, Nuclear Fusion 65 (2025), 036038

Michael Banks, China's Experimental Advanced Superconducting Tokamak Smashes Fusion Confinement Record in: Physics World, https://physicsworld.com/a/chinas-experimental-advanced-superconducting-tokamak-smashes-fusion-confinement-record/#:~:text=This%20week%2C%20scientists%20working%20on,device%20located%20in%20Hefei%2C%20China., last accessed 17 July 2025

Pietro Barabaschi/Arnaud Fossen/Alberto Loarte et al., ITER Progresses into New Baseline, Fusion Engineering and Design 215 (2025), 114990

Jonathon Baron/Rebecca Davis Gibbons/Stephen Herzog, Japanese Public Opinion, Political Persuasion, and the Treaty on the Prohibition of Nuclear Weapons, Journal for Peace and Nuclear Disarmament 3 (2020), 299–309

Rajesh Basrur, India and Nuclear Disarmament, Security Challenges 6 (2010), 69–81

Rajesh M. Basrur, Nuclear Weapons and India–Pakistan Relations, Strategic Analysis 33 (2009), 336–344

Sergey Batsanov/Vladislav Chernavskikh/Anton Khlopkov, 10th NPT Review Conference – The Nonproliferation and Peaceful Uses of Nuclear Energy Pillars, Arms Control Today 52 (2022), 13–19

Sibylle Bauer, Developments in the Nuclear Suppliers Group, in: Bates Gill/Ian Anthony/D.A. Cruickshank (eds.), SIPRI Yearbook 2011, Stockholm: SIPRI 2011, 376–386

Sabine Bauer/Cormac O'Reilly, The Comprehensive Nuclear-Test-Ban Treaty Organization (CTBTO): Current and Future Role in the Verification Regime of the Nuclear-Test-Ban Treaty, in: Jonathan L. Black-Branch/Dieter Fleck (eds.), Nuclear Non-Proliferation in International Law: Volume II – Verification and Compliance, The Hague: T.M.C. Asser Press 2016, 131–150

Claudia Baumgart/Harald Müller, A Nuclear Weapons-Free Zone in the Middle East: A Pie in the Sky?, The Washington Quarterly 28 (2004), 45–58

F. Baumgärtner/D. Ertel, The Modern Purex Process and its Analytical Requirements, Journal of Radioanalytical and Nuclear Chemistry 58 (1980), 11–28

Michael A. Bauser, United States Nuclear Export Policy: Developing the Peaceful Atom As a Commodity in International Trade Selected Developments in International Trade and Investment Controls, Harvard International Law Journal 18 (1977), 227–272

Louis René Beres, Where the Shadow Really Falls: Why Israel Must Have Nuclear Weapons, The Brown Journal of World Affairs 4 (1997), 127–138

Rudolf Bernhardt, Evolutive Treaty Interpretation, Especially of the European Convention on Human Rights Focus Section: The Law of International Treaties in the 21st Century, German Yearbook of International Law 42 (1999), 11–25

Hans Bethe, The Fusion Hybrid, Physics Today 32 (1979), 44–51

Richard K. Betts, Cruise Missiles: Technology, Strategy, Politics, The Washington Quarterly 4 (1981), 66–80

Richard K. Betts, Nuclear Peace and Conventional War, Journal of Strategic Studies 11 (1988), 79–95

John Beyer/Julian Cooper/Gerald Holden et al., The Soviet Union, in: Scilla McLean (ed.), How Nuclear Weapons Decisions are Made, London: Palgrave Macmillan UK 1986, 1–31

Sarah Bidgood, The Establishment of the London Club and Nuclear-Export Controls, Adelphi series 56 (2016), 135–162

Richard B. Bilder, A Legal Regime for the Mining of Helium-3 on the Moon: U.S. Policy Options, Fordham International Law Journal 33 (2009), 243–299

Eirik Bjorge, The Evolutionary Interpretation of Treaties, Oxford: Oxford University Press 2014

Eirik Bjorge, Evolutionary Interpretation: 'The Convention is a Living Instrument', in: Domestic Application of the ECHR: Courts as Faithful Trustees, Oxford: Oxford University Press 2015, 131–154

Jonathan L. Black-Branch, The Treaty on the Prohibition of Nuclear Weapons. Legal Challenges for Military Doctrines and Deterrence Policies, 2021 Jonathan L. Black-Branch/Dieter Fleck (eds.), Nuclear Non-Proliferation in International Law, vol V – Legal Challenges for Nuclear Security and Deterrence, Asser Press 2020

Peter Böhm, Ownership of Nuclear Materials in Euratom, The American Journal of Comparative Law 11 (1962), 167–183

Alexander K. Bollfrass, Are Nuclear Weapons an Option for Ukraine? (2025), IISS

Eric Bonds, Assessing the Oil Motive After the U.S. War in Iraq, Peace Review 25 (2013), 291–298

Julian Borger, Mohamed ElBaradei Warns of New Nuclear Age in: https://www.theguardian.com/world/2009/may/14/elbaradei-nuclear-weapons-states-un, last accessed 17 July 2025

Julian Borger, Poland Suggests Hosting US Nuclear Weapons Amid Growing Fears of Putin's Threats in: The Guardian, https://www.theguardian.com/world/2022/oct/05/poland-us-nuclear-wars-russia-putin-ukraine, last accessed 17 July 2025

Kenneth E. Boulding, The Social System and the Energy Crisis, Science 184 (1974), 255–257

Andre Bouquet, How Current Are Euratom Provisions on Nuclear Supply and Ownership in View of the European Union's Enlargement?, Nuclear Law Bulletin 68 (2001), 7–38

Dimitris Bourantonis, The Negotiation of the Non-Proliferation Treaty, 1965–1968: A Note, The International History Review 19 (1997), 347–357

Stephen Bouwhuis, The International Law Commission's Definition of International Organizations, International Organizations Law Review 9 (2012), 451–465

Pierre C. Boyer/Thomas Delemotte/Germain Gauthier et al., Les déterminants de la mobilisation des Gilets jaunes, Revue économique 71 (2020), 109–138

Alan Boyle, Soft Law in International Law-Making, in: Malcolm Evans (ed.), International Law, Oxford: Oxford University Press 2018, 118–136

Oli Brown/Robert McLeman, A Recurring Anarchy? The Emergence of Climate Change as a Threat to International Peace and Security, Conflict, Security & Development 9 (2009), 289–305

Mariana Budjeryn, The Power of the NPT: International Norms and Ukraine's Nuclear Disarmament, The Nonproliferation Review 22 (2015), 203–237

Tobias Bunde, Lessons (to be) learned? Germany's Zeitenwende and European Security After the Russian Invasion of Ukraine, Contemporary Security Policy 43 (2022), 516–530

George Bunn, Does the NPT Require its Non-Nuclear-Weapon Parties to Permit Inspections by the IAEA of Nuclear Activities that have not been Reported to the IAEA?, in: David Fischer/Ben Sanders/Lawrence Scheinman/George Bunn (eds.), A New Nuclear Triad: The Non-Proliferation of Nuclear Weapons, International Verification and the International Atomic Energy Agency, Southampton: Mountbatten Centre for International Studies, University of Southampton 1992, 44–58

George Bunn, Nuclear Safeguards – How Far Can Inspectors Go?, IAEA Bulletin 48-2 (2007), 49–55

George Bunn/John B. Rhinelander, Extending the NPT: What are the Options?, Arms Control Today 25 (1995), 8–10

Leszek Buszynski, Negotiating with North Korea – The Six Party Talks and the Nuclear Issue, London: Routledge 2013

Paula Cable-Dunlap/Lee Trowbridge/Debra Bostick et al., Comparison of Active and Passive Environmental Sampling for Safeguards Applications, Journal of Radioanalytical and Nuclear Chemistry 296 (2013), 943–949

E. M. Campbell/T. C. Sangster/V. N. Goncharov et al., Direct-Drive Laser Fusion: Status, Plans and Future, Philosophical Transactions of the Royal Society A: Mathematical, Physical and Engineering Sciences 379 (2021), 20200011

Julio C. Carasales, The Argentine-Brazilian Nuclear Rapprochement, The Nonproliferation Review 2 (1995), 39–48

Elias G. Carayannis/John Draper, The Growth of Intellectual Property Ownership in the Private-Sector Fusion Industry, Fusion Engineering and Design 173 (2021), 112815

E. G. Carayannis/J. Draper/I. A. Iftimie, Nuclear Fusion Diffusion: Theory, Policy, Practice, and Politics Perspectives, IEEE Transactions on Engineering Management 69 (2022), 1237–1251

John Carlson, SAGSI: Its Role and Contribution to Safeguards Development, Canberra: Australian Safeguards and Non-Proliferation Office 2007

John Carlson/Vladimir Kuchinov/Thomas Shea, The IAEA Safeguards System Prior to the NPT from 1959 to 1972 (The IAEA's Safeguards System as the Non-Proliferation Treaty's Verification Mechanism, 2020), Nuclear Threat Initiative

Mario E. Carranza, From Non-Proliferation to Post-Proliferation: Explaining the US–India Nuclear Deal, Contemporary Security Policy 28 (2007), 464–493

Stuart Casey-Maslen, The Treaty on the Prohibition of Nuclear Weapons: a Commentary, Oxford: Oxford University Press 2019

Stuart Casey-Maslen, The Status of Nuclear Deterrence Under International Law in Light of the Treaty on the Prohibition of Nuclear Weapons, in: Terry D. Gill/Robin Geiß/Heike Krieger/Christophe Paulussen (eds.), Yearbook of International Humanitarian Law, Volume 21 (2018), The Hague: T.M.C. Asser Press 2020, 23–57

Stuart Casey-Maslen, The Impact of the TPNW on the Nuclear Non-Proliferation Regime, in: Jonathan L. Black-Branch/Dieter Fleck (eds.), Nuclear Non-Proliferation in International Law – Volume VI: Nuclear Disarmament and Security at Risk – Legal Challenges in a Shifting Nuclear World, The Hague: T.M.C. Asser Press 2021, 385–409

CDU/CSU/SPD, Verantwortung für Deutschland – Koalitionsvertrag zwischen CDU, CSU und SPD, 21. Legislaturperiode, Berlin: 2025

Jonathan I. Charney, Compromissory Clauses and the Jurisdiction of the International Court of Justice, American Journal of International Law 81 (1987), 855–887

Renaud Chatelus, A Little Customs Glossary for IAEA Safeguards: Customs Procedures and Concepts that Matter for the Implementation of Modern Safeguards, Esarada Bulletin 47 (2012), 80–88

Abram Chayes/Antonia H. Chayes, Regime Architecture: Elements and Principles, in: Janne E. Nolan (ed.), Global Engagement: Cooperation and Security in the 21st Century, Washington DC: Brookings Institution 1994, 65–130

Mads Christensen, A Heating World Can't Afford a Cold War in: Greenpeace, https://www.greenpeace.org/international/story/60291/a-heating-world-cant-afford-a-cold-war/, last accessed 17 July 2025

Norman Cigar, Saudi Arabia and Nuclear Weapons – How Do Countries Think About The Bomb?, London: Routledge 2016

Michel Claessens, ITER: The Giant Fusion Reactor – Bringing a Sun to Earth, Cham: Springer 2020 *Marc Clemson*, Human Rights and the Environment: Access to Energy, New Zealand Journal of Environmental Law 16 (2012), 39–81

Daniel Clery, Out of Gas, Science 376 (2022), 1372–1376

Thomas B. Cochran/William M. Arkin/Robert S. Norris, U.S. Nuclear Weapons Production: An Overview, Bulletin of the Atomic Scientists 44 (1988), 12–16

M. Coleman/Y. Hörstensmeyer/F. Cismondi, DEMO Tritium Fuel Cycle: Performance, Parameter Explorations, and Design Space Constraints, Fusion Engineering and Design 141 (2019), 79–90

Lars C. Colschen, Die Internationalisierung der Tritiumkontrolle als Baustein des Nichtverbreitungsregimes für Kernwaffen: Bedingungen, Einflussfaktoren und Folgen, Aachen: Shaker Verlag 1998

Lars C. Colschen/Martin B. Kalinowski, Can International Safeguards Be Expanded to Cover Tritium?, International Atomic Energy Agency (IAEA): IAEA 1994

Congressional Budget Office, Approaches for Managing the Costs of U.S. Nuclear Forces, 2017 to 2046, 2017

Julian Cooper, How Much Does Russia Spend on Nuclear Weapons? in: SIPRI, https://www.sipri.org/commentary/topical-backgrounder/2018/how-much-does-russia-spend-nuclear-weapons, last accessed 17 July 2025

R. S. Craxton/K. S. Anderson/T. R. Boehly et al., Direct-Drive Inertial Confinement Fusion: A Review, Physics of Plasmas 22 (2015), 110501

Ion Cristescu/F. Priester/D. Rapisarda et al., Overview of the Tritium Technologies for the EU DEMO Breeding Blanket, Fusion Science and Technology 76 (2020), 446–457

I. R. Cristescu/I. Cristescu/L. Doerr et al., Tritium Inventories and Tritium Safety Design Principles for the Fuel Cycle of ITER, Nuclear Fusion 47 (2007), 458

Tarja Cronberg, For Survival, the NPT Has to Be Renegotiated in: European Leadership Network, https://www.europeanleadershipnetwork.org/commentary/for-survival-the-npt-has-to-be-renegotiated/, last accessed 17 July 2025

Derrin Culp, Part I: A Critical Examination of "The Myth of Nuclear Deterrence", The Nonproliferation Review 19 (2012), 51–68

Christophe Danielo, Quel avenir pour le Traité d'interdiction complète des essais nucléaires?, DSI (Défense et Sécurité Internationale) (2014), 52–55

Eric David, The Opinion of the International Court of Justice on the Legality of the Use of Nuclear Weapons, International Review of the Red Cross 316 (1997), 21–34

Zachary S. Davis, China's Nonproliferation and Export Control Policies: Boom or Bust for the NPT Regime?, Asian Survey 35 (1995), 587–603

Laurence Boisson de Chazournes/Philippe Sands (eds.), International Law, the International Court of Justice and Nuclear Weapons, Cambridge: Cambridge University Press 1999

Lars-Erik De Geer/Christopher M. Wright, The 22 September 1979 Vela Incident: Radionuclide and Hydroacoustic Evidence for a Nuclear Explosion, Science & Global Security 26 (2018), 20–54

Bruce Bueno de Mesquita/William H. Riker, An Assessment of the Merits of Selective Nuclear Proliferation, Journal of Conflict Resolution 26 (1982), 283–306

Erika de Wet, Governance through Promotion and Persuasion: The 1998 ILO Declaration on Fundamental Principles and Rights at Work, in: Armin von Bogdandy/Rüdiger Wolfrum/Jochen von Bernstorff/Philipp Dann/Matthias Goldmann (eds.), The Exercise of Public Authority by International Institutions, Berlin, Heidelberg: Springer 2010, 377–403

Kate Deere, The Obligations of Nuclear-Weapon States Not to Transfer Nuclear Weapons and Devices (Article I NPT), in: Jonathan L. Black-Branch/Dieter Fleck (eds.), Nuclear Non-Proliferation in International Law – Volume I, The Hague: T.M.C. Asser Press 2014, 23–45

D. Demange/R. Antunes/O. Borisevich et al., Tritium Extraction Technologies and DEMO Requirements, Fusion Engineering and Design 109–111 (2016), 912–916

Department for Energy Security & Net Zero, Towards Fusion Energy 2023 – The Next Stage of the UK's Fusion Energy Strategy, London: 2023

Sachin S. Desai/Michael Y. Hua/Amy C. Roma et al., Building a Path Toward Global Deployment of Fusion: Nonproliferation and Export Considerations (2025), Atlantic Council.

Christian Djeffal, Static and Evolutive Treaty Interpretation: A Functional Reconstruction, Cambridge: Cambridge University Press 2018

Thomas J. Dolan, Nuclear Fusion, in: Nicholas Tsoulfanidis (ed.), Nuclear Energy, New York, Heidelberg: Springer 2013, 305–342

David L. Donohue, Strengthening IAEA Safeguards Through Environmental Sampling and Analysis, Journal of Alloys and Compounds 271–273 (1998), 11–18

Oliver Dörr, Article 31, in: Oliver Dörr/Kirsten Schmalenbach (eds.), Vienna Convention on the Law of Treaties – A Commentary, Heidelberg: Springer 2018, 559–616

Assia Dosseva, North Korea and the Non-Proliferation Treaty Recent Developments, Yale Journal of International Law 31 (2006), 265–286

David Duarte/Pedro Moniz Lopes/Jorge Silva Sampio (eds.), Legal Interpretation and Scientific Knowledge, Heidelberg: Springer 2019

John. S. Duffield, Oil and the Decision to Invade Iraq, in: Jane Cramer/A. Trevor Thrall (eds.), Why Did the United States Invade Iraq?, London: Routledge 2011, 145–166

Gloria Duffy, Soviet Nuclear Export, International Security 3 (1978), 83–111

Kjølv Egeland, Spreading the Burden: How NATO Became a 'Nuclear' Alliance, Diplomacy & Statecraft 31 (2020), 143–167

Thomas Eich/Robert J. Goldston/Arne Kallenbach et al., Correlation of the Tokamak H-Mode Density Limit With Ballooning Stability at the Separatrix, Nuclear Fusion 58 (2018), 034001

Mohamed ElBaradei, Nuclear Power – an Evolving Scenario, IAEA Bulletin 46 (2004), 4–8

J. Elbez-Uzan/L. Williams/S. Forbes et al., Recommendations for the Future Regulation of Fusion Power Plants, Nuclear Fusion 54 (2024), 1–10

R. Eltayb Hassan Eltayb/I. Tsvetkov, Past, Current Status and the Future of Safeguards Implementation under INFCIRC/66/Rev.2 (2023), INMM Working Papers

Matthias Englert/Anne Harrington, Next Generation Nuclear Technologies: New Challenges to the Legal Framework of the IAEA from Intense Neutron Sources, in: Jonathan L. Black-Branch/Dieter Fleck (eds.), Nuclear Non-Proliferation in International Law: Volume II – Verification and Compliance, The Hague: T.M.C. Asser Press 2016, 187–212

Slavomir Entler/Jan Horacek/Tomas Dlouhy et al., Approximation of the Economy of Fusion Energy, Energy 152 (2018), 489–497

EUROfusion, European Research Roadmap to the Realisation of Fusion Energy (Long Version), 2018

Commission European/Directorate-General for Research and Innovation/L. Eriksson et al., Exploring Regulatory Options for Fusion Power Plants, Brussels: Publications Office of the European Union 2021

Christopher P. Evans, Questioning the Status of the Treaty on the Prohibition of Nuclear Weapons as a 'Humanitarian Disarmament' Agreement, Utrecht Journal of International and European Law (2021), 52–74

Marc Fabel/Matthias Flückinger/Markus Ludwig et al., The Power of Youth: Political Impacts of the "Fridays for Future" Movement, CESifo Working Paper 9742 (2022), 1–47

Daniel Faber, Trump's Election Victory, the Climate Crisis, and the Working Class: What Does this Mean for the Future?, Capitalism Nature Socialism 35 (2024), 1–18

F. Faghihi/H. Havasi/M. Amin-Mozafari, Plutonium-239 Production Rate Study Using a Typical Fusion Reactor, Annals of Nuclear Energy 35 (2008), 759–766

G. Federici/C. Bachmann/L. Barucca et al., Overview of the DEMO Staged Design Approach in Europe, Nuclear Fusion 59 (2019), 066013

G. Federici/W. Biel/M. R. Gilbert et al., European DEMO Design Strategy and Consequences for Materials, Nuclear Fusion 57 (2017), 092002

G. Federici/L. Boccaccini/F. Cismondi et al., An Overview of the EU Breeding Blanket Design Strategy as an Integral Part of the DEMO Design Effort, Fusion Engineering and Design 141 (2019), 30–42

Jonathan Federle/Cathrin Mohr/Moritz Schularick, Inflation Surprises and Election Outcomes, Kiel Working Paper 2278 (2024), 1–31

Clemens A. Feinäugle, The UN Security Council Al-Qaida and Taliban Sanctions Committee: Emerging Principles of International Institutional Law for the Protection of Individuals?, in: Armin von Bogdandy/Rüdiger Wolfrum/Jochen von Bernstorff/Philipp Dann/Matthias Goldmann (eds.), The Exercise of Public Authority by International Institutions, Berlin, Heidelberg: Springer 2010, 101–131

Matt FIeld, A Simple TImeline of Iran's Nuclear Program in: Bulletin of the Atomic Scientists, https://thebulletin.org/2025/06/a-simple-timeline-of-irans-nuclear-program/, last accessed 17 July 2025

Trevor Findlay, The Lessons of UNSCOM and UNMOVIC, in: VERTIC (ed.), Verification Yearbook 2004, London: VERTIC 2004, 65–86

Trevor Findlay, Unleashing the Nuclear Watchdog – Strengthening and Reform of the IAEA (2012), Centre for International Governance Innovation

Thomas Fingar, The Role of Intelligence in Countering Illicit Nuclear-Related Procurement, in: Matthew Bunn/Martin B. Malin/William C. Potter/Leonard S. Spector (eds.), Preventing Black Market Trade in Nuclear Technology, Cambridge: Cambridge University Press 2018, 48–78

Mary Finley-Brook/Curtis Thomas, Renewable Energy and Human Rights Violations: Illustrative Cases from Indigenous Territories in Panama, Annals of the Association of American Geographers 101 (2011), 863–872

David Fischer, IAEA/Euratom Agreement – An Explanation, IAEA Bulletin 15 (1973), 11–16

David Fischer, Innovations in IAEA Safeguards ot Meet the Challenges of the 1990s, in: David Fischer/Ben Sanders/Lawrence Scheinman/George Bunn (eds.), A New Nuclear Triade: The Non-Proliferation of Nuclear Weapons, International Verification and the International Atomic Energy Agency, Southampton: The Mountbatten Centre for International Studies, University of Southampton 1992, 27–43

Gerald Fitzmaurice, The Foundations of the Authority of International Law and the Problem of Enforcement, The Modern Law Review 19 (1956), 1–13

Malgosia Fitzmaurice, Treaties, in: Anne Peters/Rüdiger Wolfrum (eds.), Max Planck Encyclopedia of Public International Law, Heidelberg, Oxford: Oxford University Press 2021

Mark Fitzpatrick, Assessing the JCPOA, Adelphi series 57 (2017), 19–60

Rosemary J. Foot, Nuclear Coercion and the Ending of the Korean Conflict, International Security 13 (1988), 92–112

William E. Fork/Charles H. Peterson, Fusion Energy and Nuclear Liability Considerations, Nuclear Law Bulletin 93 (2014), 43–62

Giorgio Franceschini/Matthias Englert/Wolfgang Liebert, Nuclear Fusion Power for Weapons Purposes, The Nonproliferation Review 20 (2013), 525–544

Edward Friedman, Nuclear Blackmail and the End of the Korean War, Modern China 1 (1975), 75–91

Matthew Fuhrmann/Benjamin Tkach, Almost Nuclear: Introducing the Nuclear Latency Dataset, Conflict Management and Peace Science 32 (2015), 443–461

Fusion Industry Association, The Global Fusion Industry in 2024, Washington DC: FIA 2024

Kim Fyhr, Steering the Atoms for Peace and Development: Legal Aspects of the Board of Governors of the International Atomic Energy Agency, AUC IURIDICA 70 (2024), 31–46

Richard K. Gardiner, Treaty Interpretation, Oxford: Oxford University Press 2015

Rebecca Gibbons/Todd Robinson, Twenty-Five Years Safer? Assessing the IAEA's Model Additional Protocol and its Role in International Politics, The Nonproliferation Review 29 (2022), 1–22

Rebecca Davis Gibbons, American Hegemony and the Politics of the Nuclear Nonproliferation Regime, Washington DC: Georgetown University 2016

Rebecca Davis Gibbons/Stephen Herzog, The First TPNW Meeting and the Future of the Nuclear Ban Treaty, Arms Control Today 52 (2022), 12–17

Laura Gil, Is Africa Ready for Nuclear Energy? (2018), International Atomic Energy Agency

Andrea Gioia, Nuclear Accidents and International Law, in: Andrea de Guttry/Marco Gestri/Gabriella Venturini (eds.), International Disaster Response Law, The Hague, The Netherlands: T.M.C. Asser Press 2012, 85–102

Alexander Glaser, On the Proliferation Potential of Uranium Fuel for Research Reactors at Various Enrichment Levels, Science & Global Security 14 (2006), 1–24

Alexander Glaser, Characteristics of the Gas Centrifuge for Uranium Enrichment and Their Relevance for Nuclear Weapon Proliferation, Science & Global Security 16 (2008), 1–25

Alexander Glaser/Robert J. Goldston, Proliferation Risks of Magnetic Fusion Energy: Clandestine Production, Covert Production and Breakout, Nuclear Fusion 52 (2012), 043004

M. Glugla/A. Antipenkov/S. Beloglazov et al., The ITER Tritium Systems, Fusion Engineering and Design 82 (2007), 472–487

Braden Goddard/Alexander Solodov/Vitaly Fedchenko, IAEA "Significant Quantity" Values: Time for a Closer Look?, The Nonproliferation Review 23 (2016), 677–689

Vitaly Goldansky, Connection between Horizontal and Vertical Proliferation of Nuclear Weapons, in: Joseph Rotblat/Laszlo Valki (eds.), Coexistence, Cooperation and Common Security: Annals of Pugwash 1986, London: Palgrave Macmillan UK 1988, 21–36

José Goldemberg/Carlos Feu Alvim/Olga Y. Mafra, The Denuclearization of Brazil and Argentina, Journal for Peace and Nuclear Disarmament 1 (2018), 383–403

Bertrand Goldschmidt, La France et la non-prolifération, Relations internationales (1992), 41–50

Pierre Goldschmidt, The IAEA Safeguards System Moves into the 21st Century, IAEA Bulletin 41 (1999), 1–19

Robert J. Goldston, Climate Change, Nuclear Power, and Nuclear Proliferation: Magnitude Matters, Science & Global Security 19 (2011), 130-165

Robert J. Goldston/Alexander Glaser, Inertial Confinement Fusion Energy R&D and Nuclear Proliferation: The Need for Direct and Transparent Review, Bulletin of the Atomic Scientists 67 (2011), 59–66

Sehila M. Gonzalez de Vicente/Nicholas A. Smith/Laila El-Guebaly et al., Overview on the Management of Radioactive Waste From Fusion Facilities: ITER, Demonstration Machines and Power Plants, Nuclear Fusion 62 (2022), 085001

Thomas Graham Jr./Damien J. LaVera, Cornerstone of Security – Arms Control Treaties in the Nuclear Era, Seatlle, London: Univeristy of Washington Press 2002

Sophie Grape/Erik Branger/Vitaly Fedchenko et al., Development of Uranium and Plutonium Based Nuclear Weapons – What Impacts the Choice of Fissile Material Route?, Journal of Strategic Trade Control 3 (2025), 1–27

Michael Greenwood, Jus ad bellum and jus in bello in the Nuclear Weapons Advisory Opinion, in: Laurence Boisson de Chazournes/Philippe Sands (eds.), International Law, the International Court of Justice and Nuclear Weapons, Cambridge: Cambridge University Press 1999, 247–265

Rafael Mariano Grossi, IAEA Safeguards for International Peace and Security, IAEA Bulletin 63-3 (2022), 1-1

Rafael Mariano Grossi, Nuclear Law: The Global Debate, in: Nuclear Law: The Global Debate, The Hague: T.M.C. Asser Press 2022, 1–27

Justin S. Gruenberg, An Analysis of United Nations Security Council Resolutions: Are All Countries Treated Equally?, Case Western Reserve Journal of International Law 41 (2009), 469–511

Jürgen Grunwald, Peaceful Uses of Nuclear Energy Under EURATOM Law, in: Jonathan L. Black-Branch/Dieter Fleck (eds.), Nuclear Non-Proliferation in International Law – Volume III: Legal Aspects of the Use of Nuclear Energy for Peaceful Purposes, The Hague: T.M.C. Asser Press 2016, 171–213

Andre Gsponer/Jean-Pierre Hurni, The Physics of Thermonuclear Explosives, Inertial Confinement Fusion, and the Quest for Fourth Generation Nuclear Weapons, INESAP Tech. Rep. No. 1 1997

Andre Gsponer/Jean-Pierre Hurni, ITER: The International Thermonuclear Experimental Reactor and the Nuclear Weapons Proliferation Implications of Thermonuclear-Fusion Energy Systems, 2004

Benjamin Habib, North Korea's Nuclear Weapons Programme and the Maintenance of the Songun System, The Pacific Review 24 (2011), 43–64

David Hafemeister, Physics of Societal Issues: Calculations on National Security, Environment, and Energy, Springer 2016

Otto Hahn/Fritz Strassmann, Über den Nachweis und das Verhalten der bei der Bestrahlung des Urans mittels Neutronen entstehenden Erdalkalimetalle, Naturwissenschaften 27 (1939), 11–15

Bernd Hahnfeld, Nukleare Teilhabe ist völkerrechtswidrig – Ein Widerspruch zur anderslautenden Behauptung der Bundesregierung, Wissenschaft und Frieden (W+F) 46 (2020), 46–48

Keith Hansen, CTBT: Forecasting the Future, Bulletin of the Atomic Scientists 61 (2005), 50–57

Keith Hansen, Intelligence and Nuclear Proliferation: Lessons Learned, Paris: Ifri 2011

Jennifer Hansler/Kylie Atwood, Blinken Says Iran's Nuclear Weapon Breakout Time is Probably Down to 1–2 Weeks (*CNN*, 2024), https://www.cnn.com/2024/07/19/politics/blinken-nuclear-weapon-breakout-time/index.html, last accessed 17 July 2025

Shuichi Hasegawa, Isotope Separation Methods for Nuclear Fuel, in: Nicholas Tsoulfanidis (ed.), Nuclear Energy: Selected Entries from the Encyclopedia of Sustainability Science and Technology, New York: Springer 2013, 59–76

Mika Hayashi, NATO's Nuclear Sharing Arrangements Revisited in Light of the NPT and the TPNW, Journal of Conflict and Security Law 26 (2021), 471–491

Olli Heinonen, The Case for an Immediate IAEA Special Inspection in Syria, Washington Institute PolicyWatch 1715 (2010), 1–2

Per Helander/Craig D. Beidler/T. M. Bird et al., Stellarator and Tokamak Plasmas: A Comparison, Plasma Physics and Controlled Fusion 54 (2012), 124009 *Sondre Torp Helmersen*, Evolutive Treaty Interpretation: Legality, Semantics and Distinctions, European Journal of Legal Studies 6 (2013), 127–148

Christian Henderson, The Bush Doctrine: From Theory to Practice, Journal of Conflict & Security Law 9 (2004), 3–24

Matthias Herdegen, Interpretation in International Law, in: Anne Peters/Rüdiger Wolfrum (eds.), Max Planck Encyclopedia of Public International Law, Heidelberg, Oxford: Oxford University Press 2020

Mark Hibbs, Iran and the Evolution of Safeguards, in: VERTIC (ed.), Verification & Implementation – A Biennial Collection of Analysis on International Agreements for Security and Development, London: VERTIC 2015, 1–26

Mark Hibbs, The Nuclear Suppliers Group and Geostrategic Politics, Strategic Trade Review 3 (2017), 5–24

Newell Highsmith/Mallory Stewart, The Nuclear Ban Treaty: A Legal Analysis, Survival 60 (2018), 129–152

Mark P. Hilborne, The Non-Proliferation Treaty. Foundation of Disarmament Policy, in: Harsh V. Pant (ed.), Handbook of Nuclear Proliferation, London, New York: Routledge 2012, 251–260

Peter Hilpold, Challenging Strasbourg – The May 2025 Letter and the Pushback Against the European Court of Human Rights (2025), in: Verfassungsblog, https://verfassungsblog.de/may-2025-letter-and-the-pushback-against-the-european-court-of-human-rights/

Theodore Hirsch, The IAEA Additional Protocol: What It Is and Why It Matters, The Nonproliferation Review 11 (2004), 140–166

Mark Ho/Edward Obbard/Patrick A. Burr et al., A Review on the Development of Nuclear Power Reactors, Energy Procedia 160 (2019), 459–466

Richard Hooper, The System of Strengthened Safeguards, IAEA Bulletin 39/4 (1997), 26–30

Frank S. Houck, The Voluntary Safeguards Offer of the United States – A Review of its History and Implementation, IAEA Bulletin 27 (1985), 13–18

Scott C. Hsu, U.S. Fusion Energy Development via Public-Private Partnerships, Journal of Fusion Energy 42 (2023), 12

Michael Y. Hua/Sachin S. Desai/Amy C. Roma et al., Nonproliferation and Fusion Power Plants, arXiv:2207 14348 (2022), 1–26

Jacques E. C. Hymans, The Psychology of Nuclear Proliferation: Identity, Emotions and Foreign Policy, Cambridge: Cambridge University Press 2006

ICAN, Surge 2023: Global Nuclear Weapons Spending, Geneva: ICAN 2024

Institut de droit interational, Annuaires – Tome 44 (I) 1952 Travaux Préparatoires, Basel: Verlag für Recht und Gesellschaft 1952

International Atomic Energy Agency, Safeguards for Reprocessing and Enrichment Plants, IAEA Bulletin 19 (1977), 30–33

International Atomic Energy Agency, IAEA (ed.), The Evolution of IAEA Safeguards, Vienna: IAEA 1998

International Atomic Energy Agency, The Annual Report for 1999, GC(44)/4, Vienna: IAEA 2000

International Atomic Energy Agency, Report of the Consultancy Meeting on "Non-Proliferation Challenges in Connection with Magnetic Fusion Power Plants" (2013)

International Atomic Energy Agency, Report of the Consultancy Meeting on "Non-Proliferation Challenges in Connection with Magnetic Fusion Power Plants", Vienna: IAEA 2013

International Atomic Energy Agency, Safeguards Implementation Guide for States with Small Quantities Protocols, Vienna: IAEA 2013

International Atomic Energy Agency, Nuclear Power Reactors in the World, Vienna: IAEA 2021

International Atomic Energy Agency, IAEA Safeguards Glossary, Vienna: IAEA 2022

International Atomic Energy Agency, IAEA Nuclear Safety and Security Glossary, Vienna: IAEA 2022

International Atomic Energy Agency, IAEA World Fusion Outlook 2023 – Fusion Energy: Present and Future, Vienna: IAEA 2023

International Atomic Energy Agency, Technical Cooperation Report for 2022, GC(67)/INF/5, Vienna: IAEA 2023

International Atomic Energy Agency, Nuclear Power Reactors in the World, Vienna: IAEA 2024

International Atomic Energy Agency, Technical Cooperation Report for 2023, GC(67)/RES/9, Vienna: IAEA 2024

International Atomic Energy Agency, IAEA World Fusion Outlook 2024, Vienna: IAEA 2024

International Energy Agency, CO2 Emissions in 2022, Paris: IEA 2023

International Law Commission, Draft Articles on the Law of Treaties With Commentaries, New York: United Nations 1966

International Law Commission, Draft Conclusion on Subsequent Agreements and Subsequent Practice in Relation to the Interpretation of Treaties, in: United Nations (ed.), Yearbook of the International Law Commission, Volume II, Part Two, New York: United Nations 2018, 23–88

International Law Commission, Draft Conclusions on Identification of Customary International Law, New York: United Nations 2018

International Panel on Climate Change, Climate Change 2021: The Physical Science Basis, in: Sixth Assessment Report, Geneva: IPCC 2021

International Panel on Climate Change, Sixth Assessment Report – Synthesis Report, 2022

James Martin Center for Nonproliferation Studies, Additional Protocol (Inventory of International Nonproliferation Organizations and Regimes, 2015)

Robert Jervis, The Political Effects of Nuclear Weapons: A Comment, International Security 13 (1988), 80–90

Thomas B. Johansson, Sweden's Abortive Nuclear Weapons Project, Bulletin of the Atomic Scientists 42 (1986), 31–34

Rebecca Johnson, Little Orphan Fissban, Bulletin of the Atomic Scientists 53 (1997), 4–4

Rebecca Johnson, Unfinished Business – The Negotiation of the CTBT and the End of Nuclear Testing, Geneva: United Nations Institute for Disarmament Research 2009

Thomas Jonter/Emma Rosengren, From Nuclear Weapons Acquisition to Nuclear Disarmament – The Swedish Case, in: Ilkka Taipale (ed.), Nuclear Exits – Countries Foregoing the Nuclear Option, London: Routledge 2016, 46–63

Daniel H. Joyner, Non-proliferation Law and the United Nations System: Resolution 1540 and the Limits of the Power of the Security Council, Leiden Journal of International Law 20 (2007), 489–518

Daniel H. Joyner, Interpreting the Nuclear Non-Proliferation Treaty, Oxford: Oxford University Press 2011

Stefan Kadelbach, Nuclear Weapons and Warfare, in: Anne Peters/Rüdiger Wolfrum (eds.), Max Planck Encyclopedia of Public International Law, Heidelberg, Oxford: Oxford University Press 2019

Stefan Kadelbach, Possible Means to Overcome Tendencies of the Nuclear Weapons Ban Treaty to Erode the NPT, in: Jonathan L. Black-Branch/Dieter Fleck (eds.), Nuclear Non-Proliferation in International Law – Volume V: Legal Challenges for Nuclear Security and Deterrence, The Hague: T.M.C. Asser Press 2020, 305–322

Martin Kalinowski, International Control of Tritium for Nuclear Nonproliferation and Disarmament, Boca Raton: CRC Press 2004

Martin B. Kalinowski/Lars C. Colschen, International Control of Tritium to Prevent Horizontal Proliferation and to Foster Nuclear Disarmament, Science & Global Security 5 (1995), 131–203

Martin B. Kalinowski/Johann Feichter/Mika Nikkinen et al., Environmental Sample Analysis, in: Rudolf Avenhaus/Nicholas Kyriakopoulos/Michel Richard/Gotthard Stein (eds.), Berlin, Heidelberg: Springer 2006, 367–387

Togzhan Kassenova, Nuclear Safeguards in Brazil and Argentina: 25 Years of ABACC, AIP Conference Proceedings 1898 (2017), 1–6

Spurgeon M. Keeny Jr., The NPT: A Global Success Story, Arms Control Today 25 (1995), 3–7

Jakob Kellenberger, Bringing the Era of Nuclear Weapons to an End – Statement by Jakob Kellenberger, President of the ICRC, to the Geneva Diplomatic Corps, Geneva, 20 April 2010 (2010), International Committee of the Red Cross

Robert E. Kelley, Starve Nuclear Weapons to Death with a Tritium Freeze (*Stockholm International Peace Research Institute*, 2020), https://www.sipri.org/commentary/topical-backgrounder/2020/starve-nuclear-weapons-death-tritium-freeze, last accessed 17 July 2025

Robert E. Kelly, Liberal Norms or Coercive Counterproliferation: The American Response to Potential South Korean Nuclearization, Pacific Focus 40 (2025), 69–99

Paul K. Kerr, Iran and Nuclear Weapons Production, Washington DC: Congressional Research Service 2024

F. A. Khan, On Tsar Bomba – The Most Powerful Nuclear Weapon Ever Tested, Physics Education 56 (2021), 013002

Paul M. Kiernan, Disarmament under the NPT: Article VI in the 21st Century, Michigan State University College of Law International Law Review 20 (2011), 381–400

Wolfgang Kilb, The Nuclear Safeguards Regime of EURATOM: A Regional Cornerstone of the Verification of Non-Proliferation Obligations in the European Union, in: Jonathan L. Black-Branch/Dieter Fleck (eds.), Nuclear Non-Proliferation in International Law: Volume II – Verification and Compliance, The Hague: T.M.C. Asser Press 2016, 151–165

Shannon N. Kile/Robert E. Kelley, Verifying a Fissile Material Cut-Off Treaty – Technical and Organizational Considerations, SIPRI Policy Paper 33 (2012), 1–42

Beom Seok Kim/Suk-Ho Hong/Keeman Kim, Preliminary assessment of the safety factors in K-DEMO for fusion compatible regulatory framework, Scientific Reports 12 (2022), 8276

Daryl Kimball, What Went Wrong: Repairing the Damage to the CTBT, Arms Control Today 29 (1999), 3–9

Daryl Kimball, The Nuclear Testing Tally (2022), Arms Control Association.

David Kingham/Mikhail Gryaznevich, The Spherical Tokamak Path to Fusion Power: Opportunities and Challenges for Development via Public–Private Partnerships, Physics of Plasmas 31 (2024), 1–7

Gerald Kirchner/Stefan Oeter, Technical Limits of Verification and Their Implications for Treaty Design, in: Jonathan L. Black-Branch/Dieter Fleck (eds.), Nuclear Non-Proliferation in International Law: Volume II – Verification and Compliance, The Hague: T.M.C. Asser Press 2016, 167–186

Ingrid Kirsten/Mara Zarka, Balancing the Three Pillars of the NPT: How Can Promoting Peaceful Uses Help?, Non-Proliferation and Disarmament Papers 79 (2022), 1–18

Jan Klabbers, The Redundancy of Soft Law, Nordic Journal of International Law 65 (1996), 167–182

Jan Klabbers, Treaties, Amendment and Revision, in: Anne Peters/Rüdiger Wolfrum (eds.), Max Planck Encyclopedia of Public International Law, Heidelberg, Oxford: Oxford University Press 2006

Mackenzie Knight, TPNW2MSP: Overview And Key Takeaways (*Federation of American Scientists*, 2023), https://fas.org/publication/tpnw2msp-overview-and-key-takeaways/, last accessed 17 July 2025 *B. N.*

Kolbasov/V. I. Khripunov/A. Yu Biryukov, On Use of Beryllium in Fusion Reactors: Resources, Impurities and Necessity of Detritiation After Irradiation, Fusion Engineering and Design 109–111 (2016), 480–484

Arjan Koning/Ian Swainson/Kalliopi Kanaki et al., Physics and IAEA: Atoms for Peace and Development, Nuclear Physics News 33 (2023), 10–14

David A. Koplow, Russia, the CTBT, and International Law, Arms Control Today 53 (2023), 17–17

Vally Koubi, Climate Change and Conflict, Annual Review of Political Science 22 (2019), 343–360

M. Kovari/M. Coleman/I. Cristescu et al., Tritium Resources Available for Fusion Reactors, Nuclear Fusion 58 (2018), 026010

David Kramer, Livermore Ends LIFE, Physics Today 67 (2014), 26–27

David Kramer, DOE Prepares Major Upgrade of its Lithium-6 Operations, Physics Today 71 (2018), 29–31

Kevin J. Kramer/Massimiliano Fratoni/Jeffery F. Latkowski et al., Fusion-Fission Blanket Options for the LIFE Engine, Fusion Science and Technology 60 (2011), 72–77

Hans M. Kristensen/Matt Korda, North Korean Nuclear Weapons, 2021, Bulletin of the Atomic Scientists 77 (2021), 222–236

Hans M. Kristensen/Matt Korda, United Kingdom Nuclear Weapons, 2021, Bulletin of the Atomic Scientists 77 (2021), 153–158

Hans M. Kristensen/Matt Korda, World Nuclear Forces, in: Stockholm International Peace Research Institute (ed.), SIPRI Yearbook 2022, Stockholm, Oxford: Oxford University Press 2022, 341–432

Hans M. Kristensen/Matt Korda, World Nuclear Forces, in: Stockholm International Peace Research Institute (ed.), SIPRI Yearbook 2023: Armaments, Disarmament and International Security, Stockholm: Stockholm International Peace Research Institute 2023, 247–336

Hans M. Kristensen/Matt Korda, World Nuclear Forces, in: Stockholm International Peace Research Institute (ed.), SIPRI Yearbook 2024: Armaments, Disarmament and International Security, Stockholm: Stockholm International Peace Research Institute 2024, 271–376

Hans M. Kristensen/Matt Korda/Eliana Johns et al., Nuclear Weapons Sharing, 2023, Bulletin of the Atomic Scientists 79 (2023), 393–406

Hans M. Kristensen/Matt Korda/Eliana Johns et al., Indian Nuclear Weapons, 2024, Bulletin of the Atomic Scientists 80 (2024), 326–342

Hans M. Kristensen/Matt Korda/Eliana Johns et al., Chinese Nuclear Weapons, 2025, Bulletin of the Atomic Scientists 81 (2025), 135–160

Hans M. Kristensen/Robert S. Norris, A History of US Nuclear Weapons in South Korea, Bulletin of the Atomic Scientists 73 (2017), 349–357

Katarzyna Kubiak, Vertical Proliferation in Light of the Disarmament Commitment, in: Tom Sauer/Jorg Kustermans/Barbara Segaert (eds.), Non-Nuclear Peace: Beyond the Nuclear Ban Treaty, Cham: Springer International Publishing 2020, 59–84

Vijai Kumar, Problems of Succession to the Soviet Nuclear Arsenal and International Law, International Studies 31 (1994), 305–320

B. V. Kuteev/P. R. Goncharov, Fusion–Fission Hybrid Systems: Yesterday, Today, and Tomorrow, Fusion Science and Technology 76 (2020), 836–847

Sabine L. Perch-Nielsen/Michèle B. Bättig/Dieter Imboden, Exploring the Link Between Climate Change and Migration, Climatic Change 91 (2008), 375–393

L.B. Lanham/T.C. Runion, PUREX Process for Plutonium and Uranium Recovery (1949), Oak Ridge National Laboratory

Ralph E. Lapp, Nuclear Weapons: Past and Present, Bulletin of the Atomic Scientists 26 (1970), 103–106

Konstantin Larinov, Expanding the UN General Assembly's Role in Managing Disarmament and Non-Proliferation Challenges (*European Leadership Network*, 2023), https://europeanleadershipnetwork.org/commentary/expanding-the-un-general-assemblys-role-in-managing-disarmament-and-non-proliferation-challenges/, last accessed 17 July 2025

R. Lässer/D. K. Murdoch/M. Glugla, Tritium Accountancy Issues of the ITER Fuel Cycle, Fusion Science and Technology 48 (2005), 337–342

Rachel Lawless/Barry Butler/Anthony Hollingsworth et al., Tritium Plant Technology Development for a DEMO Power Plant, Fusion Science and Technology 71 (2017), 679–686

J. D. Lawson, Some Criteria for a Power Producing Thermonuclear Reactor, Proceedings of the Physical Society – Section B 70 (1957), 6

Richard Leaver, The Failing NPT: The Case for Institutional Reform, Australian Journal of International Affairs 59 (2005), 417–424

B. R. Leonard Jr, A Review of Fusion-Fission (Hybrid) Concepts, Nuclear Technology 20 (1973), 161–178

Trevor M. Letcher (ed.), Storing Energy, Amsterdam: Elsevier 2022

Maosheng Li/Rong Liu/Xueming Shi et al., The Project of Fusion-Fission Hybrid Energy Reactor in China, Fusion Science and Technology 61 (2012), 195–199

Wolfgang Liebert/Rainer Rilling/Jürgen Scheffran, Die Janusköpfigkeit von Forschung und Technik. Zum Problem der zivil-militärischen Ambivalenz, Marburg: BdWi-Verlag 1994

John Lindl, Development of the Indirect-Drive Approach to Inertial Confinement Fusion and the Target Physics Basis for Ignition and Gain, Physics of Plasmas 2 (1995), 3933–4024

J. Lion/J. C. Anglès/L. Bonauer et al., Stellaris: A High-Field Quasi-Isodynamic Stellarator for a Prototypical Fusion Power Plant, Fusion Engineering and Design 214 (2025), 114868

Zhu Liu/Zhu Deng/Steve Davis et al., Monitoring Global Carbon Emissions in 2022, Nature Reviews Earth & Environment 4 (2023), 205–206

Oliver Lodge, Putting the Atom to Work, Scientific American 130 (1924), 306, 358–359

B. G. Logan, Use of the National Ignition Facility for Defense, Energy, and Basic Research Science (1994), Lawrence Livermore National Laboratory

David C. Logan, The Nuclear Balance Is What States Make of It, International Security 46 (2022), 172–215

Adina Carla Loghin, Which International Authority Should Be Designated for Verifying the Irreversible Elimination of Nuclear Weapons under Article 4 of Nuclear Ban Treaty (TPNW) Scientific, Amsterdam Law Forum 11 (2019), 73–96

Taylor Loy, Speculating on Tritium Futures – Why Defense Material Should Fuel Fusion Innovation (2023), https://www.newamerica.org/political-reform/briefs/tritium-fuel-futures/, last accessed 17 July 2025

Matthew Lukacs/Laurence G. Williams, Nuclear Safety Issues for Fusion Power Plants, Fusion Engineering and Design 150 (2020), 111377

Katharine J. Mach/Caroline M. Kraan/W. Neil Adger et al., Climate as a Risk Factor for Armed Conflict, Nature 571 (2019), 193–197

Jenifer Mackby, The NPT-CTBT Connection, in: Jonathan L. Black-Branch/Dieter Fleck (eds.), Nuclear Non-Proliferation in International Law – Volume V: Legal Challenges for Nuclear Security and Deterrence, The Hague: T.M.C. Asser Press 2020, 31–52

Jean Mackenzie/Barbara Plett Usher, US and South Korea Agree Key Nuclear Weapons Deal in: BBC News, (25 February 2025) https://www.bbc.com/news/world-us-canada-65404805, last accessed 17 July 2025

Ute Mager, The UNESCO Regime for the Protection of World Heritage, in: Armin von Bogdandy/Rüdiger Wolfrum/Jochen von Bernstorff/Philipp Dann/Matthias Goldmann (eds.), The Exercise of Public Authority by International Institutions, Berlin, Heidelberg: Springer 2010, 337–339

Konstantinos D. Magliveras, The Conference on the Establishment of a Middle East Zone Free of Nuclear Weapons and Other Weapons of Mass Destruction: Too Little, Too Late?, in: Jonathan L. Black-Branch/Dieter Fleck (eds.), Nuclear Non-Proliferation in International Law – Volume VI: Nuclear Disarmament and Security at Risk – Legal Challenges in a Shifting Nuclear World, The Hague: T.M.C. Asser Press 2021, 113–133

Joseph Maina, Africa Explores Nuclear Energy as Climate-Friendly Way to Ease Power Shortfalls (2022)

Grégoire Mallard, Fallout: Nuclear Diplomacy in an Age of Global Fracture, Chicago: The University of Chicago Press 2014

J. Carson Mark/Frank von Hippel/Edward Lyman, Explosive Properties of Reactor-Grade Plutonium, Science & Global Security 17 (2009), 170–185

Pierre Mathijsen, Some Legal Aspects of Euratom, Common Market Law Review 3 (1966), 326–343

Alexander Mattelaer, Nuclear Sharing and NATO as a Nuclear Alliance, in: Stephan Frühling/Andrew O'Neil (eds.), Alliances, Nuclear Weapons and Escalation, Canberra: ANU Press 2021, 123–131

Office of the Deputy Assistant Secretary of Defense for Nuclear Matters, Nuclear Matters Handbook 2020, US Department of Defense 2018

James N Mattis, The National Defense Strategy and the Nuclear Posture Review – Committee on Armed Services of the House of Representatives, Washington DC: U.S. Government Publishing Office 2018

Noah C. Mayhew/VCDNP, Reflecting on the Annexes to the Model Additional Protocol in Support of Nuclear Governance, 2022

Garry McCracken/Peter Stott, Chapter 7 – Inertial-Confinement Fusion, in: Garry McCracken/Peter Stott (eds.), Fusion (Second Edition), Boston: Academic Press 2013, 67–81

Fred McGoldrick, The Road Ahead for Export Controls: Challenges for the Nuclear Suppliers Group, Arms Control Today 41 (2011), 30–36

Steven McIntosh, Nuclear Liability and Post-Fukushima Developments, in: International Atomic Energy Agency (ed.), Nuclear Law: The Global Debate, The Hague: T.M.C. Asser Press 2022, 249–269

Jeff McMahan, Nuclear Blackmail, in: Nigel Blake/Kay Pole (eds.), Dangers of Deterrence, Oxford, New York: Routledge 1983, 84–111

D. M. McRae, The Legal Effect of Interpretative Declarations, British Yearbook of International Law 49 (1979), 155–173

John Mecklin, Closer Than Ever: It Is Now 89 Seconds to Midnight in: Bulletin of the Atomic Scientists, https://thebulletin.org/doomsday-clock/2025-statement/, last accessed 17 July 2025

T. A. Mehlhorn/B. B. Cipiti/C. L. Olson et al., Fusion–fission Hybrids for Nuclear Waste Transmutation: A Synergistic Step Between Gen-IV Fission and Fusion Reactors, Fusion Engineering and Design 83 (2008), 948–953

Oliver Meier, The US–India Nuclear Deal: The End of Universal Non-Proliferation Efforts?, Internationale Politik und Gesellschaft (2006), 28–43

Oliver Meier, The 2015 NPT Review Conference Failure – Implications for the Nuclear Order (2015), Stiftung Wissenschaft und Politik

Lise Meitner/Otto R. Frisch, Disintegration of Uranium by Neutrons: a New Type of Nuclear Reaction, Nature 143 (1939), 239–240

Samuele Meschini/Sara E. Ferry/Rémi Delaporte-Mathurin et al., Modeling and Analysis of the Tritium Fuel Cycle for ARC- and STEP-Class D-T Fusion Power Plants, Nuclear Fusion 63 (2023), 1–34

Oliver Meyer, A Civilian Power Caught Between the Lines: Germany and Nuclear Non-Proliferation, Trier: 1998

Paul Meyer, Is There Any Fizz Left in the Fissban? Prospects for a Fissile Material Cutoff Treaty, Arms Control Today 37 (2007), 18–22

Paul Meyer, Does the Conference of Disarmament Have a Future?, Journal for Peace and Nuclear Disarmament 4 (2021), 287–294

Claire Mills/Esme Kirk-Wade, The Cost of the UK's Strategic Nuclear Deterrent, London: House of Commons Research Briefing 2023

Elizabeth Minor, Changing the Discourse on Nuclear Weapons: The Humanitarian Initiative, International Review of the Red Cross 97 (2015), 711–730

Mohd Amin Mir/Thseen Nazir, South Asian Perspectives on the Nuclear Weapons Ban: Challenges and Prospects for Disarmament, Peace Review 36 (2024), 256–266

Ralph W. Moir/Wally Manheimer, Fusion–Fission Hybrid Reactors, in: Thomas J. Dolan (ed.), Magnetic Fusion Technology, London: Springer 2013, 699–742

Christian Mölling, The Grand Bargain in the NPT: Challenges for the EU Beyond 2010, in: Jean Pascal Zanders (ed.), Nuclear Weapons After the 2010 NPT Review Conference, Paris: European Union Institute for Security Studies (EUISS) 2010, 49–70

E. Morse, Nuclear Fusion, Heidelberg: Springer International Publishing 2018

Harald Müller, The NPT Review Conferences, in: Emily B. Landau/Azriel Bermant (eds.), The Nuclear Nonproliferation Regime at a Crossroads, Tel Aviv: Institute for National Security Studies 2014, 17–26

Harald Müller, Looking at Nuclear Rivalry: The Role of Nuclear Deterrence, Strategic Analysis 38 (2014), 464–475

Harald Müller/Carmen Wunderlich (eds.), Norm Dynamics in Multilateral Arms Control: Interests, Conflicts, and Justice, Athens: University of Georgia Press 2013

M. Nakamura/K. Tobita/W. Gulden et al., Study of Safety Features and Accident Scenarios in a Fusion DEMO Reactor, Fusion Engineering and Design 89 (2014), 2028–2032

Vipin Narang, What Does It Take to Deter? Regional Power Nuclear Postures and International Conflict, Journal of Conflict Resolution 57 (2013), 478–508

Vipin Narang, Strategies of Nuclear Proliferation – How States Pursue the Bomb, International Security 41 (2016), 110–150

National Research Council, Assessment of Inertial Confinement Fusion Targets, Washington DC: The National Academies Press 2013

NATO, Factsheet: NATO's Nuclear Sharing Arrangements, 2022

Muyi Ni/Yongliang Wang/Baoxin Yuan et al., Tritium Supply Assessment for ITER and DEMOnstration Power Plant, Fusion Engineering and Design 88 (2013), 2422–2426

Irmgard Niemeyer, Perspectives of Satellite Imagery Analysis for Verifying the Nuclear Non-Proliferation Treaty, in: Gotthard Stein/Bernd Richter/Sven Nussbaum/Irmgard Niemeyer/Bhupendra Jasani (eds.), International Safeguards and Satellite Imagery, Berlin, Heidelberg: Springer Berlin Heidelberg 2009, 35–44

Georg Nolte, Subsequent Agreements and Subsequent Practice in Relation to the Interpretation of Treaties, A/CN.4/660, Geneva: International Law Commission 2013

Robert S. Norris/Hans M. Kristensen, Global Nuclear Weapons Inventories, 1945–2010, Bulletin of the Atomic Scientists 66 (2010), 77–83

Nuclear Threat Initiative/Center for Energy and Security Studies (eds.), The Future of IAEA Safeguards: Rebuilding the Vienna Spirit through Russian-U.S. Expert Dialogue, Washington DC: Nuclear Threat Initiative 2020

Gro Nystuen/Kjølv Egeland/Torbjørn Graff Hugo, The TPNW: Setting The Record Straight, Norwegian Academy of International Law 2018

Alexandre Obertelli/Hiroyuki Sagawa, Modern Nuclear Physics – From Fundamentals to Frontiers, Singapore: Springer Singapore 2021

Observatory of Economic Complexity (OEC), Nuclear Reactors in the US (2025), https://oec.world/en/profile/bilateral-product/nuclear-reactors/reporter/usa, last accessed 17 July 2025

Donald R. Olander, The Theory of Uranium Enrichment by the Gas Centrifuge, Progress in Nuclear Energy 8 (1981), 1–33

Marcus Laurence Elwin Oliphant/Ernest Rutherford, Experiments on the Transmutation of Elements by Protons, Proceedings of the Royal Society of London. Series A, Containing Papers of a Mathematical and Physical Character 141 (1933), 259–281

Frank V. Pabian/Guido Renda/Rainer Jungwirth et al., Commercial Satellite Imagery: An Evolving Tool in the Non-proliferation Verification and Monitoring Toolkit, in: Irmgard Niemeyer/Mona Dreicer/Gotthard Stein (eds.), Nuclear Non-Proliferation and Arms Control Verification: Innovative Systems Concepts, Cham: Springer International Publishing 2020, 351–371

Tae-Keun Park/Seon-Ki Kim, Tritium: Its Generation and Pathways to the Environment at CANDU 6 Generating Stations, Nuclear Engineering and Design 163 (1996), 405–411

Andrew J. Parker/Michael D. Aspinall/Colin Boxall et al., Radiometric Techniques for the Detection and Assessment of Tritium in Aqueous Media – a Review, Progress in Nuclear Energy 162 (2023), 104733

T.V. Paul, The Tradition of Non-Usa of Nuclear Weapons, Stanford: Stanford University Press 2009

Richard J. Pearson, Barriers to Fusion Commercialization: Understanding Innovation, 2020

Richard J. Pearson/Armando B. Antoniazzi/William J. Nuttall, Tritium Supply and Use: a Key Issue for the Development of Nuclear Fusion Energy, Fusion Engineering and Design 136 (2018), 1140–1148

Richard J. Pearson/Olivia Comsa/Liviu Stefan et al., Romanian Tritium for Nuclear Fusion, Fusion Science and Technology 71 (2017), 610–615

Didier Perrault, Safety Issues to Be Taken Into Account in Designing Future Nuclear Fusion Facilities, Fusion Engineering and Design 109–111 (2016), 1733–1738

Didier Perrault, Nuclear Safety Aspects on the Road Towards Fusion Energy, Fusion Engineering and Design 146 (2019), 130–134

Anne Peters, Das Gründungsdokument internationaler Organisationen als Verfassungsvertrag, Zeitschrift für öffentliches Recht 68 (2013), 1–57

Christopher Peters, Praxis Internationaler Organisationen – Vertragswandel und völkerrechtlicher Ordnungsrahmen, Berlin, Heidelberg: Springer 2016

Max-Planck-Institute for Plasma Physics, JET Fusion Facility Sets a New World Energy Record in: https://www.mpg.de/18250857/jet-fusion-facility-new-world-energy-record, last accessed 17 July 2025

Alexander Piel, Plasma Physics – An Introduction to Laboratory, Space, and Fusion Plasmas, Kiel, Heidelberg: Springer 2017 Joseph Pilat (ed.), Nuclear Latency and Hedging: Concepts, History, and Issues, Washington DC: Woodrow Wilson International Center for Scholars 2019

Pavel Podvig, Preserving the Nuclear Test Ban After Russia Revoked its CTBT Ratification, Bulletin of the Atomic Scientists 80 (2024), 75–80

Istvan Pogany, The Destruction of Osirak: A Legal Perspective, The World Today 37 (1981), 413–418

Jonathan D. Pollack, North Korea's Nuclear Weapons Development – Implications for Future Policy, Proliferation Papers 33 (2010), 7–44

Claire Portier, Le droit de la responsabilité à l'épreuve des activités de fusion nucléaire, Aix-en-Provence: Aix-Marseille Université 2022

Timothy J. Pounds, A Chronology of Comprehensive Test Ban Proposals, Negotiations, and Debates: 1945–1993, 1994

Robert Powell, Nuclear Deterrence Theory: The Search for Credibility, Cambridge: Cambridge University Press 1990

Joelien Pretorius/Tom Sauer, Ditch the NPT, Survival 63 (2021), 103–124

Joelien Pretorius/Tom Sauer, When is it Legitimate to Abandon the NPT? Withdrawal as a Political Tool to Move Nuclear Disarmament Forward, Contemporary Security Policy 43 (2022), 161–185

George H. Quester, Japan and the Nuclear Non-Proliferation Treaty, Asian Survey 10 (1970), 765–778

Howard K. Rae, Separation of Hydrogen Isotopes, Washington DC: American Chemical Society 1978

Jürgen Raeder/Arthur Weller/Robert Wolf et al., Review of the Safety Concept for Fusion Reactor Concepts and Transferability of the Nuclear Fission Regulation to Potential Fusion Power Plants, GRS 2016

Krishnan Raghunath, From Nuclear Apartheid to Nuclear Deal: The First Steps, Indian Foreign Affairs Journal 5 (2010), 85–122

Robert Rauchhaus, Evaluating the Nuclear Peace Hypothesis: A Quantitative Approach, The Journal of Conflict Resolution 53 (2009), 258–277

Paul-Henri Rebut, ITER: The First Experimental Fusion Reactor, Fusion Engineering and Design 30 (1995), 85–118

Helmut Rechenberg, 50 Jahre Kernspaltung: Transurane, Uranspaltung und das deutsche Uranprojekt, Physikalische Blätter 44 (1988), 453–459

Jörg Reckers, Tritiumbilanzierung zur Überprüfung der Nichtweiterverbreitung im Fusionsreaktor ITER, in: DPG (ed.), 72. Jahrestagung der DPG, Berlin: 2008

John R. Redick, Nuclear Illusions: Argentina and Brazil, Washington DC: The Henry L. Stimson Center 1995

Bruce Cameron Reed, The History and Science of the Manhattan Project, Berlin, Heidelberg: Springer 2019

Bruce Cameron Reed, Producing Fissile Material, in: Bruce Cameron Reed (ed.), The Physics of the Manhattan Project, Cham: Springer International Publishing 2021, 119–144

Frederick Reines, The Peaceful Nuclear Explosion, Bulletin of the Atomic Scientists 15 (1959), 118–122

Louis Reitmann, Reforming the 'London Club': How transparency and outreach can benefit the Nuclear Suppliers Group (2023), European Leadership Network

Paul Reuter, Introduction to the Law of Treaties, London, New York: Kegan Paul International 1995

Jeff Richardson, Shifting from a Nuclear Triad to a Nuclear Dyad, Bulletin of the Atomic Scientists 65 (2009), 33–42

Nick Ritchie, A Hegemonic Nuclear Order: Understanding the Ban Treaty and the Power Politics of Nuclear Weapons, Contemporary Security Policy 40 (2019), 409–434

Nick Ritchie/Alexander Kmentt, Universalising the TPNW: Challenges and Opportunities, Journal for Peace and Nuclear Disarmament 4 (2021), 70–93

J. Timmons Roberts, Global Inequality and Climate Change, Society & Natural Resources 14 (2001), 501–509

A. Robock/L. Oman/G. L. Stenchikov et al., Climatic Consequences of Regional Nuclear Conflicts, Atmospheric Chemistry and Physics 7 (2007), 2003–2012

Laura Rockwood, The IAEA's Strengthened Safeguards System, Journal of Conflict and Security Law 7 (2002), 123–136

Laura Rockwood, Legal Framework for IAEA Safeguards, Vienna: IAEA 2013

Laura Rockwood, The IAEA and International Safeguards, in: Joseph Pilat/Nathan Busch (eds.), Routledge Handbook of Nuclear Proliferation and Policy, London: Routledge 2015, 142–157

Laura Rockwood, IAEA Safeguards: Correctness and Completeness of States' Safeguards Declarations, in: International Atomic Energy Agency (ed.), Nuclear Law: The Global Debate, The Hague: T.M.C. Asser Press 2022, 205–222

Laura Rockwood, The International Atomic Energy Agency (IAEA), in: Eric Myer/Thilo Marauhn (eds.), Research Handbook on International Arms Control Law, Cheltenham: Elgar 2022, 503–529

Laura Rockwood/Noah C. Mayhew/Artem Lazarev et al., IAEA Safeguards: Staying Ahead of the Game (2019), Swedish Radiation Safety Authority

Laura Rockwood/Viatcheslav Pouchkarev/Jill N. Cooley et al., IAEA Implementation of the Board of Governors Decisions on Neptunium and Americium, Vienna: IAEA 2000

Lina Rodriguez-Rodrigo/Joëlle Elbez-Uzan/Carlos Alejaldre, ITER Licensing Process from Design and Construction to Dismantling, Fusion Science and Technology 56 (2009), 809–813

Elisabeth Röhrlich, Negotiating Verification: International Diplomacy and the Evolution of Nuclear Safeguards, 1945–1972, Diplomacy & Statecraft 29 (2018), 29–50

Elisabeth Röhrlich, Inspectors for Peace, Baltimore: John Hopkins University Press 2022

Dennis Romberg, Atomgeschäfte – Die Nuklearpolitik der Bundesrepublik Deutschland 1970–1979, Paderborn: Ferdinand Schöningh 2020

Marek Rubel, Fusion Neutrons: Tritium Breeding and Impact on Wall Materials and Components of Diagnostic Systems, Journal of Fusion Energy 38 (2019), 315–329

Maria Rost Rublee, The Nuclear Threshold States, The Nonproliferation Review 17 (2010), 49–70

Maria Rost Rublee/Carmen Wunderlich, The Vitality of the NPT After 50, Contemporary Security Policy 43 (2022), 5–23

Dean Rust, How We've Come to View the NPT: Three Pillars, in: Henry Sokolski (ed.), Nuclear Rules, Not Just Rights: The NPT Reexamined, Arlington: Nonproliferation Policy Education Center 2017, 37–101

Scott D. Sagan, The Perils of Proliferation: Organization Theory, Deterrence Theory, and the Spread of Nuclear Weapons, International Security 18 (1994), 66–107

Scott D. Sagan, Why Do States Build Nuclear Weapons?: Three Models in Search of a Bomb, International Security 21 (1996), 54–86

Ben Sanders, IAEA Safeguards: A Short Historical Background, in: David Fischer/Ben Sanders/Lawrence Scheinman/George Bunn (eds.), A New Nuclear Triad: The Non-Proliferation of Nuclear Weapons, International Verification and the International Atomic Energy Agency, Southampton: Mountbatten Centre for International Studies, University of Southampton 1992, 1–13

David Santoro, Getting Past No: Developing a Nuclear Arms Control Relationship with China, Journal for Peace and Nuclear Disarmament 6 (2023), 68–86

Leo Sartori, Effects of Nuclear Weapons, Physics Today 36 (1983), 32–41

Arman Sarvarian, The Lawfulness of a Use of Force Upon Nuclear Facilities in Self-Defence, Journal on the Use of Force and International Law 1 (2014), 247–272

Tom Sauer, Nuclear Arms Control, Harvard: Macmillan 1998

Tom Sauer, Nuclear Proliferation and Nuclear Disarmament – A Complicated Relationship, in: Harsh V. Pant (ed.), Handbook of Nuclear Proliferation, Abingdon: Routledge 2012, 317–326

Tom Sauer, How Useful Are Nuclear Weapons in Practice? Case-Study: The War in Ukraine, Journal for Peace and Nuclear Disarmament 7 (2024), 194–210

Elizabeth N. Saunders, The Domestic Politics of Nuclear Choices—A Review Essay, International Security 44 (2019), 146–184

Philipp Sauter, Russia's Withdrawal from New START – The End of a Cold War Relic, but Not the Beginning of a New Nuclear Arms Race (2023), in: Völkerrechtsblog, https://voelkerrechtsblog.org/russias-withdrawal-from-new-start/

Philipp Sauter, The Emergence of Nuclear Fusion Energy: A New Nuclear Technology, a New Chance for Nuclear Disarmament?, in: Wilfred Wan/Vladislav Chernavskikh (eds.), Expanding Perspectives on Nuclear Disarmament, Uppsala: SIPRI/Alva Myrdal Centre for Nuclear Disarmament 2023, 160–171

Philipp Sauter, European Nuclear Weapons – Europe's Nuclear Ambitions and the Constraints of International Law (2024), in: Verfassungsblog, https://verfassungsblog.de/nuclear-weapons/

Annette Schaper, Der Fissile Material (Cutoff) Treaty – ein Vertrag, der niemals kommt?, Sicherheit und Frieden (S+F) / Security and Peace 36 (2018), 86–91

Jürgen Scheffran, Verification and Security of Transformation to a Nuclear-Weapon-Free World: The Framework of the Treaty on the Prohibition of Nuclear Weapons, Global Change, Peace & Security 30 (2018), 143–162

H. W. Schleicher, Nuclear Safeguards in the European Community – A Regional Approach, IAEA Bulletin 22 (1980), 45–50

Fritz W. Schmidt, The Zangger Committee: Its History and Future Role, The Nonproliferation Review 2 (1994), 38–44

Fritz W. Schmidt, NPT Export Controls and the Zangger Committee, The Nonproliferation Review 7 (2000), 136–145

Michael N. Schmitt, Israel's Operation Rising Lion and the Right of Self-Defense in: Lieber Institute Articles of War, https://lieber.westpoint.edu/israels-operation-rising-lion-right-of-self-defense/, last accessed 17 July 2025

Michael Schoeppner/Alexander Glaser/Mark. E Walker, Detecting Clandestine Plutonium Separation Activities With Krypton-85 (2015), INMM 56th Annual Meeting Proceedings

Susanna Schrafstetter, Preventing the 'Smiling Buddha': British-Indian Nuclear Relations and the Commonwealth Nuclear Force, 1964–68, Journal of Strategic Studies 25 (2002), 87–108

Gefion Schuler, Effective Governance through Decentralized Soft Implementation: The OECD Guidelines for Multinational Enterprises, in: Armin von Bogdandy/Rüdiger Wolfrum/Jochen von Bernstorff/Philipp Dann/Matthias Goldmann (eds.), The Exercise of Public Authority by International Institutions, Berlin, Heidelberg: Springer 2010, 197–226

Gary L. Scott/Craig L. Carr, The ICJ and Compulsory Jurisdiction: The Case for Closing the Clause, American Journal of International Law 81 (1987), 57–76

Todd S. Sechser/Matthew Fuhrmann, Nuclear Weapons and Coercive Diplomacy, Cambridge: Cambridge University Press 2017

Manpreet Sethi, NPT Review: Issues and Challenges, Strategic Analysis 24 (2000), 867–881

Mohamed Ibrahim Shaker, The Nuclear Non-Proliferation Treaty – Origin and Implementation 1959–1979, Dobbs Ferry: Oceana Publication 1980

Satoshi Shimakawa/Hisashi Sagawa/Toshimasa Kuroda et al., Estimation of the Tritium Production and Inventory in Beryllium, Fusion Engineering and Design 28 (1995), 215–219

Ekaterina Shirobokova, The Netherlands and the prohibition of nuclear weapons, The Nonproliferation Review 25 (2018), 37–49

Victor W. Sidel, Vertical Nuclear Proliferation, Medicine, Conflict and Survival 23 (2007), 249–258

Fabian Sievert/Daniel Johnson, Creating Suns on Earth, The Nonproliferation Review 17 (2010), 323–346

Thomas Simko/Matthew Gray, Lunar Helium-3 Fuel for Nuclear Fusion:Technology, Economics, and Resources, World Futures Review 6 (2014), 158–171

Bruno Simma, Mainstreaming Human Rights: The Contribution of the International Court of Justice, Journal of International Dispute Settlement 3 (2012), 7–29

Jaswant Singh, Against Nuclear Apartheid Essay, Foreign Affairs 77 (1998), 41–52

Ryan Snyder, A Proliferation Assessment of Third Generation Laser Uranium Enrichment Technology, Science & Global Security 24 (2016), 68–91

Anna Södersten, Explaining Continuity and Change: The Case of the Euratom Treaty, International Journal of Constitutional Law 20 (2022), 788–817

Zsolt Sóti/Joseph Magill/Raymond Dreher, Karlsruhe Nuclide Chart – New 10th Edition 2018 EPJ Nuclear Sciences and Technologies 5 (2019), 6

Georges-Henri Soutou, La France et la non-prolifération nucléaire, Revue historique des armées 262 (2011), 35–45

Leonard S. Spector, Meeting the New Challenges to the NPT, Disarmament Topical Papers 8 (1991), 177–194

Matias Spektor, The Evolution of Brazil's Nuclear Intentions, The Nonproliferation Review 23 (2016), 635–652

Matias Spektor/Togzhan Kassenova/Lucas Perez Florentino, Brazil's Nuclear Posture Under Bolsonaro, Arms Control Today 49 (2019), 12–17

Carlton Stoiber/Alex Baer/Norbert Pelzer et al., IAEA Handbook on Nuclear Law, Vienna: International Atomic Energy Agency 2003

Tadeusz Strulak, The Nuclear Suppliers Group, The Nonproliferation Review 1 (1993), 2–10

Waldo Stumpf, South Africa's Nuclear Weapons Program: From Deterrance to Dismantlement, Arms Control Today 25 (1995), 3–8

Katalin Sulyok, Science and Judicial Reasoning: The Legitimacy of International Environmental Adjudication, Cambridge: Cambridge University Press 2020

Kumar Sundaram/M. V. Ramana, India and the Policy of No First Use of Nuclear Weapons, Journal for Peace and Nuclear Disarmament 1 (2018), 152–168

Inout Suseanu, IAEA Safeguards Under Nuclear-Weapon-Dree Zone Treaties, IAEA Bulletin 62 (2021), 8–9

Tatsujiro Suzuki, Rokkasho Redux: Japan's Never-Ending Reprocessing Saga in: Bulletin of the Atomic Scientists, https://thebulletin.org/2023/12/rokkasho-redux-japans-never-ending-reprocessing-saga/, last accessed 17 July 2025

Paul C. Szasz, The Law and Practices of the International Atomic Energy Agency, Vienna: IAEA 1970

Stefan Talmon, The Security Council as World Legislature, American Journal of International Law 99 (2005), 175–193

Karoly Tamas Olajos/Fusion For Energy (eds.), Fusion For Energy Contracting Professionals Roundtable Proceedings 2022–2023, Barcelona: European Commission 2023

Karoly Tamas Olajos/Fusion For Energy (eds.), Fusion For Energy Roundtable 2024 Proceedings, Barcelona: European Commission 2024

Tetsuo Tanabe, Tritium Handling Issues in Fusion Reactor Materials, Journal of Nuclear Materials 417 (2011), 545–550

Tetsuo Tanabe, Introduction of a Nuclear Fusion Reactor, in: Tetsuo Tanabe (ed.), Tritium: Fuel of Fusion Reactors, Tokyo: Springer Japan 2017, 3–25

Nina Tannenwald, The Nuclear Taboo: The United States and the Non-Use of Nuclear Weapons Since 1945, Cambridge: Cambridge University Press 2007

L. A. Taylor/G. L. Kulcinski, Helium-3 on the Moon for Fusion Energy: the Persian Gulf of the 21st Century, Solar System Research 33 (1999), 338

Neill Taylor/Dennis Baker/Sergio Ciattaglia et al., Updated Safety Analysis of ITER, Fusion Engineering and Design 86 (2011), 619–622

Neill Taylor/Pierre Cortes, Lessons Learnt From ITER Safety & Licensing for DEMO and Future Nuclear Fusion Facilities, Fusion Engineering and Design 89 (2014), 1995–2000

N. P. Taylor, Safety and Licensing of Nuclear Facilities for Fusion, in: 2015 IEEE 26th Symposium on Fusion Engineering (SOFE)2015

Bruno Tertrais/Ministère de la Défense, La France et la dissuasion nucléaire : Concept, moyens, avenir, Paris: La documentation Française 2017 Ramesh Thakur (ed.), Nuclear Weapon-Free Zones, Springer 1998

Judith Thorn, The UN Conference on Disarmament, in: Eric Myer/Thilo Marauhn (eds.), Research Handbook on International Arms Control Law, Cheltenham: Elgar 2022, 77–88

William Tobey, Overview: Nuclear Scientists as Assassination Targets in: Bulletin of the Atomic Scientist, https://thebulletin.org/premium/2020-11/overview-nuclear-scientists-as-assassination-targets/, last accessed 17 July 2025

Masao Tomonaga, The Atomic Bombings of Hiroshima and Nagasaki: A Summary of the Human Consequences, 1945–2018, and Lessons for Homo sapiens to End the Nuclear Weapon Age, Journal for Peace and Nuclear Disarmament 2 (2019), 491–517

Wolfram Tonhauser, The International Atomic Energy Ageny as the "Watchdog" over the Safe and Peaceful Use of Nuclear Energy?, in: Kerstin Odendahl (ed.), Internationales und europäisches Atomrecht, Berlin: Duncker & Humblot 2013, 167–184

Wolfram Tonhauser/Karoly Tamas Olajos (eds.), FELEX – Key Issue Report, FELEX 2023

Wolfram Tonhauser/Karoly Tamas Olajos, Nuclear Fusion: Legal Aspects, Nuclear Law Bulletin 2023/2 (2024), 57–74

Stephen R. Tully, The Contribution of Human Rights to Universal Energy Access, Northwestern University Journal of International Human Rights 4 (2005), 518–548

R. P. Turco/O. B. Toon/T. P. Ackerman et al., Nuclear Winter: Global Consequences of Multiple Nuclear Explosions, Science 222 (1983), 1283–1292

Phil Twyford, What Next for the Nuclear "Grand Bargain?", New Zealand International Review 47 (2022), 19–23

U.S. Department of Defense, Nuclear Posture Review, Washington DC: U.S. Government 2022

U.S. Department of Defense/U.S. Department of Energy, Memorandum for Members of the Nuclear Weapons Council – Nuclear Weapons Council Strategic Plan for Fiscal Years 2017–2042 (2016)

U.S. Department of Energy, The National Ignition Facility (NIF) and the Issue of Nonproliferation (NN-40), 1995

U.S. Department of Energy, DOE National Laboratory Makes History by Achieving Fusion Ignition (2022), https://www.energy.gov/articles/doe-national-laboratory-makes-history-achieving-fusion-ignition, last accessed 17 July 2025

U.S. Department of Energy, Fusion Energy Strategy 2024, 2024

U.S. Department of State, The Nuclear Non-Proliferation Review Conference, 2022

U.S. Government, Questions on the Draft Non-Proliferation Treaty Asked by US Allies Together with Answers Given by the United States, 1968

UK Government, Global Britain in a Competitive Age – The Integrated Review of Security, Defence, Development and Foreign Policy (2021)

Geir Ulfstein, Evolutive Interpretation in the Light of Other International Instruments: Law and Legitimacy, in: Anne van Aaken/Iulia Motoc (eds.), The European Convention on Human Rights and General International Law, Oxford: Oxford University Press 2018, 83–94

Werner Ungerer/Ryukichi Imai/I. D. Morokhov et al., Safeguards: Five Views, IAEA Bulletin 13–3 (1971), 2–13 *United Nations*, Yearbook of the United Nations 1968, New York: United Nations 1968

Marcos Valle Machado da Silva, Brazil and the Refusal to the Additional Protocol: Is It Time to Review this Position?, Carta Internacional 16 (2021), 1–26

Peter Van Ham, The European Union's WMD Strategy and the CFSP: A Critical Analysis, EU Non-Proliferation Consortium Non-Proliferation Papers 2 (2011), 1–16

Jorge E. Viñuales, Energy in International Law, Cambridge: Cambridge University Press 2022

Andrea Viski, The Status of Nuclear Export Control Regimes in International Law, Tilburg Law Review 15 (2010), 183–204

Adolf von Baekmann, IAEA Safeguards in Nuclear-Weapon States, IAEA Bulletin 30–1 (1988), 22–25

Armin von Bogdandy/Matthias Goldmann, The Exercise of International Public Authority through National Policy Assessment: The OECD's PISA Policy as a Paradigm for a New International Standard Instrument, International Organizations Law Review 5 (2008), 241–298

Paul Voosen, Pond Mud Proposed as Anthropocene's 'Golden Spike,' Defining Human-Altered Geological Age in: Science, https://www.science.org/content/article/pond-mud-proposed-anthropocene-s-golden-spike-defining-human-altered-geological-age, last accessed 17 July 2025

Kenneth N. Waltz, The Spread of Nuclear Weapons: More May Be Better: Introduction, The Adelphi Papers 21 (1981), 1–32

Kenneth N. Waltz, Nuclear Myths and Political Realities, The American Political Science Review 84 (1990), 731–745

Wilfred Wan/Vladislav Chernavskikh (eds.), Expanding Perspectives on Nuclear Disarmament, Uppsala: SIPRI/Alva Myrdal Centre for Nuclear Disarmament 2023

Rachel A. Weise, How Nuclear Weapons Change the Doctrine of Self-Defense Note, New York University Journal of International Law and Politics 44 (2011), 1331–1398

Tobias Weise, The Involuntary Watchdog: Legitimating the International Atomic Energy Agency, in: Klaus Dingwerth/Antonia Witt/Ina Lehmann/Ellen Reichel/Tobias Weise (eds.), International Organizations under Pressure – Legitimating Global Governance in Challenging Times, Oxford: Oxford University Press 2019, 130–160

Leonard Weiss, Nuclear-Weapon States and the Grand Bargain, Arms Control Today 33 (2003), 21–25

Leonard Weiss, U.S.-India Nuclear Cooperation, The Nonproliferation Review 14 (2007), 429–457

Leonard Weiss, Israel's 1979 Nuclear Test and the U.S. Cover-Up, Middle East Policy XVIII (2011), 83–95

Alex Wellerstein/Edward Geist, The Secret of the Soviet Hydrogen Bomb, AIP Conference Proceedings 1898 (2017), 020008

Ori Wertman/Christian Kaunert, Operation "Outside the Box": The Securitization of the Syrian Nuclear Reactor, in: Israel: National Security and Securitization: The Role of the United States in Defining What Counts, Cham: Springer International Publishing 2023, 123–148

Michael Wesley, It's Time to Scrap the NPT, Australian Journal of International Affairs 59 (2005), 283–299

Jeremy Whitlock, Safeguards by Design: Designing Nuclear Facilities with Safeguards in Mind, IAEA Bulletin 63 (2022), 22–22

Robert Chadwell Williams, Klaus Fuchs, Atom Spy, Cambridge: Harvard University Press 1987

Carley Willis/Joanne Liou, Safety in Fusion, IAEA Bulletin 62–2 (2021), 14–16 *Ward Wilson*, The Myth of Nuclear Deterrence, The Nonproliferation Review 15 (2008), 421–439

Joseph Windsor, The WTO Committee on Trade in Financial Services: The Exercise of Public Authority within an Informational Forum, in, Berlin, Heidelberg: Springer 2010, 405–435

Wissenschaftlicher Dienst des Deutschen Bundestages, Kurzinformation: Rechtsfragen zur atomaren Bewaffnung Deutschlands (2020)

Alexandra Witze, This Quiet Lake Could Mark the Start of a New Anthropocene Epoch in: Nature, https://www.nature.com/articles/d41586-023-02234-z, last accessed 17 July 2025

Ned A. Wogman, Prospects for the Introduction of Wide Area Monitoring Using Environmental Sampling for Proliferation Detection, Journal of Radioanalytical and Nuclear Chemistry 296 (2013), 1071–1077

Michael Wood, United Nations, Security Council, in: Anne Peters/Rüdiger Wolfrum (eds.), Max Planck Encyclopedia of Public International Law, Heidelberg, Oxford: Oxford University Press 2008

Michael Wood/Eran Sthoeger, The UN Security Council and International Law, Cambridge: Cambridge University Press 2022

W. K. Woods, LRL interest in U-233 (1966), Douglas United Nuclear, Inc., Richland, WA (United States).

Amy F. Woolf, Nonstrategic Nuclear Weapons, Washington DC: CRS Report for Congress 2010

Y. Wu/S. Zheng/X. Zhu et al., Conceptual Design of the Fusion-Driven Subcritical System FDS-I, Fusion Engineering and Design 81 (2006), 1305–1311

Samuel E. Wurzel/Scott C. Hsu, Progress Toward Fusion Energy Breakeven and Gain as Measured Against the Lawson Criterion, Physics of Plasmas 29 (2022), 062103

Herbert F. York, The Advisors: Oppenheimer, Teller, and the Superbomb, Stanford: Stanford University Press 1989

Krieger Zanvyl/Ariel Ilan Roth, Nuclear Weapons in Neo-Realist Theory, International Studies Review 9 (2007), 369–384

Fuad Zarbiyev, The 'Cash Value' of the Rules of Treaty Interpretation, Leiden Journal of International Law 32 (2019), 33–45

Hartmut Zohm, Edge Localized Modes (ELMs), Plasma Physics and Controlled Fusion 38 (1996), 105

Hartmut Zohm, On the Size of Tokamak Fusion Power Plants, Philosophical Transactions of the Royal Society A: Mathematical, Physical and Engineering Sciences 377 (2019), 20170437

M. Zucchetti/Z. Chen/L. El-Guebaly et al., Progress in International Radioactive Fusion Waste Studies, Fusion Science and Technology 75 (2019), 391–398